MURDER AT
75 BIRCH

RICHARD T. PIENCIAK

MURDER AT 75 BIRCH

A TRUE STORY OF FAMILY BETRAYAL

A DUTTON BOOK

In memory of John Cotter,
A truly professional journalist who always did things large
but never forgot his roots in the Wyoming Valley.

DUTTON

Published by the Penguin Group
Penguin Books USA Inc., 375 Hudson Street,
New York, New York 10014, U.S.A.
Penguin Books Ltd, 27 Wrights Lane, London W8 5TZ, England
Penguin Books Australia Ltd, Ringwood,
Victoria, Australia
Penguin Books Canada Ltd, 10 Alcorn Avenue,
Toronto, Ontario, Canada M4V 3B2
Penguin Books (N.Z.) Ltd, 182–190 Wairau Road, Auckland 10, New Zealand

Penguin Books Ltd, Registered Offices:
Harmondsworth, Middlesex, England

First published by Dutton, an imprint of New American Library,
a division of Penguin Books USA Inc.
Distributed in Canada by McClelland & Stewart Inc.

First Printing, October, 1992
10 9 8 7 6 5 4 3 2 1

Copyright © Richard T. Pienciak, 1992
All rights reserved

REGISTERED TRADEMARK—MARCA REGISTRADA

Library of Congress Cataloging-in-Publication Data:

Pienciak, Richard T.
    Murder at 75 Birch : a true story of family betrayal /
by Richard T. Pienciak.
        p.   cm.
    ISBN 0-525-93492-8
    1. Murder—Pennsylvania—Wilkes-Barre—Case studies.
    2. Uxoricide—Pennsylvania—Wilkes-Barre—Case studies.
    3. Wolsieffer, Glen.   4. Wolsieffer, Betty.   I. Title.
    HV6534.W6P54   1992
    364.1'523'0974832—dc20   92-52863
                                                                    CIP

Printed in the United States of America
Set in Times Roman and American Typewriter

Designed by Steven N. Stathakis

A Note on Methodology

The separate chapters of italicized discourse were drawn from in-depth interviews with Dr. E. Glen Wolsieffer, the defendant in the case. They are his words. In order to keep the text flowing smoothly, the author's questions, any improper grammar, and extraneous matter were eliminated. There also are occasions where two or more discussions about the same topic were combined and presented in accurate chronological order. The italicized copy is otherwise as Dr. Wolsieffer spoke.

In agreeing to talk to me at length for this book, Dr. Wolsieffer appealed for fairness and a chance to tell his side of the story. There was perhaps no better way to search deeper for the truth in this complex, circumstantial case than to let Dr. Wolsieffer expound. The end result is a greater body of information for the reader to rely on in deciding, as any juror must do in a circumstantial trial, whether the defendant's story makes sense, whether it follows a logical progression, whether it could have happened the way he claims. If there is no logic, there can be no credibility.

I believe the answer is in his words.

—RICHARD T. PIENCIAK

ACKNOWLEDGMENTS

A special thanks to journalist Tony Burton of the *London Daily Mail*, who provided the inspiration for me to write this book. Also a special debt of gratitude to Ronnie Rome, James M. Torbik, and Mike Cotter for providing invaluable background and insight into Wilkes-Barre, its people, and its politics. This book is dedicated to Mike's brother, John, whom I met nearly twenty years ago while both of us were employed at the Associated Press. John, who had worked at all three New York City tabloids during his career, grew up in the Wyoming Valley and followed the Wolsieffer case closely, offering me his insight whenever we talked. He had just been hired away from the *New York Post* to become managing editor of the *New York Daily News* when he suddenly died in late 1991. Daily journalism in the Big Apple will never be the same.

In the Wilkes-Barre media world, sincere thanks are in order to editor James M. Torbik, reporters Fred Ney, Dave Kaszuba, and Robert Curran and the rest of the staff at the *Sunday Independent*, and managing editor Paul L. Golias and the staff at the

Citizens' Voice. Also, a note of appreciation to those at the *Times Leader* who were very helpful in private, unofficial ways.

Many people in law enforcement circles cooperated and gave generously of their time, most notably Detective Gary Sworen of the Luzerne County district attorney's office, his wife, Corine, and Detective Robert Mitchell of the Wilkes-Barre Police Department. An extra note of appreciation is due the staff of the clerk of courts office, for facilitating access to various public court records. I also would like to extend my gratitude to Judge Gifford S. Cappellini and his tipstaff George Brussock for their kindness, courtesy, and friendship.

For their time and effort in helping me understand their actions and strategies, I thank Deputy State Attorney General Anthony Sarcione, former Luzerne County Assistant District Attorney William Keller, defense attorney Anthony M. Cardinale of Boston, Massachusetts, and defense attorney Frank Nocito of Kingston, Pennsylvania. Hopefully by the telling of their stories, the bitterness on both sides of the courtroom aisle will subside. Lawyers have a job to do, and all of these lawyers did theirs honorably.

To the always cordial and professional staff at the Ramada Hotel on the Square, I say thank you, especially to owner Tom Torbik, for enabling me to conduct my business without hindrance.

At Dutton/New American Library, I owe a great deal of thanks to Kevin J. Mulroy for his editorial care, attention, and confidence in me and the story. Also, Michaela Hamilton and John Paine aptly added their expert focus at crucial junctures.

On the personal front, I want to thank my wife, Cheryl, not only for weathering the disruptive unpleasantries that accompany extended researching and writing, but for the hours spent transcribing taped interviews, editing, proofreading, and giving her opinions—sometimes unrequested but always welcomed. I commend my two sons, Ryan and Adam, for being understanding and flexible with their lives. To my sister-in-law Edie Pienciak, I say thank you for a superb effort on the laborious task of typing transcripts into computer files. To two other sisters-in-law, Teri Beck and Joni Beck Brewer, thanks for pitching in during one of the darkest hours. As always, a profound expression of gratitude is in order to my mentor, Willard E. Lally, a very special and caring human being.

I am particularly grateful for the family members and associates on all sides of the Wolsieffer tragedies who agreed to cooperate with the understanding that I would not only tell their story but everyone else's. The most notable members of this group were Nancy Wolsieffer, Marian Tasker, John Tasker, Phyllis Wolsieffer, Lisa Wolsieffer, Carol Kopicki, and the defendant, Dr. E. Glen Wolsieffer.

There is still time for forgiveness and healing.

PART ONE

NEIL

PROLOGUE:

IN HIS WORDS

Betty and I used to kiss each other a certain way every night: three kisses, "I love you," and then I would kiss her on the nose. For some reason, I'd kiss her on the nose.

That night, Betty kind of stirred around, so I shook her and said, "Hey, I'm home."

I started making a move on her, and she said, "Oh, get away from me. You smell like beer. You smell like cigarettes. You stink."

She said, "Why don't we just go to sleep, and, you know, we'll wake up tomorrow morning?"

I said, "Okay, I understand."

If she had wanted to, I certainly would have. But she didn't.

So I said, "Okay, I'll see you tomorrow."

I gave her a kiss. She went back to sleep, and I went to sleep.

CHAPTER 1

It was barely light out when the telephone pierced the deep-sleep stillness of the master bedroom at 84 Birch on Saturday, August 30, 1986.

Nancy Wolsieffer, an enthusiastic first-grade teacher at St. Boniface Elementary School, heard the ring first. Accustomed to getting out of bed around six on school days, she understandably liked to sleep later on the weekend. Nancy glanced over at the digital clock on the nightstand. The display read 7:15. *Who'd be calling at this hour?* she wondered.

Nancy nudged her husband, Neil, a big man at five foot eleven and 230 pounds. Now he too heard the unwelcome wakeup call, so he rolled over and grabbed the receiver. His brother, Dr. E. Glen Wolsieffer, a prominent dentist and former Rotary Club president, was on the line. It was a phone call that would haunt Neil Wolsieffer for the rest of his life.

"Neil, c'mon over!"

"Why? What's up?" Neil asked, still half asleep.

"Just come over."

Neil was one of the nicest people you'd ever want to meet: soft-spoken, kind, great with kids, never had a mean thing to say about anyone. He was dedicated to his family, very protective, especially of the women, but in a good kind of way. Neil truly admired the success and popularity of his older brother, a former high school and college All-Star athlete who still shined on several softball teams.

In different ways, Neil was a success, too. A longtime employee of the city's Recreation Board, he held the title of operations director and was in line for the second-in-command's position. Neil had worked his way up the hard way, starting out as a kid working at the city's swimming pool. From his current job, Neil knew all the politically connected people. He had almost daily dealings with top city officials, the police, the Fire Department. There was always something going on that he had to take care of.

Neil hung up the phone and grabbed his sweatpants, T-shirt, and cigarettes.

"Who was that?" asked Nancy.

"It was Glen."

"What did he want?"

Neil shrugged. "Something's wrong. I have to go over to his house."

"Well, what did he say?"

"He didn't say anything. He said, 'Just come over.' "

Nancy became nervous. It was odd for Glen, who lived across the street and one house farther from the nearby Susquehanna River, to be calling so early. What could be wrong? She knew there had been marital difficulties the previous summer between Glen and his wife, Betty, but all that had been cleared up—or at least she thought so. Nancy agonized over the possibility that the problem might have flared up again.

"I wonder what's wrong?"

"I really don't know," replied Neil, heading for the steps. After a few minutes, though, he was back in the bedroom, in search of his shoes.

"Hurry up, get going," said Nancy, up now herself and getting dressed.

"I know. I'm going, I'm going," said Neil.

They walked downstairs together, and Neil went out the door.

Nancy watched intently from the downstairs window as her husband crossed the tree-lined, one-way street and walked up the driveway toward the side door of her brother-in-law's house, 75 Birch Street. The entire trip was less than fifty yards.

The phone also rang early that morning over on Gilligan Street, at the home of Marian and John Tasker, Betty's parents. Betty's brother, Jack, was calling from Lancaster, Pennsylvania, where he'd taken his wife, Dorothy, and their children for the night. The family had decided to stay in the Amish country a bit longer, so Jack, an insurance agent, would be unable to keep a golf date for that Sunday with Neil. Jack was close with both Wolsieffer boys, often joining them for a round of golf, softball, Rotary Club, or a couple of beers.

Jack explained that he was heading out early for the day with the family, so could someone call over to Neil's house later to cancel the golfing plans? John Tasker, a longtime claims specialist for State Farm Insurance, told his son that he would be glad to handle the chore.

Downtown at police headquarters, it had been a slow, uneventful night. There had been only nine calls at the dispatch desk since midnight—two loud parties, two burglaries, a business escort to the bank, an assault call, an alarm, a domestic disturbance, and a "periodic check" in the Heights neighborhood.

The calm routine was shattered, though, with an urgent incoming call at 7:18, one that precipitated a chill that the good people of northeastern Pennsylvania would not soon forget.

"Wilkes-Barre police," said dispatcher Fran Bartlomowicz.

"Ah, yes. I'm calling from eighty—, eighty-four, ah— Seventy-five Birch Street. My name is Neil Wolsieffer, and I'm at my brother's house. Someone was in his house. He's on the floor. He's about unconscious. I don't know where my sister-in-law is."

"Who is, *Glen*?" Bartlomowicz asked, knowing the two brothers and wanting to confirm the identity of the fallen man.

"Yeah," replied Neil.

The dispatcher asked Neil to repeat the address. "Seventy-five Birch." And yes, Neil responded to an additional question, he did need an ambulance.

"And you, and you're there?" she inquired.

"Is this *Frannie*?" Neil asked, then recognizing the voice.

"Yeah."

"Yeah. As soon as you can, Fran. And a couple of police or whatever. I don't know if the guy is still here, either."

"You don't? Well then, okay."

Neil put down the phone and walked toward the front of the house, toward the stairs leading up to the bedrooms. Suddenly, Glen let out a loud groan. Neil quickly returned to his brother's side. It looked like he was coming in and out of consciousness.

Glen asked for a glass of water. His brother complied.

Neil again walked toward the stairs. Just as he got near them, Glen again let out a loud moan. Again, Neil returned to his brother, unable to ascertain the whereabouts of his sister-in-law, Betty, and his five-year-old niece, Danielle. That too would haunt him for the rest of his life.

Officers Dale Minnick and Anthony George arrived at the two-story, white-sided frame home at 7:21, less than two minutes after receiving their instructions from headquarters and only six minutes after the time that Neil and Nancy Wolsieffer would cite as the moment of Glen's call to their house.

The officers were met at the front door by Neil, who seemed nervous and upset. He told them that his brother was beat up inside the house. Neil escorted the officers through the front door and into the living room.

Neil said he had entered the house through the side entrance, that the screen door had been closed but unlocked, and that the main door had been ajar. Inside, Neil said, he had found Glen spread out on the kitchen floor, the receiver from the wall telephone dangling near his head. Neil told the officers that he had called the police after Glen told him that someone had broken into the house and tried to choke him.

As the officers followed Neil into the dining room, Neil said he wasn't sure if the intruder was still in the house. He told them that his sister-in-law and niece were supposed to be upstairs, but that no one had checked on them. Neil stopped and pointed into the kitchen, at his brother sprawled on the floor. He then sat down on one of the dining room chairs.

Dale Minnick, a broad-shouldered fourteen-year veteran of the force, continued forward, while Officer George drew his gun and mounted the stairway in the dining room toward the bedrooms.

At the top of the stairs, George checked the bathroom; it was empty. He then went to his left, to the adjacent bedroom at the back of the house, a room Dr. Wolsieffer used as a home office for paperwork chores. There, the officer noticed that several drawers of a desk had been pulled open. A briefcase lay open on the floor as well. One of the back windows was open.

Working his way back to the front of the house, Officer George discovered a small girl in the middle bedroom. She was asleep and apparently unharmed.

He then headed for the master bedroom.

Downstairs, Officer Minnick had turned his attention to Dr. Wolsieffer, who was spread out, face down, right cheek on the kitchen floor. A well-developed two-hundred-pound six-footer, Glen wasn't wearing a shirt or socks, just a pair of blue sweatpants cut off around the knees.

Glen's head was directly underneath the wall phone, with his face practically against a baseboard heating unit along the wall dividing the rear of the kitchen from the family room at the back of the house. Despite the fact that Neil had used the kitchen phone to call the police, the receiver was still off the hook.

Glen seemed a little drowsy, and complained of pain. As Minnick spoke to him, Glen turned his head so that his left cheek rested on the floor. "Hey, buddy, what's wrong? Buddy, what's wrong?"

"Someone was in my house. Someone tried to choke me," Glen said. Asked what happened next, he explained: "I kicked him in the balls."

"Is there anyone else in the house?" asked Minnick.

"My little girl and wife are upstairs," said Glen.

Just then Officer George summoned Minnick from the top of the stairs.

"Dale, you'd better come up here."

*   *   *

Upon entering the master bedroom, George had discovered the body of Betty Wolsieffer, thirty-two, resting on the floor alongside the bed, a blanket beneath her, a pillow next to her. She was face up, but positioned in the opposite direction—her head toward the footboard. A stuffed teddy bear lay nearby.

The victim's rose-colored nightgown was gathered above her waist. She was not wearing any undergarments. Her diamond ring and wedding band were still on her left hand.

A twenty-four-inch floor fan was running at high speed, blowing air across the victim's unclothed abdomen and lower extremities. The left front window was open about eight inches from the bottom. A light was on.

George tried for a pulse on the wrist. He found none. He tried her neck and got the same results. He was not surprised, though; the facial skin had already started to turn blue. The body was cool to the touch, too; rigor mortis, the stiffness of death, had begun to set in.

It was obvious that Betty Wolsieffer had been murdered. There were scratches and bruises about her arms and face, unequivocal evidence that she had been beaten. There were dark red marks on the neck, abrasions really, and she had foamed heavily from the mouth. It looked like strangulation.

When Minnick joined George upstairs, he confirmed his colleague's gruesome findings. Using his two-way police radio, Minnick reported a 10-45, a call for the coroner. He also requested the presence of the watch commander and some detectives. On the opposite side of the bed, away from the body, Minnick noticed an empty handgun holster on the floor.

Their anxiety heightened even more, the two officers drew their weapons and began an urgent canvass of the house.

There was a killer on the loose.

CHAPTER 2

Veteran firefighters John Ostrum and Richard Powell responded to the emergency call in the Fire Department's ambulance, outfitted with a trauma box filled with bandages and stethoscopes, oxygen, and several bags of cardiac arrest equipment. The men had been working since four o'clock the previous afternoon and were scheduled to be relieved at seven that morning. The only problem was, their replacements had not shown up when the Wolsieffer call came in.

Powell, certified as an emergency medical technician following 121 hours of training, had answered thousands of calls in his career, including several hundred involving trauma. With Ostrum driving, the two men sped to Birch Street, arriving just minutes after officers Minnick and George.

Powell leaped up the front steps and was met on the porch by Neil Wolsieffer, who explained that his brother had told him he had been in a struggle with someone who had attacked him in the dark, tried to strangle him, then hit him on the head.

Walking through the living room, Powell immediately noticed

a shirtless man lying facedown on the kitchen floor. He was unattended; the cops were nowhere in sight.

At first Powell thought the injured man was unconscious. But as he advanced, Glen's eyes appeared to be open, as if he was laboring to see who was approaching. Then, as Powell got within ten feet, the man closed his eyes.

Powell knelt down beside him. "What's his name?" Powell asked Neil.

"Glen," the younger brother replied.

"Glen!" shouted Powell, giving him a shake in an attempt to rouse the seemingly incapacitated form slumped before him.

Glen opened his eyes, and with that, Powell commenced with some rudimentary questioning in an effort to ascertain the extent of the injuries.

"Are you okay? What happened?"

Glen, thirty-three, turned his head and coughed a bit. It appeared that he was having a hard time swallowing. It sounded as if he also was having a hard time talking. Picking his head up slightly, Glen managed to reply that he'd been in a fight with a prowler. He explained that sometime during the night he had heard a noise in the house. He said he took his handgun and went to check around when he was attacked by someone who tried to strangle him. Glen said he tried his best to fight it off, but couldn't. After fighting for a few moments, he said, the attacker struck him on the head.

Still facedown, Glen complained that his neck hurt, so Powell made a quick check. The paramedic found some redness, like a light abrasion, around Glen's neck, but couldn't find any lacerations or contusions—or anything worth noting other than the redness.

Glen, though, kept moving his neck from side to side, almost more of a nervous habit, for he didn't grimace or display any sign of discomfort that would indicate he was suffering from pain. Instead, he kept making noises from deep in his throat.

"Can't you do anything for him?" asked Neil as his brother started to gag. Glen managed to request another glass of water; again Neil obliged.

"Is there anything else wrong?" Powell asked.

"My head hurts," said Glen.

Powell palpated Glen's scalp and located a small lump, between the size of a quarter and a half dollar, on the back of the head, near the midline. The bump wasn't lacerated, and it wasn't open. There was no sign of blood on the floor or on Glen's head. Examining deeper, Powell noticed several superficial scratches on Glen's back, near his shoulders, and on his chest. But there was no blood coming from them either.

Although Glen had explained that he had lost consciousness as a result of a blow to the head, he didn't complain of nausea, numbness, or dizziness—the usual symptoms. His eyes were not dilated, and they didn't seem glassy. Also, he was immediately able to recall the attack. As a result, Powell concluded that Glen had not sustained any serious swelling or trauma to the brain.

Surveying the area, Ostrum looked beyond the kitchen to the family room. There he noticed a revolver on the floor. He went over to investigate and determined that it looked real. Not knowing the intentions of the man lying on the floor, Ostrum positioned himself between Glen and the gun.

At that moment the police officers summoned Powell upstairs into the master bedroom. Listening at the bottom of the staircase, Neil heard somebody on the second floor pronounce: "She's dead."

Just then a child came out of her room and into the hallway. Danielle, known as a deep sleeper, had been awakened by a man's voice. She thought it was her father's, but as she walked toward her parents' bedroom, she realized that it wasn't. One of the cops yelled at her to get back into her room. Danielle did, but not before stealing a peek at her mother lying motionless on the bedroom floor.

Across the street, Nancy Wolsieffer grabbed a cup of coffee and looked out the window at Glen's and Betty's. Seeing two police cruisers out front, she became really nervous. What could be going on over there?

Her two-year-old daughter, Bryn, was upstairs sleeping in her crib. Nancy was afraid to leave her. But, keeping her front door open, she ran across the street to investigate.

Walking into 75 Birch, Nancy spotted Glen lying on the kitchen floor, under the phone, with a big man standing over him.

As she walked toward the back of the house, Neil met her in the dining room.

"What happened to Glen?" Nancy asked.

"I don't know," said Neil. "Someone got in and knocked him out."

The house was eerily still, and Nancy was trembling from alarm. Leaving her husband, she started to go upstairs. Whatever was going on here, at least she could take Danielle.

Just then, from the top of the stairs, Nancy heard one of the cops yell: "Will someone get that kid out of here!"

"That's why I'm here," said Nancy. The cops looked down at her, about halfway up the steps, and screamed at her to stop. Nancy froze in her tracks. She had no idea they were trying to preserve a crime scene. She was just trying to help by getting Danielle out of the house.

Officer George handed Danielle to Nancy on the stairway. "Everybody who doesn't belong here, please leave the house," Minnick instructed.

"Where's Betty?" Nancy asked with panic in her voice.

No one answered.

Nancy left quickly, taking Danielle back to her house, where she deposited the child in front of the TV. Then she just stood there by the front door, watching the police cars across the street. There wasn't much else she could do.

Ostrum told Minnick about the gun he had noticed, and the officer went into the back room to pick it up with a pen through the trigger guard. It was a six-shot, .22-caliber Ruger revolver containing three loaded shells.

The family room held another possible clue: an ottoman had been tipped on its side, and a coffee mug lay on the floor.

Minnick returned to Glen, again asking him what had happened. Glen again told the officer about the intruder. He said he had been knocked unconscious. He complained of pains to the back of his head and neck area. Minnick also noticed the scratches around the neck and shoulder.

Minnick then sat Neil down in the dining room for a heart-to-heart chat. Neil explained that Glen had come over to his house around 10:00 the night before, asking if he wanted to go out for a couple of beers. Neil said the next time he heard from Glen was a little after 7:00 that morning, when Glen called him to come over.

He stated that he never once went upstairs, and that he had no idea what had happened, if anything, to Betty or Danielle. He said Glen appeared to be groggy, slipping in and out of consciousness. Neil said he noticed the cellar door open and the door to the dry sink in the dining room ajar. He listened but heard nothing, even at the bottom of the steps to the bedrooms. Then he heard the police cars arriving.

Upstairs, Powell had walked over to the body, where he knelt down and checked futilely for any sign of life. Froth had collected around the victim's mouth. Returning to the others in the kitchen, Powell quietly told Ostrum that there was a dead woman upstairs who appeared to have been strangled. The two firefighters then helped Glen sit up on the floor. He complained that he was very cold.

"How are my two girls?" Glen asked.

"Don't worry about them. Just worry about yourself," Minnick replied.

The cop attempted to help Glen stand up, but he went limp. As Minnick picked up Glen by his shoulders, he slipped from the patrolman's hands. Glen did not fall unprotected to the floor, though. He braced himself and fell on his palms, as if in a push-up position.

"Get up!" Minnick yelled loudly. Glen sat himself up against the wall.

The ambulance crew moved in to attend to him. Just then Glen began groaning, as if in pain.

"He does have a lump on the back of his head," Powell explained.

But Minnick was skeptical of the scene unfolding before him. "From the way this looks, he better have a lump on the back of his head."

Powell and Ostrum helped Glen to walk into the family room, where he sat in a soft chair. From what he could tell, Powell felt Glen did not require emergency treatment and Glen said he didn't want to go, but Minnick strongly suggested that Glen make the trip. In fact, others would later recall, Minnick raised his voice considerably when making the recommendation. "If you have pain, it's the best thing you can do. You never know. If you got hit in the head, the best thing to do is to go to the hospital," Minnick advised.

Glen relented, and so Powell and Ostrum brought in a litter and opened it flat on the kitchen floor. As Glen was putting on a pair of pants in the family room, he again asked about his two girls.

"What two girls?" asked one of the cops.

"My daughter and my wife," Glen replied.

"They're upstairs."

Glen complained of still being cold, so Ostrum went out to the ambulance and got a sheet to wrap around him.

Loaded onto the litter, Glen was carried outside to the ambulance, his upper body positioned almost in a sitting stance. He kept turning his neck from side to side, and he seemed drowsy. Coughing, Glen complained again that his throat was dry. He asked Officer George, "How's my daughter?"

"Fine," answered the patrolman.

With superiors and other officers arriving to assist, George was instructed to follow the ambulance to the hospital. Glen was apparently the only witness to that morning's tragedy. Whoever had murdered Betty and bopped Glen on the head just might try to finish the job.

With the loading operation completed, George took Powell aside. "Try to remember everything that he says on the way to the hospital, okay?"

Powell nodded, then hopped into the back of the emergency vehicle and radioed to alert the emergency room. They were less than two minutes away.

As Ostrum pulled away, Glen asked: "Who's in here with us?" Powell explained that Ostrum was driving, and that it was just the two of them in the rear of the ambulance. Powell paused, then added: "But the police are right in back of us." Uncertain of the full import of the events unfolding around him, the last thing Powell wanted was for his patient to bolt out the back door.

Glen lay there silently, without expression.

Seeking to ascertain if Glen's level of consciousness had improved any, and to confirm the method of injury so he could relay the information to the emergency room staff, Powell again asked Glen what had happened inside the house.

Glen added several new details. He explained that there had been an intruder, that he had seen the man at the top of the stairs, and that he had gotten his gun and gone down after him. He said that at some point, after he had gone downstairs, the intruder—whom he described as "a large man"—grabbed him from behind. Glen said the man had tried to strangle him and had knocked him unconscious.

There wasn't time for Powell to get any more of the story. The ambulance had arrived at the hospital.

Over on Magnolia Avenue, Glen's mother, Phyllis, walked out onto her front porch for the morning newspaper. She heard, and then saw, police cars headed down Academy Street in the direction of Birch. She wasn't even back in the kitchen before the telephone started ringing. It was Nancy.

"There's something wrong over at Glen's," Nancy said. "He called for Neil to come over."

"I'll be right there," said Phyllis, hanging up the phone.

Glen's other sibling, Lisa, an analyst for a public utility, had just bought a new 1986 Subaru. Mother and daughter jumped into the car for the brief trip, only several blocks. Along the way, though, the car kept stalling.

Phyllis jumped out and started running.

Out of breath as she approached 75 Birch, Phyllis saw a police officer and paramedic putting someone into the back of an ambulance. Because she knew Glen had called Neil, she assumed that something had happened to Betty. One of the neighbors told her it was Glen who was being taken to the hospital.

Phyllis wanted information, but no one would give it to her. "Nobody knows what's going on, nobody's coming out of the house, nobody's allowed in, nobody knows nothing," she recalled of the moments before being informed that Betty had been murdered.

Neil walked out of 75 Birch and was besieged by neighbors. "How's Betty?" asked Tom O'Connor, a neighbor who had waved to her as he drove by on his way to work the night before.

Neil didn't answer at first. O'Connor persisted, though, and Neil blurted out, "She's dead."

Still in the dark about her sister-in-law's murder, Nancy had been watching from her front door as Neil walked up to O'Connor. Suddenly, the man started to walk away from Neil and began making a weird noise. At first Nancy thought he was laughing. Then she realized he was crying.

She stepped outside to meet Neil. "Where's Betty? What happened?"

"She's dead," said Neil.

"Dead?"

"Yeah."

Nancy reacted with a stunned emptiness. "Oh," she said. "How did she die?"

"Someone got in the house."

"Oh, my God," said Nancy. She didn't ask any details. She didn't want to ask.

At her suggestion, Neil went upstairs and called Brian Lavan, a Wilkes-Barre police officer who was married to one of Nancy's sisters, Sharon. The county district attorney, Bernard A. Podcasy, was married to one of Lavan's first cousins. Lavan and Neil had been friends for years, long before the marriages. Making the call seemed like the thing to do.

"Brian, can you come down to Glen's house? It's a holy mess down here," said Neil.

"What happened?" asked Lavan.

"Glen's been robbed," Neil explained, not daring to mention that Betty had been murdered. Neil grabbed a sweatshirt and headed back to Glen's house.

Lavan remembered that Glen and Betty had made plans to travel to Syracuse, New York, for the weekend. That fact, combined with Neil's cryptic call, led him to assume that Glen and Betty had left the night before and that the house had been vacant when the burglars struck. Lavan dressed quickly and made it over to 75 Birch within fifteen minutes. Getting out of his car, he noticed three Wilkes-Barre city police cruisers. He also noticed Phyllis Wolsieffer standing across the street, almost in front of Neil's house, with her daughter, Lisa.

"What could happen next?" asked Phyllis. There had been a

break-in attempt on her house just a few months earlier. At that point, Lavan had the same thought as Glen's mother, but was under the impression that 75 Birch had been "wiped out" by burglars, not that a murder had occurred.

Lavan walked into the house and immediately spotted Minnick seated at the dining room table with Neil. "What's up?" Lavan asked Neil. Neil didn't answer.

Lavan looked around the room and was surprised to find nothing out of place. At least Glen hadn't been totally cleaned out.

"What's up?" Lavan now asked Minnick.

"We have a homicide," the officer replied.

Stunned, Lavan went over to chat with one of the sergeants, then climbed the stairs. Inside the master bedroom, he recognized the victim immediately.

"I know her. I can identify her," Lavan told Officer James Wardle, who was standing guard. Not wanting to disturb the crime scene, Lavan walked back downstairs and told the others he would be outside if anyone needed him.

A short time later, Chief of Police Joseph Coyne and Chief of Detectives William Maguire arrived. Captain Maguire, a friend of both the Wolsieffer and Tasker families, was surprised to see Brian Lavan in street clothes and Phyllis Wolsieffer standing outside. Lavan gave the captain a quick rundown, and Maguire immediately put him on duty. The officer provided Maguire with two suggestive facts about marital turmoil inside 75 Birch: There had been problems in the Wolsieffer marriage, and as he knew the story, up until the previous year Glen had been involved romantically with his former dental assistant. Lavan said he didn't know her name, but believed she lived in Nanticoke. Lavan also told Maguire that Glen had been a patient at First Valley Hospital, the psychiatric facility on Dana Street, about a year ago.

Maguire walked into the house, and he too saw Minnick at the dining room table chatting with Neil. Maguire, a native of the same South Wilkes-Barre neighborhood, had known Neil for twenty-five years; they had played Teeners baseball together. They had also dealt with each other in their official capacities. In Maguire's mind, Neil Wolsieffer was a top-notch guy.

As Maguire and the chief surveyed the scene, Lavan realized

that no one had informed Betty's immediate family, who lived only a few blocks away. He mentioned this to his superiors and was dispatched, along with Maguire, to handle the uncomfortable task.

By this point, the scene outside 75 Birch was becoming chaotic. Neighbors were streaming out of their houses. Reporters and camera crews were arriving by the carload. As George Cook, Betty's elderly next-door neighbor, later recalled: "That was a confusing day. There were so many people on the porch. I couldn't tell who was a detective, who was a policeman, who was a reporter, and who was a busybody looking around."

Scuttlebutt spread through the crowd quickly that a portion of the side screen door of the Wolsieffer home had been cut away the week before. Several neighbors confirmed that they had heard the story firsthand. Much of the chatter pertained to other recent break-ins throughout the South Wilkes-Barre neighborhood. The most popular conclusion held that the bandits must have wanted to get into Dr. Wolsieffer's house specifically. Since he was a dentist, maybe they were looking for drugs.

George Cook returned home to 77 Birch to wake his wife. "Come quick," he said. "No fooling around. Now! Come quick." Mrs. Cook, a frail soul, hobbled out of bed, put a bathrobe over her pajamas, and walked downstairs. "Something's happened to Betty. She's dead," he announced. Mrs. Cook peered out her front door. The front lawn was under siege.

Looking out back, George Cook noticed a rickety wooden ladder leaning against the Wolsieffers' family room. He had seen that ladder before. Glen stored it on the ground between the two garages. It had been left behind by the previous owner.

Spotting Neil walking by, George Cook headed out for more information. Cook mentioned something about Betty having been shot.

"She wasn't shot," Neil snapped back. He told the old man to go home.

Little Danielle's attention was fixed on the Saturday-morning cartoons. She was still unaware of her mother's murder, and acted oblivious to the circus developing across the street.

In the meantime, Nancy picked up the phone. First, she called her parents. They said they'd be right down to help with the kids. Then Nancy turned businesslike. She called up to Jamesville, New York, to the Wilkies, to tell them Glen and Betty would not be coming.

Craig Wilkie had met Glen about seven years earlier at a golf tournament. He and his wife, Eileen, were school teachers in East Syracuse. The two couples went on skiing trips and to the New Jersey shore together, and the families visited each other's homes. Nancy and Neil had met the Wilkies through Glen and Betty. The three men played in a golf tournament in the Poconos every June.

"Something terrible happened this morning," said Nancy. "Someone broke into Betty and Glen's. Betty is dead and Glen is in the hospital." She explained that the police were at the house and that no one was allowed in. Nancy said she didn't even know the condition of the house.

Nancy also placed a call to one of Glen's three offices—the one he worked in on Saturdays, on Green Street in Nanticoke. She told Mia the receptionist what had happened and that Glen would not be coming to work as scheduled. Mia and another co-worker, Pam, took the news very hard and started crying. A short while later, Deborah Shipp, Glen's former longtime dental assistant, stopped by for a visit. They gave her the bad news.

It didn't take too long for Nancy's phone to start ringing. In the midst of the growing mayhem, Betty's father called. Nancy's mother answered, then handed the phone to her daughter. "It's Mr. Tasker."

Nancy was horrified. She couldn't believe he was calling.

"Hello," she said.

Ever the storyteller, John Tasker started the conversation with a joke. It was obvious he didn't know about Betty yet. Nancy just stood there, holding the phone, unable to listen to the joke. She felt so bad for him.

"Well, anyway," Mr. Tasker said, "the reason I called is that Jackie and Neil were supposed to golf together tomorrow. Jack's away and he won't be able to make it."

Nancy was as short as possible. She couldn't get him off the phone quick enough. Thank God Brian was on his way over there. What a mess.

Several minutes later, John Tasker answered his doorbell. At first, he thought the grim-faced visitors were going to tell him that his car had been stolen or vandalized. But the news, of course, was much worse.

Lavan and Maguire talked with Betty's father for a few minutes, then called his wife downstairs. Marian Tasker was told she'd just lost her only daughter.

CHAPTER 3

With the assistance of Officer George, Glen was wheeled into the Mercy Hospital emergency room. In the monitors section, he was placed in a gown, put on another litter, and taken to Room 3, a separate area off to the side. A scant twenty minutes had passed since Neil's call to the police.

Glen again asked George, "How's my daughter?" He was assured that Danielle was fine.

Inside the emergency room, a duty nurse started an EKG. Glen complained that he was cold and said he wanted a blanket. One was promptly supplied. His vital signs were all within normal ranges, with his blood pressure at 144 over 86. He complained of pain in the neck. A soft cervical collar was applied.

"Are you having any trouble breathing?" Glen told the nurse that he was, and added that his throat was dry. In response to questions, he provided basic background information. Asked if he was married, Glen answered yes, he had a wife and a daughter. Asked if he had any other pain, Glen said he did, "the back of my head."

Next the nurse asked Glen to tell her what had happened at his house. He gave her the same basic story while saying he had knelt while proceeding to the bedroom door so he would not be seen, and that the intruder wore a mask.

When the nurse left, George started his own round of questioning. "What time did this happen?"

"When it was first starting to get light."

"What woke you up?"

"I heard a bang, like metal crashing in the back of the house on the second floor." Glen explained that he kept a fan running in his room, so he couldn't hear much.

"What did you do then?"

Glen said he didn't know if he had woken his wife, but he grabbed a gun from the dresser next to the bed and went to the doorway, carefully, because he didn't want anyone to see him. Looking out, Glen said, he saw a man at the top of the steps, just his upper body and head, then saw him go down the steps.

George asked Glen to describe what the man looked like.

"I couldn't tell. He had a mask on." It wasn't a ski mask, Glen explained. It was "a clear thing, like tan or something."

Glen said that he watched as the man headed downstairs. "I waited awhile and then went downstairs too." He said he didn't see anybody and eventually made his way to the room at the rear of the house, the family room. Just then he heard a noise from behind. He knew it wasn't in the kitchen because he had checked that room, so the intruder must have come from the side, behind the wall separating the kitchen and the family room.

Then, Glen said, he felt something around his neck. He struggled to get it off. It was a chain or a rope, something like that. "I tried to get loose. I couldn't. He must have been bigger than me. I kicked him in the groin."

"He was still behind you?" asked George.

"Yeah. I kicked him backwards. The thing on my neck got loose," said Glen. "Then he must have hit me with something. I blacked out."

The next thing Glen said he remembered was waking up, feeling cold. He said he knew he had to contact someone. He didn't know the police phone number, so he called his brother.

"Then what happened?"

Glen said Neil came over but he didn't remember too many details, other than that he was lying on the floor and Neil called the police. He remembered paramedics talking to him. And then there was Officer George and a big, tall cop—an obvious reference to Dale Minnick.

George wondered about the assailant's height. Glen said he couldn't tell from looking at him across the upstairs hallway, but said that when the man grabbed him downstairs, "he was bigger and taller than me. He also was strong."

At 8:15, Dr. Paul Witt, an emergency room physician, arrived to examine Glen. Citing physician–patient privilege, Dr. Witt asked George to leave the room, and he did, standing just outside the curtained area, not far from where several members of Glen's family had already gathered.

Dr. Witt was due to go off duty, so he conducted a quick examination. He found Glen to be alert and oriented. He also found a six-by-six centimeter hematoma on the occipital area, in the back of Glen's head. Glen said he was not certain if he had been hit about the head with an object or by a fist.

The doctor ordered that Glen be taken to the X-ray Department.

Detective Robert James Mitchell, a soft-spoken veteran of ten homicide investigations, got the call from the dispatcher's desk at the Wilkes-Barre Police Department shortly before 8:00. Mitchell had been a cop for twenty-one years, the last nine as a detective. He showered and quickly drove to 75 Birch, where his superiors put him in charge of the police department's investigation.

Gary Walter Sworen, a former local police chief with the rank of lieutenant detective in the Luzerne County district attorney's office, had been out late the night before with his fiancée. He was sleeping soundly when his phone rang. He'd had no intention of getting up early, since he and Corine had plans to go to a wedding that evening. But as is often the case with cops and investigators, Sworen's work would come first that Saturday. So he jumped out of bed and headed over to the homicide scene, where he was assigned as chief investigator on the case for the D.A.'s office.

Within an hour of Neil Wolsieffer's call, the crime scene was teeming with other law-enforcement personnel. First, with the help of a couple of sergeants and patrol officers, Minnick secured the general area. No one was allowed in the house. Yellow plastic police lines were erected.

Mitchell quickly gathered a team of four detectives, and before morning's end, six members of the Luzerne County district attorney's office also appeared on the scene, headed by District Attorney Bernard A. Podcasy.

A call went out to the state police at Troop P, the Wyoming Station, for an identification officer. Corporal Eugene J. Centi arrived just before 9:00. He proceeded to take color photos of the victim in her original position in the master bedroom, as well as color shots of the interior and exterior of the home. The crime scene was processed for latent prints, and two partial palm prints were detected on the top of the desk, a few inches to the right of center, in the rear office on the second floor, near the window—the room Dr. Wolsieffer had said he heard the noise coming from. The prints came up as soon as Centi dusted, an indication to him that they were fairly new, certainly less than twenty-four hours old.

By this point, Minnick was pretty convinced that Dr. Wolsieffer had killed his wife, so he focused his energies on finding something that would connect the dentist with the murder. The officer could not understand why neither Wolsieffer brother had checked on Betty and Danielle. Minnick's suspicions were heightened by the fact that every time he had asked Dr. Wolsieffer if anyone had checked upstairs, he appeared to suddenly be in pain and complain about his injuries.

Taking his hunt for evidence outside, Minnick ambled over to the cars parked in the driveway. The weather conditions were far from routine for a summer's day. The temperature had plunged to a record low 38 degrees. The relative humidity, meanwhile, had ballooned to more than 90 percent. The convergence of these meteorological conditions resulted in the formation of lots of wet, nippy dew. Unlike Betty's Chevy, though, there was no dew on Glen's black Subaru, not even on the windshield.

Minnick found the Subaru's doors unlocked, so he looked inside. He retrieved a gold belt, later logging it as a piece of evidence. Looking further, he noticed a packet of chewing tobacco.

Walking around to the back of the house, Minnick discovered a wooden ladder resting against the rain gutter above the flat porch roof of the family room. Looking above the roof, Minnick noticed that the window of the second-floor back bedroom was open.

The ladder's surface was spotted with powdery dark red paint that came off with a finger's touch. Because of the severe oxidation, Minnick thought that if the ladder had been used recently there should have been marks on the rungs, but there were none. Moving the ladder, Minnick also noted that there was no indentation in the ground beneath the ladder or on the chalky rain gutter where the ladder had been resting. With the help of other officers, Minnick erected an aluminum ladder next to the wooden one and climbed it in order to view the roof. There were no footprints in the morning dew. Instead, there was a screen on the roof, apparently removed from the window in the back bedroom. There was a hole punched in one corner of the screen, adjacent to the screen-locking device. Although he certainly wasn't an expert at such things, Minnick was certain the screen had been punched out, not in. Peering in, Minnick spotted several curly hairs on the windowsill. He collected them for evidence.

Returning inside the house, Minnick noticed that in the back bedroom, the drawers to Glen's desk were open, but an AM-FM portable radio-cassette player appeared to be untouched. In the master bedroom, the drawers to Betty's jewelry box were pulled out, but still filled with gold items and watches. A night table, the one on Glen's side of the bed, was open, and an empty Bucheimer holster was nearby.

Downstairs in the kitchen, a drawer was open, but again nothing appeared out of the ordinary. Small amounts of money were visible in the kitchen; Danielle's bank was undisturbed in her bedroom.

When Mitchell arrived, he first toured the house. Finding no signs of forced entry, he too went out back to check out the wooden ladder, which he had spotted from the window. Like Minnick, he was a bit mystified about the ladder. To him, it looked like no one had been on it. There was green-colored moss on the rungs, undisturbed. It also bothered him that the aluminum ladder had made a mark on the rain gutter, whereas there wasn't any mark where the wooden one had rested against the house. The wooden ladder also was cracked in the middle. He tried pushing the ladder into the ground to see if there was an indentation made in the grass. When he stepped on the first rung of the ladder with his 210 pounds, it made a mark in the soft soil. The sole of his shoe made a footprint on the rung itself. As another experiment, several officers climbed the aluminum ladder and went onto the roof. As they sauntered across the surface, Mitchell noticed that his men left grass cuttings from their shoes on the roof as well as several footprints in the dew.

Mitchell now checked the outside surfaces of all the doors and windows. He found everything in order, except for a three-inch, inverted-L-shaped cut in the screen on the side door.

Trooper Centi dusted the rear side door, the outside of the upstairs window, the window frame, and the screen frame. There had been so much traffic by the time he arrived that he didn't even bother with the front door. He deemed the ladder too pitted and rotted to be processed.

To Mitchell, the whole scene was very curious, especially when he got the word that the victim's husband had been involved with another woman. He had seen and heard enough for now, though. The others could continue processing the scene. Mitchell thought he could make better use of his time at the hospital. He wanted to hear firsthand what the dentist had to say for himself.

"Don't worry, Mom, everything will be okay now. Bill Maguire's here," said Neil Wolsieffer.

As the investigators looked for clues that morning, Glen's mother went for a walk around the neighborhood with Nancy Wolsieffer's mother. "Glen will never survive this," said Phyllis. "This will be so tough on Glen without Betty."

One of Phyllis's friends then drove Phyllis and Danielle to Phyllis's house. Little did the youngster know that her grandmother's house on Magnolia Avenue would be her home for the next few years.

City Councilman Bob Reilly, a longtime friend of Neil's, joined several other buddies and Gary Stinson, a cousin of the Wolsieffer boys, in Neil's backyard. "If they can't place a third party in the house, Glen's it," Reilly told Neil. He suggested that the family think about getting Glen an attorney. The idea seemed preposterous to Neil.

Upon returning from the Taskers, Brian Lavan took measurements of the back roof and helped Officer Wardle videotape the outdoor crime scene. The video showed the ladder, which had been moved quite a bit by that point, resting backwards against the rain gutter of the family room roof, its steps angled in the wrong direction. It would have been very difficult for anyone to have climbed the ladder that way. Also, the bottom of the ladder was pulled out too far for anyone to mount it without breaking it in the middle.

In the meantime, Detectives John Gonos and Wayne Cooney started canvassing the neighborhood. Gonos began next door with Jule and George Cook, both retired and in their sixties. They had nothing but pleasant things to say about the "nice and kind" Wolsieffers, especially about Betty, "a very giving person" whom they viewed "almost like a daughter."

Mrs. Cook, known as Peggy, had met Betty years ago, when Betty was a student at Wilkes College and Mrs. Cook worked in the school bookstore. Once they became neighbors, Betty gradually assumed a daughter-figure role, especially after Mrs. Cook became ill with cancer. Betty frequently shopped and cooked for the Cooks. When Mrs. Cook was hospitalized, Betty bought and prepared Mr. Cook's meals.

As a result, the Cooks saw Betty and Glen almost every day. Neither of them had ever heard Betty and Glen argue outside, nor did they ever hear arguments coming from inside the house.

Both Cooks said they spent a lot of time on their front porch, and that in the past year they'd noticed "a lot of strange people in the neighborhood, especially male youths." As Gonos would later write in a report: "Mr. Cook stated within the last months two black males [were] selling a cleaner going from house to house. At this time they [the black males] did not go to the Wolsieffers' or the Cooks'." The Cooks went on to tell Gonos that during the day, they had noticed "young males, youths, looking into homes, like if they were looking to see if anybody was home." They lived in fear, they said, because of the strange people frequenting the neighborhood.

George Cook said that a week ago Saturday, Betty had

showed them a cut on her back screen door. Betty had asked if the Cooks had heard or seen anyone around the door or the house. They told Gonos, as they had told Betty, that they heard nothing.

Both of the Cooks said that they had been receiving strange phone calls lately, callers asking for the names of people who didn't live there. Most of the time, the callers were male. They said they felt the callers were checking to see if they were home. The Cooks said Betty had never mentioned that she had ever received strange phone calls.

Gonos and Cooney knocked on some more doors. The stories were pretty much the same, with several others recalling strangers lurking in the neighborhood and receiving crank telephone calls. As for the Wolsieffers, they were described as nice people who appeared to get along well. No one had heard them argue or fight. And no one had heard any strange noises during the night. Only Ron and Josephine Slusser, of 80 Birch, had a possible clue. At about 2:00 that morning they had heard a car pull into the driveway on the west side of their home. The vehicle left approximately fifteen minutes later. They didn't look to see what type of car it was, but they knew that a college student had moved into 82 Birch within the last week. Also, they had seen Glen at Burger King that Tuesday and he told them that the screen on his side door had been cut or ripped last week. They had also seen two strangers sitting in a car parked outside their house on June 14, more than two months before.

By this point, Dr. George E. Hudock, Jr., the Luzerne County coroner and medical examiner, had arrived at 75 Birch. Dr. Hudock had been around for years, winning reelection to his post with ease. He was a fan of Sherlock Holmes, right down to appearing in public with the pipe and hat.

Entering the master bedroom, Dr. Hudock noticed the twenty-four-inch fan on the floor. None of the police had turned it off. The frothy material coming from the victim's mouth was an indication of asphyxiation.

The coroner then began a cursory examination of the body's exterior, finding "rigor of the mandible and partial rigor mortis of the upper extremities." He detected no evidence of rigor mortis in the musculature of the thorax, abdomen, or lower extremities. But Dr. Hudock did find evidence of livor mortis—the discoloration of the body caused by the settling of blood by gravity—in the face, which blanched slightly on pressure. Also, there was livor mortis of the rear of the body, which blanched slightly, but not completely, on pressure. Touching Betty's cheeks with the back of his right hand, Dr. Hudock observed that they were cold. It was a rudimentary test. The rule of thumb says if the cheeks are cold, the body has been dead more than four hours.

Gathering information that he hoped would help him pinpoint the time of death, Dr. Hudock recorded the room temperature at 10:40 A.M. at 22° centigrade—about 71.6° Fahrenheit. Seven minutes later, he measured the rectal temperature of the deceased at 31.5° C, or 88.7° F. At 10:55 A.M., the temperature had dropped to 31.2° C, or 88.16° F.

Temperature comparisons are normally very useful when determining time of death. But the fan blowing cool air toward the body for who knew how many hours was muddying the waters. Still, Dr. Hudock could make a reasonable estimate: he figured Betty had been dead for four to eight hours prior to his arrival, meaning that she had been killed between 2:30 and 6:30 A.M. He wasn't going to be able to do any better than that.

The body was officially identified by Deputy Coroner William Lisman, a close friend of Glen and Neil from the neighborhood and Rotary Club, and it was transported to the Mercy Hospital morgue.

Several of Glen's friends and relatives stood watch at the hospital, including Phyllis Wolsieffer's sister, Mary Stinson, a nurse who had formerly worked in the emergency room for six years. Lisa and Mrs. Stinson asked to see Glen, but were told they couldn't. Finally, word came that he was going to be all right. Later, they saw him as he was wheeled by on his way to the X-ray Department. "How are my girls?" he asked Aunt Mary.

Upon his return from X ray, just before 9:00, Glen's blood pressure was 144 over 72. He asked a nurse to tell his relatives to call his office so they would know he would not be in. Otherwise, Glen rested comfortably.

Based on Glen's comments, Lisa realized he still did not know Betty was dead. She insisted that someone from the family tell him because she didn't want a stranger to do it. "You don't understand," Lisa said. "The only thing I remember when my father died was that they came to tell me. You always remember how you are told and what was said. For some reason, it sticks in your head." But the family was ushered to a private room, where they were joined by two priests from the hospital.

Lisa called Neil, who by this point had been escorted back to his house by Officer Minnick and was sitting in his backyard. Neil said he would be right down.

Meanwhile, Dr. Dennis J. Gaza, a practitioner in internal and emergency medicine for five years, took over for Dr. Witt. Since Dr. Wolsieffer was complaining of neck pain and increased headache, Dr. Gaza started with a neurological examination. Glen's mental status was tested by, among other methods, what is known as serial sevenths, where the patient is asked to subtract seven from a number, then seven more, and so on. Glen went through five consecutive subtractions without a miss, so Dr. Gaza stopped the test.

Glen knew where he was and what day it was. He was able to respond when asked about past and present presidents, as well as who was the present mayor of Wilkes-Barre. Then it was on to several proverbs, such as "A penny saved is a penny earned." Glen had to explain what they meant to him, and his replies were appropriate.

Dr. Gaza then conducted a complete physical examination, from the top down—eyes, ears, nose, head, and throat, for starters. In the left occipital region of the back of the head, a sensitive area vulnerable to serious disruption of brain functions, Dr. Gaza found some swelling and the same bump noticed by the paramedics. There was no bleeding, however. It looked instead like a hematoma, a collection of blood under the scalp.

Glen's eyes appeared to be normal; the pupils were equally reactive to light, indicating that the pathway to the brain remained intact. There was no pinkeye or cloudiness in his eyes, either. As for vital signs, blood pressure was within the normal range, the pulse slightly elevated.

On the neck, Dr. Gaza found tenderness in the muscle and a two-millimeter semicircular abrasion on the back portion. There was no such mark or injury on the front of the neck, however. In fact, the rest of Glen's body had no additional lesions or abrasions.

Still, Dr. Gaza ordered another round of X rays immediately. The doctor also wanted a CAT scan of Glen's cervical spine to rule out any injury that might have been missed by the X rays. He ordered a CAT scan of the head so he could rule out any cranial injuries. Ice packs were applied to take down the swelling.

Detective Mitchell walked into the Mercy Hospital emergency room shortly before 10:00 and was directed to a glassed-in area off to the side. Briefed by Officer George, who had continued to shadow his charge, Mitchell approached his prey.

Glen was lying on a small bed in Room 3, a small cubicle within the emergency room area. There were no intravenous tubes in him; a white sheet covered his lower body.

"Hi, Bob," said Glen.

Mitchell was taken aback because he had never really met Glen Wolsieffer, save for a quick introduction several years previously at a Christmas party.

Mitchell proceeded to ask Glen a series of questions about exactly what had happened back at his house that morning. Seemingly alert, Glen started to tell the same story he had told Minnick and George—about the intruder with a transparent mask—only with more details.

Glen said that when he arrived home after visiting two local bars, about 2:00 A.M., he tried to enter through the back door. He said he opened the screen door, but when he put his key in the main door, it wouldn't unlock. According to Glen, he then went to the front of the house, where he found the screen door locked. Unable to gain entry that way, Glen said, he returned to the back door, where he jiggled the key in and opened the door. He said he had a glass of juice, removed his clothes in the upstairs back bedroom, and left them there. He said he put on a pair of cutoff sweat pants, then went to bed.

Glen said that about daybreak a clang coming from the rear upstairs bedroom woke him. He said he grabbed his .22-caliber gun from a nightstand, left Betty asleep, and began to check out the noise. As he got near the hallway, Glen said, he saw a man walking down the steps to the first floor. He said he followed the man downstairs and was attacked at the end of his room-to-room search. Someone wrapped something around his neck from the rear, trying to strangle him. As he fought and kicked, Glen said, he was struck on the head with a hard object, became dizzy, and his "eyes went black."

The next thing he knew, he woke up on the floor feeling very cold. He said he then summoned Neil on the phone. When Neil arrived, he said, he was still on the floor. He said the ambulance and police arrived a short time later.

Asked to describe the man he followed down the stairs, Glen said he was about six feet tall, two hundred pounds, race unknown, wearing a transparent mask over his head, and wearing a dark sweatshirt.

Under more questioning, Glen recounted his Friday night out with the boys. He said he had consumed four bottles of Miller with his cousin, Gary Stinson, and friends at Bud's Place, a neighborhood shot-and-a-beer tavern in the City Heights section of Wilkes-Barre. Later that evening, Glen continued, he drank a single Jim Beam and soda at the Crackerbox Palace, just across the river in Kingston.

The Crackerbox was a cross between a middle-aged pickup joint and a fistfight-in-the-parking-lot type of place. The bar hopped on Friday nights, though—heavy mascara, chain smokers, beer bellies, gold chains, and cheating hearts. It was there, at the Crackerbox, that Glen ran into two attractive blonde friends from aerobics class, Joyce Marie Greco and Carol Ann Kopicki, and Carol Ann's husband, Mark, a funeral director. Glen spent part of the time grumbling about his job, a frequent pastime. "I wish I was even a mailman, because I'd be outside then," he told them.

Glen made a point of providing Mitchell with the names of all the male friends he had run into at the two bars, but he made no mention of his encounter with the Kopickis and Greco.

The detective then asked Glen what he had worn for his night on the town. Glen said blue jeans, a long-sleeved blue shirt, blue jean jacket, and boots.

Mitchell looked down at the patient and noticed two scratches on the left pectoral area of his chest, then a smaller one on his left rib area. Glen showed Mitchell a pink mark on the back of his neck. The mark ran from one side of the neck straight across to the other side of the neck. Glen also showed the detective a raised mark on the back of his head. A bit of loose skin was sticking up.

Glen said that he had had about $1,300 in a drawer in the back room of the second floor. He said about $940 of it might have been in a check. He said he hadn't had a chance to deposit the money.

Especially because it had been a cool evening, Mitchell asked Glen about the fan that had been running on the floor in the master bedroom. Glen replied that he always slept with the fan on, "summer or winter." He said he slept better with it on. "It keeps down the noise."

Armed with the scuttlebutt from the scene, Mitchell asked Glen if he had been having an affair with someone from his office. Glen replied that he had had one, but that he had broken it off about a year ago. He identified the woman as his dental assistant, Deborah Ann Shipp. In response to questioning, Glen said she was about twenty-seven years old, and he provided Mitchell with her address and telephone number.

About twenty minutes into the interview, Mitchell and Glen were joined by Assistant District Attorney Peter Paul Olszewski; Bill Lisman, the deputy coroner who had identified Betty's body; and Detective Sworen.

"Glen, I am here officially," Lisman told his friend. "I have to tell you that Betty has passed away."

"Oh, fuck," Glen said, turning away to his right, toward the wall. He started to sob, then just as quickly stopped. It was hard to tell if he was in shock or putting the others on. After about forty seconds, Glen rolled back toward his visitors and resumed talking.

Lisman explained that there was going to be an autopsy, and that there was a lot of police activity at the house. "The investigation is ongoing right now," Lisman assured him. "I'll be in touch with you after the autopsy to make some kind of funeral arrangements." Glen told Lisman to do what was necessary, and if he needed to select a funeral director, to get someone from the Rotary Club.

Sworen wanted to see what he was dealing with. He asked Glen if he could see the head injury. Glen leaned forward and moved his hair to the side in order to provide a better view. It really didn't look that bad.

The interview was interrupted so Glen could be taken to the

second floor for the CAT scan. George went along, and en route he offered Glen his condolences.

"I should have realized something was wrong when you called for the coroner," Glen replied.

To George, this meant that Glen had heard Minnick make the radio call for a coroner from the second floor of 75 Birch while he was still sprawled on the kitchen floor, seemingly incoherent. Something wasn't right.

Felix Kwiatek, a Mercy Hospital employee, had called security guard William Emmett on his walkie-talkie around 9:00. He asked Emmett to meet him immediately in the first-floor emergency room. When Emmett got there, he found his colleague standing by the time clock in the stairwell.

"Do you know Glen Wolsieffer?"

Emmett said he did.

"His wife's been strangled, and Glen's here."

Emmett asked where.

"In E.R.," replied Kwiatek.

The cops were in Glen's room, so Emmett couldn't go in to see him. He stood outside, in the emergency room's kitchen area, for more than an hour.

When Glen went up in elevator number seven to the CAT scan room, Emmett accompanied him and George because the assigned hospital aide didn't know where the room was located. The test took only ten minutes—he'd kept George company in the waiting room—then it was back downstairs.

Glen turned to Emmett, his friend from the Mercy Hospital softball team, and started talking sports. He praised Emmett for having hit the ball so well that year. "So this is what life's all about," Glen continued. "I thought it was playing ball with the guys and having a good time. We'll have to play golf some time."

Glen started to cry. "I'll go outside if you want," Emmett said.

"That's all right," said Glen. "I don't mind you seeing me like this."

Emmett went to get Glen a container of chocolate milk. Glen seemed to relax. Without prompting, he started talking about the previous night's events, about how he'd been at the Crackerbox.

"I felt like getting into a fight, but I never expected this." Glen started crying again. "Poor Betty, she's gone. And I was almost a goner too."

Glen told Emmett that he'd been on the living room couch when he heard a noise like someone had tripped. He said that he always put a fan on when he slept on the couch. Glen said he had a gun. "I could have got him, but I tried to get the chain from my neck. I felt myself going and the next thing I felt myself being hit in the head." Glen said the intruder had been "a big dude with a mask on," but that it was dark in the room. "I should have known she was dead when I heard them talk about the coroner. I should have known. Poor Betty, she's dead."

A call went out to Dr. Robert Czwalina, who was filling in for Glen's regular family physician, Dr. David Kistler. Dr. Gaza told Dr. Czwalina that Glen was clinically stable, but he felt it best because of the head injury that the dentist be admitted to the hospital for observation. Dr. Czwalina agreed. He said he would be in to see Dr. Wolsieffer as soon as possible, but was tied up at another hospital with a cardiac patient.

The working diagnosis for Glen was possible severe concussion, multiple abrasions, a possible cervical sprain, and the trauma he was exhibiting from the apparent assault. The patient had to be watched closely for the next twenty-four hours to make certain his condition did not deteriorate.

Glen was transported to the Progressive Care Unit on the fifth floor, an area serviced by extra monitoring equipment and specially trained nurses. He was served a bowl of spaghetti for lunch, and complained to Officer George, who had followed him from the emergency room, that the food was cold.

CHAPTER 4

At the very moment that Glen Wolsieffer was being admitted to the hospital, Dr. Hudock was beginning a two-hour autopsy of Betty in the morgue several floors below. The pathologist was joined by Chief Deputy Coroner Joseph M. Shaver, Deputy Coroner Harry Hyman, Detective Mitchell of the city police, and detectives Mike Dessoye and Sworen from the district attorney's office. This had quickly become an important and sensitive case.

The victim before Dr. Hudock was a well-developed brown-haired female. By now, the abrasions on her body were more pronounced, as they always are in death.

Dr. Hudock found reddish-purple rigor mortis present on the left side of the face and small petechial, or pinpoint, hemorrhages in the white part of the eyes. There also were petechial hemorrhages along the upper and lower eyelids. The hemorrhages were an indication of asphyxiation, the denial of intake of oxygen and one's inability to exhale carbon dioxide. Betty's tongue was protruding about one-quarter inch beyond her teeth, another possible indication of asphyxia.

In the corners of Betty's eyes, Dr. Hudock found a dry pale-yellow matter, that secretion of the glands commonly called "sleepers." It appeared Betty had been asleep for much of the night prior to her death.

He found a superficial abrasion on the victim's nose, the type of wound often caused by an object such as a baseball bat or fist, or when the body part comes in contact with a stationary object, such as a wall or floor. The mouth-lip area appeared to have sustained a beating. The neck also was bruised, with extensive superficial abrasions and ecchymoses, or blood in the tissues from ruptured blood vessels. There were abrasions on the front and back of the neck.

From a pathological point of view, Dr. Hudock was bothered by the relatively clean condition of Betty's upper body. Virtually all of the abrasions would have caused bleeding. Yet there was no blood on her face. Someone must have wiped her clean.

There were other injuries on the upper body: a superficial abrasion to the lower right ear, an L-shaped abrasion on the left shoulder, and a brush burn on the right shoulder. When he palpated the Adam's apple, Dr. Hudock found the neck difficult to turn, and it made a grinding sound. The cartilage of the larynx had been damaged.

Under the left shoulder, Dr. Hudock found two reddish-brown linear streaks that appeared to be blood, significant because of the lack of blood found on the face and neck. Looking closer, he also found the same material on the left index finger and thumb. There were little cuts on the back of her left ring finger and left middle finger.

At Dr. Hudock's direction, Dr. Shaver, his chief assistant, clipped each of Betty's fingernails. He also cut samples of her head and pubic hair. Dr. Hudock drew two vials of blood from Betty's heart. Tests conducted at the state police laboratory would subsequently fail to detect any traces of alcohol or drugs.

Dr. Hudock also took cotton swab samples from her mouth, vagina, the posterior part of the throat, and the anus. There appeared to be no injury to the vaginal or anal areas, but the swabs would be tested for semen.

Turning the body over, Dr. Hudock found a blue washer-type object on the sheet. He detected an indentation in the skin near the back of Betty's neck. The mark matched the dimensions of the object, indicating to Dr. Hudock that it had been embedded in Betty's skin. He turned the object over to investigators, along with the victim's nightgown and two rings taken from her fingers: a fourteen-carat white wedding band, engraved "EGW to EJT, 11–27–76," and a white diamond ring.

Internally, the forensic pathologist found a hematoma, a bump or swelling filled with blood, on the left side of the scalp, and hemorrhages in the muscle running from the side of the neck to the shoulder blade. There were hemorrhages around the Adam's apple, too, but the thyroid cartilage was intact. As he worked his way through the various body parts, Dr. Hudock also uncovered small petechial hemorrhages near the heart.

Dr. Hudock concluded the messy part of his job and proceeded to the analytical. His major pathologic diagnoses: Betty Wolsieffer had died from "asphyxia due to strangulation" as well as a beating that left "multiple contusions, abrasions on the skin of the face and neck."

It was obvious that some type of force had been used on Betty's neck; Dr. Hudock just wasn't certain what that force had been. Surely some of the pressure had been manual, but he wasn't sure what else, if anything, had been used. Maybe someone would be able to discover what that blue object embedded in Betty's neck had been.

The process of collecting evidence at 75 Birch continued throughout the day. The ladder was seized, as well as the window screen. In addition, the police, led by Detective Bernard Banas, had seized a gray belt from the second-floor banister, the empty brown holster from the bedroom floor, and the Ruger .22-caliber revolver along with the three cartridges from the first-floor family room. In his hunt for possible murder weapons, Banas filled two bags with twenty-eight assorted belts. He proceeded to take the blood-stained pillow and blue-and-white pillowcase from the floor of the master bedroom murder scene. He also took the flowered green, brown, and yellow mattress sheet, also bloodstained. A white blanket, with hairs attached to it, a blood-spotted white bedspread, and a flowered bedsheet also were seized. From the master bedroom closet, he seized a plastic bag containing thirteen more belts of varying colors, a brown carrying strap, a black carrying strap, and red suspenders.

Moving to the second-floor bathroom, Banas seized four towels from the door, including two orange ones. He took a brown towel from the first-floor powder room. A videotape was made inside the house, with the camera going from room to room.

By midday, Danielle had been briefly interviewed by Detective Henry Kmetz. She still didn't know her mother was dead. Danielle said she'd been watching "Love Boat" on TV the night before with her Mommy and Daddy when her father's friend Richard came over to "ask Daddy to go for some beer." When the program ended, Danielle said, she went upstairs to lay down in Mommy's bed. She said she didn't hear any noises in the house that night. She also said she was not certain how she ended up in her bedroom, but when she woke up, she saw a policeman standing in the hallway outside of her room. Danielle would later worry that perhaps she had knocked her mother off the bed while moving around, after she had fallen asleep watching TV the night before.

Kmetz also interviewed Nancy, who confirmed that Glen had called her house at about 7:15 that morning asking Neil to come over. She said Neil told her that Glen did not give a reason. She told the detective she was aware that Betty and Glen had been experiencing marital problems, and that a former employee of Glen's was the third party. But, Nancy insisted, the matter had been resolved last January, when the employee was dismissed by Glen. Nancy said she had never heard about any violent arguments between Betty and Glen or of Betty being struck by Glen. If there had been any such incidents, Nancy said, she was sure Betty would have told her.

In the meantime, Neil drove down to the hospital in an unsuccessful attempt to see his brother. There were to be no visitors, on orders of the police. He then headed to police headquarters for additional questioning in the interrogation room by Detective Kmetz and Assistant District Attorney Larry Klemow.

The law enforcement team was far from convinced that Neil was telling all he knew. Maybe Glen had floated in and out of consciousness, and maybe he couldn't have gone upstairs to check on Betty and Danielle. But Neil hadn't been attacked. How could he have found his brother lying on the floor, claiming that someone had tried to strangle him, and not have gone upstairs to check on the others?

Neil, though, essentially repeated what he had told the cops in his brother's dining room, adding that when he first spotted Glen he had to "tap him a little bit, and say, 'What happened?' He really didn't know, he just said all he really knew was that he was being choked or strangled." He said Glen had not described the assailant or indicated whether there were more than one of them.

Kmetz wondered if Neil had gone to any other parts of the house besides the kitchen. Neil said he had walked into the living room, "then just came back out." He didn't mention Glen's sudden groaning. Instead, Neil simply told Kmetz that he resumed "trying to talk" to Glen, to "see what was going on."

Neil said that the entire time he was there alone with his brother, Glen never got up off the floor. As for his state of consciousness, "he was in and out. He was conscious and then, ah, I'm not sure if he went completely unconscious but, ah, he could talk sometimes and then he would just sort of moan." Again, Neil did not let on if he was at all bothered by the timing of his brother's wails.

"Did he say anything about his family?" Kmetz asked.

"Ah, let me think, no, I don't think so. I remember him saying something about the girls but I can't remember exactly what it was."

At this point, Kmetz let some of his skepticism show. "Okay, you come into this home—your brother, I figure you're worried about your brother—he's on the floor, okay. Your brother's married, is he not?"

"Yep."

"He has a child?"

"Yeah."

"Were you interested in these people?"

"Yeah, I was."

"Did you make any indication that you were interested in them when you were in the house waiting for the police to come?"

"Just my brother. I was listening, ya know, I was trying to hear any kind of noises or anything."

"Did you go up, did you go upstairs to see where the child was?"

Neil said he had not.

When Kmetz sought a reason for the lack of action, Neil first said he didn't know why, then added that he had been scared to climb the steps. "I was afraid that the guy was still in the house. I was listening for any noises upstairs, I didn't hear anything. I was afraid what I was gonna find, ya know, I just didn't know what to do."

Again, Kmetz's curiosity was aroused by Neil's response. "What did you think you might have found?"

"Well, I heard no noises, and seeing my brother's condition, I didn't know." It sounded as if Neil was afraid that Betty and Danielle were dead, but Kmetz neglected to ask the question directly.

"Did you ask your brother about his wife or his child?"

No, Neil said, he hadn't.

"Did your brother say anything about his wife or child?"

"Not that I can recall—I know when he was leaving he said, 'Take care of the girls.' "

Neil was asked how much time had passed between his call to the police and their arrival. He estimated about "three minutes or so."

"So you're saying for three minutes you stayed down by your brother? You weren't aware of what happened upstairs?"

"No, I had no idea," Neil insisted.

Kmetz tried to review the extent of the injuries, and lack thereof, to Glen's person. No, Neil said, his brother was not bleeding. As for any marks, Glen had told him the intruder had tried to strangle him. Neil said he didn't look very closely, that all he saw was some redness around the neck. He said he didn't notice anything else until the paramedics found the bump on the back of Glen's head.

After Neil described the conversation involving his decision not to join his brother for a couple of beers the night before, Kmetz asked Neil if Glen normally went out on Friday nights. Neil sighed, then replied: "No, I'd say he goes out maybe once every two weeks or so." Neil professed not to know that much about his brother's social life. Aside from a neighborhood tavern or two, he said, "once in a while" Glen would go to the Locker Room, a bar across the river in Kingston. "That's all I know," said Neil, making no mention of the Crackerbox.

Neil explained that Glen and Betty had had marital problems in the past—"he was seeing somebody else," someone he worked with—but everything had been worked out. Just like Nancy, Neil said that as far as he knew, his brother had fired the woman and they were no longer seeing each other.

Kmetz wanted to know if Betty had known about the other woman. Neil said that last year, "about this time," Glen had told her, "trying to get everything cleared up." As far as Neil knew, Betty and Glen had straightened everything out, and "everything seemed fine."

When Kmetz switched his interest to Glen's temperament, Neil described his brother as very levelheaded, not someone with a short fuse. In their ten years of marriage, Glen and Betty seldom argued, he said.

Circling back, Klemow asked Neil again about the woman in Glen's life. He said he only knew her as Debbie, that she had stayed on the job for a while after the romance ended, but that things got too sticky. "He tried to keep it platonic, I guess, but it wasn't working out. So, ya know, she was getting on his nerves or something, so he let her know it would be better for her if she just left."

Neil said Betty had known about the affair before Glen ended it. "They wanted to work it out. They wanted to get it out in the open." Neil said he did not know of any other extramarital affairs involving his brother.

By this point the interview was turning into an interrogation, as if Neil was a suspect, his credibility on the line, his responses subject to follow-up questions. But his position in all of this was crucial. He possibly held the key to what had unfolded at 75 Birch that morning.

Klemow wondered if he had told the cops to go upstairs. "I might have. I don't know," Neil replied. "I don't remember."

"Well, do you remember what if anything you may have said to them about upstairs?"

Again, Neil's memory went blank. "No, I don't. I don't. —I might not have said anything, I don't know."

"At that point did you know if anything was wrong upstairs?"

"No, I didn't," Neil told Klemow.

"When did you first find out that there was a problem?"

"Well, when Officer George went upstairs and he yelled down to Dale Minnick, 'Dale, ya better get up here.' "

Still, Neil insisted, he didn't know what Officer George meant. He said he didn't know Betty was dead until later, when he listened in on the upstairs conversation between the cops.

"You could hear them from the kitchen?" asked Klemow.

"I could hear them, yeah," Neil replied. Just as fast, he changed his answer. "No, no—I'm sorry. I was, I was in the living room."

"And what did you hear them say?"

"I heard them say that she was dead."

"And what did you do?"

"Nothing. I walked around. Then I heard my niece, and then they said, 'Will somebody come up here and get the child out?' "

Hunting for a clue to the murder weapon, Klemow asked about the lamp in Danielle's room—unplugged, without the shade on. Neil said he didn't know anything about it. He said he was pretty sure Danielle used a night light, but that he hadn't been in her present bedroom since she'd moved from the back bedroom, the one Glen now used as an office. "I would say she probably slept with a night light on, because she never liked to sleep alone, let alone in the dark."

Shifting gears like a prosecutor or defense attorney might do on cross-examination at a criminal trial, Klemow deftly inquired about Glen's business. Neil explained that his brother was in practice with two partners, was doing fine financially, hadn't appeared depressed or anxious in the past few months, and didn't have any enemies who might have committed the murder. He said Betty didn't have any enemies either.

Klemow wanted to know if Neil had any idea what time Glen got home the night before. Again, Neil sighed. "No, I don't. I'd just be speculating." But, he explained, their cousin Gary Stinson had come by his house that morning, after the police cars showed up and all, and told everyone that he had been with Glen at Bud's Place until 1:30.

There were a few questions about sports and Glen's drinking

habits, described as light. Then it was back to the ex-girlfriend. Neil said he was "pretty sure" that Glen had gotten counseling up at First Valley Hospital for the problem between his wife and the woman. He said that at first Betty was mad, but "after awhile they seemed to be working it out—and then it was great as far as I could see."

Next it was on to the ladder found behind the house. Neil said he had seen the ladder leaning against the house that morning. He had walked out back after one of the cops announced in the house that there was a ladder up in the back. Neil said he believed it was the ladder his brother kept between his garage and the Cooks'. He said it was in "terrible condition. It was just bendable. It was broken in one spot." Neil said he did not think the ladder was usable. In fact, he said, Glen often borrowed his ladder for things like painting.

He said Glen did not give him details about the attack. "All he said to me was, 'All I can remember is being choked. And then I kicked him in the groin.' That's all he said about the whole thing." He said he had not seen anything around Glen's neck, like a belt or a cord.

"How was the phone? I think you said it was off the hook, laying by him?" asked Klemow.

"Right."

"Was there any sound coming from the phone, like when you leave a phone off the hook sometimes it makes some noises?"

"No, I didn't hear it. I know the first thing I did, I picked it up, hung it up, and called the police."

Neil was not asked why he had failed to hang up the phone *after* he used it to call the police.

As Klemow's interrogation wore on, Neil got noticeably testy. As fast as the oncoming other half of a wrestling tag team, Kmetz took over the questioning, switching to Glen's dress habits. Neil said Glen didn't wear any kind of jewelry. He told Kmetz that Glen didn't use drugs, either. He had seen him intoxicated "once or twice." Glen only drank beer, so it would probably take him eight or nine beers to get drunk. But he had never been so drunk that someone had to drive him home. Neil said his brother's mood was not related to the amount he drank.

Klemow took over again. "Did your sister-in-law have any expensive jewelry?"

"No," said Neil. "We were just talking about that this morning, my family and I, and we couldn't figure out why, ya know, all we could figure out why anybody would want anything from their house is that there's a dentist, after his name in the telephone book. It happened to him before in Virginia, where he had got broken into and there was a large amount of cash laying around and at that time nobody took the cash, I think they were either looking for gold or maybe prescription pads, or something like that."

Klemow inquired about Glen's prior mental problems.

Trying to put the best foot forward, Neil replied: "Well, like I said, last year when he was having that problem, he was depressed and then I think then he went to see somebody up there," meaning the hospital on Dana Street.

"Was this different than the marriage counselor?"

"No, same one I guess."

"Well, did *he* go, or did they both go?" Klemow asked.

"They both went," said Neil, explaining only part of the story, leaving out that Glen's inability to decide between Betty and Debbie had led to his being admitted for psychiatric observation for several days.

Klemow wondered if Glen was a violent man. "Nothing out of the ordinary," said Neil, "scuffles at a softball game, but nothing other than that."

Kmetz shifted back to Debbie Shipp. Had Glen ever talked about the affair? "Not really," Neil replied. "He was ashamed of it, and I think he felt that I wouldn't look at it too well." As Neil explained all this to Kmetz, Glen's lack of candor to his brother became apparent. Although most who knew them believed the two men were inseparable confidants, here was Neil mistakenly explaining that Glen's affair had lasted no more than a year and that it had ended. Clearly, Glen had misled his brother about these personal matters.

Klemow was winding down now, firing queries all over the lot—loose ends. You never knew what might hit.

"Did your brother ever indicate to you that he was sorry that he was married?" Neil said no.

"The gun that was in the house, do you know why he had a gun?" Neil said it was for protection, and that he believed his brother had obtained the weapon after the burglary in Virginia.

They had been talking for forty minutes. Klemow told Neil to contact him, Detective Kmetz, or anyone in the police department if he remembered anything important or if any of the neighbors passed on something they might have heard.

Detectives Wayne Cooney and John Gonos had headed over to 35 Coal Street in Nanticoke for a chat with Deborah Ann Shipp.

A Luzerne County Community College student, Shipp acknowledged that she had been employed as Dr. Glen Wolsieffer's dental assistant from 1981 until February of 1986. She said she had worked at all three of his offices.

It quickly became clear that Glen and Debbie had not parted ways, as Glen had told Detective Mitchell at the hospital. Debbie said she had talked to Glen the day before, right here in her house. She said they had had lunch. In fact, she said, they usually had lunch together every Friday.

Debbie said that she and Glen had been involved in "a close relationship" for the past two years. They were in love with each other, she said. During the affair, both she and Glen had discussed his leaving Betty for her, Debbie said. Yes, she knew Betty; she had met her at the dental office. She said Betty had known of the affair for the last twenty months. No, she and Glen had never discussed anything going on at home between Glen and his wife. And no, Glen didn't do drugs, as far as she knew.

As the conversation progressed, Debbie loosened up, and the detectives circled back for a second round of questions about the previous day's lunch date. Debbie now acknowledged that she and Glen had also gone to bed. She further revealed that on that Thursday, Glen had also visited for lunch, and that they also went to bed and made love.

Debbie said that on both days Glen had appeared to be in a good mood, "comfortable, relaxed, not uptight or disturbed about anything." As he was leaving after Friday's lunch, she said, Glen promised: "I'll call you tomorrow." Of course, with Glen now in the hospital and his wife dead, the call would not be made.

According to Debbie, she and Glen had talked many times

"about their future, about being together, about a divorce." Glen had given her Christmas presents in the past, including a watch and earrings. She said she had bought gifts for him in return.

Debbie explained that sometimes she and Glen checked into a motel for sex, the Imperial Inn most of the time.

Recalling one particularly significant incident, on a Saturday in February 1986, Debbie said they had registered at the Red Roof Inn at about 11:00 A.M. and stayed overnight through Sunday. She said Glen had told his wife he was leaving her that weekend. Debbie said she thought that she and Glen were finally going to set up shop. But come Monday morning, when Glen returned home to see his daughter, Danielle, she was quite upset that he had been away all weekend and that he had not spent any time with her. Glen returned home and the plans were postponed.

Debbie confidently told the detectives it was impossible to even consider that her man had killed Betty. "He's not capable of doing something like that."

CHAPTER 5

By midafternoon, Dr. Wolsieffer was resting comfortably in the Progressive Care Unit, but still complaining of a headache. The hematoma had shrunk considerably, now described as the size of a quarter. The neck injury was described as only a "line-type reddened abrasion." X rays of the skull and cervical spine were negative. The CAT scan was fine, too.

His mother, Phyllis, was allowed in the room for a ten-minute visit. Her son was crying when she entered. "Mom, they suspect me. They think I had something to do with it."

Now they were both crying. "Betty's dead. I can't lose any more people I love," Glen continued. Mrs. Wolsieffer was told to leave the room.

The hallway outside of Glen's room looked like a law-enforcement convention. Assisting District Attorney Bernard A. Podcasy were several of his top aides, the city police chief, a captain, and a couple of detectives. Mostly they were milling around, hoping they would learn something crucial to the case.

Podcasy and his first assistant, Larry Klemow, decided a more complete statement was needed from Dr. Wolsieffer, provided, of course, he was still willing to talk. It was agreed that Sworen, Mitchell, and Assistant District Attorney Olszewski would make the attempt. The young prosecutor was a newcomer to the scene, a lawyer for less than two years, but he was smart and politically connected.

There were several important areas to cover: the seemingly ongoing status of Glen's extramarital involvement with Debbie Shipp; the substance of the statement he had given Detective Mitchell at the hospital that morning; and the history and circumstances of the dentist's mental health treatments.

While the investigators and prosecutors reviewed their laundry list, other members of the Wolsieffer family, still waiting for an opportunity to visit with Glen, discussed the frenzy of police activity with Glen's mother. She, in turn, called Neil, who, by this time, had returned home from police headquarters and was beside himself. It was obvious Detective Kmetz and Klemow the prosecutor thought Glen had killed Betty. Neil couldn't consider the possibility with even his wildest imagination. No way! It was preposterous.

But it looked like his opinion didn't matter. As a result, Neil started to seriously worry about what he should do. This thing was getting out of hand. He couldn't believe the questions he had been asked at police headquarters. It sounded like they thought that even he was involved. *Why didn't he go upstairs? Why didn't he do this? Why did he do that? Didn't he care about Betty?* Neil knew that Kmetz and Klemow were just doing their jobs, but the stuff about Betty was bullshit. He had loved Betty like a sister. He saw her and Glen every day. He and Nancy went out with Betty and Glen all the time. They were tight. They were family. He thought the world of Betty. Of course he cared about her. He still couldn't believe that she was dead, and here these guys were practically accusing Glen of having done it.

Chain smoking as usual, Neil paced around the kitchen and dining room of 84 Birch, stretching the telephone cord as he spoke to his mother. "Mom, I'm going to call Schooch," he said, using a nickname for Mark Ciavarella, a Wilkes-Barre attorney and good friend. "I don't like the way this questioning is going." A few minutes later, Ciavarella picked up Neil and they headed for the hospital.

When Mitchell, Sworen, and Olszewski entered Glen's room, the prosecutor had Mitchell extract a small card from his wallet containing the Miranda warnings against self-incrimination. If Dr. Wolsieffer had been involved in his wife's murder, the investigators weren't going to take any chances blowing the case on a technicality.

After reading the warnings, Mitchell asked Glen if he was willing to speak to them. Glen replied that yes, in fact, he *wanted* to speak to the investigators.

Glen substantially gave the same statement he had provided to Mitchell in the morning. But somehow in the course of the ensuing hours, he had been able to remember additional physical attributes of the intruder: the man had dark eyebrows, a dark mustache, and dark hair under the mask.

Olszewski asked Dr. Wolsieffer how he had spent the day before, Friday the 29th. Glen responded that he had worked all day at his dental office, until about 4:00 P.M.

Armed with the appropriate tidbits from the Debbie Shipp interview, Olszewski asked Glen if he had made love to his wife that night. Glen said he had not. Asked if he had seen Debbie Shipp the day before, Glen admitted that he had been in her company that Friday afternoon, only hours before Betty's murder.

"Did you have sexual relations with her when you saw her?"

"Yes," Glen conceded.

Mitchell said he didn't understand. That morning, in the first interview, Glen had contended he had broken off the relationship a year ago. No, Glen said, he had *fired* Debbie as an employee on February 3, 1986. But even that didn't make sense, because February was nowhere near a year ago.

Then Glen let on that about a year ago he had been treated for his "mental problem" at a hospital in Wilkes-Barre. Looking up angrily at the investigators, Glen said he had been told by one of the physicians that he was suicidal. He assured the law-enforcement officials that he was going to get his records changed to delete that diagnosis.

When the conversation turned to details of Glen's whereabouts that Friday evening, Olszewski asked him what time he had left the Crackerbox.

Just about closing time, Glen replied, about 2:00 A.M. Glen said he had gone directly home. As he had done earlier, he described his drinking that evening as moderate.

Glen said that when he arrived at 75 Birch he went upstairs, to the master bedroom in the front of the house, where he found Danielle and Betty asleep. He said the television was still on, so they must have fallen asleep while watching it together.

"What, if anything, did you do with your daughter?"

Glen said he had picked her up and carried her into her own bed, in the adjacent room. After placing Danielle in bed, Glen said he changed from his jeans into a pair of cutoff sweat pants, then went to bed. He said he did not have a conversation with his wife or daughter, a claim he would subsequently contradict.

"What happened next?" asked Olszewski.

Glen proceeded to tell essentially the same story he had been telling all morning, with additional details here and there: the clanging sound, from the rear of the second floor, it was just beginning to get light out, the intruder walking immediately from the back room down to the first floor.

Glen contended that he too went down the hall, and then down the stairs. Olszewski wasn't satisfied with the degree of description on that response, so he dug deeper. "How'd you get down the hall? Did you run down the hall? Did you walk down the hall? Did you crawl down the hall?"

"Yeah, I crawled," said Glen, adding that he had gone from his hands and knees to flat on his stomach, with the gun still in his right hand.

"Why'd you do it that way?" asked Olszewski, given the fact that the intruder had already made his way downstairs.

"I don't know," Glen replied.

Olszewski then wondered if Glen could have shot the intruder with his gun. Glen replied yes, he could have. The prosecutor wondered if Glen had ever shot a firearm before. Glen said he had. "Have you ever fired that particular weapon before?" Again, Glen said yes.

"Was the gun loaded?"

Glen said there were live rounds in the cylinder, but he didn't know if there had been one in the chamber ready to fire.

"Why didn't you just shoot the guy?" Glen said he did not know.

"Couldn't you have yelled to the guy to 'halt'?"

Again, Glen said yes. And again, when asked why he hadn't taken that action, Glen simply replied: "I don't know."

Trying to get the narrative back on track, Olszewski asked Glen what he did next. Glen said he went down the steps. "How'd you go down the steps? What did you do with the gun? Where was the gun at this point? In what position?"

Glen said he didn't crawl down the steps, that he had walked, with the gun pointed down, toward the first floor.

"Before you went down the stairs, did you have any idea where the intruder might have been?" He said no.

"Do you think it was possible for the intruder to have left the house without you knowing it?" Again, Glen said no.

"Why not?"

Glen said he would have heard anyone leaving through the front or side door. The intruder couldn't have gone to the basement, either, he added, because the steps were very squeaky and the door made a loud noise when it was opened.

Olszewski asked Glen if he heard any noises at all once he got downstairs. Glen replied in the negative, that there was quiet throughout the entire house.

In response to a question about what he had done next, Glen said he had looked around near the steps in the living room, but the intruder was not there. He said he then made his way back, into the dining room.

Olszewski interrupted at that point. "Are you absolutely positive that this intruder wasn't in the living room or in any part of the front of the house?"

Glen said he was certain.

"Was the intruder in the dining room?" Again, Glen said no. And again, he said he was "absolutely positive."

Working his way to the back, Olszewski asked Glen where he went next. Glen said he then entered the kitchen. Given the search of the other rooms that Glen said he had conducted, Olszewski wondered where the intruder possibly could have been.

Glen said the only possibilities were the kitchen or the family room behind it.

"Are you absolutely, one hundred percent sure that the intruder couldn't have somehow been behind you, upstairs or in the living room or in the dining room?" Glen said such a scenario was impossible, that the intruder would have had to have been somewhere in front of him.

Realizing that the intruder *had* to be in front of him, Glen said, he then repositioned the revolver from his side to a ready position, a little above his shoulder, but with the barrel pointing upwards, toward the ceiling. Once in the kitchen, though, he was certain the man was not there either.

Olszewski again focused on the door to the basement, located in the kitchen. Was it possible the intruder had gone through that door and down those steps? Glen said it was impossible; surely he would have heard the man on the noisy steps.

That left the family room at the back of the house.

Olszewski again wanted to make sure what Glen was telling him. "Going through everything you just told me, is there any way this person could have been in the kitchen, in the dining room, in the living room, or upstairs?"

"No," said Glen.

"Is there any way he could have gotten out of the house?"

"No." Glen said he was certain that the intruder had been in front of him.

But then Glen explained that as he continued to walk toward the family room, someone came up behind him, grabbed him around the neck, and began to choke him.

"What did you do?"

"I dropped the gun." He said that he reached back with his right hand to try to grab his assailant or the thing that was choking him. He said he also tried to attack the man's groin, with "a backward type of kick," but the end result was that he got hit on the top of his head and was knocked out.

Glen said he did not remember anything else until he woke up and called his brother, and during the entire struggle he had never turned around to get a good look at the intruder.

"When this person first started to choke you, why didn't you use your gun and shoot him?" asked Olszewski. Glen didn't answer. Again the prosecutor asked Glen if he could have shot the person, and again Glen responded that he could have. When pressed, he said he didn't know why he didn't shoot—other than that his response to the choking was to get both his hands in between his neck and the object choking him.

Mitchell asked Glen what he had worn the night before. Glen told him about the blue jeans, shirt, and jean jacket, and where he had put them—in the back bedroom. Mitchell asked if he could take the clothing; maybe it would be of some help in tracking down his wife's murderer. Glen said of course the police could have the clothing.

The scratches on Glen's chest and rib area were again discussed. He was asked how he had gotten them. Glen's response was bizarre. "I didn't wear anything on top. I should wear a T-shirt to bed." He continued that Betty, however, had worn a nightgown to bed. Asked if he had made love to her that evening, Glen said he had not.

About two-thirds of the way through the conversation, defense attorney Mark Ciavarella appeared at the door of Room 40. There wasn't a need for introductions; Ciavarella and Olszewski knew each other.

Ciavarella relayed that he was representing Dr. Wolsieffer and wanted the interview to stop until he had an opportunity to talk privately with his client. The law-enforcement team left the room and went off to brief Podcasy and the others.

After several minutes, Ciavarella motioned the men to return to the room, where he informed them that Glen wanted to continue with the conversation and would answer all questions as best he could. Ciavarella took a chair at the back of the room.

Mitchell concluded by asking Glen if he would mind providing some samples of his hair in a container. They too might help catch the intruder. Glen readily agreed, and a nurse was summoned to assist.

With hair in hand, Mitchell returned to 75 Birch to seize Glen's clothing. He also took a checkbook from the First Eastern Bank, issued in the names of E. Glen and Elizabeth J. Wolsieffer, a dark red leather woman's clutch purse, and a white cloth woman's handbag containing credit cards, cosmetics and other personal care items.

Mitchell then took a ride down by the banks of the Susquehanna River, just two blocks from 75 Birch. Perhaps the killer had ditched the murder weapon or some bloody clothing. But the search turned up nothing.

At 4:00 P.M., about a half hour after the cops left, Glen's blood pressure was checked again. It had zoomed up to 158 over 92. Glen complained again of headache. Apparently the medication was not relieving any of the pain. Another call went out to Dr. Czwalina. The nurse told him the patient was "somewhat despondent, and was demonstrating flat affect," meaning he was unemotional, without spark, sullen, and withdrawn. He still wasn't showing any grief. There was no telling how or when it might come out. Dr. Czwalina ordered a suicide watch.

Glen, though, ate a full dinner. He washed himself and shaved. Family members visited in pairs to check on his condition and pay their condolences about Betty.

Richard Miscavage, Glen's close friend and frequent companion, came to visit about 6:00 and asked some questions of his own. "Was he black or white?" Glen said he could not tell. "Did you turn on the lights?" Glen said he had not.

Asked for more details, Glen pointed to the cord on the window drape and said the ligature that had been wrapped around his neck "felt something like this." Miscavage then asked, "Doc, the house is open downstairs. Where could he hide?" Glen did not respond, saying instead that the intruder had been about six feet tall, very strong, and wearing a mask.

Nancy and Neil Wolsieffer also visited that evening, just before the arrival of Betty's brother, Jack, and his wife, Dorothy. Neil stood next to the bed while Nancy sat in a chair. Glen looked so pitiful lying there. There wasn't much talking. Neither one of them dared ask for details about what had happened. That was the furthest thing from their minds. Nancy thought to herself how awful it must be to lose a spouse at such a young age.

When Dr. Czwalina finally arrived at about 6:30, he found his patient sitting in a chair near the window, wearing a cervical collar. He promptly debriefed him and conducted a thorough physical examination. "He was not in any obvious distress," Dr. Czwalina later observed. "However, he was markedly shaken by the course of events which had ensued prior to the admission."

Glen provided a misleading explanation for his hospitalization at First Valley, attributing it to "nervous exhaustion." Dr. Czwalina observed that the bump on the rear of Glen's head was "tender to the touch" but had shrunk to less than the size of a nickel in diameter. He characterized the neck wound as superficial, less than one-sixteenth of an inch in width. Unlike the police, Dr. Czwalina did not detect any scratches, at least any worth mentioning in his reports, which did note Glen's persistent complaints of headache, pain in the left rear of his head, and stiffness of the neck. He repeatedly grumbled about the "ring around my neck."

Of course, the ring was not *around* his neck. The numerous physicians had detected an abrasion only on the *back* of the neck. The front of Glen's neck showed no sign of distress or injury.

Over the next several hours, as the parade of visitors dwindled, Aunt Mary the nurse prepared to spend the night in a chair at Glen's bedside. He still showed no signs of grief.

A sleeping drug, Halcion, was administered. Glen was in for a quiet, peaceful night. Under the advice of his attorney, Glen also was about to become silent concerning the circumstances of the night before.

Darkness had begun to settle in over the city of Wilkes-Barre when the investigators from the D.A.'s office and the city police department sat down to exchange notes. Around the table, they voiced a healthy dose of suspicion about the story told by Dr. Wolsieffer: a middle-of-the-night, second-story break-in, of an occupied house with two cars in the driveway; the use of a cruddy ladder, just laying there between two garages, to get to the darkened second-floor roof; Dr. Wolsieffer's failure to have shot at the intruder; the lack of serious injury to his body when compared to the brutality of the attack on his wife; the call to his brother rather than police; the wound on the back of the neck but not the front.

There was the lie about the girlfriend, too, but that could be expected. Anyone with otherwise clean hands who had the misfortune to end up in the middle of a police investigation couldn't be expected to open his heart and soul about his side action, at least not immediately. But this was a murder investigation, perhaps a spousal murder at that. Innocent or guilty, it didn't help Dr. Wol-sieffer that he had had sex with a mistress just hours before his wife's murder. Debbie Shipp certainly qualified as a motive for murder.

There were differences in the statements Glen had given that day, too. But were the subtleties that significant? Glen had told Officer George he didn't know if he'd woken his wife when he got up to investigate the clanging noise; he told Detective Mitchell in the morning interview at the hospital that he remembered his wife was asleep when he left the bed. Glen's description of the assailant got more specific with each interview. But none of the descriptions had been contradictory.

This was going to be a tough one, reasoned Podcasy. There was a considerable inventory of circumstantial evidence—but an equally large number of unanswered questions. Podcasy, the only one with the authority to approve an arrest, concluded the sum total of evidence to be nowhere near enough to convict in a court of law.

There would be no arrest—at least for now.

CHAPTER 6

IN HIS WORDS

August of '85, that was when I told Betty originally. I guess I wasn't certain if I felt strongly enough about Debbie to give up my wife and my daughter. And that was a very big concern of mine—if anybody, whether it was Debbie or anyone else, was worth giving up that happy home.

It was just that Debbie was around and she enjoyed me and I enjoyed her. It was at work, or if we did go out, it would be on a Friday night. We would go somewhere, whether it was a hotel or her mother's apartment or something like that.

After a few years, I started feeling guilty about doing it and I told Betty, "You know, I'm seeing somebody. I'm involved sexually with somebody else." And she said, "Who is it? Is it Debbie from work?" And I said, "Yeah." She said, "I thought so." That was as far as she took it. She didn't say, "Somebody told me" or "I saw you."

I don't know if anybody had told her or anything. I wanted to be the one to tell her, to admit to it. She didn't accept it. It certainly wasn't the right thing to be doing, but I told her, "I don't know what I'm going to do. I don't know if I want to be with her or if I want to stay with you and Danielle." There were a lot of things that were going on in my head.

I didn't want to just up and leave her. It wasn't Danielle, you know. A lot of it was Danielle, but a lot of it was Betty too.

One Sunday I was lying in bed and I looked at Betty, thinking, "She doesn't deserve this shit, you know, I'm being an asshole about this." So I figured before anybody else—I didn't know if she knew about it or not—but I kept thinking to myself, "I owe it to her before anybody else tells her, or she finds out. I should be the one to tell her." At least I could be that honest with her. If I've been screwing around on her, at least I can do that for her.

So we talk about it and I'm crying my head off, I don't know what the hell is going on, and she calls Neil over and he's worried. He doesn't know what's been happening. Then I explained it to him.

I really didn't know what to do. I was really distraught. I said, "I don't know who to talk to, I just need some counseling of some type."

So immediately she called her mother, not to squeal on me or anything, but her mother worked in a hospital, so maybe she knew a doctor. So she called somebody.

Next thing I know, I'm going up to this place where people really need help. There's some wild people up there.

It turns out I sign up for this place, and I'm there for three days trying to get out. I said, "What do I have to do to get out of here? I'll work it out with my wife, you know, things are fine or they will be fine."

I ended up like being a counselor for the time I was there. They would have these group sessions and I'd be helping these other people out, talking to them, "Hey, it isn't so bad, you know."

I went back to Debbie again.

I was thinking, "Well, maybe I will leave." I packed my bag and said, "I'm going away for the weekend." Debbie was in school, so on Monday I dropped her off at school, and I told her I would pick her up. "In the interim," I said, "I'm going home to see Danielle." So I went home to see Danielle, and Betty was there.

We talked some more. She didn't ask me where I was, who I was with, but I'm sure she probably suspected I was with Debbie.

She and Danielle were in the back room and I'm looking at them thinking, "How can I be doing this to you people?" I'm ruining their lives and I said, "I'll be back. I'm going"—I don't know if I told her "I'm going to see Debbie" or what. But I said, "I'll be back."

So I picked Debbie up and told her, "Hey, look, I can't go through with any plans with you. I love my wife and daughter and that's where I'm going to be." So I went back home. I thought that Betty had put up with that, with me, that I wanted to be loyal to her, and I loved her. There were no two ways about it.

Then I fired Debbie, and then Betty and I sort of—we even talked about having another kid, that kind of thing. But we didn't get any better. I wanted to work it out with her. But then we just kind of stayed the same as we were before I had told her.

Betty was very supportive at that point. I mean, she was the one that drove me to the hospital. I'm sure she wanted to get me straightened out as much as I did.

I said, "I really don't want to leave. I love you. I love Danielle. And I love what we have here." I guess I was maybe trying to say to her, "I wish you and I could have something that would keep me away from someone else."

CHAPTER 7

Betty and Glen were high school sweethearts and each other's first love. They married in 1976 while he was studying dentistry at prestigious Georgetown University in Washington, D.C. They lived in suburban Virginia, and Betty worked hard to support them during those years. They moved back to their Pennsylvania hometown, located just west of the honeymoon havens of the Poconos, in the fall of 1981, shortly after the birth of their daughter, Danielle. When they decided to return to Wilkes-Barre, they were motivated most by a desire to be near their respective families, especially on Glen's part.

In addition to their kin, Glen and Betty were reunited with a storied community founded in 1769 during the bloody Yankee-Pennamite Wars, and named after two Europeans sympathetic to the Yankee cause, John Wilkes and Isaac Barre. In recent times, Wilkes-Barre, the seat of government for the seventy-five municipalities in Luzerne County, has tried to forget its coal-mining past despite unmistakable daily reminders—Coal Street Park, Anthracite Street, Mineral Street, and Miner Street.

The locals also try hard to forget the destructive Agnes flood of 1972. More than twenty-five thousand people in the Wyoming Valley lost all or part of their homes. The area around Birch Street was inundated with up to thirty feet of water. Miraculously, only six died. The Mennonites and Amish came to help. So did the students from the nearby colleges. "Rebuild We Will" became the rallying cry. The catch phrase "The Valley with a Heart" also caught on, surviving to this day.

For a city its size, about fifty thousand, Wilkes-Barre is a place where everyone knows everyone, but at the same time it is a cultural extension of New York City, 130 miles away, without the proportionate crime, drugs, and violence. That is not to say that Wilkes-Barre—with its motto, "The Industrial Center of Northeastern Pennsylvania"—is not without its problems. The elegance of the good old days is gone. Nothing really took the place of coal. As with so many aging cities, suburban malls sucked away substantial sales from the downtown business district.

But all in all, as Betty and Glen made their pilgrimage north to their roots, Wilkes-Barre was still a very nice, quiet, peaceful community to raise children.

It was home.

Elizabeth Jayne (Betty) Tasker was born in Wilkes-Barre on January 17, 1954. Growing up, Betty was a Girl Scout, studied voice and piano, sang in the Mozart Club, and was a member of the First Baptist Church. She loved daisies. Blessed with an inexhaustible reserve of energy, Betty was a member of the Meyers High School Student Council, an honor student, a strutter in the marching band, and a member of the girls' basketball team. She spent those early years in a house on Wood Street in the South Wilkes-Barre section, with her mother, Marian; her father, John; and her brother, Jack.

Hazel-eyed, brown-haired, and bubbly as could be, Betty was a member of the Queen's Court for her senior prom, escorted by Glen, her football hero. "She was a great girl," said her dad. "Intelligent, charming—she'd do anything to help people out." In fact, Betty spent a large portion of her days assisting people in need: neighbors, friends, relatives, whoever. That was Betty's way, always there to lend a helping hand. It was not unlike Betty to show up unannounced at her parents' house to cut their lawn or help them put up their Christmas tree.

Then there was the day Neil and Nancy brought their newborn, Bryn, home from the hospital. Betty spent the morning at 84 Birch baking banana bread, so the house would smell good. Betty and Danielle, then four, decorated the front porch with streamers and a huge, homemade heart-shaped "Welcome Home Bryn" poster. "The cradle was set up and the house was all straightened. She even had prepared a casserole for that evening's supper," Nancy recalled.

Or the day when Nancy told Betty how upset their neighbors Marilyn and Tom O'Connor were about an accident their son had had at work. Betty immediately went home, cooked up a meal, and sent it over to them. "She was always doing things like that," said Nancy. "That's the way she was."

Strong and taut at five foot six, one hundred forty pounds, Betty worked hard at staying in shape by jogging almost daily and attending classes at the popular Lesley McCann's Aerobic World in Forty Fort, just across the Susquehanna River. She made many friends through her aerobics class, which she sometimes attended with Glen and even Danielle. By virtue of her husband's occupation, Betty also became very involved in the county dental society auxiliary, which afforded her an entrée into a more exclusive slice of the community.

An enthusiastic, driven spirit permeated Betty's entire life, whether it was her involvement in the dental auxiliary, aerobics and jogging, gardening, or homemade crafts. She was always the life of the party. "You knew that if Betty was going to be there, you'd have a really good time," recalled Nancy. For a wedding or baby shower, Betty would organize the entire program. If someone was needed to emcee, Betty would volunteer and handle the chore without the slightest display of nervousness. She loved to talk and socialize, just not on Friday nights in taverns, like her husband. "Hi, I'm Betty. Hi, I'm Betty," she'd say in greeting each guest at a Rotary Club function. If she wasn't consumed, she wasn't happy. And she never did anything halfway. Sometimes she expanded and improved relatively minor projects until they became major efforts. But she always saw the project through to fruition.

There was a soft spot in Betty's heart for animals, too. One day she brought a basket up from the basement and a mouse jumped out. She had to be convinced to set a trap and then, when the mouse was caught, Betty cried and wanted to let it go.

Betty was closely attached to the family dog, Rocky. The springer spaniel slept at the bottom of the bed and was treated as a member of the family. In the spring of 1983, Rocky was hit by a bus and rushed to the veterinarian. That June, while still recovering, the dog died after being hit by a police car in front of Meyers High. Betty and Danielle took the loss very hard, and frequently visited the gravesite, near the SPCA building. During one visit, Danielle asked her mother to write "Rocky" on a large rock, then placed it on the ground as a headstone.

The choice between a career and full-time motherhood was ultimately an easy one for Betty. She was content as a housewife and handled her role with considerable ease and comfort, given the fact that growing up she was rarely near small children. With Danielle starting kindergarten in the fall of 1986, though, Betty did begin to consider going back to work. Another child would have completed her life, but Glen wasn't ready. Also, she figured any employer would provide health-care benefits, which would ease the family budget since Glen had to purchase the insurance on his own.

To a fault, Betty covered for Glen and for the state of their marriage. She protected his image and didn't want anyone to think badly of him. In the end, above all else, Betty loved Glen no matter what he did. When she found love letters from his mistress, she kept them hidden. She always wanted people to believe that everything was perfect. If she was depressed, she wouldn't show it for fear of putting a damper on everyone else's good time. She was almost always smiling, ready to lend a helping hand to friends and neighbors, especially those in households where both parents worked.

She never once gave divorce serious thought, even when she threatened Glen. There was no way she was going to give up on him. She promised herself she would never let her daughter be bounced back and forth. "Mommy, if you and Daddy get divorced, I'll be an orphan," Danielle had told her one day. Betty also was terrified of the prospect. She had no job. She had no money of her own. Where would she go? What would she do?

On the days when things weren't going right, Betty often sang the words to Madonna's song "Borderline," always the verse, "You keep on pushin' my love over the borderline, keep pushin' me, keep pushin' me." Still, she always tried to be understanding with Glen and think positive for the future.

After Neil and Nancy learned of Glen's affair with Debbie Shipp, Betty begged them, "Don't be mad at him." Despite evidence to the contrary, Betty tried for as long as she could to downplay Glen's infidelity, at first even accepting Glen's claim that the relationship with his employee was not sexual but akin to brother and sister or father and daughter. When it came to Glen, Betty was always willing to put things in their best light.

Phyllis Duffy and Edward Wolsieffer were high school sweethearts before he joined the Navy in 1950, and they married in 1952. Stationed in Maryland, Ed told Phyllis he thought it best if she stayed behind in Wilkes-Barre, and so she did, living with her mother. Glen was born eight months later, but mother and son moved soon thereafter; his grandmother was spoiling him so.

Ed came home as frequently as possible on weekend leaves, and before long Phyllis was pregnant again, with Neil. "When we got married there were the two of us; when he came out of the service there were four of us," Phyllis recalled years later. "It never was the two of us anymore."

Shortly after Ed's discharge, they purchased a house at 14 Magnolia Avenue in South Wilkes-Barre, a house Phyllis still lives in. Like everyone else in South Wilkes-Barre, they endured the flood of 1972, when the water level reached the baseboard of their second-floor bedrooms. They rebuilt with a low-interest government loan.

Ed went into sheet-metal work, a field he would stay in the rest of his life. He traveled a great deal in those early years, often to the Binghamton, New York, region. "He busted his balls," Glen recollected. "He was a perfectionist, too." The elder Wolsieffer frequently told his children: "If you think you're right, I'll back you to the wall. But if you're wrong, you are on your own."

Glen's father also was a nervous man, to the point where the stress of his job led him to seek therapy. "We were more or less private people," said Phyllis Wolsieffer. "I think that was my husband's problem. He kept everything in, you know. His job was so stressful. He'd get mad on the job. These guys weren't doing things the way he wanted, he ended up doing it himself, that kind of thing, but he kept it all in. I remember he went to the psychiatrist a few times. He came home, he said, 'That's enough of this bullshit. This is costing too much money.' " As Phyllis recalled the period, her husband pulled himself together without any additional help.

There were other hardships. In the mid-1960s, when Lisa, the third and youngest Wolsieffer child, was still an infant, Ed almost lost his life in an industrial accident, breaking bones in his face and temporarily losing hearing in one of his ears. "They don't know if he missed his footing or if the flooring became weak, but the ladder toppled and he went through two stories and landed in a concrete basement," said Phyllis. "Had he landed a couple of inches to his right he would have been speared with conduits that were sticking up."

Neil and Glen didn't see their father very much back then. For many years, he came home only on Wednesday nights and on the weekend. These were the days before Interstate 81, so he had to drive the country roads from upstate New York. It wasn't until Glen was almost a teenager that Ed got a supervisory position that allowed him to stay in Wilkes-Barre all week long. "I really think that he pushed for that because then the boys started becoming very active in baseball and he wanted to be right there. Naturally, he became the manager of the team," said Phyllis. "He was a wonderful father."

Born March 20, 1953, Edward Glenn Wolsieffer, a Roman Catholic, spent his first six years of schooling at St. Aloysius with the Sisters of Mercy and practicing for Little League. He then switched to public school for better opportunities to play sports. In high school, Glen lettered in baseball, basketball, and football. Nicknamed "Wolf," he was an honor student and treasurer of the Student Council in his senior year. On Sundays, he was a reader at St. Theresa's Church on Old River Road.

In his adult life, Glen had many acquaintances, but few really close friends. He felt uncomfortable in crowds and often came across as laid back, almost indifferent. From childhood on, he had a desire to be liked. It was important to Glen what others thought of him. Muscular, fit, and handsome, Glen loved the attention the women at aerobics class paid him.

Glen paid the household bills, but Betty often had to push him into making major decisions, like buying 75 Birch instead of continuing to rent it. Yet there was a decisive arrogance to Glen in the way that he sometimes treated Betty. "Friday nights are mine," he had been heard to lecture her when she complained about his going out with his friends.

Glen's dental business was solid, although no one would ever accuse him of being a workaholic. He always found the time to play on several softball teams, including the Mercy Hospital squad, get in a round of golf, or have a few beers with the guys.

By all accounts, Glen was highly professional and a perfectionist when it came to dentistry, this despite the fact that he had grown to dislike his profession. Glen said he wished he had a job like his brother's because Neil came in contact with so many people and liked what he was doing. To Glen, dentistry was the same boring routine while Neil got to experience something new and different every day.

Whereas Neil was content with his rather uncomplicated life, Glen always appeared to be waiting for better times. As one of Glen's friends said years later, "He was just never satisfied. No matter what he did, no matter who he was with, he always wanted something else."

Glen and Neil were inseparable during their childhood years, though they often settled their disputes by putting on boxing gloves. They loved to play cowboys and Indians, and Zorro. They shared a bedroom, which for a time was wallpapered with horses.

Although he was the older one, Glen often sought comfort and protection from Neil. "I can remember Glen sometimes having a bad dream, and saying, 'Neil, can I come over with you?' and they would end up sleeping together," their mother recalled.

The boys were opposites in many other ways, too. Glen loved school, Neil hated it. On many mornings, as their mother watched from the front porch, Glen would push Neil up the school bus steps. "Neil would be holding back. Glen would say, 'Come on, get on.' He'd get up, come down the steps, and he pushed Neil up the steps."

Neither boy posed a discipline problem, though; they were

good kids. Ed Wolsieffer never laid a hand on his boys; his large frame and stern commands were enough. He sat you down and talked to you. That was sufficient.

That's not to say that Glen the toddler never went astray. "I remember one time, Glen getting on the kitchen table and I was ironing and he picked the hanger up off the table and put it in his mouth," said Phyllis. "Instead of him pulling it out of his mouth he pulled it through his cheek. He kept pulling. I was trying to stop him. There he was, pulling it and yelling."

Of the two, Neil was definitely quieter. "He just sat on the floor. He had a little stagecoach with horses and he'd crawl all along here playing with them," Phyllis said, contending that Neil was more like her and her husband, keeping his true feelings to himself.

A love of sports was perhaps the strongest bond between brothers, as well as between father and sons. Relatives and friends remember the devotion that both Neil and Glen paid to athletics dating back to their early grammar-school days, an interest no doubt buoyed in the teen years by Ed Wolsieffer's involvement in youth baseball programs.

Many would say that Neil had the better athletic ability, but Glen had the greater drive. He wanted it more. As captain and starting catcher, Glen led the Meyers Monarchs high school baseball team into the third round of the state playoffs, being named All-Scholastic his last two years. "Neil had the natural ability in everything, academically, too," their mother contended. "But you know, I think Neil was like I am. We get in our own little cushioned nest and we're comfortable and we don't push for anything better. We are happy with what we have."

Betty and Glen grew up just a few blocks from each other. At first they socialized within a clique of about twenty friends, dating each other's acquaintances. Then, during their senior year, 1970–71, they fell in love. They were one of the high school's most popular couples. They went to dances together. They went to the movies together. They walked home from school together, hand in hand. They took romantic strolls along the promenade of the Susquehanna.

After high school, Betty wanted to be a veterinarian, while

Glen wanted to be a dentist. He enrolled at the University of Scranton on a four-year room-and-board athletic scholarship, where he studied pre-med and continued his exploits on the baseball diamond. Named to the All-Middle Atlantic Conference team, he hit nearly .300 while playing first base.

It was in college that he finally fixed on precisely what to call himself. He had replaced his real first name, Edward, with his middle name, Glenn, in high school, contending that people kept mixing him up with his father. During his years in Scranton, he shortened the name to Glen. "I figured I had enough letters in my last name, I didn't need another N," he explained.

In the meantime, Betty enrolled at Wilkes College, located in downtown Wilkes-Barre. She found the pre-veterinarian work too much to handle, however, especially the chemistry courses. She graduated with degrees in sociology and education, in between working part-time at the college and raising money for the United Way.

After graduating, Glen studied dentistry at Georgetown University, renting an apartment in Arlington, Virginia, with three buddies and commuting back to Wilkes-Barre on weekends to see Betty. When Phyllis and Ed drove Glen to his new school, Ed, who had never missed one of Glen's college games, even the ones in Florida, took Glen's departure especially hard. On the way home, Ed inexplicably began crying, so much so that he had to pull into a rest stop. He suffered a heart attack about two weeks later.

By this point, Betty had begun to carry two jobs—switchboard operator at a local hospital until 6:00 in the morning, then substitute teacher at one of the local high schools—a rigorous routine that enabled her to save money for the anticipated wedding. She would do anything for Glen, and often did—that was the depth of her dedication.

With the permission of the Roman Catholic Church, the high school sweethearts were married by a minister at the First Baptist Church in Wilkes-Barre on November 27, 1976, the Saturday after Thanksgiving. Neil served as best man. A friend of Glen's father, a priest, also participated in the ceremony. A reception followed at a local American Legion Post Home, complete with a polka band and attended by nearly three hundred people.

There was a civil coolness between the two families, a condition that would provide the foundation for the emotional tumult that ensued ten years later in the wake of Betty's murder. Her father thought well of Glen and believed that his daughter was destined for a bright, happy future, but he wasn't enamored with his son-in-law's pedigree. There was no mistaking that the father of the bride and the father of the groom could not stand each other. Over the years, petty things caused friction, too. The Wolsieffers frequently complained that the Taskers were always late. The Taskers felt as if their every move was being timed by a stopwatch.

Betty and Glen spent their wedding night in a Wilkes-Barre hotel, then left for Arlington, Virginia, to set up their new life together. Glen had to be back at school on Monday.

"We didn't think we'd get married while I was in dental school. Everyone said, 'Wait until you get your degree,' " said Glen. "But I was driving back and forth, and she was working up here. We figured, 'We love each other, let's do it.' "

As with most newlyweds, money was tight during those early years. Betty and Glen lived in an apartment furnished with hand-me-downs from relatives and friends as well as Betty's creations, products of her love for flower arranging and needlepoint. Betty was an impeccable housekeeper. Everything always had to be just perfect.

While going to school, Glen worked part-time in a U.S. Food and Drug Administration lab while Betty toiled as a contract executive for Xerox, mostly investigating unpaid accounts on government contracts. During those years, Glen almost always turned down invitations from his buddies to go out for a beer. He was in too much of a hurry to rush home to Betty.

Upon graduation in 1979, Glen joined a dental practice in Virginia with one of his instructors from Georgetown. The following year, the Wolsieffers purchased a home for $140,000 in Fairfax, Virginia, which Betty decorated with reconditioned crates from Louisiana. They both had to work to keep up with the mortgage.

At this point in their lives, Betty and Glen began trying to have a child. In early 1980, Betty miscarried. They kept trying and by that summer, Betty was again pregnant. Danielle was born on March 29, 1981.

It was about this time that Glen grew homesick. For her part, Betty was torn because she had grown to like Virginia. The issue of housing costs, and the overall cost of living, was the deciding factor for them, since the prices of houses near the nation's capital were among the highest in the country. Glen wasn't making that much money. Betty was going to have to go back to work. But she didn't want to put Danielle in day care. Something had to give.

Both of them had grown up in close families. Furthermore, they figured the family setting would benefit Danielle, too. In August 1981, Betty and Glen moved back to the South Wilkes-Barre neighborhood where they each had been raised—a two-minute walk to the Susquehanna levee, renting the trim, two-story house at 75 Birch.

How proud Ed and Phyllis Wolsieffer were to have their professional son return home, setting up a practice—and with their first grandchild, too. Ed visited virtually every night, eventually to read Danielle a book before she went to sleep.

Oddly, Glen resented the attention his father paid to Danielle, surely much more attention than he had received at that age, with his father first in the service, then on the road for work. Perhaps subconsciously, Ed Wolsieffer was trying to make up for those lost moments through Danielle, but Glen cut him no slack. Most nights when his father arrived right after dinner, Glen abruptly excused himself and took the dog for an unnecessarily long walk. He needed his space.

A beautiful child, Danielle wore her brown hair long in the back. She told relatives she wanted her locks to grow just as long as Crystal Gayle's, the country-western singer. She and her mother were like a team, whether it be baking a cake, combing their hair, applying fingernail polish, going to aerobics class, arranging flowers, doing arts and crafts, or waiting for Daddy to come home.

Still very active in sports, Glen hung a basketball hoop over the garage door in the backyard. He also attended aerobics classes, sometimes with Betty, played on two softball teams—usually at third base—and was a 10-handicap golfer, often playing with Neil and his brother-in-law, Jack Tasker. Glen's contacts with other members of the Tasker family were quite minimal, however.

Professionally, Glen joined up with two other dentists who

operated offices in three outlying communities and worked his way up the ranks to be president of the South Wilkes-Barre Rotary Club, succeeding his brother-in-law, Jack, who had succeeded Glen's father, Ed.

Although quiet and moody, Glen appeared to be content. But underneath he wasn't, frequently wondering, "Is this all there is to life?"

The spirited and energetic Betty joined the Luzerne County Dental Society Auxiliary and subsequently served on the state membership committee of the Pennsylvania Dental Society. Then there was racquetball or aerobics, sometimes followed by a luncheon date. With the entrée into this more elite social world, Betty took on a considerable work load. Before long, she was spending countless hours planning educational programs about dental care for young children, and eventually was elected recording secretary of the county group. Put in charge of a statewide workshop on "Dental Health Week," Betty drew on her love of exercise and concocted "Toothercise," a combination of aerobics and dental hygiene education to the melodies of a Disney record album, *Mousercise,* and presented it at the Wyoming Valley Mall. When a child deposited a token into the project's huge refrigerator box, someone came out to explain the finer points of brushing to the youngster. Betty won statewide recognition for her efforts.

In fact, Betty's main problem was that she had a difficult time turning down requests for her time. She just couldn't say no—whether it was the dental auxiliary, Rotary Club, or her elderly, infirm neighbors. Even her brother, Jack, said she spread herself too thin helping others and had advised her to slow down. It wasn't that she was taken advantage of as much as she enjoyed helping others. But sometimes her largesse went too far. "Sometimes she overextended herself, giving 150 percent. And that bugged Glen," said Nancy.

The assessment by Glen's sister, Lisa, was less kind. "Betty said no to no one, then bitched because she had to do it all. She was always late because she was always doing a million things. She was a real good person, but I wouldn't call her saintly as she has been described.

"Betty always had a headache. She was so tense from all these demands. If she didn't go to exercise every day she was miserable," Lisa added. She went on to recall that in the midst of her busy day, Betty managed to salve her guilt by buying Danielle a present every day. "It drove me crazy," said Lisa. "Every day she got something, I guess because she had to go to all these places. And wherever Betty had to go, Danielle had to go. So to pacify Danielle, because she didn't want to go, Betty would say, 'I'll buy you this.' It got to the point that no one else wanted to take Danielle shopping because she was real demanding."

In late 1983, the Wolsieffers purchased 75 Birch for $42,700. They didn't make any money selling the house in Virginia.

Several months earlier, Neil and Nancy had purchased a house almost directly across the street, at 84 Birch.

With Glen back in town, the two brothers were frequent companions. They shared their dreams and disappointments. They played ball together. They hung out together. They drank together.

Brothers. As close as brothers could get.

It was like old times.

CHAPTER 8

The marriage of Betty and Glen Wolsieffer gradually developed on two incompatible levels. On the one, they spent a great deal of time together. They went skiing in the Poconos and often took trips to visit friends in places like Boston and New York State. They went out for dinner almost every weekend, often with Neil and Nancy. On Mondays, when Glen was usually off, the two of them went grocery shopping together. They even took dance lessons together. A common backyard scene would have Glen shooting basketball with Betty gardening nearby. They appeared to be a happy couple while out in public.

On the other level, though, they were off on their own separate ventures. Betty spent much of her free time alone with Danielle, or with her friends and the dental auxiliary, while Glen hung out with "the boys"—golfing, hunting, softball, the Rotary Club, or at one of several neighborhood taverns.

Obviously, something was wrong. Perhaps they were high school sweethearts who outgrew each other. Betty hurt more than she let on about Glen's infidelity. When she did reveal the unsatisfying aspects of her marriage to friends, she only told them bits and pieces. "She kept the facade that they had a great relationship," said Nancy Wolsieffer.

Glen's insatiable desire for more out of life escalated after the birth of Danielle. He wanted the secure life-style of being married and having a family, but he also wanted the freewheeling social life of an eligible bachelor.

Like his father before him, Glen developed a habit of going out every Friday night without his family. Sometimes he would take Betty and Danielle out for dinner—usually a quick pizza. But then he would drive them home and head out on his own. Of his customary Friday-night disengagement from family life, Glen explained that it was a tradition. In fact, on some Friday nights he ran into his father while bar hopping and joined him for a few. "We would go to our different bars. A bunch of the fathers would be at one place, so we would hang out with them for another hour or so," Glen explained.

It was usually quite easy for Glen to get away alone; Betty wasn't interested in bar hopping. A woman of simple tastes and pleasures, she preferred to stay at home. She didn't like to stay out late. She didn't drink much at all.

She also despised her husband's Friday-night ritual because it seemed that every time he went out lately, she was awakened by an anonymous telephone call. When Glen and Neil went out together, Nancy often received a call as well, usually when the men were at a place called Sofa's Bar & Grill. Most of the time the women heard only breathing. But on one occasion, the male caller told Nancy, who had an unlisted number: "I know you're home alone." The calls, which always came around 1:45 A.M., just before closing time, were worrisome enough to Neil that he had stopped going out as much.

When Betty, who didn't like the nightlife, protested that she thought it inappropriate for a married man with a young child to be out partying at singles bars like the Crackerbox, Glen assured her he meant no harm, that he just needed to relax a little. Anyway, he told Betty, he was always home by 2:00 A.M., when the bars closed.

Of course, the good-looking dentist was often busying himself with more than just a couple of bottles of beer. Instead, he was fighting a losing battle to keep his sexual desires in check.

Glen's roving eye began to affect his marriage when the family returned to Wilkes-Barre in the fall of 1981. With Betty occupied caring for the newborn, Glen turned his attentions elsewhere. He hired Deborah Ann Shipp, who was twenty-two at the time, as his dental assistant. The attractive, dark-haired woman took care of his instruments, X rays, and appointments. It wasn't long before she also was taking care of more personal matters.

Debbie drove herself whenever she worked at Glen's offices in Nanticoke or Hanover Township. But on Tuesdays, her day to report to the office in Shickshinny, Debbie was picked up in the morning by Glen. Within weeks the chitchat in the car turned romantic. There was electricity in the air. The two became intimate in time for Christmas of 1981.

Glen and Debbie saw each other every work day. Then, once almost every week, always on Friday night, they went to a local motel, the Imperial Inn, for sex. Month after month, then year after year, the secret relationship continued. In fact, the affair would endure until at least November of 1988—more than two years *after* Betty's death.

The relationship never seemed to get past the sex, though. Debbie was looking for more, but she understood that it was difficult for Glen to make a commitment. Debbie sympathized with her lover's plight, always figuring in the back of her mind that someday they would be together.

While Glen's love affair blossomed, the duplicity gradually started to eat away at him. Then two unrelated events added more stress. On March 16, 1984, Glen's father died of a heart attack at the age of fifty-three. He hadn't taken care of himself after his first attack, going back to smoking and eating the things he'd been told to stay away from. And then there was the stress, always the stress of the job.

Phyllis remembered that Neil went to Glen's office to break the news; then the two of them drove over to inform her. "I was getting ready for work, I came downstairs, I saw the two of them at the back door and said, 'I know what you want to tell me, your father is dead.' They said, 'Mom, how do you know?' I said, 'I just know it.' And I don't know how I knew it."

A month after his father's death, Glen's best friend, the Georgetown instructor who had helped set him up in practice after graduation, died in an automobile accident, killed by a drunken driver. The tragedies struck like a double whammy. Friends recall that Glen was never the same. He grew more quiet, sometimes sullen. He stopped going to church every Sunday, and he stopped going to confession altogether. As a consequence of his losses, Glen grew even closer to his brother. In discussing his losses one day, Glen put his arm around Neil and told him that he was his new best friend and role model. Neil felt sorry for Glen. They spent more time together than ever.

That fall, Debbie enrolled at Temple University in Philadelphia to study physical therapy. Her relationship with Glen didn't end, however. She came home nearly every weekend, and almost always spent Friday nights with Glen, still at the Imperial, never out in public having a good time. As usual, Glen left to return home about 2:00 A.M., the time the bars closed.

During these sex sessions, Glen repeatedly begged Debbie to return to the Wilkes-Barre area full-time. He echoed that same plea in almost daily telephone calls. Her absence was depressing him considerably. At times he was frantic. He claimed he couldn't make it without her.

Debbie relented that December during the year-end holiday break; she not only returned to Wilkes-Barre but resumed working full-time in Glen's dental offices. Glen gave her pearl earrings as a Christmas present. The Friday-night forays continued, only now they took place at Debbie's house instead of at the Imperial. There would be other love presents forthcoming—a watch, a bracelet, diamond earrings—for Debbie's birthday and other special occasions. There was talk of the future.

But Glen never got a divorce. Instead, as Debbie explained, Glen was "concerned about not being with Danielle and not seeing her."

Betty knew about none of this, however. She only knew that in addition to Friday nights "with the guys," Glen had his Monday-night Rotary Club meetings, softball, golf, and working late on Wednesdays (Debbie did too).

The more time Glen spent outside the home, the more time Betty spent preoccupied with the dental auxiliary and lending a hand to whoever needed it. They were running from each other and their marriage.

In early August 1985, with Danielle now more than four years old, Betty discovered a cache of love letters Debbie had mailed to Glen's office while she was away at Temple. As Betty would later relate, she kept her discovery a secret for several days, then confronted her husband, who at first denied any infidelity, then insisted the affair was "nothing." Glen said he somehow needed Debbie to get over the death of his father the year before. He also promised Betty that he would end the relationship immediately. Of course, Glen neglected to tell Betty that he had started up with Debbie nearly three years before his father died. He obviously also neglected to tell her that he and Debbie had talked about his getting a divorce, and that he and Debbie had recently looked at an apartment. Glen did tell Betty that he was thinking about getting an apartment on his own, for a trial separation. "If you walk out that door, you're not coming back," Betty told him.

Forced to address his double-dealing, Glen jumped back and forth between leaving home and forgetting about Debbie to work on his marriage with Betty. Debbie threatened to kill herself. Betty held the trump card, little Danielle and visitation rights.

With each day the strain increased. Glen started to lose weight. He couldn't sleep. Betty found him crying uncontrollably for no apparent reason. His stomach was upset. His internal system was out of whack, with abnormally frequent bowel movements. He really didn't know what to do. He couldn't go on like this. He even thought of suicide.

Late on the morning of August 25, 1985, Glen tried to check himself in at the NPW Medical Center. Glen explained that he was physically exhausted and began crying. He said he had been depressed for the past four to five months over an extramarital affair. He said he had told his wife two weeks ago that he was going to leave her, but had not yet followed through. He reported being depressed about the recent losses of his father and best friend and that approximately one year ago he had suffered through a bout of depression when his mistress left the area to attend school. For the past year, Glen explained, he had been suffering from insomnia and confusion. He admitted to fleeting thoughts of suicide over the past month but had not developed a plan or method. He said his brother was a major source of support.

An initial diagnosis of "major depression—recurrent" was made, and after consultation with psychiatrist Steven R. Kafrissen, Glen was referred to First Valley Hospital, Wyoming Valley's mental health unit, in downtown Wilkes-Barre. There, a battery of medical and psychiatric personnel commenced a round of examinations. As part of the admission workup, Glen was required to sign a document acknowledging that he understood he had to give seventy-two hours notice in writing if he decided to leave before being officially discharged.

Glen explained in one session that he needed "time to re-evaluate life," that he had to decide whether to stay in his marriage or leave for the "woman I love." The admitting psychiatrist, Dr. Kafrissen, wrote in a report that Glen had talked "about feeling preoccupied with guilt feelings and has had vague passive suicidal thoughts." Dr. Kafrissen's report also noted that Glen's father had suffered a "nervous breakdown" about twenty years earlier, and that Glen had suffered through the loss of his father and his best friend within the past year. The psychiatrist observed that Glen was "especially concerned because of his four-year-old daughter, who would be traumatized by the separation and divorce."

Dr. Kafrissen also wrote: "He continues with very ambivalent feelings about what to do with his life and states: 'I don't want to hurt anyone.' "

The admitting diagnosis was given as "adjustment disorder with mixed emotional features." Dr. Kafrissen noted three items on his initial problem list: "depressed mood with sleep and appetite disturbances, vague past suicidal thoughts, and serious interpersonal difficulties." On a hospital questionnaire, Glen listed under personal strengths "active in sports and a caring individual." Under special interests and hobbies, he listed "sports."

He told Brian Wlazelek, his assigned therapist, that he had decided two weeks ago to leave his wife, but had not done so yet. He said he was angry with himself for "being in this predicament." Glen said he felt little support since the deaths of his father and best friend. He said he was "confused about what to do," found himself sleeping only five or six hours instead of seven, and frequently woke up at 4:00 A.M. thinking about his situation.

It didn't take long, however, for Glen to feel uneasy in his temporary home. When a nurse attempted to administer a dose of Norpramin, an antidepressant, that evening, Glen refused, stating that he was unsure of his intentions to stay on for treatment. He said that he would talk to Dr. Kafrissen in the morning about being discharged. Glen then asked to sign the seventy-two-hour notice form to get the ball rolling for his departure. After a discussion with hospital personnel, however, he was persuaded to wait until the morning. Before going to sleep, Glen participated in a community group meeting, and it was noted that he displayed no suicidal thoughts.

He slept well that night, but refused to have his blood drawn for a comprehensive workup in the morning, stating that he planned to leave the hospital. He then requested to be allowed to sleep through breakfast. The request was denied, and Glen soon got up and ate with the others. But that was the extent of his interaction. After eating, he secluded himself in his room.

Throughout the afternoon, Glen was depressed. He was described as cooperative, but focused on his desire to leave so he could "take care of 'outside' problems." He remained ambivalent about his treatment.

Then Glen and Betty met with Wlazelek to discuss the supposed key problem areas in their marriage, namely "communications and distance in the relationship." Even before the hospitalization, Betty had felt that Glen didn't communicate with her and didn't reassure her enough that everything was okay. In her mind, Glen preferred to avoid such conversations, which led to her keeping silent for fear it would upset him. It was an unproductive cycle that needed to be worked out.

Later that day, under orders from Dr. Kafrissen, the Minnesota Multiphasic Personality Inventory test was administered to gauge Glen's personality functioning. Glen scored fine, but the results generated skepticism as to his sincerity. "This profile should be interpreted with a degree of caution," the examiners wrote in a report. "Examination of the validity scales reveals that this patient was not completely honest in answering test items, suggesting some motivation to deny problems." The examining psychologists recommended that Glen begin therapy to confront the denial of his true feelings and explore the underlying feelings of dissatisfaction and depression.

Glen's attitude changed for the positive following the session. He expressed a willingness to stay in the hospital, but only for a short time. He wanted to work his problems through on an outpatient basis.

He again slept well throughout the night. In the morning he finally agreed to have his blood drawn. He continued to keep to himself before breakfast, though, interacting only with his roommate. Then, just as suddenly, he told Wlazelek that he again wanted to sign the form giving seventy-two-hour notice to leave the facility against medical advice. Glen explained that he had decided to stay with his wife, though he stated that he had made his decision "primarily out of a sense of responsibility."

That afternoon, Dr. Kafrissen talked to Glen about his intentions. Glen told the psychiatrist he wanted to return to his wife, but, Dr. Kafrissen noted, Glen was "still very guilt-ridden" about his duplicity. After a discussion, Glen withdrew his notice to leave and agreed to have a therapy session with Betty and possibly one with Debbie.

That night, Betty again came to visit, and Glen seemed in a better mood. He appeared comfortable with his decision to rescind the seventy-two-hour withdrawal notice, and he attended a community therapy session with other patients.

On August 28th, Glen's fourth day in the hospital, he awoke in a bright mood after yet another good night of sleep. He remained in his room until breakfast time, though, again declining to mingle with the others. Clearly, Glen was still bothered by his marital dilemma. Following a meeting between Glen, Dr. Kafrissen, Wlazelek, and Debbie Shipp, the psychiatrist observed that Glen was "still having a problem making a decision" about leaving "his paramour." Glen had managed to give Debbie the bad news, but, as Dr. Kafrissen observed, "he had a very difficult time telling her he would not see her anymore." Continued therapeutic support was promised for Glen. Debbie refused all offers for outpatient counseling, though.

Later that afternoon, Betty visited Glen, and he was observed interacting well with other patients. The next morning, he attended

another community meeting and was very cooperative with all involved. He renewed his request to be discharged.

When Dr. Kafrissen looked in, he found Glen's depression
and "intense conflicting feelings" to have lifted. Glen promised he
would live with Betty and not see Debbie Shipp anymore. He also
committed to continuing with marriage counseling.

Glen and Betty met with Wlazelek that afternoon and reviewed follow-up plans for counseling. Glen agreed to individual
as well as marital therapy. He was advised to avoid all contact
with Debbie Shipp, and to work at understanding the dynamics of
guilt.

Accompanied by his wife, Glen Wolsieffer was discharged
from the hospital on August 29, 1985. It would be exactly one
year later that Betty was murdered.

CHAPTER 9

Betty was adamant: she wanted Debbie fired. She knew that Debbie's presence in her husband's office was the equivalent of offering an obese dieter a piece of New York cheesecake. Glen agreed to the demand. But in the ensuing days, he told her that he couldn't fire Debbie because she was going to nursing school and needed money for tuition. Glen put his arm around Betty and told her what she wanted to hear, that he loved her, that Debbie was unimportant. It helped that Betty was unwilling to believe the depth of the affair, and Glen successfully continued to downplay it to her. She didn't want to push the issue. Besides, Glen had told her the affair was over. Glen's charm had not lost its magic with Betty. She bought the explanation and went along. Betty told friends she knew Glen loved her and that they would be able to work things out.

In fact, Glen and Debbie did agree that their relationship would be confined strictly to the office. He told her he was going to try to make his marriage work. However good their intentions might have been, though, the two lovers were back in bed together in less than two months, again enjoying their Friday-night trysts, again planning to build a new life together.

As usual, whenever Betty asked, Glen lied about Debbie.

It was unavoidable that family members and friends learned of Glen's hospitalization. Those who hadn't known beforehand also learned about Glen's relationship with Debbie Shipp. For Betty, this was a source of deep embarrassment. She told friends she "hated Debbie for screwing up their lives." She couldn't eat. She was vomiting. She stayed away from aerobics for a while, for fear her demeanor would give away her disappointment, or worse, someone might ask her about it. She wondered, "Am I the last one to know?"

Glen, too, wasn't comfortable with the situation becoming public, in even a limited circle. In deference, most of his friends never brought up the subject; it just didn't seem like the thing to do.

Neil's wife, Nancy, remembered that Glen had told Betty that he had grown close to Debbie because "she was needy, that he took her under his wing like you would take your daughter. He always made it like that, so it wasn't his fault. He could never be at fault."

Glen's sister, Lisa, was very close to Betty, and she was extremely upset over her brother's adultery. Whenever she couldn't do it herself, Betty got Lisa to drive around to various locations to see if Glen's car was where it was supposed to be.

In time, Betty shared parts of her calamity with her closest friends, but rarely told anyone the whole story. For instance, there was the day Barbara Wende, Betty's close friend from the dental auxiliary, lamented about what a terrible summer she'd been having.

"If you think yours was bad, I bet you I can beat that," said Betty. She told her friend that she and Glen had been having problems, that Glen had suffered a breakdown and had been hospitalized. "Glen wants out of the marriage, but I'm going to fight to keep him," Betty said, professing her undying love for her husband. She said she had offered to get a full-time teaching job so Glen could take a job in construction or something less stressful than dentistry, which, she said, Glen hated. In truth, when he wasn't at the office, Glen often dressed casually. With a flannel shirt on and a wad of chewing tobacco in his mouth, several people said that when they first met him, they mistakenly assumed he did work outdoors, as a woodsman or construction worker.

Betty said she realized that she and Glen had to work out their problems. She had no intention of divorcing him. She also thought that Glen's breakdown had been precipitated by his inability to grieve properly over the death of his father.

Betty went on to explain that Glen was angry about all the time she had been spending on dental auxiliary functions and meetings and conferences. In fact, to quiet things down at home, Betty was careful not to discuss auxiliary business on the telephone when Glen was in the house. She said he had asked her to "set me free. I should have known this was coming. He'd been spending so much time out." Betty did not mention anything about Debbie Shipp or Glen's affair, however.

Thinking it best to be a true friend and not pry, Wende left it at that and wished Betty well.

That fall, Betty suffered a miscarriage. On the advice of Glen's counselor, she didn't tell her husband. He hadn't even been told about the pregnancy, and there was some concern over how he would react.

That November, Betty and Lisa held a large crafts party at 75 Birch. "A million people were there. We sold all this stuff. It went really well," said Lisa. Friends and acquaintances came from all over, including two blondes from aerobics class, Carol Ann Kopicki and Joyce Marie Greco. When the presentations and selling were completed, Glen brought home pizza.

As Debbie and Glen continued to work—and play—together, Debbie escalated her efforts to snag her man. Her crusade reached a crescendo on February 1, 1986, when Glen finally left Betty, if only for a weekend. The morning after one of his Friday nights out, Glen came home, packed a suitcase, and drove over to Debbie's place. From there, the two had plans to attend the wedding of one of her cousins. And from there, the couple had plans to hit the Red Roof Inn for a weekend of illicit sex.

At last, this was to be the start of their life together.

While Glen headed over to the motel, Betty set off for the *Sunday Independent* to drop off a press release for the dental auxiliary. Obviously, the news from Glen that morning had upset her badly. As she was walking down the steps of the newspaper office, Betty suddenly became weak, her knees buckled, and she began hyperventilating. She had pains in her chest. An ambulance was called, and Betty was rushed to the NPW Medical Center.

In the emergency room, Betty admitted to the attending physician that she had been under "a lot of stress lately." Within ninety minutes of testing and examination, Betty calmed down, and she was given some Valium.

Unable to locate Glen, hospital employees called Betty's parents, who in turn called Glen's dental offices. Nancy spent a good part of the day trying to track him down as well. Eventually, one of Glen's employees traced him to the Red Roof. Betty later told her mother that Glen had taken off to "get his head screwed on straight."

Glen went to the hospital to pick up Betty, but instead of taking her home, he dropped her off at her parents' house. He then returned to the motel, and to Debbie, to pick up where they had left off.

On Monday morning, Glen drove Debbie to classes at Luzerne County Community College, where she had enrolled to resume her studies, now toward a degree in nursing. He then drove himself over to 75 Birch to grab another suitcase of his belongings.

When he arrived, Betty was livid. She wouldn't let Glen see Danielle. She also threatened, once and for all, to file for divorce. The marriage counseling had been a farce; Glen had stopped attending. There was no point in her going by herself. Things couldn't continue like this.

Glen picked up Debbie after classes and informed her that he *had* to return home. Betty had threatened that he would never see Danielle again. As of that afternoon, Glen told Debbie, she no longer worked for him. And, he added, their relationship was terminated.

Though Debbie never worked for Glen again, their carnal entanglement resumed within two months. The scenario played pretty much as before: Debbie's house for sex, always on a Friday night, Glen always home by 2:00 A.M., to coincide with when the bars closed. In earnest, Debbie and Glen resumed their plans for his divorce from Betty. Glen told Debbie he had even discussed the matter with an attorney. But, again, there was to be no divorce.

Glen's relationship with Debbie continued on the sly throughout the summer of 1986. When Debbie pressed for a more stable relationship, Glen promised he would leave Betty at the end of August, which turned out to be the weekend of Betty's murder. "Glen said he was leaving that weekend," Debbie recalled. "We were going to go away for a few days, to the Shadowbrook Lodge in Tunkhannock."

As usual, Glen couldn't keep his promise. On the Sunday before the planned weekend, Glen called to say he had to cancel because someone had tried to break into 75 Birch—they had made a slit in the screen of the side door. Playing the role of faithful husband and father, Glen apologized that he had to stay home to make sure Betty and Danielle were safe, or he would never forgive himself. He assured his lover that as soon as the matter was taken care of, they would go on with their plans for him to leave Betty and get a divorce.

Weary of Glen's inability to keep his word, Debbie was very angry that Sunday night, but still, she took it. She accepted that this was not an easy situation for the man of her dreams.

In fact, Glen *had* called the Wilkes-Barre Police Department that Sunday morning to report a slit screen on the side door. It was a call that certainly raised no eyebrows, given the fact that the neighborhood around Birch Street had borne the brunt of a rash of break-ins in the previous few months. Screen doors had been cut through. Windows had been used to gain entry. On one occasion, a would-be burglar was seen erecting a ladder against the back porch when the home's owner looked out the window.

"I didn't see any other attempt to enter," Glen told the dispatcher when he called. "I just didn't know if I should report it or not. So I just wanted to see what you thought." Glen was instructed that if he wanted a report to be taken, an officer would be dispatched to the house. Perhaps he would be satisfied if his call was noted in the official ledger so patrol cars could make periodic checks of the house and yard?

"Yeah. I think that would be the best idea," Glen replied. "Because we haven't seen anybody around. But you know, there must have been somebody here."

"Okay, no problem," the dispatcher said. "It's 75?"
"Seventy-five Birch," said Glen.

Maybe they couldn't go away for the weekend, but that didn't stop Debbie and Glen from getting together during that week. On Thursday, they met at her place for lunch. Then they made love. Later that day, Debbie received an anonymous telephone call from a male who talked "very low." She couldn't understand what he was saying, so she hung up.

That night, Glen joined Betty for a romantic dinner at Villa Roma, out at Harveys Lake. There, they ran into Mark Ciavarella, the attorney who had handled the closing on their house.

On Friday the 29th, Glen and Debbie again rendezvoused at lunch. Again they had sex. Later that day, Debbie received two more anonymous calls from a male. Again she could not understand what he was saying.

Before they could meet for lunch again, Betty was dead.

CHAPTER 10

Glen's deception with his wife did not stop with Debbie. A worse blow to Betty would have been the knowledge about his other lover, Carol Ann Kopicki.

One of Glen's friends from aerobics class, she was the woman he'd run into with her husband at the Crackerbox Palace the night of Betty's murder, the woman who had attended Betty's home-made crafts party the previous November, the woman who sometimes sat around chitchatting with Betty after aerobics about Glen's likes and dislikes.

Tall, thin, blonde, former high school cheerleader, stylish clothing, plenty of makeup—Carol was everything Betty and Debbie were not. The category "future" in her high school yearbook read "undecided." But in April 1977, during her senior year of high school, Carol married football player Mark Kopicki and soon gave birth to a daughter, Megan. Another child, John Paul, was born the following October.

Glen and Carol met in mid-1983, at Aerobic World, though their friendship didn't start to develop until 1985. While Betty and

Glen both attended exercise classes, strangely, when they attended the same class, they exercised separately most of the time—he on one side of the room, she on the other. Also, Betty attended only one aerobics class; Glen did a double session, starting ninety minutes before Betty, leaving him even more room to maneuver. Most mornings Glen positioned himself next to Carol and another friend, Joyce Greco. Another Aerobic World attendee, Barbara Wende, a close friend of Betty's, recalled that when Betty arrived, "The whole little threesome would split up."

Glen had let his lustful desires for Carol be known during one of his Friday-night visits to the Crackerbox Palace when he asked her to dance. As they snuggled for a slow number, Glen began kissing her on the neck. Carol got the picture that Glen was interested in her, but she wanted to take things slowly. The first kiss occurred in November 1985, less than three months after Glen's psychiatric stay at the hospital, and within weeks after he had started up with Debbie again.

Not until the following March—just weeks after Betty's collapse—did Carol allow herself to be encircled in the amorous clutches of the Romeo of Birch Street. The encounter, later described as a chance meeting, again occurred at the Crackerbox. In the midst of a conversation, Glen asked Carol to go for a ride. She agreed, and several minutes later, while stopped at a red light, Glen leaned over and passionately kissed her on the lips. Another sexual relationship was about to be launched.

At about 10:30 on the evening of April 25, 1986, Carol slipped away from her husband—they had just finished with their daughter's birthday party—to meet Glen at the Busy Day Motel, a spartanly appointed facility just across the Susquehanna from the Luzerne County Courthouse. Over the years, the Busy Day had served as a discreet retreat for hundreds of couples engaging in an hour or two of unsanctioned passion. In this case, the meeting had been Glen's idea, but Carol was all for it, too.

Now Glen wasn't only cheating on Betty; if it could be called that, he was also cheating on Debbie.

Two weeks later, following the wedding of Nancy Wolsieffer's sister, Sharon, to police officer Brian Lavan, Glen and Betty—usher and bridesmaid—departed for Disney World with Danielle. Glen said the trip would mark a new beginning. But even the Magic Kingdom didn't help. Friends later quoted Betty as saying she'd had a lousy time.

When he returned, Glen met Carol at the Busy Day Motel for another Friday-night session of sex. He told her that he loved her. "We both have problems with our marriages. We're lacking something." He described himself as "a wimpy dentist," miserable over being cooped up in an office. He wanted some excitement.

Carol still wanted to move slowly. She told Glen they were "just like friends." But the assignations continued. When he and Carol didn't go to the Busy Day Motel, they used the Red Roof Inn or other inexpensive motels on the outskirts of Wilkes-Barre. They often brought wine coolers. Almost always they convened on a Friday night.

Glen and Carol were sometimes accompanied by Joyce Marie Greco, their blonde friend from aerobics class, and Glen's long-time friend Richard Miscavage. Joyce, the mother of two, and Richard also were playing around, having started their affair about the same time as Carol and Glen.

One Friday night shortly after Glen's Florida trip, the two couples met at the Busy Day Motel. Miscavage registered for two rooms. As subsequently reconstructed, the couples then paired off. The following month, the two couples again visited the Busy Day Motel. They thought it would be nice if they got the same rooms, and so they did.

With or without company, Carol and Glen did not confine their heated yearnings to a tacky motel room. Occasionally they visited one of Glen's dental offices. On one such occasion—just before midnight on the Friday night before Father's Day, 1986— Glen took Carol to his office in Shickshinny, the one he worked in on Tuesdays with Debbie Shipp. Sex was on the agenda that night, but Carol said they had important business to discuss first. She explained that Joyce Greco had discovered that her husband had been following her. Carol said Joyce had been caught with Rich Miscavage. As a by-product, Carol said, Joyce's husband also had learned about their affair.

"I'm scared," she told Glen.

Her lover assured her everything would be all right. "We'll just have to be careful."

They proceeded to have sexual intercourse on the office floor.

Sometime in midsummer, Carol returned Glen's proclamations of true love. Unbeknownst to Carol, her words were spoken in the same time frame that Debbie Shipp was turning up the heat on Glen to make a firm commitment to her. In between, Glen took Betty and Danielle to the New Jersey shore for a vacation.

To Carol, Glen was quiet, sensitive, and understanding. He told her he felt bad he didn't spend more time with his daughter. In between assignations, Carol watched Glen play softball for the Mercy Hospital team at Kirby Park. Once or twice she watched him play for the Heights team, too.

Carol felt sex with her husband, Mark, was boring, while her love with Glen was "new, exciting, and passionate." Each morning after, Glen dutifully called to assure her that "everything was all right when I got home last night."

Still, she felt comfortable with Mark and figured that her affair would not be a long-term one. She had good reason to think that way. Unlike Glen's display of largesse toward Debbie, Glen never bought Carol any gifts. He never spoke of commitment or expressed thoughts of leaving Betty. Carol never brought up that subject either. Glen explained that he couldn't put Betty through the garbage he'd put her through during an old affair he'd had with somebody at the office.

If truth be told, the dental auxiliary *was* taking up a great deal of Betty's time. In the spring of 1986, she was installed as the group's recording secretary. Sometime after the Fourth of July, 1986, Betty went out of town for the group. She really didn't want to go for fear that Glen would be out fooling around. She was right.

It was Thursday night, but Carol and Glen didn't let the calendar deny them the extra opportunity. They met at Joyce Greco's house, then headed for the Red Roof Inn.

During the months of July and August, Carol and Glen got together at least three other times, at the Granite Motel in Mountaintop. Carol would later assert that her last sexual encounter with Glen prior to Betty's death took place at the Granite on

August 22, the Friday before the murder. Carol and Glen did not return to their respective homes until 3:00 A.M.

The following Tuesday afternoon, Betty was angry when her friend Barbara Wende called to ask about some information she needed for a dental project. Wende started out by inquiring if Glen was home, because she knew that he got angry when Betty spent time on the phone talking auxiliary business.

"Don't worry about if Glen is home," said Betty. "I'm tired of worrying about what bothers him and what doesn't bother him anymore." That sounded like a new Betty to Wende, who'd been encouraging her friend since the previous fall to stop letting people take advantage of her.

Betty couldn't help but remember the events of a year before, Glen's posthospitalization promises to stop screwing around and be a good family man. Wende asked how the marriage counseling was coming along. Bitterly, Betty explained: "Glen quit going a long time ago. There's no reason for me to continue going by myself."

Betty went on to say things were bad again between her and Glen. Fridays were especially gloomy, with Glen always staying out "to the wee hours of the morning. I'm fed up."

Wende suggested that Betty join Glen on his Friday-night jaunts. "Glen knows that I don't drink, and that I wouldn't be able to stay out as late as he does," she responded.

"Why don't you say something to Glen instead of just being quiet?" asked Wende.

"Well, if he comes in late this Friday, I'm going to take a stand. I *am* going to say something," said Betty. "I'm not going to allow myself to be stepped on anymore."

Betty spent a good portion of the final day of her life assisting her friend Eileen Pollock with preparations for Eileen's daughter's birthday party. Betty had arranged for a performance by Pat Ward, a magician she had previously recommended to other friends from the dental auxiliary and aerobics class. When Ward started to set up his equipment at the near end of the swimming pool, Pollock asked him to move to the other side. Ward wasn't excited about lugging everything across the yard, but Betty, who had returned from picking up the birthday cake, offered to lend a hand. "Don't worry. I'll help you," she said. "I'm healthy, I'm strong."

Ward performed a trick called the Professor's Nightmare, using three pieces of rope of varying lengths. When he was finished, he distributed the clothesline to Danielle and two other youngsters. He told them to put the rope under their pillows so the Magic Rope Fairy could visit that night.

After the party, Betty was late getting home because she volunteered to drop off several of the young partygoers who needed a ride. Pollock called the Wolsieffer home around six-thirty to ask Glen a question about her teeth. She made an appointment for the following week. Glen said Betty wasn't home yet.

About two hours after the call from Pollock, Richard Miscavage, Glen's friend of two decades, stopped by to say hello. Over the years, the two men had played baseball and softball together. They had lost touch when Glen moved to Virginia, but since his return, the friendship had resumed in earnest. The two men were pals and drinking buddies. In the spring of 1986, they joined an aerobics class at Lesley McCann's. There were hardly any guys there, and they got to observe the great-looking women.

Miscavage said he wouldn't be going out that evening, unlike many other Friday nights. The two men chatted for about a half hour with Betty, who had arrived home by then, and Miscavage departed.

Glen was itching to get out. He wondered if Neil was ready for a little action. He had asked him that afternoon if he wanted to go out for a few beers. Neil had told him he would think about it. There was no rush, Glen thought. It was still early, not even ten yet.

Over at 84 Birch, Neil Wolsieffer was watching TV with Nancy and his sister, Lisa. They ordered out for pizza; then the two women went to pick it up. Returning with the food, Nancy spotted Betty and Glen on their front porch carrying in a large flowerpot. "Bring your plants in, it's going to be cold tonight," advised Betty, already dressed for sleep in a pink nightgown and striped robe.

Nancy noticed that it *was* quite cold for August, even for 10:15 P.M. "Okay," she replied. "I'll talk to you tomorrow."

Glen walked over to Neil's to see if he'd take a ride up to Bud's Place on Amber Lane. Neil was unwavering, though; he said he was going to stay put.

The brothers exchanged small talk: Glen was going to work the next day until about noon, then pack up the family for a trip to friends near Syracuse, New York—the Wilkies—to help them dig a pool in their backyard. Neil said he was going to work on the addition he was finishing in the rear of his house. He and Nancy had hired contractors to build the shell, but financially strapped, Neil was completing the interior work himself.

Unaccompanied but undaunted, Glen departed on the short trip over to Bud's.

Betty crawled into her own bed to watch some TV with Danielle, a Friday-night custom when Daddy wasn't home. It wasn't long before they both were sleeping soundly.

Glen stayed at Bud's about an hour, drinking beer and talking with his cousin Gary Stinson and several pals. By all accounts, Glen appeared to be in a good mood.

"Where's Neil?" asked Ronald Rebo, an off-duty Wilkes-Barre police officer and longtime friend of Glen's brother. Glen said Neil was at home.

"Why don't you call him?" Rebo suggested.

"No way," Glen replied, knowing he had already made his best effort.

Around 12:30 A.M., Glen headed across the Susquehanna River into Kingston, en route to the Crackerbox Palace. As usual, the singles bar was packed. Glen Wolsieffer was certainly not the only buck in the valley who lived by the credo, "Friday nights are mine."

When Stinson, who had driven over from Bud's in his own car, noticed Glen in deep conversation with Joyce Greco, Carol Kopicki, and Carol's husband, Mark, he drove back to Bud's by himself. Shortly before 2:00 A.M., Glen headed for home.

When he arrived at 75 Birch, Glen drank some juice, changed his clothes, and carried Danielle from the master bedroom into her own room.

In a story he would later change, Glen maintained that he then went to sleep without talking to Betty, and remembered nothing more until he was awakened by a clanging, metallic sound emanating from the rear second-floor bedroom about the time it was starting to get light out.

CHAPTER 11

IN HIS WORDS

Betty and I were very close in a lot of things, but sex was not one of them. I don't think it was one of her priorities. She was the first woman I ever made love to, and I thought it was the greatest thing going. I wanted it as much as I could. But it seemed that as soon as we were married, the intimacy ran out. I couldn't figure out why. It was almost like a drag to her, more of a chore than fun.

I believe she had sex just to satisfy me—and if she got anything out of it, fine. If she didn't, no big deal. We did our mandatory once a week or so, and I thought that was how she wanted it. But that's certainly not what I was interested in.

I would want to do things and she would be embarrassed, whether it was oral sex or—I tell you what, that was basically the

*most confused I ever got with anybody as far as sex goes. She
would be embarrassed by anything of that nature. Basically, we just
did missionary stuff.*

*I wasn't physically attracted to Betty. But as a person, as a
human being, as a woman and my wife, I loved Betty. She was a
friendly person.*

*Even though I had gone out with Debbie a long time, it was still
exciting. Different types of sex. It was just that she enjoyed it, and
I enjoyed it. I felt some guilt, but not enough that I would stop.
She and I did things that Betty and I weren't doing.*

*Debbie had started working for me, and basically, things
weren't that great with Betty and I sexwise. One day I went into the
x-ray room, Debbie was in there, and I kissed her. She didn't know
what to do, we were kind of fumbling around. One thing led to
another, and we ended up intimate—not at that time, but a couple
of weeks later. Then I would see her on Friday nights, not every
one, and then at the office.*

*We wouldn't say, "Okay, it's Thursday, today's our day." If
Debbie was going somewhere, or I had something to do, then we
would go home and that would be it. We never did it in the chair,
no stirrups or anything. Just on the floor. We'd get everything
straightened up, start making out, and then end up doing it.*

*Debbie would initiate certain things, you know, to get me
going. She was basically shy, except when it was just she and I
together. When there was a chance that you might get caught, or
that you were doing something that you shouldn't be doing, that
was the excitement of it. If a woman is excited, then I get excited.
That's the best way that I can tell you. She was on the pill. I didn't
use anything.*

*I kept stringing her along, I guess, knowing that I wouldn't be
leaving. But if Debbie wanted to hang on, then that was up to her.
She was a big girl.*

*I cared for Debbie, and I thought I might have loved her. But
my heart never said, "I'm in love with you."*

*I was physically attracted to Carol. I thought she was really a good-
looking woman, and I really wanted to get to know her intimately.
It took a while, but I did. She and I had a real, very exciting sex*

life. Nothing I would say kinky, but a lot of good, different things that I had never done with anybody.

Once I met Carol it was like, "Man, this is how you are supposed to feel with a woman. You are supposed to be able to laugh and have a good time." Then, if you want to be intimate, fine. If not, then no big deal. No pressure. I felt, "God, this is the kind of woman I want."

Still, I wasn't getting serious with Carol. But then I realized that maybe I wasn't that serious with Debbie. I became less interested in Debbie at that point and more interested in Carol.

I knew Carol was married. She knew I was married. We knew that we weren't going to leave each other's spouses. It was like a flirtation. It wasn't, "Well, you know, I'm not going to see you anymore if you don't leave Mark" or "if you don't leave Betty." It wasn't anything like that.

I basically pursued Carol, I'm not going to deny it. She is the first woman that I really had to pursue. I don't like to be one of those guys who come on too strong. I would rather wait for the right moment. I never get into that real macho come-on stuff.

CHAPTER 12

The morning after Betty's murder, the *Sunday Independent* scored a scoop by virtue of being the only Sunday newspaper in town at the time. The newspaper's reporters and editors, led by James M. Torbik and Fred Ney, jumped all over the story. HOMICIDE RULED IN DEATH OF WILKES-BARRE WOMAN, blared the front-page headline. BODY FOUND IN BEDROOM; STRANGULATION CITED, ran the second tier. WOLSIEFFERS WERE PROMINENT FAMILY, said the accompanying sidebar.

"If God ever created a saint, Betty Wolsieffer was it," Mrs. Jule Cook, the victim's next-door neighbor, told the *Independent.* "She was like a second family to us."

Several of the inside stories revealed the panic gripping Birch Street in the wake of what many considered the latest escalation in the neighborhood's crime wave. One resident likened the South Wilkes-Barre area to "a battle zone." Another asked: "What's happening to our neighborhood?" Mrs. Samuel Bloch, Jr., of 90 Birch, said: "I've been here sixty-one years and I'm scared stiff." Another Birch Street resident said her door had been kicked in and that another family had been robbed. "You can check the police reports and find out the number of attempted burglaries this past year," said neighbor Jane Decker. "But never did we think someone would be murdered here."

The *Sunday Independent* coverage, which spanned several pages and included a dozen photographs, marked the beginning of what would be a vigorous, sometimes embarrassing battle among the Wyoming Valley's news media outlets. With two-newspaper cities becoming nearly extinct, it is exceptional for a city the size of Wilkes-Barre to have two dailies and one large, separate Sunday newspaper. The newspapers, along with the region's major television stations, also headquartered in Wilkes-Barre, all wanted a piece of the Wolsieffer story. The cutting edge of the competition would not be the content of the coverage as much as the rancor of the stories. In the case of one newspaper, the *Times Leader*, there would be a drastic departure from commonly accepted practices of fundamental fairness and protecting a defendant's right to a fair trial. That newspaper's arrogant machinations would become a sometimes embarrassing story unto itself, climaxing in the arrest of the publisher, editor, managing editor, and star columnist under the state's wiretapping statutes.

The media war over the Wolsieffer story could be traced in part to the purchase of the *Times Leader* by Capital Cities/ABC Inc. and a bitter union-busting dispute that began in 1978. In fact, the other daily newspaper in Wilkes-Barre, the *Citizens' Voice*, was started by *Times Leader* strikers. During the ensuing years, animosity had run so strong in the prolabor valley that more often than not, the paid circulation of the *Citizens' Voice* had been larger than the financially stronger *Times Leader*.

The most controversial aspect of the *Times Leader* coverage would be the columns of Steve Corbett, a relatively inexperienced but forceful reporter appointed a columnist in the early stages of the Wolsieffer story. Corbett, a former bouncer, had worked on a string of weekly newspapers in Harrisburg, the state capital, before coming to the *Times Leader* in 1985. He was known to tell other outsiders in Wilkes-Barre, "This is my town." He also was known to tell anyone who would listen that the Wolsieffer story was his story.

*   *   *

Dr. E. Glen Wolsieffer, the person who would draw so much media attention in the coming months, woke up in his hospital bed the Sunday after Betty's murder complaining of stiffness in his back, a "dull soreness" in the back section of his head, and persistent headache. But an examination failed to detect any adverse change in his condition. He requested, and was given, a painkiller. The cervical collar remained in place.

Glen was neurologically stable, so Dr. Czwalina told him that depending on how his neck felt, he would probably be released in the next day or two. Glen said being discharged was probably the best thing for him, then continued: "Well, I will just have to have my wife bring in my jogging outfit and shoes."

Dr. Czwalina was taken aback by the remark. "What did you say, Glen?"

"Oh, she can't," said Glen.

"What do you mean?" asked the doctor.

"She's dead."

Concerned about his patient's flat tone of voice, as if he were still in a shock-like state, Dr. Czwalina offered Glen psychiatric counseling. Perhaps remembering the last time he accepted psychiatric assistance, Glen replied that he thought the best form of therapy would be to interact with his family. He said he could handle the situation himself. Dr. Czwalina decided to go along, but made sure the nursing staff remained on the lookout for any signs of grief reaction. But there would be none. It was as if Glen was without emotion.

Soon thereafter, Bill Emmett, Glen's security guard friend, stopped in to see him during his morning break. Glen introduced his Aunt Mary to Emmett, and they exchanged pleasantries.

Glen looked out the window toward the clear blue sky. "Boy, it's a good day for golfing," he told Emmett. "We'll have to get out sometime."

Emmett didn't stay long after that, feeling awkward with Glen's relative in the room. He would later say the only other part of the conversation he remembered was Glen telling his aunt that the night of Betty's death, he had locked all the windows in the house before going to bed.

Two by two, family members began to file into Glen's room to pay their condolences and inquire about his health. Lynn McGinty,

Betty's first cousin, came to visit with her husband, Terry. They both embraced Glen, and Mrs. McGinty cried. She later noted with curiosity that Glen had not.

Glen sat back down in his chair by the window, next to the bed. He was wearing a cervical collar and hospital garb. Mrs. McGinty asked Glen to explain to her what had happened. His story was consistent with what he had told the police. Adding a little detail, though, he said the man was wearing a clear mask, "like pantyhose," and had thick eyebrows, more like one continuous eyebrow straight across. In telling this version, Glen said he believed the object used to choke him was a rope. It struck Mrs. McGinty that the entire time she and her husband were talking with Glen, he never looked at them.

Once he was alone again, Glen requested, and was granted, permission to take a shower. Neil came to visit. He told Glen he was devastated by Betty's death. He had really liked her and felt close to her.

Neil didn't question his brother about his story. He still didn't doubt him. How could he doubt his brother? He had the utmost faith in Glen. But deep in his mind, a little something must have been nagging at him. As he had told his close friend city council member Bob Reilly: "If there weren't two intruders, my brother's story makes no sense."

All of the law-enforcement parties involved met that Sunday morning, the day after the discovery of Betty's body, at Chief Coyne's office for a strategy and planning session. The thinking among the investigators was that forensic analysis and Neil Wolsieffer, the dentist's brother, offered the best shots at clearing things up. But the scientific testing of possible bloodstains and the hair, the ladder, the screen, et al. could take weeks, if not months. That left Neil. Perhaps there was something important he had remembered overnight. Perhaps there was something he knew all along and would now be willing to reveal.

There was a group in the police department willing to suggest that Neil had been part of the murder. They thought that not only Glen should have been arrested immediately, but Neil, too. If cops got to make all the decisions, though, there would be no need for district attorneys, judges, juries, and courtrooms.

Detectives Mitchell and Sworen, who both realized they had a great deal of legwork to do, headed back to South Wilkes-Barre to reinterview Neil. They conducted the session inside 75 Birch, which at that point remained under the control of the Wilkes-Barre Police Department.

Neil told the same story he had told several times the day before. Along the way he added nuances—he had run over to the house after the telephone call, Glen appeared groggy when he first went over to him in the kitchen, Glen said he had managed to kick or knee his assailant in the groin.

Neil also said that he had entered the house through the side door, a potentially key point since Glen had said when he got home the front screen door had been locked. Neil said he had opened the front doors for Officers George and Minnick from the inside. He said he could not remember if both doors were locked, but assumed that they were.

Sworen and Mitchell learned nothing else new, however. On the way out, Mitchell asked Neil point-blank if Glen had told him he had killed Betty. Neil said his brother had not told him anything like that. Even if he did, Neil continued, he certainly wouldn't tell Mitchell. "But he didn't tell me," said the one brother of the other.

After the police collected a few additional items that might possess evidentiary value, Mitchell turned 75 Birch over to Neil. In return, Glen's brother gave the detective a written acknowledgment.

Everyone was becoming more official—and considerably less friendly.

The second morning after the discovery of Betty's body, Glen again showered without assistance. He ate breakfast without any problems or distress, though the wound on the back of his neck mysteriously appeared to have reddened. The area was administered to, and the cervical collar reapplied.

There was no medical reason for Glen to remain hospitalized. He had stayed neurologically stable throughout his entire hospitalization. All of the tests had shown negative. Dr. Czwalina signed the discharge papers, releasing Glen to the care of his Aunt Mary. He wrote Glen a prescription for Soma Compound for pain, while

Aunt Mary was given five Halcion tablets to parcel out in case he had difficulty sleeping.

Aunt Mary and other family members were advised to keep a close watch on Glen to make sure that he didn't—in Dr. Czwalina's words—"decompensate emotionally." The doctor placed no restrictions on Glen, who specifically asked—permission granted—to be able to "exercise and run off his tension." In an attempt to avoid a pack of news media, Neil drove his brother to their mother's home in a car borrowed from a friend.

"I was in the kitchen when Glen came in," recalled Phyllis Wolsieffer. "He was a zombie. He had on my husband's brown windbreaker, too big on him of course, and the white blanket they give you in the hospital. He walked toward me with such a stare I just couldn't believe how he looked, so horrible. He had no color whatsoever, he was ashen, and he said, 'Mom, would you drive me to the cemetery?' I said, 'The cemetery?' He said, 'Yeah.' "

At first, Phyllis didn't know what cemetery Glen was referring to, whether he wanted to go where Betty was going to be buried the following day or to where his father was buried. It turned out Glen wanted to go to St. Mary's Cemetery to visit his father's grave. "He stood there and he cried pitifully, pitifully. People around were looking," she said.

From there, Glen and his mother went to the Tasker home on Gilligan Street. "There's young Jack sitting out on the front steps with a beer and a couple of his cousins, and I opened the door for Glen to get out of the car because he had a collar on his neck, and he had a lot of pain," said Phyllis. "So I opened the door and he got out and stood up. Jack Tasker looked at him, young Jack, and said, 'Jesus, Phyllis, he looks like hell. Do you think they should have let him out of the hospital?' That's his words. And then I took him in the house and I can remember Betty's mother took him by the hand and took him in a room by themselves. Then I brought him home."

Accompanied by his mother, Glen later that afternoon walked over to Neil's house, where a group of friends had gathered around the swimming pool in the backyard. After Ed Wolsieffer died, Phyllis had a little money and decided to buy a pool for her children. Neil's yard was the largest, so he and Nancy got the fun of fighting the algae and entertaining unexpected guests.

Several of the guys told Glen that he shouldn't be out walking, but Glen said he needed some air. Feeling comfortable around his friends, Glen appeared to relax. He removed the cervical collar. When someone suggested a ride up to Rich Miscavage's father-in-law's hunting cabin, everyone agreed and started walking toward the street. As Glen proceeded, though, he stopped short, turned around, and returned to the backyard to retrieve his collar, as if realizing that he needed to wear it in public.

Miscavage would later recall that the group discussed hunting and fishing on the ride. Glen professed to get cold during parts of the day, and put a blanket around himself. To his friends, Glen appeared "depressed, lost, and drained emotionally as well as physically." He cried twice during the trip, when he talked about *how* Betty had died, and how he knew what she went through because "it" had hurt his neck too. Otherwise, Glen never discussed Betty or what had happened to her. None of the others asked questions. It just didn't seem like the thing to do.

While Glen was traipsing around the woods, his attorney, Mark Ciavarella, was busy protecting his client's right to remain silent. He declined Detective Mitchell's invitation for Glen to return to 75 Birch for more questions and to reenact Saturday morning's events before a police video camera. Ciavarella said it was obvious that Glen was a suspect.

Other detectives chatted again with Debbie Shipp and Nancy Wolsieffer. Even threats of criminal charges for withholding evidence failed to turn up anything significant.

Mitchell and Sworen interviewed Dr. Dennis J. Gaza at police headquarters regarding his examination and treatment of Glen in the Mercy Hospital emergency room. Dr. Gaza noted that Glen had a small hematoma and abrasion at the back of the head, and a red abrasion from the side of the neck to the back of the neck. He said he detected no hemorrhages in the eyes and no evidence that Glen had been choked. He had determined that Glen sustained "a probable severe concussion," but acknowledged that he had based that conclusion only on what the dentist had said happened to him. Dr. Gaza told the detectives he would not have admitted Glen to the hospital if Glen had not said he had been knocked unconscious. Also, Glen had complained of neck tenderness, but the doctor went on to say that being unconscious was not consistent with the type of mark on Glen's neck. More puzzling, the marks were on the wrong side of the neck if Glen had been attacked from behind as he had claimed. Regarding the bump on Glen's head, Dr. Gaza said one could easily self-inflict such a lump by banging one's head against a wall, or hitting oneself on the head with a hand.

Now, that's interesting, thought Mitchell and Sworen. The hematoma might not be that important after all. Or looked at another way, it might crack the whole case.

CHAPTER 13

The funeral director was asking John Tasker if he wanted his daughter's casket open or closed. Tasker recoiled. His face had a terror-stricken look, as if to say, *"What?????"*

"Oh," the mortuary man said. "She was pretty well beaten up, large bruises and a cut lip."

Jesus Christ, Tasker thought to himself. *Why? Why would anybody want to do it?*

The decision was made to keep the casket closed.

After returning from his trip to the hunting cabin, Glen joined the rest of the family at a private wake. As everyone was preparing to leave, he asked the undertaker to open the coffin so he could look at Betty. Several other family members peered in as well. Despite the preparation, Betty looked horrible. "You had to look away. It was terrible," said Nancy. "It wasn't a bruise here and a bruise there. It seemed blended, and her face seemed distorted. It just didn't look like her." It was clear to anyone who looked at Betty's face that she had been a victim of violence, a fact that would prove significant as the investigation unfolded.

The following morning, three days after her murder, Betty was laid to rest in Mount Greenwood Cemetery in Trucksville, Pennsylvania, following a private service at the funeral home attended by more than fifty people. Before leaving the funeral parlor, Glen stayed behind for a final look at his murdered spouse. Following the service, everyone went to the home of Marian Tasker's brother, William May, for a repast. Jane Ann Miscavage, a close friend of Betty's, would subsequently claim that Glen was "the first person to eat and pass the food around."

Danielle did not attend. At first, the child was led to believe that her mother had been hospitalized with an illness. It was only after the funeral that Glen took his daughter into his mother's backyard and told her that the people at the hospital had not been able to make Mommy well.

Relations were civil between the Taskers and Wolsieffers between Betty's death and her funeral. They mourned together, even prayed together. Bill May and Lisa Wolsieffer made many of the arrangements—ordering the funeral cars, making the appropriate calls. Phyllis Wolsieffer was crushed nearly as much as Marian Tasker. She was still getting over the loss of her husband, and now Betty was gone.

If the Taskers had any nagging doubts about Glen's story, they submerged them and concentrated on getting through the ordeal of the funeral. No one thought to ask for more details about what had happened inside 75 Birch. It just wasn't the thing to do.

Once the service was out of the way, though, tensions began to rise. The Taskers couldn't understand why Glen's lawyer was telling him to remain silent. What they really couldn't understand was why Glen had a lawyer in the first place.

Part of this resentment was fueled by newspaper headlines: MURDER VICTIM'S HUSBAND WON'T COOPERATE and WOLSIEFFER WON'T TALK TO POLICE. Attorney Ciavarella angrily rejected suggestions that his client was being uncooperative, pointing out that Glen had "answered all their questions as best he could" during the two interviews that Saturday at the hospital. The attorney said Glen also had provided a description of the intruder, estimated what time the break-in occurred, explained that he had been rendered unconscious by the intruder, and allowed police to remove physical evidence from the house. "I advised Dr. Wolsieffer not to answer any more questions," Ciavarella said. "I feel he has cooperated enough. He's been questioned twice and I don't think he should have to answer the same questions a third time."

Citing a police news blackout, both daily newspapers addressed the most obvious question in the only way they could. The *Citizens' Voice* quoted a veteran police officer as saying: "Burglars fear ladders, feeling they could get trapped using this type of device. They would rather kick in a door." The *Times Leader*, meanwhile, quoted Detective Mitchell casting aspersions at the usefulness of Glen's description of the intruder. "It's very vague," said Mitchell. "I don't know if anyone could get anything out of that or not. I certainly couldn't."

The Wednesday after the murder, Glen stopped by the Tasker home. Betty's father told Glen he was displeased with the advice that Ciavarella was giving him, and asked Glen why he wasn't cooperating with the authorities.

"I told the police everything I know," Glen replied. "I just wish I could have done more."

Maintaining his silence, Glen moved into his mother's house, so there was no reason for anyone to set up camp outside of 75 Birch. That left the pursuers—the police, media, and curiosity seekers—to go after the residents of 84 Birch, especially Neil. As the first known outsider to enter his brother's house the fatal Saturday morning, Neil realized that the attention was reasonable. But as the pressure built—the police alone called or asked for a follow-up interview nearly every day—Neil soon felt hounded.

Day and night, photographers and TV crews camped outside 84 Birch. Reporters rang the front doorbell unannounced, uninvited, at any time of the day and night. Neil and Nancy couldn't walk out the front door without tripping over the press corps. At first, the pair was obliging, even providing photos of Betty and Glen and Danielle. But handing over the photos begot questions, and answering one led to five more. "We were just deluged," said Nancy. "I guess as soon as you give one interview, then everybody thinks 'Well, they're open.' I know they were doing their job and I really tried to be compassionate, but we were in the height of this grief and I felt the media didn't belong in our private lives.

It was too much. They would ring the doorbell at nine o'clock at night. It was Grand Central Station."

As the weeks unfolded, Neil and Nancy grew to despise certain members of the Wilkes-Barre media, especially for what the couple viewed as the reporters' unfairness, duplicity, and dishonesty.

Selected by default as the front line of defense for the Wolsieffer family, Neil and Nancy were expected to have all the answers. They began to feel as if they were on trial, that their every word or action, or lack of action, was scrutinized and challenged.

Feeling they had nothing to hide, Neil and Nancy didn't hire a lawyer, though they did go as far as scheduling an appointment, then canceling. "I had a terrible feeling," said Nancy. "I thought, 'What are our rights here? Are we allowed to be badgered like this?' We weren't treated with respect. I didn't like it at all, and Neil hated it."

Nonetheless, they supported Glen having an attorney. They thought he was getting blamed for something he didn't do and therefore had every right to legal representation. "I was glad that he did have a lawyer. I didn't think there was anything wrong with that, so I never questioned it."

Many others in the community did, though, including the police.

The Wolsieffer investigation settled into a deliberate, meticulous routine of pursuing leads, tips, ambiguities, and unanswered questions. Lab tests were done. The gun was fired and found to be in working order. Innumerable interviews were conducted revealing Glen's prolific sex life.

The morning after Betty's funeral, Mitchell and Sworen interviewed Barbara Sharp, a part-time receptionist at Glen's Nanticoke office. She described Debbie Shipp as "a nice girl," and said she believed Glen loved both his wife and his hygienist.

Next, Mitchell and Detective Cooney sat down with Glen's buddy Rich Miscavage, who recounted his visit to 75 Birch the night before the murder. Mitchell asked Miscavage why he had gone to the murder scene after learning of Betty's murder. Miscavage replied that he wanted to know in his own mind if Glen had killed Betty. When he arrived, Miscavage said, he spoke with

Glen's cousin, Gary Stinson, and Stinson's father, Jerry. They only knew that Betty was dead, nothing more.

As Miscavage began to recount Glen's version of events to him, Mitchell noticed that his interview subject had started to sweat very heavily. Miscavage said he felt faint. Bizarrely, he dropped to the floor, lying there for about five minutes. Then, just as suddenly, he said he felt better, and resumed the interview with the detectives.

He went on to tell several lies to cover up for his friend. As far as he knew, Miscavage said, Glen spoke to Debbie once after he got out of the mental hospital, and "that was the end of it." What's more, Miscavage said he didn't know of any other girl-friend of Glen's.

The next morning, Miscavage called Captain Maguire at po-lice headquarters, asking if he could come in for a second inter-view. Maguire, of course, was only too willing to oblige.

When he arrived, Miscavage explained that he had "not told the truth about a few things." First, Miscavage explained that al-though he had previously told Mitchell that he had asked Glen if he had killed Betty, he was now certain that he had wanted to ask the question, but had not. Miscavage said that when he saw Glen at Mercy Hospital and subsequently, Glen spoke only of the time period from when he saw the intruder to when he was hit on the head. Second, Miscavage revealed that Glen did have a second girlfriend, and that her name was Carol Kopicki. Miscavage said he had called Kopicki to tell her he had spoken to police and that she told him she was very worried. Miscavage did not say so to the police, but Carol later said she told him that her attorney, John Moses, had told her to tell the truth. "You should do the same," she instructed. And so he did, giving police a fertile lead.

Miscavage said Glen had met Carol at aerobics class and that as far as he knew, their relationship was ongoing up to the day of Betty's murder. Miscavage also related Glen's behavior during the ride up to the hunting cabin earlier that week, that he cried twice, but never said anything about Betty, or about getting the people who had killed her.

Glen's social life obviously wasn't the only avenue being pur-sued by investigators. Clearly, the local cops needed forensic help if they were going to build a case against Glen. Captain Maguire drafted an official request to the FBI to analyze the evidence seized at 75 Birch. Maguire's letter, which requested "immediate attention," laid out the basic claim of the second-story break-in by use of a ladder and the attack on Glen from behind. The letter contained crafty nuances that approached misrepresentation—a technique that Captain Maguire would employ frequently during the Wolsieffer investigation and would contribute to the suggestion by other investigators that he grew obsessed with the case. For example, nowhere in any police report did Glen Wolsieffer describe the intruder as six foot two, 220 pounds. Nowhere did it state in any reports, as Maguire contended in his letter, that Glen Wolsieffer "assumed" that the intruder had returned to the second-floor bedroom to strangle Betty. Based on Glen's story, the possibility of more than one intruder couldn't be ruled out. Then there was the impression left that Glen had gone down the stairs directly behind the intruder, which is not what he told those who interviewed him. Perhaps the nuances were designed to assist the FBI in Maguire's ultimate quest: "A request is made by this Department to determine whether or not husband's account is factual."

Detective Bernard Banas was personally dispatched to the FBI Laboratory in Washington, D.C., to deliver two boxes and two bags of material seized from 75 Birch.

Assistant District Attorney John C. Eichorn, one of two ADAs assigned full-time to the investigation, asked Mark Ciavarella if Glen planned to submit an inventory of any items allegedly taken during the break-in. At first Ciavarella said that some money had been taken from a desk in Dr. Wolsieffer's office, and, after checking with Glen, stated that his client had discovered the following items missing: approximately $1,300 in cash, a gold necklace with diamond pendant, a gold chain, an extra house key, and a V-shaped gold necklace with diamond.

The police department issued a press release that stated, in part, that investigators were not focusing on a particular individual "to the exclusion of others." The public was assured that "every possibility into the exact manner in which this crime could have occurred" was being examined.

Behind the scenes, Eichorn, Assistant District Attorney Dan-

iel Pillets, and Detectives Mitchell and Maguire agreed that Neil
Wolsieffer should be interviewed again. He was their best hope.
He *had* to know more.

A call went out to Neil, and he agreed to come in.

Gathered around the victim's brother-in-law, the investigators
told Neil they didn't believe he was telling them the entire story,
that he had not acted in a normal manner the day of the murder.
The way they figured it, he was holding something back.

Neil was beside himself, bordering on distraught. He insisted
he had already told them everything that he knew. Eichorn asked
Neil if he would take a lie detector test. Neil said he was afraid
it could somehow hurt his brother. Eichorn wondered if Neil was
interested in hypnosis or sodium pentothal. Perhaps he would remember something important while under the trance. Neil said
he wasn't interested in any tests, and the interview was quickly
terminated.

All was not lost, however. Miscavage's information about
Carol Kopicki had the potential to dramatically move the case
forward. If Debbie Shipp wasn't the motive, maybe Kopicki was.
Maybe both women were.

Wondering if their homicide investigation was about to ex-
plode into a soap-opera cesspool, Mitchell and Sworen headed out
to the Sunshine Store office on Route 315 to interview attractive
Joyce Marie Greco. She told the detectives she had met Rich
Miscavage and Glen during a party at Leslie McCann's Aerobic
World in May 1985. According to Greco, she had started seeing
Miscavage about four months before the murder. She said she
knew both men were married.

On the Friday night of Betty's murder, Greco said, Kopicki
called from the Locker Room Lounge in Kingston to inquire if
she was going to come over. Greco told the detectives that after
she finished work she indeed went to the bar, meeting Carol and
her husband, Mark Kopicki, about 11:45 P.M. She said they stayed
at the Locker Room for about an hour or so before heading over
to the nearby Crackerbox Palace. When they arrived, she said,
Glen was already there. He came over to them, they all talked,
and Glen bought her a drink, club soda with lemon. She insisted
that Glen had only one drink in their presence.

According to Greco's recollection, Glen left the bar first.

"Well, I have to go," she quoted him as saying about 2:00. When the lights came on inside the Crackerbox, she, Carol, and Mark headed out to Ollie's Restaurant in Edwardsville for breakfast. Then they went home.

Shifting to more personal matters, the detectives quizzed Greco about her knowledge of the relationship between Carol and Glen. She said Carol had started seeing Glen about the same time she and Miscavage had started their affair, four to five months earlier.

In drips and drabs the story of Glen and Carol's relationship emerged, along with details of how the Greco marriage had disintegrated in the wake of her numerous motel visits with Miscavage. Greco explained that her own affair "was not as hot and juicy" after she was caught by her husband's private eye, but that she continued to see her lover in the weeks leading up to Betty's murder.

Greco quoted Carol as saying that she and Glen "laughed a lot together," that Glen said he loved his wife and daughter, and that Glen was easy to talk to. More intriguing to the detectives, she quoted Carol as telling her that Glen was a jealous person, angered whenever she showed the slightest bit of interest in another man. Sworen and Mitchell also found it interesting when Greco told them that Carol had quoted Glen as having said: "I don't think I was ever meant to be married."

According to Greco, Glen had been cautious in his relationship with Carol, while Carol had not been. "She didn't think before she acted," she said of Carol. "Glen would leave the exercise class, and right after Glen left, Carol would follow." Greco said she had warned Carol that her behavior did not look good, but Carol failed to change her ways.

She said Rich Miscavage had told her that Glen used to have another girlfriend, a dental assistant. The relationship had been described as serious. According to Greco, Miscavage didn't like Debbie Shipp, especially when he heard that Glen was thinking of leaving Betty for her. Greco said Debbie had "put a lot of pressure on Glen." She added that Betty had been very hurt, so Glen broke off the relationship with the intention of continuing his marriage.

Even the detectives were taken aback with the next bits of

news: Greco said she had become friendly with Betty Wolsieffer the previous October, and that Carol Kopicki knew Betty even before she did—from aerobics class—where the three of them sometimes sat and drank coffee after the exercise session. In fact, Greco recalled, she and Carol and Betty had engaged in conversation on the Wednesday before the murder. Not addressing the possibility that Betty had been playing detective that day, Greco said she didn't think Betty knew anything about the affair. As for the other participant in the chitchat, Greco explained: "Carol was able to handle the situation."

Carol Ann Kopicki wasn't anxious to talk, although she eventually agreed to answer questions at the offices of her lawyer, John Moses. This interview was potentially so important that Mitchell and Sworen were accompanied by Pillets. Mark Kopicki, Carol's husband, decided to hire Moses, a prominent criminal attorney in Wilkes-Barre, immediately after Carol told him about her affair with Glen.

Nervous at first, Carol laid out the basic chronology of her "exciting and passionate" relationship with Glen. She told the homicide investigators that Glen had told her of a previous affair, long since ended, but added that he had neglected to give her any details. At that point Mitchell broke the bad news: Glen's affair with the dental assistant had continued right up until the day Betty was murdered.

Carol started to cry. In an understatement of classic proportions, she volunteered that under the circumstances, she thought Glen had "put up a facade."

Although she insisted she had had no contact with Glen since Betty's murder, Carol admitted that she had indeed seen Glen at the Crackerbox Palace on the 29th, the fatal Friday night. She emphasized that their meeting, just like the encounter that led to the kiss at the red light, had been a chance one. Asked about his possessiveness, Carol contended that she and Glen never fought, but she said she did consider him a jealous man. If she talked to another man at exercise class, Glen often told her, "Stop teasing me."

She recalled that the day of Betty's murder, she told her husband, Mark, "You don't know how this is affecting me," referring to the homicide.

"I know Glen loves you," she said her husband replied. "I saw how he looked at you last night at the Crackerbox."

So here was Glen Wolsieffer telling two women—neither his wife—that he loved them dearly. He was going to leave, he wasn't going to leave. He bought one presents, never bought the other a thing. He mentioned Debbie vaguely to Carol, but in the past tense, not even her name, not even that she'd worked for him. But he never dared mention Carol to Debbie.

Murderer or not, here was a Romeo gone wild, a love triangle with too many points.

CHAPTER 14

As difficult as he found it to even consider, John Tasker had to
face the possibility that Glen had murdered his daughter. Glen's
story didn't make much sense. He couldn't understand his silence.
And, worst of all, he'd been hearing abundant rumors of extramarital affairs. They needed to talk again.

On Tuesday, September 9, a week and a half after the murder, Betty's brother, Jack, called Neil to set up a meeting at the
Tasker home. Glen knocked on the front door that afternoon,
with Neil in tow for moral support.

Glen was again asked why he wasn't cooperating with the
police. Glen stated that his lawyer had advised him not to make
any more statements, and that he was merely following his lawyer's
advice.

But why, the Taskers wanted to know, was that his lawyer's
advice? Glen kind of shrugged; he had no answer.

The elder Tasker then turned the conversation to the swirl of
rumors he'd heard in the ten days since his daughter's murder. He
had heard about Debbie long ago, but had been assured, just like

Betty, that the relationship had ended. He told his son-in-law that since Betty's murder, however, he'd been hearing that Glen's affair with Debbie had never ended. Incredibly, Betty's father continued, he'd also been hearing rumors that Glen had been carrying on with some blonde from aerobics class, right under Betty's nose.

Faced with the Taskers' bounty of information—it was as if they had a pipeline to the police investigation—Glen admitted that his affair with Debbie had been ongoing right up until the day of Betty's murder. Under persistent and well-informed questions, Glen had little choice but to admit to his affair with Carol Kopicki as well.

Even Neil appeared shocked, pounding the back of the couch with his head and a clenched fist. He was being bombarded with heartbreak. First Betty's murder, and now this.

Glen admitted that he had been wrong to cheat on Betty. "I don't know why I do those things. You must hate me but please don't take it out on Danielle," he said. "I did some wrong things, having a couple of affairs. But that doesn't mean I'd kill my wife."

Betty's brother, Jack, spoke up. "Sometimes I feel you are responsible for Betty's death and other times that you're not." Glen said nothing. The younger Tasker kept pressing for details of the night Betty died. "Glen, you gotta come up with some answers." But Glen had nothing specific to say, contending he had told authorities all that he could.

Neil stood up and banged the back of his head against the wall. He took several deep breaths, but he too had nothing to say. How could he? He also was wondering what was going on.

"We have nothing more to discuss," the elder Tasker told his son-in-law.

With that, the two Wolsieffer boys left.

Little did the Taskers know that Glen and Debbie would be back to their sexcapades before the end of the month. Resumption of the relationship did not go smoothly, however. Detective Mitchell had told Debbie about Carol. That prompted Debbie to call Glen to inquire if he was indeed seeing someone else. Glen told her he had been, but wasn't anymore. Glen followed up with a note, and Debbie met him at his office. The sex resumed, and again they talked about their future. "Nothing definite," Debbie would later say, although she acknowledged that she was under the distinct impression that with Betty gone—the tragic manner in which she died notwithstanding—Glen was finally going to marry her.

The same day Glen and Neil visited the Taskers, investigators called Neil and asked him to report to police headquarters for another round of questions. He readily complied.

During the interview, Maguire told Neil that the focus of their investigation had led them to Glen, and that they felt he had to know something about his brother's actions. Assistant District Attorney Eichorn warned Neil that he could be arrested and charged if he had participated in a cover-up after the fact.

But Neil would have none of it. He insisted that he knew nothing.

In a typed report Maguire filed about the session, the captain wrote that based on the way Neil was acting, he felt he was withholding information. Maguire wrote that he had told Neil to do what was right, that he understood how hard it would be to tell on his brother, but that he had to take care of himself and his family. Maguire played a tape of Neil's call to the police the morning of the murder. Putting his spin on what had sounded like a nervous caller, Maguire told Neil he could not understand how Neil could have sounded so calm if he thought someone might still be in the house. "At this point Neil started to cry," Maguire wrote in his report. "Reporting officer put his arms around Neil and said, 'Neil, just do what you think is right.' At this point Neil asked, could he tell the reporting officer something 'off the record.' Reporting officer replied, 'No. Anything you say that incriminates your brother will be used against him.' "

Maguire said that at that point, Neil told him he trusted him, but added: "I just don't know what to do." He said he would go home and talk to his wife. Maguire said he put an arm about Neil and told him, "You have to understand, no matter who it is or what has to be done, we'll do it. It's a murder case and it will not go away. It will get worse. Think of everybody involved, and get back to me."

Maguire filed several other police reports that week, based on conversations he had with Betty's father and brother. In one document, the younger Tasker was quoted as having reported that he had told Glen he "just wanted to hear it from him, if it was a heat of passion thing he might understand. If that's possible he wanted Glen to say if he's guilty." Betty's brother said Glen replied: "It's not for me or you, Jack, or your father, to say who killed her. It's up to the police to find out."

When Glen continued by contending that he did want to find out who killed Betty, her brother asked, "Then why won't you talk to police?" Glen again cited his lawyer's advice, then added, "I don't have to prove I'm innocent, they have to prove I'm guilty."

Detective Mitchell stepped into the fray next, taking a call from Nancy Wolsieffer, who claimed that Neil was ready to snap. She told Mitchell that Neil had woken up in a rage, mumbling something about Captain Maguire wanting him to take a lie detector test. Nancy said she was not going to allow Neil to talk to investigators anymore. "I'm begging you, keep us out of it," she said. "I can't stand it anymore. Just leave him alone." At that point, Captain Maguire interceded. "If Neil doesn't want to come in, he has to tell us. I don't want his wife telling us."

That afternoon, Neil drove to police headquarters, but only got as far as the parking lot. He sat there for a time, staring off, then drove back to work, where he sat in a chair and again stared off into space. A coworker brought Neil home because he felt Neil was incoherent, had no idea what was going on, and was in no condition to drive.

Neil was in a rage. "Who did this to my family? Who's responsible for this?" he demanded. Nancy calmed her husband down and convinced him to go upstairs to take a rest.

In the midst of all that, Neil managed to call Captain Maguire to inform him that he would not be taking any kind of test, nor would he speak to any of them again. As Maguire later recalled the conversation, he then asked Neil: "Is this on the advice of your lawyer?"

Neil said he didn't have a lawyer. "I just feel I don't want to talk anymore," Maguire quoted Neil as saying. "I could only hurt people. I don't want to hurt people."

According to Maguire, he ended the conversation and ceased further contacts with Neil.

In the meantime, Chief Coyne announced that the FBI had accorded the Wolsieffer case "top priority" status, and the detectives working the case on a day-to-day basis continued their search for more information about Betty and Glen Wolsieffer.

On the forensic front, Dr. Hudock, the county coroner, said he had determined that Betty had been strangled between 4:00 and 7:00 A.M. with a soft object such as a tie, scarf, or belt. The time frame was within Glen's claim that it was starting to get light out when the intruder supposedly broke in, but not the optimum range if the murder was committed shortly after last call. Dr. Hudock said it appeared that Betty had been struck several times about the face, that her cheeks were swollen and scratched, and that authorities had detected no other signs of a struggle in the master bedroom.

Though this information was still too vague, the investigators had better luck in their search for additional information about Glen's affiliation with Carol Kopicki. A check of registration records at the Busy Day Motel indicated that on April 25, a "Glen Wilson" registered for Room 206 with a guest, giving his address as 88 Birch Street in Wilkes-Barre, and the license plate on a Subaru as LYY-371 (Glen's Subaru was LYY-341). At the same time, a Richard Miscavage and guest checked into Room 209. The occupants checked out at 1:25 A.M.

Additional examination of the motel records indicated that on May 16, a "Richard Potsko" rented the same two rooms "Wilson" and Miscavage occupied in April. Detective Dessoye ran a check on the license plate listed on the registration cards and discovered that the Oldsmobile was registered to Jane Ann Miscavage, Richard's wife.

Navin Bhojani, the motel manager, said he remembered the foursome and was quite certain they had visited the facility on other occasions. He said he was quite surprised at being unable to find more registration cards for them. Perhaps they had used other names.

At the Granite Motel in Mountaintop, Dessoye tracked down Glen on three registration cards—for July 25, August 8, and August 22—all within a month of Betty's murder. Glen had signed his real name and gave 75 Birch as his address.

Investigators Mitchell and Sworen, meanwhile, interviewed Betty Wolsieffer's closest friends and associates—Lesley McCann, Barbara Ryan Dombroski, Eileen Pollock, and Jane Ann Miscavage—in their quest for a nugget of circumstantial gossip that would help them crack the case. As a byproduct, additional details about the rocky state of the Wolsieffer marriage in the year prior to Betty's murder also emerged.

McCann, the operator of Lesley McCann's Aerobic World in Forty Fort, told the investigators that on the days Glen attended class in the morning, he often arrived alone a half hour or more before the start of the 9:15 class, as did Carol Kopicki.

She also said that Betty had quietly checked herself into a hospital in November 1985 for a miscarriage and called her the next day for a ride home. She said Betty never even told Glen about the pregnancy because of concern that the news would be "too much for him to handle." According to McCann, Betty had some sort of blood disorder shortly before her death and "took a lot of pills." McCann quoted Betty as saying she wanted to have another baby, but Glen didn't.

She said Betty expressed compassion for her husband during his stay at the mental hospital, quoting Betty as having explained that Glen was "having a hard time dealing with what to do" about choosing between her and Debbie Shipp. McCann said Betty was "always concerned about Glen being able to shoulder any pressure over this incident," and so she was careful to shield him. Upon Glen's release, McCann said, Betty had asked her to "make a fuss" over Glen, to make him feel good.

Turning the conversation to Glen's buddy Rich Miscavage, McCann said she was aware that Rich and his wife, Jane Ann, were having marital problems, that they were very competitive and sometimes argued in class. McCann said that on about ten occasions, Glen had told her, "If Rich is having problems, he should get out."

Barbara Dombroski, wife of Glen's office partner, Dr. Stanley Dombroski, made a disturbing addition to previous anecdotal information. She stated that sometime between Glen's hospitalization and February of 1986, Betty had blood in her urine, attributing it to a damaged spleen. When asked for an explanation, Betty contended that she'd "flipped out about Debbie" and banged herself against a wall. On another occasion earlier that year, Betty had sported large bruises on the inside of her arms.

When Dombroski asked her what had happened, Betty tried to pass it off. "I think I'm going to die," she said with a laugh.

Dombroski also knew of Betty's miscarriage, telling the detectives that afterwards, Betty went on birth control pills, which made her ill. "Betty would have had a child in a minute if Glen wanted one," Dombroski explained.

The next afternoon, September 10, Mitchell and Sworen headed out for a more in-depth interview with Eileen Pollock. Recounting the story of Betty's discovery of Glen's affair and his subsequent visit to First Valley Hospital, Pollock added a new twist for the investigators: Betty had discovered some love letters in Glen's briefcase that proved he was having an affair with Debbie. Betty was very upset and confronted Glen about the letters. This led to arguments. The arguments led to Glen's checking into the hospital. As Pollock told the story, Betty would wake up in the middle of the night and find Glen sitting on the edge of their bed crying. Pollock had also heard Betty's explanation about the damaged spleen, that she'd hit the wall in anger over Glen and Debbie. But, Pollock said, she didn't believe that was how Betty had sustained the injury. Other parts of Pollock's story also were consistent with what the detectives had heard elsewhere: Betty had a hard time getting pregnant; Betty and Glen had blow-ups, especially when Danielle was not home; holidays were bad for Glen, to the point that Betty once found him crying in the shower; Betty tried to keep things quiet about her problems with Glen, often softening the story.

The last of the friends interviewed on that round, Jane Ann Miscavage, recalled that Betty was especially angry over Debbie one year when Glen had a Christmas party for his employees and specifically did not ask Betty to attend.

The case was starting to blow the community apart. There were those clamoring for Glen's hide pitted against those accusing the police of harassment against Glen and the rest of the Wolsieffer family. Police Chief Coyne reiterated his confidence that an arrest would be made in due time. He said investigators were awaiting results of tests on evidence sent to the Pennsylvania State Police Crime Laboratory and to the FBI laboratory. The media would just have to be patient, he warned. In an interview with Fred Ney

of the *Sunday Independent*, Coyne bristled at reporters who had
been calling his office asking for "all the test results" or demanding
to know who police thought was their "most likely" suspect.
"When have the police ever labeled an individual as a 'suspect'
before an arrest?" Coyne asked rhetorically. He noted that police
could be held civilly liable for making false accusations and the
news outlets could be guilty of libel or slander, especially if someone else was eventually arrested. Little did Coyne know that as
the investigation unfolded, he would have to eat his words about
premature identification of a suspect.

As the weeks turned to a month, the morale of the investigators and their superiors turned downward as the district attorney,
Bernard A. Podcasy, adamantly refused to authorize an arrest.
Podcasy had been appointed to the D.A.'s post in January by a
panel of local judges when the incumbent left to go into private
practice. The new D.A.'s father, Judge Bernard J. Podcasy, did
not participate in the vote, but the appointment nonetheless led
to accusations of nepotism. In the recent past, whenever the sitting
D.A. left before his term expired, his top deputy—the first assistant D.A.—was appointed to the job. Podcasy the son had been
working in the D.A.'s office, but as a mere assistant. When Podcasy's appointment was announced, first assistant D.A. Joseph Giovannini resigned in protest. He would be heard from again before
the Wolsieffer saga ended.

Increased pressure from police headquarters notwithstanding,
the decision of whether to arrest was Podcasy's call to make, for
in 1981, the Pennyslvania State Supreme Court had approved a
rule of criminal procedure allowing local district attorneys to designate certain crimes, including murder, that mandated consent from
the D.A. before an arrest could be made. The regulation was
enacted to minimize police errors on legal documents. In this
case, Podcasy insisted that investigators keep digging. He maintained that despite gut feelings and common-sense suspicions, they
were nowhere near to having enough to carry out a successful
prosecution.

There were other considerations, too. Podcasy's chief assistant
had just quit, and the weekly criminal court calendar sometimes
contained as many as seventy-five cases. The D.A.'s office was
already in the midst of several complicated, high-profile trials, and

Podcasy could ill afford to have a technical, circumstantial case like this one against Dr. Wolsieffer take up one hundred hours or more of trial time, only to see a guilty man acquitted because the case was rushed.

That left Mitchell and Sworen, who also had plenty of other cases to work on, spinning their wheels in the hopes of miraculously uncovering the big break. From the start, one possibility had been the lab tests. Perhaps the crucial damning piece of evidence could be unraveled in the bags and slides of hair, blood, towels, and fingernail clippings.

In late September, Chief Coyne and Captain Maguire told reporters that 80 percent of the FBI tests had been completed and that they expected the last 20 percent to be finished by the middle of the following week. They gave no official indication as to whether the test results were going to be of any help. But "one source close to the investigation" left the impression that authorities were closing in, that something of significance had been uncovered. "The emphasis right now is determining, from a legal point of view, whether certain evidence can be entered into the record during a trial. And that requires a lot of legal research," the source was quoted as saying in the *Sunday Independent*.

In fact, the tests were more of a dead end than anything. The FBI experts concluded that dark brown Caucasian head hairs microscopically like Glen's hair (hair comparisons do not constitute a basis for absolute personal identification) were indeed found in various samples, including the hairs removed from the windowsill and bed linen. Those findings had little evidentiary value, however. So Glen's hairs, if they were his, were all over the master bedroom, *his* master bedroom. There was no telling when they had been dropped there.

The news wasn't any better when FBI experts compared Betty's hair to the various samples. Brown Caucasian head hairs microscopically like Betty's were found on the mattress sheet, the blanket, the bedspread, and a bed cover sheet. Again, no surprise, given that Betty had slept in that bed on a nightly basis.

All was not lost, however. Two of the hairs found on the blanket, and sex-typed as male, had been "forcibly removed from the scalp," according to the FBI report. "The above-mentioned hairs could have originated from Glen Wolsieffer." While that sounded significant, depending on various factors the technical term "forcibly removed" can sometimes apply to hairs pulled while combing or brushing.

Potentially troubling for investigators was the FBI's disclosure that other head hairs, exhibiting "similarities *and* differences" to Glen's and Betty's hair, had been found on the blanket, bed-spread, bed cover sheet, and an orange towel. If a case was ever to be made against Glen Wolsieffer, evidence suggesting the presence of an outsider's hair on the bed wrappings would present a daunting dilemma for prosecutors. Had someone else been sleeping in the bed? Had the intruder lost several hairs during a struggle? Had the police or paramedics sullied the crime scene? There would be no easy answers. As the FBI report observed: "No conclusion could be reached as to the possible origin of these hairs."

The results of the FBI's other tests were equally murky. Blue cotton fibers "microscopically like those" from Glen's denim jeans and jacket were found in three of the fingernail clippings removed from Betty's body during the autopsy. But again, the FBI experts were forced to dilute what on first blush appeared to be a significant discovery. "Although these fibers could have originated from these specimens, it should be noted that blue cotton fibers like those comprising denim clothing are commonly encountered."

Finally, although Minnick had made a big deal over the hole in the upstairs window screen having been punched out from the inside, toolmark examinations of the ends of the wire strands around the hole by the FBI experts "did not indicate whether that hole was produced from the inside or the outside" of the screen. "Further, the type of tool or object used to produce this hole could not be determined."

For now, that was it. While the hair on the windowsill was consistent with Glen's, and the fibers in his jeans were consistent with the ones scraped out of Betty's fingernails, D.A. Podcasy still felt there wasn't nearly enough to make a solid case. Both pieces of evidence left plenty of reasonable doubt.

CHAPTER 15

Four years into their marriage, Nancy and Neil Wolsieffer bought the house at 84 Birch Street as a prelude to having a baby. They were happy and content. Neil was moving up the bureaucratic ladder at the city's Recreation Board; Nancy was professionally satisfied teaching. They both thought it was great to be living so close to Glen and Betty. Never did they imagine that the proximity of their residences, and the familial intimacy that developed, would lead to their becoming embroiled in a sensational murder case.

Nancy Woods met Neil Robert Wolsieffer and fell in love with him when she was fourteen and he was sixteen. By the time of Betty's murder in 1986, they had spent half of their lives together. Neil was the only guy Nancy ever dated.

Neil worked part-time, then full-time, for the Recreation Board. He had started when he was fourteen as a basket boy at one of the city pools. Neil rose from attendant to lifeguard to manager of the Aquadome. He later ran the city's softball program and was considered the unofficial assistant to the Recreation Board's executive director.

After high school, Neil enrolled at Luzerne County Community College, where he obtained an associate's degree in 1975. He then transferred to East Stroudsburg State College, intending to major in physical education. That same fall, though, the city of Wilkes-Barre opened an ice skating rink, the Ice-A-Rama, so named following a valley-wide contest. They needed a manager. "Whatever makes you happy," Neil's father advised. It was a tough decision. Teaching positions were low-paying, and Neil wasn't even sure that he wanted to teach. There weren't many other options for a guy with a phys ed degree. With the first semester not even completed, Neil dropped out of East Stroudsburg and became manager of the rink, which operated from October to March. He spent the rest of the year running the parks and playgrounds, supervising the summer employees, mostly college students.

Nancy, meanwhile, attended the local community college, where she graduated with a two-year degree in child development. As Neil was establishing himself in the Recreational Board's hierarchy, Nancy enrolled in Bloomsburg State College, where she eventually obtained a bachelor's degree in elementary education.

Nancy's leaving Wilkes-Barre figured to be a good test of the seriousness of their relationship. In high school, infrequent spats had lasted only a few days. "We'd have a fight and say, 'This is it.' I had his high school ring and I'd say, 'Here, you take it back.' That kind of thing," said Nancy. As she prepared to leave home for Bloomsburg, though, she was a tad apprehensive. "I thought, 'This is going to make us or break us, when I go away.' " Neil told her she would probably meet someone else while at school. "No, I won't," Nancy had promised. "It'll be you."

In fact, she came home from Bloomsburg every weekend. They spent as much time together as possible.

"He had a great sense of humor, and that was real attractive," Nancy remembered. "He was shy. It was more like I had to pursue him because he was shy—and I never really knew how he felt because he didn't always say. That was a challenge to me. But that shyness was also something that I admired about him. And he was very deep and compassionate. You know, as quiet as he was, he had a heart this big and that was probably the number one thing, just really caring about other people."

On several occasions when friends were in financial trouble, Neil withdrew money from his credit union. He trusted his friends and knew they would pay him back as soon as they could. "If I had a pipe break or if something happened, I would just have to make a phone call and he was here," said Neil's mother. "Glen wouldn't get excited about it, you know, I never called Glen first. Oh, don't get me wrong, Glen would come, but I would call Neil first."

Neil proposed to Nancy at the end of her junior year. The following May, Nancy graduated. After eight years of courtship, on July 21, 1979, they were married. Nancy was twenty-two, Neil twenty-four. Nancy's dream was old-fashioned traditional: a white picket fence in front of a modest home, two children at her side while she cooked and baked. That's all she really wanted out of life.

Glen was the best man, and the reception was held at the American Legion, the same as Glen and Betty. The newlyweds went to Bermuda on their honeymoon, and didn't really fit in. "We weren't this real romantic, gushy couple and the island was filled with people like that, that just got married and were walking around hugging and kissing," said Nancy. "We were ready for our twenty-fifth anniversary." Nancy and Neil were more than just mates. They were the best of friends. "We put in so much time," she said. "We went through everything."

Polite, caring, considerate, down-to-earth people. The kind of people who could be relied on in a pinch. The kind of people easily taken advantage of.

In fact, the police had been after Neil unceasingly to cooperate. He kept insisting he had told them all he knew, but few believed him. It was a trying time for Neil and Nancy. Both of them had been close to Betty. They couldn't believe that Glen had been involved in her death. Sure, there were questions to be asked, but they didn't feel right asking them; they didn't want Glen to think they were doubting him. More important, there was no question in their minds that Glen was innocent. There was no way he could have killed Betty.

"We didn't really come home at night and talk about the murder. We talked about life without Betty," Nancy explained.

"That's when I really was able to cry and feel. Betty was gone and she wasn't running in here ten times a day like she used to. We didn't sit around talking about Glen and the murder."

Although they gave it more thought, Neil and Nancy again decided against hiring their own attorney for two reasons: one, they felt they still didn't need one—they'd done nothing wrong and had nothing to hide; two, they couldn't afford one—they were still paying off the loan for the two-story addition on the back of their house. Neil was busy every chance he had finishing the inside of the job.

Nancy subsequently concluded that they were mistaken not to get an attorney, whatever the cost. "Neil could have said, 'No, I'm not coming in. I don't want to answer any more of your questions. I've told you over and over.' But he said, 'How will that look, if I tell them, "No, I'm not coming in"?' "

But it didn't matter what he told them. The investigators, especially Maguire, refused to believe that Neil didn't know anything. Pursuit by the police was literally driving Neil crazy. He was supposed to have all the answers. Yet if Glen hadn't called that Saturday morning, he wouldn't even be involved. "It was like everyone's life was going on but ours," said Nancy. "We would just sit here and we wouldn't even have the TV on. There'd be one small light on. We couldn't even talk. It was just so—I don't even have words to say what it was like. You can't believe that this is happening to you, this normal happy life that you had is gone."

Nancy thought frequently about the loss of Betty, and how tough it had to be for Glen to have lost a spouse at such a young age. She was torn over who needed her more, her husband or her widower brother-in-law. "The hard part was seeing Glen all the time. I would look at him and think, 'How do you survive without a wife?' I couldn't imagine if something happened to Neil. I couldn't imagine what that felt like. I felt so sorry for Glen."

Glen, who visited day and night, had to see how the pressure was tearing Neil apart. Although they were supportive of Glen's legal stance, Nancy decided to talk to Glen about how his silence was adversely affecting Neil.

"Glen, this is killing him," said Nancy. "How long can we go on like this?" Nancy was concerned about Neil's job. He was up for a promotion and was afraid all the publicity might hurt him. "He's so torn," Nancy continued. "And I can't stand this. You have to do something."

"How would you like to be me?" Glen replied. "What about what I'm going through?"

"You're right," said Nancy. She then thought to herself: "How selfish of me to even think that. Here's this poor guy with no wife, and I'm telling him what we feel like."

Even as the days turned to weeks and virtually everyone in Wilkes-Barre began to doubt Glen's innocence, Neil and Nancy remained supportive. If a doubt about Glen's story ever entered their minds, they immediately became furious at themselves. "It'd be like, 'How could you even think that?' " said Nancy. "When you trust somebody, and take them at their word, you are not going to second-guess every single thing."

Like Nancy, Neil never confronted his brother. "You wouldn't say, 'Well, what about this?' or 'Could you explain that?' Never," said Nancy, "because you felt too sorry for him and you didn't want to be wrong."

Those feelings didn't bother the police, though. Nor did it stop them from asking questions as if Neil and Nancy were part of a Wolsieffer family cover-up. Neil grew weary of the constant pressure. He started to become seriously depressed and withdrawn. Several close friends would later recall that they found it difficult to get close to him during this time period, "as if Neil didn't trust anyone." Some days he came home from work early, mentally exhausted. He just had to lie down. He hardly ever wanted to go out anymore. When he did go out, like when his friends dragged him to a Penn State game, he acted as if he was very uncomfortable and really didn't want to be there.

In the weeks following Betty's death, Glen spent a great deal of time with Neil. Friends would suggest that on several occasions, it appeared as if Glen was chaperoning his brother. "Neil felt better with him there. Glen was trying to help Neil and do whatever he could, to see how everything went. It was a brotherly kind of thing, you know," said Lisa, offering the family's explanation. "It's just the way we always were. Something's going on—you go to whoever needs the help at the moment." Unaddressed in that explanation was the fact that Neil needed help because the police were hounding him instead of his legally represented and silent-as-could-be brother. "They hounded Neil so bad that I will never forgive them for what they put him through," said his mother.

Everywhere Neil went he said he saw different cars following him. "He drove a lot of the time looking in his rearview mirror," said Nancy. "He went for pizza one night, two blocks away, and he was followed. And this was always on his mind, that someone was following him." Neil didn't know who or why, but blamed the police and reporters.

Paranoid or not, Neil did have a genuine fear that there was a killer on the loose and that that killer, for whatever reason, was after the women in the Wolsieffer family. In the days following Betty's funeral, he became obsessively protective of his wife, daughter, mother, and sister. Phyllis said Neil was "so suspicious of everybody. He thought that we were all going to be killed, I think. He must have called me fifty times a day to see if everything was all right here."

One evening, Lisa came to Neil's house to watch "Knots Landing" with Nancy. As Neil was about to go upstairs to watch something else on the other TV, he looked down at Nancy in his silent, protective mode. As Lisa recalled, "She said, 'Neil, I will be all right.' He just looked at her. What he was saying was, 'I don't want to go up there and leave you down here.' Finally, he went up."

Lisa, however, contested suggestions that Neil was paranoid. "He functioned. He did everything. He went to work," she said. Added his mother: "That seemed to be the thing that he focused in on—how everybody was against him."

Neil didn't confine his concerns strictly to safety issues, either. Phyllis remembered babysitting Danielle and Bryn one afternoon at a local park. "They were interviewing kids for the Special Olympics at that park, and Channel 15 was there. Neil knew I was going to that park and he happened to drive by. When he saw the TV people there, he jumped out of that car and made us go home."

What really bothered Nancy was all the people who criticized Neil and her for their actions on the Saturday of the murder, especially in Neil's case. "It kills me how they tell us what we should have done," Nancy lamented. "How do they know what they would have done? They even made a big deal about 'Why did Glen call here? Why didn't he just call the police?' which God only knows. I wish he had. But at the time, that wouldn't have been out of character at all because we were always calling back and forth."

Nancy said if she had known Betty was beaten and strangled upstairs, "I wouldn't have been walking out saying, 'Oh, where's Betty?' I would have been upstairs, saying, 'What went on in here? What happened?' We didn't know that. And they took everything prior to the time that we learned she was dead and scrutinized it."

One particularly sensitive issue was Neil's failure to go upstairs at 75 Birch the morning of the murder. "I never wanted to see what was up there. Thank God I didn't go upstairs," Neil said after learning of the condition of Betty's face and body. As police skepticism about his inactions persisted, though, Neil said he wished he had gone up, "only so they would get off me about not doing it."

The investigators also were skeptical of the claims from 84 Birch about how much time had transpired between Glen's call to Neil and Neil's call to the police. They wondered if Neil had gone over to 75 Birch hours earlier to help concoct a cover-up, perhaps with the help of Nancy, too. "I really resented that, that I was not believed, and so did Neil," said Nancy. "He said, 'How many times can you tell the truth?' "

As the police advanced their theory on the fan blowing air on Betty's body, they let it be known that they believed their main suspect had positioned it toward the bed to keep rigor mortis from setting in and to make it more difficult to ascertain the time of death. But, in fact, Nancy later said that Glen and Neil both slept with fans on—even in the winter. It was a subject she and Betty had discussed on many occasions. "We hated it," said Nancy, "because it would be freezing. Neil would have his on a stacked table, in the bedroom, blowing on the bed, and I would be up in the night freezing. In the winter, all year 'round, and Glen was the same way, five below zero they'd have the fans on."

Investigators also found it hard to believe that Nancy hadn't asked Glen for details when she visited him in the hospital after Betty's body was discovered. "The police said, 'Well, did you talk about what happened in the house that day?' I would never have asked him that in the hospital. That was the furthest thing from my mind. I mean, it was the first time I had seen him since Betty died and I felt so bad."

Neil was grieving as well, and as the persecution by the police escalated, he began to act more and more erratically. One afternoon, Marguerite Delaney of 83 Birch spotted Neil standing in the middle of the street. "Come on in the house," she heard Nancy call out. When Neil didn't budge, Nancy came out of the house, took him by the arm, and led him inside. A short time later, Neil came out of his house again, walked several houses down the sidewalk, then abruptly turned around and walked back into his house.

On another afternoon, Neil ran into an old friend, Wilkes-Barre patrolman Ronald Rebo. During the conversation Rebo realized that the barrage of newspaper articles was deeply affecting Neil. To Rebo, Neil looked "mentally and physically destroyed." Neil said he couldn't sleep and often found himself up most of the night wandering around. "When this is all over, they're all going to have egg on their face," Neil said emphatically. Then, looking over at 75 Birch, he added: "That house has to go."

On more than one occasion, Paul McDermott, who lived several doors away at 100 Birch, looked across his backyard to watch Neil conducting an early-evening ritual. Neil would walk five paces forward, then five paces backward, without ever turning around.

Just before noon on September 18, Neil was spotted walking back and forth on his front porch by Mike Hersik, who lived next door. Something seemed to be bothering Neil, so Hersik asked if he could be of any assistance. Neil asked if he could use the telephone. Hersik said yes, but instead of coming into his neighbor's home, Neil walked into his house. A short time later, Neil returned outside, walking back and forth on the porch. Then he walked off the porch, only to pace back and forth on the sidewalk.

Finally, Neil sat down in a chair on the porch. Hersik and a buddy started to play catch with a football in the street. A short time later, Hersik heard a noise. Looking toward Neil's porch, he spotted his neighbor lying on the wooden floor. Hersik immediately called for help.

Word traveled fast that day. Detective Mitchell arrived a few minutes later as well.

Jay Delaney, one of the paramedics, found Neil lying face-down with his head resting on his arms, which were folded as if for sleep. Delaney rolled Neil over, but couldn't get any response from him. However, in the process of being rolled over, Neil moved his body to get in a more comfortable position. A few moments later, Neil opened his eyes and stared straight ahead. Still, he wouldn't respond verbally.

When he was lifted up onto an ambulance litter, police officer Edward Grenevicki noticed that Neil again shifted his body to become more comfortable. His arm had fallen over the side of the litter, but Neil lifted it up and positioned it across his chest. To the officer, it appeared that Neil "did have control over his body movements," but he "would not respond to questions as to what [had] happened."

Unable to determine at the scene what was wrong, the paramedics took Neil to Mercy Hospital, where he was examined by Dr. Dennis Gaza, who had treated Glen in the emergency room back in August. After a series of tests, Neil, a chain smoker, was admitted for observation. There was a possibility he was not getting enough oxygen to the brain. That could cause a blackout. He stayed for several days, during which time he was treated for bronchitis and stress.

"When I got to the hospital there was Mitchell. Before me!" said Nancy. "He comes right in—and he wants to talk to the doctor. He had no right to even be there.

"That really bothered me. Everything about the way they treated us bothered me. They weren't respectful at all."

The most difficult part of Neil's inner struggle about Glen's guilt or innocence was that he did wonder: "Why are they saying all these things if they are so untrue?" But he worked hard at pushing his doubts aside. Glen was family, and that's what really mattered. "I don't think there's a person alive who could say that they didn't question Glen," said Nancy, "but we always gave him the benefit, like I am sure anybody in a close-knit family would do."

Neil rationalized that if Glen had killed Betty he would have made a glaring mistake in his cover-up, something that would have conclusively proved he was the killer. But there was no such glaring piece of evidence.

He frequently replayed in his mind and with Nancy the key issues from that Saturday morning, like his finding the cellar door open. "I thought somebody could have still been in the cellar. I was scared, I was truly scared," he said. "But when I said I was scared to the police, they said, 'A big guy like you?' They made a fool out of me. If I had known that someone had killed Betty, I wouldn't have cared what I had to do to them. But I didn't know that. So now everyone knows the story, Betty is dead. She was strangled. And I look like this coward that wouldn't even go upstairs."

The pressures were intense, heavy, and crunching. How does one cast aside family feelings and honor and loyalty and examine with objectivity and clear conscience? Surely, it is never an easy task. Uneasily, Nancy informed Neil one day, "I'm sorry to say this, and I hope it doesn't cost me my marriage, but sometimes things really bother me about Glen's story."

Neil looked at his wife and revealed a painful innermost thought: "There are certain things that bother me, too." As a surprised and relieved Nancy listened, Neil detailed his two biggest concerns, things that he never would have thought about discussing with the police: Glen's moaning on the kitchen floor and his request for a glass of water.

Why, Neil questioned, when he walked toward the dining room steps to the bedrooms that Saturday morning, had his brother suddenly started moaning, as if on cue? "Glen was lying on the floor and every time I walked away, Glen moaned," he observed to Nancy.

Neil also couldn't understand why Glen was well enough to ask for a glass of water but somehow unable or disinterested in asking how his wife and child were doing.

But after extensive debate, Neil and Nancy pushed the questions aside. "So what if he asked for a glass of water?" Nancy decided. "I don't think there is a person who hasn't looked at both sides of it—you have to," she later said. "If it was your own son, you would do it. You analyze it to death. I think all of us did that. But the bottom line is, we kept coming up saying there was no way he could have done it. No way."

At that point, things like the moaning didn't seem so critical. "That's not something you're going to go to the police and say, 'Well, you know, maybe and maybe not.' You're not going to discuss your doubts with the police. And so, ninety-nine percent of you believed in your brother; that's how it was," Nancy explained.

As time went on, though, Glen's moaning became more difficult to dismiss out of hand. "That moaning just bugs me," Neil told Nancy one day in late September. He wanted desperately to continue to believe his brother, but Neil's private misgivings had begun to tug at him.

The disquietude—no matter how minor—began to eat at his heart and soul. He became even more depressed, sullen at times. Slowly, but steadily, Neil Wolsieffer was dying inside.

CHAPTER 16

Surely it would have been difficult for Neil Wolsieffer to reveal even the mildest of doubts. While he wouldn't have been directly accusing his brother of murder, such comments would have been tantamount to familial sedition.

Trying to bring his life back to normal, Neil got out of bed on Sunday, October 12, 1986, and went golfing. Nancy woke up and grabbed her usual cup of coffee. Turning to page 3 of the *Sunday Independent*, she immediately realized it was going to be another miserable day.

NEIL WOLSIEFFER BALKS AT LIE DETECTOR TEST screamed the headline across the top of the page. The story began: "The Betty Wolsieffer murder investigation is 'far from over,' according to Wilkes-Barre police sources who are beginning to express private concern over the refusal of Dr. Glen Wolsieffer, the dead woman's husband, and Neil Wolsieffer, Glen's brother, to cooperate with city detectives. Sources said yesterday that Neil Wolsieffer has 'refused to take a lie detector test' and that Dr. Wolsieffer had denied a police request to reinterview his six-year-old child,

Danielle." After providing several paragraphs of background—including the fact that Neil and Glen had both failed to go upstairs and check on Betty and the child—the story continued: "One police source said investigators want to give Neil a lie detector test 'simply to ask him if everything he told us is the truth.' He said Neil has refused to cooperate with the request."

The only police official quoted in the story was "Wilkes-Barre Detective Captain William Maguire."

Nancy put down the paper and dialed the number of Dorothy Tasker, Betty's sister-in-law. Nancy wanted Dorothy and the other Taskers to know that Neil wanted the murder solved as much as anybody. "He's not hiding a thing." The part about Neil not being willing to take a lie detector test was true, Nancy said, explaining that he didn't want to submit to a test he had been told could show him to be a liar even if he was telling the truth.

"Please tell Betty's parents because we feel terrible being separated from them at this time. Before this, we were all very close," Nancy said, explaining that Neil was "really caught up" in the mess, and really couldn't do anything about it. "I just wanted you to know, and the Taskers also, that we feel sorry for them and we're behind them."

Little did Nancy know that her call had started a fateful chain of events.

The Wednesday after the newspaper article, John and Marian Tasker received an official update on the case, including a review of the FBI tests conducted on the various pieces of physical evidence. During the course of the discussion, Betty's mother stated that Nancy had told Dorothy the newspaper story had wrongly reported that Neil had said he wouldn't take a lie detector test, but that the police had just never gotten back to him.

Maguire explained that in the six weeks since Betty's murder Neil had consistently stated that he would not take a lie detector test. Assistant D.A. Eichorn explained that even Nancy Wolsieffer had called police recently to state emphatically that Neil would not take any tests.

The Taskers, however, insisted that they had been told differently. "We could clear this up right now," said Maguire. "I could give Neil a call."

Everyone agreed, and so Neil's longtime friend called 84 Birch.

"Neil, this is Captain Maguire."

"Yes, Bill—or should I say Captain?"

"Bill is all right."

Maguire explained that at that very moment he was having a meeting with the Taskers about the investigation. "Neil, somebody is calling somebody a liar," said Maguire.

Neil had no idea what the detective was talking about.

Maguire proceeded to tell Neil the Tasker version of the conversation between Nancy and Dorothy the previous Sunday, including Neil's supposed willingness to take a polygraph.

"No, Bill," said Neil. "She never said that."

"Who?" asked Maguire.

"My wife. I don't think my wife ever said that."

Maguire asked Neil if he would take the test. As always, Neil said he was not interested. "I could only hurt my brother."

Maguire asked: "Will you at least come in and talk? Will you talk to Mister Tasker?" With that, Maguire handed the phone to John Tasker, who told Neil he couldn't understand why he wouldn't cooperate with the police to find Betty's killer.

Marian Tasker asked for the phone, and she implored Neil to please help the police with any information that he had. "Neil, I loved you like a son. We were all together, and you feel like a son to me. Just please help. Why isn't anybody saying anything? This isn't normal."

The phone now back in Maguire's hands, the detective asked Neil: "Will you speak to John?"

"John who?"

"John Eichorn from the district attorney's office."

"I don't want to speak to anybody from the district attorney's office," said Neil. With that, the phone went dead.

For several minutes after the call, Neil and Nancy discussed the matter. In their view, these people couldn't get a story straight or were deliberately screwing things up. Angrily, she called Assistant D.A. Eichorn back to straighten him out about her conversation with Dorothy Tasker. She insisted that she had never said Neil would take a lie detector test, but rather that Neil would talk to the police, only they hadn't gotten back to him.

Nancy said she had been told that lie detector tests were not always accurate. "Who told you a lie detector was no good? They can't be used in court anyway," Eichorn replied. "We just want to find out if what Neil told us is the truth. It will help us to believe Neil." But Neil was not going to take a lie detector test, and that was that.

"Will Neil, in fact, talk to us?" asked Eichorn, grasping for straws. "Can I speak to Neil?"

Nancy handed the phone to her husband. Eichorn asked Neil if he would be interested in undergoing hypnosis. "Will you do anything? Will you come in and talk?"

Neil said he did want to cooperate. Mrs. Tasker's comments about them all being so close before Betty's death really hit him hard. He wanted to do what was best for everyone. Pressed by Eichorn, Neil hesitated, then stated that he would be willing to come in, again, to answer additional questions.

"Will you come in and talk now?"

No, Neil replied, now was not a good time.

"How about tomorrow morning?"

Neil agreed, and the appointment was set for 10:00 at the district attorney's office.

When he hung up, Eichorn relayed the conversation to the others, explaining that Neil still wasn't interested in taking any tests, lie detector or otherwise, but was willing to talk.

It was better than nothing.

The investigators had genuine hopes that Neil would finally tell them what they thought he knew. For a change, the mood at the D.A.'s office was upbeat and sanguine.

There was a strange kind of optimism inside 84 Birch that night as well. Neil had hoped he was done with the police. Their recent silence had been welcome. But here out of the blue was Maguire coming on like a ball of fire, essentially accusing Neil of having called him a liar.

"How many times can I tell them the truth until they believe me?" Neil asked. "I don't know what else they could ask me that I haven't told them already. I don't know how to prove to them that I'm telling the truth."

"Go down and try it again," said Nancy. "If they don't believe you, at least you'll have tried."

"I will," said Neil. "I want to."

"Then tell them to leave us alone," she added.

Nancy rose at 6:15 A.M., the time she always got up on a school day. As usual, Neil slept another half hour, getting a cheerful "rise and shine" from his wife when she was finished using the bathroom.

Before she left for St. Boniface, at about 8:00, they talked briefly about his going in to see the authorities. Neil said he felt confident, and said that after work he was going to pick up some stain for the woodwork in the addition to the back of the house.

About fifteen minutes later, he also departed, first to his mother-in-law's house to pick up Bryn, who had spent the night there. He then took her to his mother's house for the day.

"You're early this morning," said his mother.

"Yeah," Neil said, without further explanation.

He asked if he could borrow ten dollars. "I'll give it back to you later," he said, turning toward the door.

"Oh, Neil, there's a spot on the back of your sport coat."

"I have a couple of them I have to get cleaned. I'll get them to the cleaners," he said. With that, Neil walked outside to chat with his brother, who was about to take Danielle to school. Outside their mother's earshot, the brothers chatted about Neil's plans. After leaving Magnolia Avenue, Neil dropped from sight for the next hour or so, except for being spotted back at his house by one of his neighbors, then by Jack Tasker, Betty's brother, driving through town.

Down at the county courthouse, Eichorn, Maguire, Chief Coyne, and Detective Mitchell gathered just before 10:00 to await Neil's arrival. About ten minutes after the hour, Eichorn called the Recreation Board to see if Neil was there. He wasn't. Then a call was placed to the Ice-A-Rama. He wasn't there either.

Everyone began to wonder whether Neil was going to show up after all. The promise of the previous evening was fading with each passing minute.

At 10:30, Detective Sworen from the D.A.'s office knocked on the door. "I think Neil Wolsieffer was in a fatal car accident on River Road." The room fell silent. The investigators and prosecutors were in a state of shock.

Mitchell and Sworen rushed to the scene.

Shortly after 10:00, Neil was driving his 1978 Honda CVCC north on River Road, past the county courthouse and out of the city. It was a two-lane road, and paved berms lined both sides of the roadway. Two solid yellow lines ran down the middle of the thoroughfare, indicating no passing in either direction.

As Neil drove by Saylor Avenue, about four miles past the courthouse, a cement truck pulled out onto River Road. The truck was crawling along, its driver working his way up the lower end of the ten-speed manual transmission. Neil, whose car also had a manual transmission, pulled out, then returned to his own lane after passing the truck.

Subsequent accounts of what happened next were far from consistent. Inexplicably, though, as Neil Wolsieffer's car approached a left curve in the road, traveling at an estimated forty to forty-five miles per hour, within the speed limit, the vehicle smashed into the front of an oncoming twenty-two-foot Mack truck.

The crash was excruciatingly violent.

The car was pushed and crushed and crinkled into an ugly junk ball. Neil's skull was shattered, and his heart was torn from its proper position. He died instantly.

Pennsylvania State Trooper John Yencha was in the third vehicle behind the truck when he saw what appeared at first to be an explosion. It was 10:14 A.M. He immediately radioed his barracks in nearby Wyoming, where a dispatcher informed the local authorities. As a result, Chief Frank Mudlock of the Jenkins Township Police Department arrived within minutes.

The truck had actually mounted the Honda, crushing it in the process. The Honda was resting in the wrong direction in the center of the northbound lane, some sixty feet back from the point of impact.

The truck was stopped off the southbound shoulder in a grassy gully, its front end one hundred and seventy feet forward from the point of impact. It had traveled forward three times the distance the Honda had been pushed back. Clearly, the truck had not stopped immediately.

The officers working the accident were shocked when the license plate check came back: the car belonged to Glen Wolsieffer's brother, Neil. But the victim's injuries were so extensive that it was impossible to immediately make a positive identification.

According to a police report later filed by Chief Mudlock, the driver of the truck, Anthony G. Shatrowskas, said the Honda had been traveling north at what "appeared to be a high rate of speed." Shatrowskas said that when he initially saw the car, referred to as Unit Number One in the police report, it was in its own lane of travel. "Driver of Unit Number Two stated that Unit Number One looked like he was going by him, the next thing he heard was breaking glass and felt a jolt, applied his brakes, his vehicle continued to its final resting place. Driver of Unit Number Two stated in his opinion Driver of Unit Number One intentionally turned into him." Shatrowskas estimated that he had been driving at a speed of no more than thirty-five to forty miles per hour, claiming that he had just looked at his speedometer because he'd noticed the state police officer to his rear. Judging from the comments attributed to Shatrowskas in the written police report, however, it seemed that, incredibly, he had not actually seen the crash.

Beth Kelly, driving directly behind the truck, said she was driving toward Wilkes-Barre when the Honda "cut directly in front of" the truck. She stated that it looked as if the Honda "was going to pull across the street." Just behind her, witness Mike Ulichney, a courier for Wilkes-Barre General Hospital, corroborated her statement.

Luzerne County Deputy Coroner Michael Yeosock pronounced the driver of the car as dead at the scene, attributing his demise to "multiple traumatic injuries." The body was subsequently transported to Mercy Hospital for an autopsy to be conducted by Dr. George Hudock, the county coroner.

At St. Boniface School, Nancy couldn't leave the classroom for a phone call except in an emergency, so she had told Neil to call during the noon hour to let her know how his session with the homicide investigators had gone. Entering the office, she asked if her husband had called. The secretary said he hadn't. Nancy called the Wilkes-Barre Recreation Board office on Coal Street, and learned that Neil still hadn't shown up for work.

A little concerned, Nancy called home, then the ice rink, Kirby Park, and Phyllis. But Neil wasn't around. The lunch period was over. Full of anxiety, Nancy returned to her classroom.

Soon thereafter, a fourth-grade teacher came to the door of Nancy's classroom. "You're wanted in the rectory," she said.

Walking from the school over to the priests' residence, Nancy figured that they had finally arrested Glen. "Every day we waited. 'Is today going to be the day that Glen's arrested?' " Nancy later recalled. "So logically, Neil goes in for questioning, Neil can't be found, Glen's arrested. It's just the way I put the picture together."

At the rectory, Nancy was met by the Reverend Joseph Meighan, Deputy Coroner Bill Lisman, and state Trooper Yencha. It didn't fit. "Why would a deputy coroner be sitting in the rectory?" she asked herself.

"Sit down," said Father Meighan.

Nancy looked at him blankly.

Father Meighan took her by the arm. *"Sit,"* he instructed.

Nancy had a horrible feeling. She sat down and turned to Lisman. "Bill, just tell me this isn't about Neil."

Lisman put his head down. "It is," he said.

He started to explain the details as he knew them—that Neil's car had gone into the other lane—but Nancy tuned him out; she was in shock.

Father Meighan squeezed Nancy's arm tightly.

"He was killed instantly," Lisman said. Nancy heard that much, but nothing more, not the when, or the where.

"Please, get my parents here," pleaded Nancy, a widow at age twenty-nine.

Phyllis Wolsieffer remembered getting a call about midday from Nancy, asking if she had heard from Neil. She said she told Nancy she hadn't. It was only then that she found out about Neil's appointment with the investigators that morning.

Mark Ciavarella called a little while later, Phyllis said, asking, " 'Do you know where Neil is?' and I said, 'No, I don't, Mark. Why?' I said, 'Nancy tells me he had to go for an interview.' He said, 'Did he take counsel with him?' And I said, 'No.' And he said, 'Oh Jesus,' and he hung up."

"He's already dead and I don't even know it," said Phyllis. "I had a candle up in my bedroom burning ever since Betty was killed, a candle in front of my Blessed Virgin statue. Do you believe when I went upstairs that candle was shattered? The glass was shattered. The pendulum had fallen off my clock that day. My clock has never chimed since. Then I get a clock man in here and he's from Switzerland—he doesn't know one thing about any of this history—he said, 'You know, in Switzerland it's a bad omen if a pendulum falls down.' I couldn't believe it."

In the meantime, Ciavarella had reached Glen at one of his dental offices. They immediately set off for Phyllis's house.

Glen walked in the back door. "Danielle, take Bryn upstairs."

Then he changed his mind. "No, you watch Bryn down here. Mom, come upstairs with me."

Glen proceeded to give his mother the bad news. "Mom, there's been an accident. They're pretty sure it was Neil."

In fact, the authorities would require the assistance of Neil's dentist to positively identify the body found in Neil's Honda. The dental records matched. The victim was Neil Wolsieffer.

Glen, of course, had been his brother's dentist.

CHAPTER 17

IN HIS WORDS

Neil was the kind of guy who didn't like anybody to be mad at him. He wanted to help everybody. He liked to be everybody's friend. And I think he sacrificed a lot of his privacy, a lot of his own self, by giving too much to others—like Betty. They robbed themselves of their own time, and their own responsibilities, trying to please everybody.

Neil thought for sure people were following him. He started making me paranoid. I didn't give a shit who was following me— follow me wherever you want. Tap my phones, I don't give a shit.

Neil knew the cops were trying to stick it up my ass, and he was friends with some policemen. He figured if he could help the police find who killed Betty, he could help his brother. But they weren't satisfied with that. They believed that he knew what happened. They figured, "This guy is soft, and we're going to keep pressuring him." They kept hounding him. They were on him. He became real nervous. He was smoking a lot.

My thought was he could have blacked out that day. If he was upset, he was probably smoking his brains out. He was up to five packs a day of Marlboros.

One time he came home for lunch at his house and he blacked out on the porch. Mitchell heard it on the police radio and was at the hospital. He heard "man down on Birch Street." He must've thought, "Oh geez, it must be Glen Wolsieffer." I get to the hospital—and I knew Neil's physician—I said, "What's wrong?" He said he had a severe case of anoxia, no oxygen to the brain, because his lungs were so screwed up from smoking. It knocked him right out.

He could have blacked out. No oxygen to the brain. Anoxia. That is what I think, to be honest with you. And let's face it, a guy going to take a lie detector test—if you are going to be nervous, that is when you are going to be nervous, no matter what you are going to say. That is what I think, you know. He was no more nervous, and no less nervous, that morning than he was since Betty was killed.

I was at his house the night before, and we were talking about it. The Taskers called Neil crying and saying "Why won't you cooperate? Why won't you help the police?" Neil was close with these people. Neil was the one who dragged me up to their house, to talk to the both of them—the father and the brother. If it wasn't for him, I wouldn't have gone up there.

So he said, "I am trying to help out, other than taking a polygraph. I'm trying all I can." Maguire says "someone from the Taskers told me you're saying something different about the polygraph." Neil was upset. He said, "I'm trying to do all I can, and now he doesn't think I'm doing enough."

So Maguire says, "Hey, Neil, what's the story? What are you going to do? The Taskers are here. They want you to take a lie detector test to help them out, to get the truth out." So then he agreed. He said, "All right, I'll do it." Basically, Neil was going through with that lie detector test to keep the Taskers shut up.

He was concerned about the accuracy. "What if I'm too uptight?" I said, "All you gotta do is go in there and tell the truth. You know as much as I do about this stupid case."

And he said, "I'm just afraid if the lie detector test is not admissible, then it's inaccurate. What if I go in there nervous, and something comes out the wrong way, you know, they're going to use it against me."

I said, "Well, I don't know what else to tell you than to go in and tell them everything you know. Just tell them the truth." After about twenty minutes of just saying, "Just do what they want you to do to ease their minds, and you can get them off your ass, that's what you got to do," finally, he said, "All right. Fuck 'em. Let's do it. I'll take it."

I said, "Good. That's the only way they're gonna get off your ass." We had a beer. He felt better.

Then they set up the arrangements for the next morning. He said, "You know, you're right."

I knew him like he was myself.

He had this feeling, "We're gonna turn this thing around. We'll finally make these people believe we're not lying."

I said to him, "What have you got to lose?"

PART TWO

NANCY

CHAPTER 18

Neil's burden was now Nancy's to bear. Now it was she who supposedly held the key to solving Betty's murder. Now she was supposedly withholding information. Now she was supposedly protecting Glen. Nancy responded with equal hostility. Her heightened animosity toward all law enforcement, especially Maguire and Mitchell, only pushed her to support Glen more than ever.

If she had believed Glen's story ninety-five or ninety-nine percent before Neil's death, now she believed it one hundred percent—"because I knew he would never have let his brother die."

In Nancy's eyes, the police were out of control. She felt like accusing *them* of murder. Not only were they wrongly implicating Glen in Betty's murder, but as a result, her husband—the only man she ever fell in love with—was gone.

There was finger-pointing and name-calling over Nancy's refusal to let a state trooper search 84 Birch to look for a suicide note. To make matters worse, at first she had agreed, then was convinced to change her mind by Glen's attorney, Mark Ciavarella, and Glen's cousin Gary Stinson.

Nancy conducted her own search because she feared those against the Wolsieffer family would forever say, "She wouldn't let us in the house." Nancy's inspection turned up nothing, as she knew it would, but her words didn't silence the skeptics.

More than ever, wild rumors swept through Wilkes-Barre. The sensational gossip that Neil had been involved in a cover-up of Betty's murder now grew to include the allegation that he had actually committed the crime, and that he and Betty had been romantically involved. Others suggested that Neil had been murdered to keep him from revealing what he knew about his brother's guilt.

The antagonistic emotional battle between the Wolsieffers and the Taskers was painfully magnified by Neil's death. On the one hand, some of Glen's defenders blamed the Taskers along with the police for Neil's death. And on the other, the Taskers felt cheated. Their hopes of finally seeing Betty's killer captured had been cruelly snatched from their grasp. "The one person who may have known something is dead," lamented John Tasker to reporters. Added Betty's mother, Marian: "Neil was under pressure—not from us, but from something he knew. Neil was going to tell what he knew. He said he would, and I believed him."

The possibility of suicide as the cause of Neil's death was swiftly planted in the minds of the public. The morning after the crash, the *Citizens' Voice* quoted Dr. Hudock, the county coroner, as saying he had "no reason to believe" that Neil had committed suicide, but the *Times Leader* took a more conjectural approach, providing a nameless investigator with the means to disseminate what would become the party line on Neil's death. "A law-enforcement official close to the case speculated Thursday that Wolsieffer, a Wilkes-Barre resident, drove past the courthouse, proceeded north on River Road and then intentionally drove his car into the path of the oncoming truck. Wolsieffer's maroon Honda 'just cut into' the path of the truck, according to township police chief Frank Mudlock."

The story also quoted a "police source" who said he spoke to Neil the night before his death and had "pleaded with him" to talk. The source—Maguire was the only police department representative who spoke with Neil that night—quoted Neil as agreeing to talk by proclaiming, "OK, I trust you."

The speculation and self-serving comments further angered Neil's widow. "They always have 'somebody close to the investigation' saying something," she said. "We weren't being believed and we couldn't prove it, and there was nothing we could do."

Meanwhile, two houses were empty on Birch Street now, for Nancy immediately moved into her parents' home with two-year-old Bryn. Due to the circumstances, Nancy was compelled to request an unpaid leave of absence from her teaching job. Already, she had been absent at the start of the school year due to Betty's murder, and then she had taken time off when Neil was hospitalized. School officials, concerned about the adverse effect her absences might have on the first graders, wanted her back in the classroom. "I said, 'I can't even get out of bed, let alone come back to work.' I couldn't imagine how I was going to go to work and work with these kids." The principal graciously called the Diocese of Scranton, where Roman Catholic higher-ups granted Nancy's request for a one-year unpaid leave. She was guaranteed a return to her teaching position in the fall of 1987.

Nancy's father turned off the heat inside 84 Birch, and he winterized the pipes. Plastic sheets separated the unfinished addition in the rear from the original front rooms. Over the course of that winter, Nancy returned frequently to her bone-chillingly cold dwelling, alone—save for a Thermos of coffee—to sit, and think, and cry. "I couldn't really show the way I felt at my parents' house because they got so upset. If they saw me really losing it, then they did too, and I felt responsible for triggering that. My daughter was there all the time and I was trying to put on a facade around her all the time. She was so clinging—and she knew every time I was having a really bad day."

In those days immediately following Neil's funeral, Nancy's grief was often transformed to anger at some of the things being written and spoken about her husband, like the repeated contention by police officers, most often Captain Maguire, that Neil hadn't cooperated with the police. "He 'didn't talk' because he didn't say 'My brother told me,' " said Nancy. "They were all waiting for that big confession and because he didn't have that, then he didn't cooperate."

From the start, Nancy and Neil had felt like they had done nothing wrong and had been forced to endure innuendo, suspicion, accusation, and a loss of privacy because of something they had no control over. Now, Nancy found herself violated even more. "When you lose your husband, it's so private and personal," she said. "But I was never afforded that opportunity to grieve privately. There were reporters and all at the funeral, it was horrible. Plus front-page pictures. I didn't think things like this existed. I just hate how I feel about the media."

Family members were especially angry over suggestions that Neil had committed suicide. His mother insisted that his death had been an accident, attributing his lack of attention at the wheel to nerves and stress. "Neil *was* upset. And I've experienced very often over these past years these—I call them anxiety attacks," said Phyllis. "You get so bad that you think you are coming right out of your skin. And I've gone through red lights, I've done a lot of goofy things under the stress and that's what happened to Neil, I know it. He loved all of us too much to ever put us through a suicide."

After a well-publicized appeal, the driver of the cement truck Neil had passed just before the accident was located, and Trooper Johnson Miers told reporters: "This is the first person we've been able to identify who was in the position to actually see the impact. All the others were traveling behind the Mack truck and therefore couldn't really see anything."

The success of the hunt for the driver provided Assistant D.A. Eichorn and Captain Maguire the opportunity to explain their behavior in the days preceding Neil's death. "I want to make it clear that there was no pressure or harassment involved in the conversation we had with Neil," said Maguire. "We simply talked and asked him to come in. He agreed. It was voluntary on his part and at no time was he ever considered a suspect in this investigation."

Eichorn added: "I have to believe that Neil was going to tell us something. If he had nothing more to say than what he already told us, why would he agree to a meeting?"

Of course, to the Wolsieffer family, the posturing by Maguire and Eichorn was ridiculous. "God Almighty, nobody can describe that feeling—the hatred of knowing that somebody drove somebody to the point of this stress," said Neil's mother. Like Nancy, she held Detective Mitchell and Captain Maguire most responsible, especially Maguire, who supposedly had been her dead son's friend. "Little did I know, Maguire turned a knife in Neil's back," she said. "I think that he wanted to climb up the ladder. He thought he was the best cop that ever came down the pike."

A week after the accident, the police asked to interview Nancy. "I just couldn't believe they wanted to see me, to talk about business after everything that happened."

The investigators promised to send just one person. Using her next-door neighbor, attorney Richard Ferguson, as an intermediary, Nancy specified "no Maguire and no Mitchell." But when she showed up for the appointment, she was greeted by Eichorn, Sworen, and Maguire. Using a tortured logic that only angered Nancy more, the investigators tried to convince her that not only should Maguire be present, but she should speak with him privately. "They said, 'Bill knows Nancy better, so how about if Bill and Nancy go in a room and talk?' "

"No way," said Nancy, aware that Maguire had used the same buddy-buddy stunt with Neil. Maguire was forced to leave the room; the interview was conducted with Sworen and Eichorn.

To Nancy, Maguire represented everything that was wrong with the police tactics. She viewed him as a hotshot recklessly obsessed with solving the case at any cost. It was a view some colleagues in the Wilkes-Barre Police Department and D.A.'s office did not disagree with. "He thought Neil knew something," said Nancy, "and he was hell-bent on getting it out of him. No matter what he had to do, he was going to get that information."

With Neil no longer around to harangue, the investigators turned their spotlight on Nancy. "Everything was questioned, from the phone call straight through until Neil died. Every move we made, or every move that Neil made, was questioned," she said. "They made a claim, 'Well, at least you asked about Betty.' In other words, Neil looked bad because he didn't ask about her. Maybe he did ask about her. I don't know. But every word we said was scrutinized. I told them, 'You don't know how you would react.' "

As far as she knew, Neil had never confronted Glen. He had told her nothing concrete to point to Glen's guilt. Nancy felt that she had known Neil better than anyone, and was convinced that at his death he still knew nothing that would prove Glen had killed

Betty. She also remained convinced that Neil's behavior was the product of a distressed and confused individual, not a co-conspirator. "I spent half my life with him. I would know how he reacted to things, and I thought he was acting in character. He wasn't outspoken, and he was very sensitive. Things bothered him, publicity bothered him. Everyone was so good at saying what they would have done."

For Nancy, there were more questions about why she had failed to press Glen for details about the intruder. "They said, 'Well, why didn't you ask?' You just don't ask. When I found out Neil got killed I didn't ask, 'Well, tell me how it happened.' I didn't want to know. I just knew he was dead. Until anybody is in that situation they'll never understand."

Nancy said she tried explaining all that to the investigators after Neil's death, but they refused to believe her. "They didn't like what I was saying." she said. "I was contradicting totally what they had to make fit. So, of course, I was their enemy."

Little did Nancy and other members of the Wolsieffer family know that when Maguire sat down to write a three-page report about the meeting with the Taskers and the telephone conversation with Neil the night before he died, the detective put the strongest possible spin on his paraphrase of Neil's comments. "Neil stated that if he took the test it would hurt his brother. Also, he stated, 'I could help you guys and I could hurt my brother.' "

The Wolsieffer and Tasker families settled into their respective bunkers. Acrimony increased to the point where words were no longer exchanged face to face, replaced by letter writing. A week after Neil's death, Glen wrote to Betty's parents, thanking them for coming to his brother's wake. He also sought to explain his stance with the investigators, and he reiterated his innocence in Betty's death.

     I wish I could, but I know I cannot remove from your minds what the detectives and DA's have placed in there. I don't know what they have told you from the beginning and in the past weeks. Apparently I have no right to know or to speak my piece. What I did tell them was apparently dismissed. That's why nothing has been solved or resolved. I have not been given a chance from the beginning with anyone because the detectives formed their own opinion, looked only for what they wanted to look for, and now are trying to make the circumstantial evidence fit. It is a complete travesty, for now I don't believe we will find out what happened to my wife and your daughter.

Glen said he realized that attending Neil's wake must have been "a most difficult thing to do," and expressed his appreciation to the extended Tasker family "for the sake of Neil, Nancy and my mother."

My heart aches for you because I can only imagine how I would feel if anything like this ever happened to Danielle. I would certainly want justice to be served and I would probably follow the impulses which made me feel better.

No matter what you think now or before, I loved and will always love Betty. She was my wife as well as my friend and nothing will ever change the way I miss her and hold on to her memory. She was the only one who could understand me and accept me for what I was. I try to deal with her loss in my own way. Apparently I don't grieve in the proper manner, but I am a man alone now, and I must deal with it however I can.

Glen promised that as far as Danielle was concerned, the Taskers were free to see her whenever they wanted. "She is our link to Betty and as long as we have her, we will never be without Betty," he wrote. "Danielle is what she is today, because of Betty's influence and love. We must keep her that way. When I say we, I mean your family and mine."

Glen said there was no necessity for anyone in the Tasker family to see him in connection with Danielle's visits. But he assured Betty's parents, "Please don't feel that I don't want to see you. I have nothing to keep from you or from anyone." Oddly, for a man not under arrest, he concluded by saying he would keep his faith in God "and our justice system."

Prompted by Thanksgiving and what would have been the tenth wedding anniversary at 75 Birch, Betty's Aunt Marilyn, wife of Marian Tasker's brother, wrote Glen an emotional request for him to cooperate with the police. The letter, which she later gave to Detective Mitchell, spoke volumes about what most, if not all, members of the Tasker family were thinking.

Marilyn May told Glen he could give Betty a terrific holiday present by cooperating fully with authorities in their efforts to apprehend those responsible for Betty's vicious murder.

Betty's aunt went on to recall how Betty had supported Glen financially while he studied dentistry at Georgetown, and how she had provided him with a loving home and a sweet little daughter. She wrote longingly of Betty's ever-present smile, her affable personality, and her perpetual willingness to lend a hand to anyone, friend or stranger, in need of assistance.

Tugging at her burning family passions, May wondered what Danielle's opinion would be of her father in later years, questioning whether she would be able to rationalize why her father had not done everything possible to assist the police investigating her mother's death.

She lamented the great loss suffered by Betty's immediate family and challenged Glen to focus his thoughts on how much love and assistance they had provided to him throughout his marriage to Betty.

Aunt Marilyn also bemoaned Neil's death, suggesting that Danielle would grow up to recognize the enormous pressure that Neil had felt prior to his demise. She said that it seemed to her that Neil had been prepared to help authorities, but that the true answer to that question would remain a mystery in the wake of his death. May told Glen that she had been unaware he was such a spineless and uncaring individual. She promised that she would continue to pray daily that he would eventually find the backbone to collaborate with the authorities.

She concluded by observing that while Betty was gone forever and that things would never be the same, she remained hopeful that at some point in the future, with the guidance of the Lord, everyone involved would somehow manage to gather up the necessary fortitude to put the tragedies behind them and resume a satisfying and meaningful existence.

Glen's written response the following week only served to increase the rancor between the families. He said he wished that members of Betty's family had witnessed the questioning he had endured at the hospital. "Maybe then you would realize that everything that the police wanted or needed was given to them by me. I went over everything that I knew with at least 5 different people on 5 occasions." He said that when he realized that the police were "not looking for any real evidence," he realized that they were not interested in anything that he had to say. "They wanted to solve the crime that day, even if they got the wrong person, so that they could wrap it up and go home to polish their badges."

They could care less about cars parked in front of our house the weeks before, which the neighbors have provided; or phone calls Betty and Nancy would get if Neil and I were out; or screen doors being cut, or any number of things which have all been provided to them. I don't think that the police source, from which your information comes, is complete nor is it all truthful. But as it stands, I'm sure everyone will believe what they want to hear.

Glen said he ceased cooperating with the police because his efforts were "falling on deaf ears. They feel that they can solve the crime first and hopefully make the evidence fit. If it does not, then I'm afraid that my wife's killer will be off free and sitting laughing at me for taking his blame."

Believe me, I think of Betty's family, when I realize how much they have lost. I only wish that things could be as they were last Thanksgiving or Christmas or *our* Anniversary. I also wish that everyone could realize that my family and myself have also suffered a tragic loss with Betty. That seems to be forgotten sometimes.

Glen said he thought frequently of Betty and all the things she did for him. "To think of her being gone, especially tragically, sickens me even more." He suggested that "everyone stop with the self-pity" and think of Betty "and how much she is missing by not being around her loved ones." His muddled train of thought continued as he launched into his fractured reconstruction of their marriage.

We were finally to a point in our lives, which we both worked up to, where we could have the things that we wanted and that she deserved. You are right, she worked very hard for us to get where we did, but we did it together with a little hard work on my part. We were proud to say that we did it on our own!! That's the only way we wanted it and the only way she would have it. I'm glad that we did it together and that she was the one.

Glen shifted gears to his brother, contending that Neil had told the truth but had been manipulated and pressured by the police into thinking he wasn't helping as much as possible. "Please realize that Neil loved Betty also, and he did everything that he could to solve the crime. It wasn't enough for the police, the DA and whoever else, to put him in the hospital."

In closing, Glen said he longed for the love and support that Betty's family had showered on Betty and him in the past. "Believe it or not, I really miss that right now." He promised to resume cooperating with the authorities when they realized they should be looking for someone else.

The following week, Lisa wrote the last in the series of letters, nine handwritten pages to Marilyn May. It was by far the most bellicose. She said she was tired of being told to feel sorry for Betty's relatives, and promised she would never forgive them for what they had done to her family, especially her two brothers. She said Glen was innocent and Neil had known nothing because there was nothing to know.

Lisa said that if Glen knew anything else, he would have told the police a long time ago. "He would have never involved anyone else in this. He certainly would NOT have allowed his Brother to *Die* for him."

She said she had never known more "selfish and narrow-minded people" than Betty's relatives, adding that any emotional ties had been "ripped apart by you and can never be put back together. I'll never understand how Betty ever came from such a family. She would be ashamed at how you are all treating *her husband.*"

Lisa then lashed out at the Tasker family for making what she characterized as "a side-show" out of Neil's wake, ignoring

Glen while "asking Nancy for forgiveness to make yourselves feel better. I realize that guilt does funny things to people, but that was totally uncalled for."

She concluded by observing that concerns about Danielle were unnecessary, that Glen did not kill Betty, and that Neil had not committed suicide. "I no longer have any sympathy, respect, or anything but contempt for Betty's *entire* family."

Of all the words flung back and forth, Marilyn May's dismal assessment of relations was certainly the most difficult to challenge: Things would never be the same.

CHAPTER 19

Dr. Hudock, the county coroner, was unwilling to make the politically charged determination of how Neil Wolsieffer had died, so he announced that a coroner's inquest would be convened in January. An elected official, Dr. Hudock said he didn't have sufficient information to make the decision himself. He would later contend, however, that he believed all along that Neil had committed suicide.

Under Pennsylvania law, a jury of six persons would be selected, hear information about the circumstances surrounding Neil's death, and then determine, if possible, the manner in which he died. The choices would be homicide, accidental, suicide, or unknown. A majority vote would be required.

The next day's *Times Leader* story about the inquest carried the now obligatory paragraph: "Law-enforcement officials have speculated that Wolsieffer, 31, of Wilkes-Barre, intentionally drove into the path of the truck." The article also pointed out that Jenkins Township police had said they were unable to find any skid marks on the road to indicate that Neil had tried to stop his maroon Honda.

Chief Mudlock and Trooper Miers were given the assignment of interviewing Neil's coworkers "to try and assist in determining his frame of mind prior to the accident." Several of the women in his office said he had been in a better mood in the days before his death, seeming to lift himself out of the depression following Betty's murder. "He was returning to his usual self," said one. "He was in a pleasant mood," said another. A third, Denise Thomas, said Neil had specifically ruled out suicide as a solution to anyone's problems. "Suicide is a cop-out. There is always an answer," Thomas quoted Neil as having told her.

John Majikes, another coworker, said Neil's car did not handle properly, that it vibrated when traveling more than twenty miles per hour. He told Mudlock and Miers that Neil also did not take proper care of his car.

Nearly a month after Neil's death, Chief Mudlock and Trooper Miers also sat down for an interview with Nancy at her attorney's office. She related the events of the morning that Neil died, telling them that she believed Glen had been the last one to talk to Neil. She was insistent that her husband's concerns about cooperating with the police were related to his fear that something he said could be misunderstood, not that he felt his brother had been involved in Betty's death. She told the officers that her husband had been followed, that they had been receiving strange telephone calls, and that Neil was under a doctor's care at the time of his death for stress and other ailments. She was unbending in her belief that Neil's death was an accident.

Nothing in the interviews pointed toward suicide. If anything, the information pointed in the other direction. The consensus among Neil's colleagues was that while he had been depressed immediately following Betty's murder, he had been feeling and acting much better in the period immediately before his death. He had spoken out against suicide. And, as Nancy had told the investigators, although he was nervous, he had been looking forward to his interview at the courthouse because he wanted to convince everyone, once and for all, that he had already told them everything he knew.

On January 8, 1987, Dr. Hudock convened a coroner's inquest in the Luzerne County Courthouse. Officially, the accused was

Anthony Shatrowskas, the truck driver, but in reality, Neil Wolsieffer was serving the role of suspect from his grave.

Nancy was represented by Richard Ferguson, her attorney neighbor. William Degillio, another local attorney, represented Shatrowskas. Joseph Giovannini, the former assistant D.A. who quit when the judges gave Podcasy the top post, served as counsel for the coroner.

Giovannini had told reporters that the inquest would not be focused on Betty's death, but solely on the facts directly related to Neil's crash and those relative to Neil's state of mind at the time of his death. Dr. Hudock had said the jury would consist of six persons, selected from the regular jury list. It developed that eight persons were selected, with the additional two identified as alternates. Little regard was paid to whether potential jurors had read the extensive newspaper coverage about Betty's murder and Neil's death.

Unlike a criminal trial, the questioning of witnesses was one-sided, posed only by Giovannini on behalf of the coroner or by the coroner himself. If one of the other attorneys wanted to ask a question, they had to submit it to the coroner's team, whose approval was far from automatic. There was no judge to raise objections to, no cross-examination to probe the other side of testimony, no one to challenge leading questions or scientific conclusions that might not be supported by the facts, and no accident reconstruction expert to discuss important factors like the angle of impact.

Having ruled out natural causes, Dr. Hudock asked the panel to pick from among the remaining four "manners of death," homicide, suicide, accidental, or undetermined. "From the information and facts presented here today, if you feel you are unable to rule on the manner of death, you will have to rule 'undetermined,' " he told the jurors.

The first witness was Frank Joseph Mudlock, the Jenkins Township chief of police. Testifying that he had investigated about 150 accidents in his career, Mudlock said he was summoned to River Road at around 10:15 the morning of October 16, 1986, arriving within minutes of the accident.

With Giovannini's prodding, Mudlock produced an artist's rendition of the accident scene. Standing over the diagram, Mudlock explained the scene as he and other officers had found it. "At the point of impact, which we determined from the evidence on the roadway, gauges and so forth, Unit Number One, which was the Wolsieffer vehicle, was directly in the center of the southbound lane of traffic."

"Are you conclusive from examining the physical evidence at the scene, together with the witnesses who saw the accident, that it occurred completely in the southbound lane?"

"Yes," replied Mudlock. "In the lane going towards Wilkes-Barre." He said the physical evidence and damage to the roadway was all confined to the southbound lane.

The chief said the road was not narrow, had no visible defects, was dry and relatively new. He said neither driver had been speeding or drinking, and both had unobstructed views, on a clear day. He said the curve in the road just prior to the point of impact was only "slight."

Giovannini asked if either driver had tried to avoid making contact. "No, I don't think either driver made any evasive action," said Mudlock, adding that there "was no indication" that either driver had applied his brakes prior to impact.

"That is one of the reasons this inquest is being held," said Giovannini. "We cannot determine from the physical evidence at the scene or from the witnesses how this collision occurred."

Through Mudlock's replies, Giovannini enlightened the jurors on Neil's missed appointment with the investigators, and that the courthouse was situated between Neil's house and the location of his death—about 1¼ miles from Birch Street to the courthouse, another four miles or so to the accident site.

"But we don't know his direct route?" asked Giovannini, presenting an air of neutrality. "No," Mudlock replied.

"We only know he ended up at the accident scene?"

"Yes," said Mudlock, "about fourteen after ten A.M. on the 16th of October, on River Road, Jenkins Township."

A great many photos were introduced into the proceeding—aerial shots, frontal shots of Neil's car, of the truck, of the truck and the car, ground-level overviews from both directions—by Trooper Eugene McDonald, a twenty-two-year police veteran who helped process the scene. Coroner's Exhibit 9, a photo of the rear of Neil's car and its license plate, curiously showed damage to the right rear of the vehicle, a point Giovannini needed to clear up. "From the investigation, Trooper, was it determined how a front-end collision caused damage to the rear of the vehicle?"

"It is believed that the truck passed over the top of the vehicle, and the wheel came down and struck the rear of the vehicle and top of the bumper," said McDonald.

As Giovannini circulated eleven photos to the jury, he turned his attention to the post-accident analysis McDonald had conducted on parts of Neil's car and on the soles of the victim's shoes. The trooper explained that by comparing the impressions on the soles with the clutch, brake, and accelerator pedals, investigators can sometimes determine the course of action, or lack of action, on the part of the vehicle's operator.

On a broadside or rear-end collision, impressions are rarely found, he said. But in a head-on crash, the competing physical forces from opposite directions often create markings.

Displaying the shoes Neil was wearing when he died, McDonald said he found scuff marks and cuts on the soles of both shoes. He also noted several cuts and scuff marks on the top of the right shoe, but could not associate any of those with the markings of any particular pedals or other objects in the car.

On the left shoe, however, McDonald said he found "an imprint on the smooth surface of the arch area." In comparing the mark with the brake pedal and the clutch pedal, he found the impression on the shoe to be similar in design to the pattern on the brake and the clutch. "A further examination showed that on the clutch pedal, on the upper left corner, there were some horizontal lines. My conclusion is that at the time of impact, his left foot had made contact with the clutch pedal." Of course, it would have made no sense for Neil's left foot to have been on the brake. The standard method of driving a stick shift calls for the right foot to alternate between the gas and the brake, and the left foot to operate the clutch. "It would be a natural reaction to brake with your right foot in the standard shift," the trooper explained. "You wouldn't bring your left foot over to the brake."

Seeking to minimize any significance to the fact that Neil had engaged the clutch at the time of impact, Giovannini asked if one would have to depress the clutch "in order to stop the vehicle." No, said McDonald, that wouldn't be necessary.

Of course it wouldn't be necessary. But isn't it natural to depress the clutch when applying the brakes? Who stops a car with a manual transmission without stepping on the clutch? Unspoken, but of even more significance, was the fact that with the clutch pedal depressed, Neil could not possibly have been accelerating.

"Is there any way to determine where his right foot was at the time of the impact?" Giovannini asked.

"No, sir, I can't make that determination."

Nancy's lawyer, Ferguson, got Giovannini to ask if he could positively rule out that Neil's right foot was not on the brake at the moment of impact.

"I can't say that," the trooper acknowledged.

Giovannini felt compelled to hold his ground on that one. "You can't say one way or another? You just don't know where his right foot was at just prior to the impact?"

"That is correct."

Trooper Truman Brandt, a State Police garage inspector who had examined Neil's car for possible mechanical defects, testified that he and George Legezdh, the barracks' chief mechanic, had been unable to find any deficiency that could explain the accident. "There were no parts found to be broken or disconnected prior to the accident," he said. The brake linings were well within safety standards. "The complete braking system was in good condition." He reviewed the list of parts found to be broken, but insisted "this was all due to the impact with the truck."

There was one unusual discovery, though, Giovannini pointed out. Hadn't the inspection team found the volume control on the AM-FM cassette player set at almost maximum? "What does that contribute?"

Brandt confirmed the finding, but then conceded he could not be certain that the dial hadn't been bumped up during the crash sequence.

As with the prior witnesses, Giovannini asked if the jurors had any questions. Again, they did not.

Legezdh, the chief mechanic, testified next, basically confirming what Brandt had said. Asked to theorize on the strut, or stabilizer, found broken on the right side of the car, Legezdh said he was certain it broke on impact.

"If Mr. Wolsieffer had earlier complained about the vibrations of his motor vehicle, would the strut be a material factor?"

"No, not for vibration," Legezdh told Giovannini. He said such a vibration could have been caused by a bad ball joint. "I would say that vibration could be caused by either the balancing of a vehicle, the tires of the vehicle—and that vibration would only be caused between thirty-five and fifty-five miles per hour."

He then acknowledged that the right strut had recently been repaired, but contended there was no possibility the repairs could have affected control of the car.

"But suppose the part was defective?" asked Giovannini. "Could you say if the part was defective prior to the accident, or was not working properly, would that affect the steering or his control of the automobile?"

"I couldn't tell if it was defective."

"But suppose it were?"

"It would only be for the suspension to hold the car in a level position. If that suspension were not on, it would make the vehicle lean to the right side."

Trooper Johnson Miers, who figured he had investigated about 1,700 traffic accidents in his seventeen years with the Pennsylvania State Police, testified that he and Chief Mudlock interviewed a number of eyewitnesses as well as Neil's coworkers because they were "unable to determine from physical evidence at the scene as to what had actually transpired."

Instead of calling Neil's coworkers directly, Giovannini had Miers recall what they told him regarding Neil's state of mind prior to his death.

"There was some suggestion, was there not, whether it be by law enforcement or by the public, that Mr. Wolsieffer had committed suicide, isn't that correct?" Giovannini asked, raising the specter in the unlikely event any of the jurors hadn't read about or heard about Neil's death and the plethora of gossip and rumor.

"Yes, sir," said Miers. "We were trying to determine, one way or another, if this was the cause of the motor vehicle fatality."

The trooper summarized the interviews with Neil's widow and coworkers, about his mood and his vibrating car. He recounted his conversation with the Recreation Board employee who said Neil had specifically spoken out against the concept of suicide.

Miers recounted Nancy's detailing of Neil's fears in dealing with the police, how her husband became incoherent following a visit to the police station less than two weeks after Betty's death, and how she believed Glen was the last one to speak to Neil. "She indicated that Neil was deathly afraid to take a lie-detector test and answer questions relative to the murder investigation, mainly because they might be taken out of context, and he might harm his brother," Miers testified. "She further stated that Neil felt that Glen did not commit the murder or anything of that nature." He said Nancy told him that Neil was under a doctor's care "because he had blacked out and had to be transported to the hospital" because of stress stemming from the murder investigation.

The rules changed slightly for the next witness, truck driver Anthony Shatrowskas. He was read his rights against self-incrimination. "It is not an indication, it is not to be inferred in any way by the jury, that you are in any way culpable," Giovannini explained. "However, it is customary in a coroner's inquest for all operators of the motor vehicles involved, or indirectly involved, in the collision, to be informed of their constitutional warnings." The witness acknowledged he was accompanied by an attorney, and that despite the Fifth Amendment, he was prepared to give his version of events.

He said the first time he spotted the Wolsieffer vehicle approaching was "almost at Saylor Avenue," about a quarter mile away. Giovannini asked whether anyone had been in front of Shatrowskas. No, he said. Was there anyone behind Neil's car? He said he didn't see anyone, but added that after the accident a cement-truck driver told him the Honda had passed him just before the crash. Shatrowskas then confirmed that there were several vehicles behind him but made no mention, nor was he asked, about his sighting of the state police car.

"I find it interesting," Giovannini continued, "that you said you put your foot on the clutch. Is that normal?"

"It is normal when you are at an accident. It is normal to put one foot on the clutch and one foot on the brake," Shatrowskas said. "If you just put it on the brake, you will just keep on jerking, and the truck will keep on moving."

"So in a sudden emergency, it is common to put both feet on both pedals, is that right?"

"Yes," said Shatrowskas.

Asked to describe the moments immediately preceding impact, Shatrowskas said he saw Neil's car approaching from "maybe fifty or one hundred yards away." He said there was a curve in the road, requiring him to go more to the right, to keep from going over the center line. "I thought he was going by me, like a normal car," he said. The next thing he knew, he heard a crash.

"Did you notice Neil's car jerk, as if he was reacting to the turn in the road?" Giovannini asked.

"No," the witness said. "There was no jerking. All it was, I heard the glass and I felt the impact. Then my feet automatically went to the brake and the clutch. And to this day, I don't know when he went under, at what point he started to go under my truck."

This was hardly a sterling eyewitness. It sounded like he didn't really know what had happened. "Mr. Shatrowskas, you didn't notice him gradually coming into your lane? Getting close to the double yellow line?" Giovannini asked. "He wasn't just gradually moving over?" The witness said no.

"Was that a sharp turn which would require a sharp turning of his steering wheel?"

"No, it was very gradual," he said.

"Did you ever have any previous experience with motorists having a tendency to wander into the wrong lane at that point?" The question from Giovannini would have never been allowed in a regular court of law for the simple reason that even though he said he drove River Road twenty times a week, Shatrowskas was far from qualified to be an expert witness on such a potentially crucial issue.

"No, not down there," Shatrowskas replied. "The turn was so slight, I didn't notice it."

At that point, one of the jurors joined the questioning. "You saw the car from a distance and the next time you saw it, you felt the impact?"

"I seen him about one hundred yards away, and then I thought he passed by. And the next thing I heard was the glass, and I felt the impact."

Again, it sounded like Shatrowskas was admitting he didn't really know what happened.

He was asked if, after noticing the car approaching from one hundred yards away, he had lost eye contact with the vehicle. "I thought he passed me. And the next thing I heard was the glass. Then, after the truck stopped, I jumped out to see how he was."

Giovannini asked Shatrowskas how the accident had affected him personally. "I am going to a hypnotist because I am having bad dreams about it. I want to find out in my own mind, how it happened. I still can't figure it out in my own mind."

"That's why we are here today, to try to find out how it happened," Giovannini interjected.

But clearly, Shatrowskas's testimony had raised more questions than answers.

The fog didn't lift any with the next witness, either—Fred Matani, the cement-truck driver whom Neil had passed. "I think I was in third gear. I went through two sequences, from second to third. I saw this car pass me out on the left-hand side and proceed down the road, not completely in the right-hand lane. He just proceeded down the road." The witness said he had pulled out despite seeing several cars approaching because he thought the cars were far enough away.

"You said the vehicle went into the southbound lane to pass you out?"

"Definitely," said Matani.

"It had to go on the other side of the double yellow line?"

"Yes, sir."

"Then what happened? Tell us."

"He started to proceed back, heading north. There were no cars on the road. He proceeded, and he seemed to be taking two lanes. It was like taking his half out of the middle of the road."

"So he took his time getting back to his side of the road, is that what you are trying to tell us?" asked Giovannini.

"Yes, that's it," said Matani.

Matani said he did not think the Honda was speeding, adding that he was only going twenty miles per hour when he was passed.

"When did you finish shifting?" asked Giovannini.

"To be honest with you, I don't believe I completed it, because I bent down to grab a sandwich. I went back and the first thing I saw was this vehicle coming toward me, or coming in a half spin toward me, with parts flying all over."

Matani said he was about thirty to forty yards away from Neil's car when he saw it hurtling toward him. "That's all?" said Giovannini critically. "That's pretty close, isn't it?"

"Like I said, I wasn't paying much attention, you know what I mean?"

Giovannini handed Matani a photo and asked him to mark where his truck was located when Neil's car passed by and where his truck was located "when you saw the impact."

"I did not see the impact," Matani shot back.

"Where were you when you *heard* it? When you heard it, you looked up immediately, didn't you?"

"Right." Matani put an *X* on the photo to note where his truck was when he heard the impact. Giovannini now guessed the distance to be about fifty yards.

"You said you didn't see the impact," Giovannini said. "You *didn't* see the collision?"

"No."

"You reached down for a sandwich? What did you reach with, your right hand?"

"Yes," he said. The sandwich was on the floor? Yes, "in a bag."

"You had your left hand on the steering wheel, I suppose?"
"Yes."

"And your right hand was used for shifting the gears?"
"Yes."

Continuing through the body parts, Giovannini asked and Matani answered that his left foot was on the clutch, and his right foot on the accelerator, to help him shift up. "And then you reached down and picked up a sandwich, during all that activity?"

"I had it in second gear, and there wasn't anything on the road. It was clear. In the meantime, I just reached down for the sandwich."

"Did you complete your shifting process with the sandwich in your hand?"

Matani said that he had indeed.

"Do you do that normally?"

"I do it every day."

"Are you *sure* you didn't see the impact?" Giovannini asked.

"Not a bit of it."

Even though his star witness was leaving him at the lunch table, Giovannini made a final attempt at scoring points with the jury. "Did you hear any brakes?" Matani said he had not.

"Did you see any of the vehicles make any evasive maneuvers?" Matani said he had not. Of course he hadn't. He had been too busy reaching for his sandwich.

"Just prior to impact, were you sure that Neil's vehicle was back in the right lane, where he belonged?" asked Giovannini.

"That I don't know," said Matani. "I didn't even observe it."

"So you don't know?"

"I don't know."

"When you last saw Neil Wolsieffer's vehicle, where was it? Just prior to impact, where was it on the roadway? What lane was it in?"

"The last time I saw it, he was riding right down the middle of the road. He had the yellow line straddled."

Giovannini was finished. Dr. Hudock turned to the jury. "Members of the jury, have you any questions?"

There was silence in the room. The man who supposedly had the best view of the accident had been eating a sandwich.

The next two witnesses had been driving behind Shatrowskas. Beth Kelly of Duryea, driving the family station wagon with her three-year-old daughter in tow, said she had witnessed the collision from directly behind Shatrowskas. But when asked for precise details, she was very sketchy. "The first time I seen the car and the truck was when it was on impact with each other," she said. "Everything happened so fast. The car just came right over into the southbound lane—and that's where they collided." Asked if she actually saw the Honda leave the northbound lane and go into the oncoming lane, she replied: "Yes. It came over so fast, just like he was going to make a U-turn. It was like someone was going to turn around and go back. That's what it seemed like."

"But it was in front of the truck?" asked Giovannini, seeking to establish the head-on aspect of the crash. "It was down a little farther past the truck. It was like in the center of the trailer," Kelly replied.

The young mother wasn't helping much. "Do you understand my question?" Giovannini asked. "How close were the two objects when the motor vehicle started to turn left?"

"Right in the center of the truck," Kelly replied, again challenging the head-on theory.

But had she noticed Neil's car leaving the northbound lane and going into the southbound lane? Again, her answer was qualified. "I seen it just as it came into the lane and as they collided. I was behind the truck and I couldn't see everything." Giovannini wondered if Kelly had seen Shatrowskas's truck run over the top of Neil's car. "No. I just heard the noise and saw the glass was flying. I put my foot on the brake and I just swerved. I went off the side of the road, and that's where I stayed."

It was clear that Kelly hadn't seen much, either. "It happened so fast," she said.

Asked to give his version, Mike Ulichney, who was in the second car behind the truck, told the jury: "Like she said, basically just a car coming down the road, and it looked like it was going to make a U-turn. And just like she said, it happened so fast. There was nothing the truck driver could have done."

Ulichney said he did not see the truck driver make any evasive maneuvers. "After the accident, he told me that he thought the car had hit him right behind the cab."

Had he seen the actual impact? "From my angle, the car seemed to disappear when it went toward the truck. It was like underneath it. And I couldn't see the actual impact, but I did see the car swerve." From that testimony, it sounded like the car swerved into the side of the truck and got gobbled up underneath the heavy weight and large tires.

"Where was it when you last saw it?"

"It was outside of its lane, into the left lane," Ulichney replied.

"Was it something that occurred suddenly, or was it something where the motor vehicle gradually drifted into the wrong lane?"

"It was very sudden, like a second."

Again, the jury had no questions.

That completed testimony about the accident. The focus of the inquiry shifted back to Neil's state of mind. How had Betty's death and the subsequent investigation affected him? Had it driven him to his death?

Officer Brian Lavan, Nancy Wolsieffer's brother-in-law, said that before Neil died he appeared "preoccupied most of the time." He said it seemed that Neil handled Betty's death the same way he had handled his father's, very quietly. "But Neil wasn't a talkative man from the beginning anyway. Neil was a man of few words," said little Bryn Wolsieffer's godfather. "Neil was the kind of a person who would handle his own emotions. He didn't need anybody else's help."

"But," Giovannini continued, "you think something was bothering him as a result of that? After his sister-in-law's death?"

"Yes," said Lavan. "But I didn't know what it was."

Giovannini got Lavan to give a summary of his activities the day Betty was murdered, beginning with the telephone call he received from Neil. This guaranteed that all the jurors now knew about the homicide case, and Neil's call.

"Can I add something?" Lavan asked. Dr. Hudock told him to elaborate. "As long as I knew Neil, he was a loving husband and he had no reason to take his life. He loved his wife more than anything. If there was one person that made him feel like a million dollars, it was his daughter, Bryn, and there was no way in the world that he would leave her."

Dr. Hudock said he had one more question. "Can you say with any certainty that Neil was the kind of a person who would do things on the spur of the moment? From your knowledge of him, did he do things spontaneously? Did he do things on the spur of the moment?"

"No," answered Lavan.

William J. Lavan, Jr., Brian's brother and Neil's best friend, said Neil was "definitely a changed individual" after the murder. He was quiet to begin with, but after the murder "it was almost to the point of no conversation with him at all. He seemed the same—exactly the same—as when his father died several years ago. Very distant, extremely quiet."

At times trying to sound as if he had been Neil's best buddy, Captain Bill Maguire told of a meeting a week after Betty's death between himself, Detective Mitchell, and two assistant D.A.s at which they decided Neil's story "just didn't seem right to us as the investigators." Maguire contended that because Neil had been the only person alive in the house other than Glen and Danielle when police arrived, the investigators decided they wanted to re-interview him. "We basically told Neil we felt that he wasn't telling us the whole story. We felt from what he had said, from what we knew of him, he just didn't react in a normal way the day of the murder and we wanted to know if he could tell us any more."

With no defense attorney to object, the detective told of Neil's refusal to take the lie detector test. "He asked several questions about a lie detector test and said, 'No, no. I would just hurt my brother.' We asked him, 'What do you mean by that?' But he just wouldn't say. He only said, 'I just don't want to take it. I could only hurt my brother.' "

Maguire said that during another interview he had told Neil that the investigation led to his brother, and that police felt Neil knew more than he was saying.

Maguire's comments took everyone in the courtroom by sur-prise. His seemingly casual remark represented the first official confirmation that Glen Wolsieffer was the prime suspect in the murder of his wife. And this testimony, in a room filled with reporters, would be trumpeted on the evening newscasts. So much for Chief Coyne's policy statement to reporter Fred Ney several weeks earlier: "When have the police ever labeled an individual as a 'suspect' before an arrest?"

Again, under the rules of the coroner's inquest, there was no one to object to Maguire's testimony, and so the detective kept on talking, giving the jury as much as he chose to. In his written report, Maguire had made no mention of Assistant D.A. Eichorn or any other participants at the meeting, as if he had met alone with Neil. Now, however, he freely pointed the finger at Eichorn as having put the squeeze on Neil. "Attorney Eichorn advised Neil that if he had anything to do with the murder after the fact, he could be arrested if he was hiding anything. And again this seemed to bother him," Maguire opined. In fact, not only had Maguire's report failed to mention Eichorn, it had failed to note in any manner that Neil had been warned about possible criminal charges for participating in a murder cover-up after the fact.

"I told Neil, 'We are at the point of the investigation, with everybody's actions up to this point, pointing in the direction of your brother, Glen. We can't talk to your brother, Glen. We did not put you in this predicament. Your brother called you. If your brother had called the Police Department, you wouldn't be in this state you are in.' "

The jurors were soaking it all up, following Maguire's every word. " 'You have to remember, you were the witness at the scene of the homicide. This is a homicide. It won't go away.' I said, 'I know we are friends. I think I am your friend. I don't know how you feel about me, but there are no friendships in a murder investigation. Whatever has to be done, has to be done.' At which point, Neil said to me, 'Can I talk to you "off the record"?' I said, 'No. Anything you say, if it incriminates anybody, you are here in a court of law.' At this point, he started to cry. I went over and I put my arms around him. In fact, I had a few tears in *my* eyes. I felt bad for the condition he was in. I said, 'Neil, think of your wife, think of your kid, and you do what is right. You know the truth, and you are going to have to say it.' "

Neil had told Maguire he would go home, talk to his wife, and "get back to him" about taking the lie detector test. But in Maguire's testimony and official reports, the comment was interpreted another way—that Neil was going to go home and think about coming in to confess to all that he knew.

Sitting there listening, Nancy Wolsieffer was livid. This was the first she had heard of this. She was convinced that it never happened that way either. "I think Maguire thought that he was going to break Neil down, so he slanted the whole report to look that way."

She said Neil could have requested to talk to the detective "off the record," but in a totally different context. He could have revealed that he had questions of his own, and wasn't really sure what had happened at his brother's house. "He may have said, 'I'm scared. I don't know what to do.' These are the things he wanted to say—not 'My brother killed his wife, but don't tell anybody.' How absurd is that?"

Before he left the stand, Maguire was asked about Neil's unkept appointment the day he died, whether he had cooperated with the police, and whether the police had harassed him, as Nancy and her family had so vigorously alleged.

The detective said there was "a state of shock in the room"

when the assembled group was told of Neil's death. He explained with a wide brush that Neil was supposed to come to the D.A.'s office "for an interview of his involvement, or his brother's involvement, in the Wolsieffer murder case."

Maguire acknowledged that Neil "was with the Police Department a minimum of three or four times," coming nowhere near the actual number. "And he was talked to on the phone besides that." The detective was vague when asked if authorities had gone to his home, but conceded there was "a good possibility." Contradicting the police propaganda that had repeatedly been leaked about Neil, Maguire now conceded that "there was never any question" from the time of the murder up until their last interview "that Neil would talk to police." But, Maguire continued, "he wasn't saying anything when he was talking."

Perhaps more for himself than the jurors, Maguire sought to explain his aggressiveness toward Neil: " 'You and your brother and a child were the only people in the house when the police got there. We can't speak to your brother. He won't speak to us.' So we had to speak to Neil."

It was impossible to tell if there was even a tinge of guilt or remorse in the explanation.

When Nancy Kathleen Wolsieffer took the stand, Giovannini sought to relax and reassure her. "Mrs. Wolsieffer, the questions I am going to ask you may be personal or might even be painful, but I assure you that all the questions I ask you are in an attempt to get to the truth."

The attorney quickly had Nancy confirm that her family had two cars, the Honda and a Chevy Cavalier, both stick shifts. Neil used the Honda; they had had it for more than two years.

Nancy said she personally was unaware of any mechanical difficulties with the Honda in the weeks before Neil's death. She said she believed the car had been worked on the past summer. In response to questioning, she said that Neil had complained to her about a vibration. "He said it would shimmy at a certain point." As far as she knew, the shimmy was never repaired.

Giovannini moved on to Neil's mental state following Betty's murder. "Neil and Betty were very close and he was devastated by her death. He was also worried about the investigation. He was

ABOVE: *Glen and Betty celebrating Brian Lavan's birthday in August 1982.*
BELOW: *Labor Day, 1981: Betty and Glen with six-month-old Danielle.*

The Wolsieffer family at Neil and Nancy's wedding on July 21, 1979. From left are Ed Wolsieffer, Lisa, Glen, Betty, and Phyllis.

CLOCKWISE, FROM UPPER LEFT: *Nancy and Neil play with Rocky, Betty and Glen's dog, inside 75 Birch in 1981, just after Betty and Glen returned from Virginia. Neil Wolsieffer and his daughter, Bryn, in 1985. Neil Wolsieffer's Honda after the fatal crash on River Road in October 1986.* (WARREN RUDA/*CITIZENS' VOICE*)

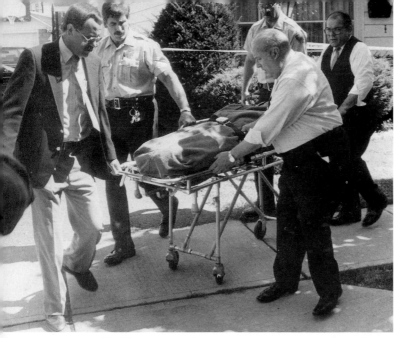

ABOVE: *Police and deputy coroners remove Betty Wolsieffer's body from 75 Birch.* (SUNDAY INDEPENDENT)
BELOW, LEFT: *Police squad cars parked outside 75 Birch the morning of Betty Wolsieffer's murder.* (SUNDAY INDEPENDENT)
BELOW, RIGHT: *The roof and upstairs rear window Dr. Wolsieffer claimed was used by intruders to enter 75 Birch. The aluminum ladder was placed against the rain gutter by police.* (SUNDAY INDEPENDENT)

RIGHT: *Deborah Shipp, Dr. Wolsieffer's hygienist, at the murder trial.* (JACK KELLEY/*CITIZENS' VOICE*) BELOW: *Carol Kopicki with her attorney, John Moses.* (JACK KELLEY/*CITIZENS' VOICE*)

ABOVE: *Marian and John Tasker, Betty Wolsieffer's parents, talk to reporters during a recess in their son-in-law's preliminary hearing.* (JACK KELLEY/*CITIZENS' VOICE*) BELOW: *Marian Tasker, distraught after particularly graphic testimony. Mrs. Tasker is consoled by Corine Sworen, Luzerne County victim's rights coordinator.* (*CITIZENS' VOICE*)

OPPOSITE, FROM TOP: *The prosecution team of Assistant District Attorney William Keller and deputy state Attorney General Anthony Sarcione on their way into the courtroom. The Wolsieffer defense team:z Frank Nocito, on the left, and Anthony M. Cardinale of Boston. Cardinale went on to gain national publicity representing John Gotti's codefendant in a major Mafia trial in New York City in 1992. Frank Nocito confers with his client in the hallway outside Courtroom Four while Lisa Wolsieffer follows.* (JACK KELLEY/*CITIZENS' VOICE*)

ABOVE: *Dr. Wolsieffer in handcuffs as he is escorted out of the Wilkes-Barre police headquarters.* (JACK KELLEY/*CITIZENS' VOICE*) BELOW: *Dr. Wolsieffer and defense attorney Frank Nocito are besieged by the media on their way to a court hearing following the arrest. Police Chief Joseph Coyne is in the foreground.* (*CITIZENS' VOICE*)

caught up in that and he felt that he tried everything in his power to explain that he didn't know anything other than what he had already told the investigators countless times. He couldn't understand why they didn't believe him. He kept saying, 'I don't know what I have to do for them to believe me, that I am telling the truth.' He talked about the lie detector test and we got advice from our neighbor, who is now my attorney, and Neil said to him, 'Could you tell the truth and still fail a lie detector test?' And he said 'Yes.' Then Neil said, 'I am not going to take that chance then.' That was the only thing he didn't want to do. He wanted to go in for questioning, he didn't mind that. But he just said, he didn't feel that he wanted to take the lie detector test. He felt it wasn't reliable and he said he was too emotional and he might fail it—and he didn't want to do that. He had a permanent city job and he was worried about it, the publicity surrounding it. There were headlines because he didn't take the test and he thought what if he did take it and didn't pass it, what would that do from the point of view of his job? He said, 'I wish they would believe me on my own.' He said, 'I would never lie about something like that.' "

Nancy said Betty's death and the subsequent investigation had obviously affected her and Neil. "We lived just across the street from them and we wondered how we were going to live there without them being there. It was real hard to even go out the front door and look at their house and know that she was gone."

Witness and interrogator quibbled over the definition of "depressed," and Nancy finally conceded, "He was sad and he was grieving." Also, there were times when he had trouble concentrating on his duties.

"He was eating okay and he was sleeping okay. But he was worried about the murderer. He put locks on the windows, which we didn't have before. He wouldn't let me go out of his sight. He wouldn't let me go food shopping at night. I couldn't walk down to our neighbor's house without him waiting on the porch, and I had to call him when I was leaving so he could come and meet me on the porch. He feared for our lives. At night he just put little traps around the yard to see if whoever did this would come back. He was scared."

Neil never told her who the person was, because he "had no

idea" who had been responsible, she said. "Betty and I both were receiving phone calls at that time. He was worried about that. We just received these anonymous phone calls. . . . It was always when Neil or Glen had been at this certain bar, that we would get these phone calls. Since that time the bar closed and the phone calls stopped. But he was worried about it and he thought about it a lot, because Betty and I would get them on the same night."

Nancy said she was certain the caller had been a male, but she wasn't sure she could identify him "because it was a unique voice." She said she never called the police or the phone company to complain. "I had problems like this once before, not with this same situation, we lived somewhere else when it happened. I called and reported it. Going by that last experience, it didn't prove anything."

The Friday-night calls were "an entirely different situation," not worth reporting at the time, Nancy explained. "It happened to me about five times maybe, throughout the winter. We were just trying to come up with somebody that could have done this. And these phone calls stood out in my mind. I thought if Betty was getting them and I was getting them, too, something might happen to me."

Giovannini wondered if Neil had been suffering from anxiety, from fear. "Yes, he was fearful," she replied, then added, however, that she felt the pressure had lifted after September 11, when she called investigators and asked them to leave Neil alone. "He just wanted them to believe him, and they didn't seem to believe him. Over and over and over again, it went on and on and on—and that was the hardest part. And I was in for questioning, too, and I know what it's like. It was really hard for us to imagine that we were in this situation. But what were we going to do about it? How were we going to prove that we didn't know anything? And then after that stopped, I was sitting in the room when Neil made that phone call."

"Which phone call?" asked Giovannini.

"The call to Captain Maguire at four o'clock, when he called him back, when he didn't want to take the lie detector test. He said, 'Bill, I just don't know.' " Nancy maintained that she had told Maguire, " 'I want you to leave him alone,' " and that Maguire had replied: " 'I need that in writing.' From what Neil understood, he never refused to cooperate, because he would go to work, day after day, and he would wonder if they would call him that day and what else could they possibly ask him. They never called him again and that's what made him wonder why they weren't calling him anymore. Then we read the accounts in the newspaper that he refused to cooperate. To his knowledge, he did not refuse to cooperate and I guess that was misinterpreted that day on the phone call.''

Asked if her husband had continued to maintain his normal duties at work during this trying time, Nancy brought up Neil's hospitalization, on September 18th, after he blacked out on the front porch of 84 Birch. "Originally, they thought he had a blood clot in his lung, but it turned out that that wasn't it, and Dr. Kish thought he was suffering from the pressure he had been under. He explained it to me one day, he said, 'It is your body's way of reacting to stress. It happens to a lot of people.' He said, 'If somebody faints at the sight of blood or at the sight of a mouse, it is the body's way of shutting down.' ''

According to Nancy, Neil was treated for bronchitis and hypertension and was on five medications, including a steroid. She said Neil had been administered the medicines while in the hospital and had been told to keep taking them at home until they ran out. She said she was pretty sure Neil took his medicine the morning that he died. She said by that point, he was down to three kinds: one for high blood pressure, an antibiotic for his bronchitis, and a third for congestion in his lungs.

Had Neil complained of any side effects? "Yes, I think it was the steroid that caused him to perspire and caused him to want to eat. He was hungry all the time and it caused his hands to shake. If I remember, while he was in the hospital, he went to cut his food and his hands would be shaking and the nurse said it was a side effect of the medication he was taking. I am not certain if he was still taking it that day. He was weaned off, he had to take five, four, three a day until they were all finished.''

Overall, Nancy said, Neil didn't have a history of physical ailments before the blackout, other than a trick right knee that went out on him every now and then despite having been operated on. And no, she replied to Giovannini's questioning, Neil had not been delusional.

"Did he have any false beliefs? Do you think that something he believed in was totally unreasonable, or false?" She said no.

"Now, you lived with him for seven years. In the last few weeks prior to his death, did you find him hallucinating? Did you find him seeing things that were not there, or talking to people that weren't there either?"

This was starting to sound like an inquisition. Again, Nancy insisted those scenarios had not taken place.

"Or talking to himself?" Again, she said no.

"Do you ever remember your husband having any history of blackouts?"

"Well, that's what caused him to be admitted to the hospital on September 18th."

"Was that the only time?" Yes, she replied, though he had complained of dizziness on many occasions in the weeks prior to his death, when he got out of bed too fast. He complained of dizziness two days before his death and on the day he had blacked out.

Giovannini wondered if Neil had gone to see his physician or obtained any new medication to relieve the dizziness problem.

"No," said Nancy. "It wasn't a serious enough problem. He had an appointment to go back to the doctor a week after the accident."

"So he was still being treated by his physician for hypertension at the time of the accident?"

"Yes," said Nancy, and for his bronchitis.

Nancy already had been on the stand longer than anyone else, but Giovannini was nowhere near done. Now they went through the story about her call to the D.A.'s office, the one she made after Maguire told Neil somebody was calling somebody a liar.

Nancy then explained how she got up first on the morning of the accident and had listened intently as her husband spoke optimistically of his appointment with the police. She said she had told him to take his medicine, and that they had chatted about his plans to purchase supplies for a home-repair project that evening. As she described Neil's actions in the hours before his death, he didn't sound like a man contemplating suicide. The night before his death, he had brought money home for a down payment for carpeting for the downstairs. Nancy recalled how Neil had left the funds for her, instructing her not to forget to deposit the money on her way home from work so that the carpet could be ordered.

Of course, she couldn't testify directly about Neil's final conversation with Glen. No one had witnessed the chat. And only one of the participants was still alive.

Giovannini asked Nancy how she knew about the conversation. "His brother, Glen, told me."

"Did he tell you what they discussed?" Nancy said she did not ask.

"You weren't interested in what they said to each other?" Giovannini asked with incredulity.

"It was the day Neil died, and I just had some questions about who saw him last," she replied.

"You weren't interested in what they discussed?"

"I'm not saying I wasn't interested. I was just upset and I wondered who saw him last."

She denied that Neil had seemed distraught that morning. Instead she said, he "seemed relieved almost. He wanted to go back in. He thought maybe this time they would believe him."

Giovannini then popped the all-important question, forcing Nancy to give her opinion on whether Neil had in fact taken his own life. "Absolutely he did not," she said. "I am sure he did not." Echoing the suggestion of two of the eyewitnesses, Nancy continued: "I wouldn't be surprised if he took a U-turn and went back to the courthouse. He was very conscientious, and if he had an appointment, he would keep it—or he would call and say why he couldn't keep it. It could have been that he was just driving around, thinking about what he should do, totally preoccupied. I don't think he should have been driving a car. I don't think his mind was on driving."

Giovannini wondered about Neil's mood the morning he died. "He was upset. He was angry. That's the way he had been acting," said Nancy. "But I know when it got right down to the time to go in, he was scared and he didn't want to go. It happened before, when he was supposed to go, he just changed his mind.

"And another thing that I think is very important, weeks prior to the accident, Neil was being followed. He didn't know by whom or why. He had license numbers," Nancy said.

Through his questioning, Giovannini sought to belittle Nancy's explanations, suggesting at one point that maybe Neil had been hallucinating. Nancy retorted that she had seen the cars out in front of their house herself. Besides, it did not matter whether Neil in fact was being followed; he thought he was. "The point remains that Neil talked about it all the time," she said.

Giovannini was finished. Dr. Hudock wanted to know if Neil had made any references to his father in the week before his death. Nancy said he had not. Nor had he actually seen Betty's body the morning of the murder.

Asked if there was anything else she could add to assist in the investigation of Neil's "sudden death," Nancy took the opportunity to defend her husband's honor. "I just know he wouldn't have taken his life. He had no reason to do that. He loved me and he loved our daughter. Our little daughter was his whole life. We spent every night talking about her when he got home for supper. He was a good Catholic. He went to church every week. He felt that his faith really helped him through the death of Betty. He had very strong faith and that would have been totally against his religion to do anything like that. He had no reason for that. He was hiding nothing at all and it is just the way Neil handled things. He did become strong and quiet. He was quiet by nature. He got more quiet. He didn't express his feelings. And he wasn't acting out of character at all."

If not, why had she prevented a state trooper from looking around the house for a suicide note? "That was the last straw. I was outraged that they would even think that. We have had so much since August 30th between the police and the investigators. I remember Neil saying we are just too honest. We tried to do things and we were really upset that they didn't believe what we were saying. I thought, 'Nobody is going to go rummaging through my house the day my husband died and look for a note,' but I went and looked myself. I knew it wouldn't be there, but I looked to carry through on it."

Finally, Nancy was finished. It had been an exhausting experience, but she thought she had handled herself well. Surely, she thought, the jury would vote accidental.

The testimony-taking portion of the inquest was not over yet, however. It was time for the jury to hear from Glen, officially identified just hours ago in the same courtroom as the prime suspect in his wife's murder, and just minutes ago as the last person to talk to Neil before the fatal crash. Glen confirmed that he had talked to his brother twice that morning, inside his mother's house and out by his car. "When we were in the house, I tried to keep it kind of light. I didn't want to upset my mother about anything. I also knew that Neil was kind of preoccupied with all the questioning that he was going through. I asked him what we would do that weekend, were we going to play golf? He said no, he didn't want to play golf because he had some work to finish up on his house. There was some staining and he was going to have some carpeting put in. That was the gist of the conversation. After we left the house, Neil got into his car, which was parked in front of my mother's house, and I asked him if he was going in for questioning that day. He said, 'Yes. Maybe we will get this thing straightened out.' " Glen said he told his brother to "go in and do your best. Do what you have to do."

Giovannini asked Glen how he knew of the possibility of Neil going in for questioning. Glen replied that his brother had spoken to him about it the night before.

Glen said he and his brother parted ways about 8:30 that morning, and he headed for his office in Nanticoke. "That was the last time I saw him."

"Did he seem apprehensive or distressed in any way?"

"Not really," said Glen. "He seemed almost resigned to the fact that he was going and maybe he could shed some light in any way he could. I don't know how he could, because of what he had told them already."

Giovannini recalled for Glen the prior testimony concerning Neil's apprehension about talking to the police, and wondered if Glen knew why his brother felt that way.

"You can only tell the truth so many times, and not have people believe you—then you get a little frustrated. Neil wasn't a man who would lie to anybody." As a practicing Roman Catholic, "anything dishonest bothered Neil," said Glen.

"Did he seem to have changed his personality after the death of your wife?"

"He was upset, as we all were. He and Betty were like brother and sister. We lived across the street and we did a lot of things together. He was upset, yes."

"Did his personality change?" Glen said yes, Neil had been down in the dumps for "I would say maybe a couple of weeks, as far as being really obsessed with finding out what happened."

"Did he seem to have come out of it after a while?"

"Yes, we did some things. He and I talked every day, me trying to help him, him trying to help me, you know. Console each other on the loss. I don't know what else I can tell you."

Glen said that as time passed after Betty's murder, Neil began to lighten up and talk more about what was bothering him: "The fact that he had been through so many investigations and nobody would believe him, the fact that he had a public job and the newspapers were blasting him all over the place, as well as myself."

Since Glen said he saw Neil every day, Giovannini inquired if he had noticed any special change in his brother after the call to investigators the night before his death. "It was the same way that he acted any other time before he went in for questioning. He was nervous, that kind of thing. He had a couple more cigarettes than usual."

Shifting the focus to Neil's medical problems, Giovannini got Glen, who had taken pharmacology courses in school, to explain the different types of medication his brother had been taking and their possible side effects. "I guess this was even when he was in the hospital, he would take what he called breathing pills. I assumed it was the ones that took the swelling down in the lungs. As Nancy had stated, he would shake. He couldn't tie his shoe, couldn't eat his dinner, and he knew exactly when it was going to happen. When he took the pill he would say, 'Now in a half hour I am going to shake.' " Glen said he could only assume that Neil had been told not to take the medication just before operating a motor vehicle. "I didn't follow his medication schedule after he was out of the hospital." As for the condition of Neil's Honda, Glen said his brother hadn't mentioned anything specific to him that morning, "but I had driven that car and it wasn't the most steady vehicle on the road."

Giovannini was done. Dr. Hudock asked the jurors if they had any questions. There was no response.

"If there is anyone in the courtroom who wishes to add anything concerning this case, we would ask them to come forward now," Dr. Hudock said.

The room stayed silent, and so Dr. Hudock began delivering his instructions to the panel. "Ladies and gentlemen of the jury, the purpose of this inquest is twofold. One is to determine whether the death of Neil Wolsieffer resulted from a criminal act or criminal negligence of any person other than the deceased. And second, to determine the manner of death. And to determine whether it was accidental, homicide, suicide, or unknown. You have heard all of the evidence. Consider all the facts and circumstances in this case, and we want you to consider only the evidence presented to you here today. In doing so, of course, you must also consider and weigh the credibility of each witness and decide for yourself what testimony you will believe and what you will not believe. Keep in mind his or her biases and prejudices.

"In the course of your deliberations, if you have any questions which you cannot resolve among yourselves, please notify me immediately—and then please notify me when you have reached a verdict."

Members of the Wolsieffer family, in discussing how well the proceedings had gone, were sure the vote would be for accidental.

In just short of an hour, the jurors returned to the courtroom. Inexplicably, all eight of them had signed the tally sheet, indicating that the two alternates had voted. The foreman announced: "We, the jury, find that Anthony Shatrowskas, truck driver, was not guilty of criminal negligence; and in the case of Neil Wolsieffer, we determine that the manner of his death on October 16, 1986, was suicide."

Nancy began to cry loudly. She couldn't believe it. She buried her head in her hands as family members sought to console her. How could the jurors have reached such a decision? With what evidence?

For his part, Glen stood frozen. Jack Tasker, Betty's brother, walked over to him and Ciavarella. "One of these days we're going to have to talk," he yelled at Glen, who stood there and nodded. Tasker then confronted the defense attorney, accusing him of being the main problem and of enjoying the limelight. "You made this guy more guilty than he could ever be guilty on his own."

As he departed the courthouse, Glen told reporters he was certain his brother had not committed suicide. "I knew my brother. He wouldn't do that. He wasn't that kind of guy." He continued that Jack Tasker wasn't the only one upset. "I lost a wife and a brother. I guess I'm upset too."

A TV reporter inquired if Glen expected to be arrested soon for Betty's murder.

Glen exploded. "No, but I think I'm gonna beat the shit out of you."

Ciavarella grabbed Glen's arm and led him away.

CHAPTER 20

Nothing specifically suggesting Glen's possible involvement in his wife's murder had been written in the city's newspapers before the inquest. But the rules changed drastically following the coroner's proceeding for two reasons: the verdict itself, and Captain Maguire's sworn testimony identifying Glen as the prime suspect. The focus was now inescapably on Glen, which precipitated the start of his public lynching at the hands of the *Times Leader*.

Certainly coverage of the inquest by two of the papers was fair. The *Sunday Independent* pointed out that the inquest had produced a suspect in Betty's death. Bernard A. Podcasy, the district attorney, emphasized that law-enforcement officials had been heretofore precluded from publicly identifying a suspect, but characterized Captain Maguire's comments at the official proceeding as appropriate because he was describing a conversation he had with Neil prior to his death. Although privately he was angry about Maguire's tactics, Podcasy was quoted as explaining that Maguire's discussion of the conversation—in which he told Neil that Glen was a suspect—was relevant because it demonstrated aspects of Neil's frame of mind prior to his death. "So it was an indirect naming of the suspect," said Podcasy, trying to wiggle out of the predicament he had been placed in.

A lengthy summary of the inquest testimony in the *Citizens' Voice* omitted that Maguire had identified Glen as a suspect, but provided evenhanded coverage of the various witnesses. Two weeks later, the newspaper unabashedly printed a letter to the editor from Phyllis Wolsieffer's sister, Mary Stinson, thanking the publication for its unbiased accounts. "Your coverage has been complete but not all one-sided. The *Citizens' Voice* reporters have not appointed themselves jury and executioner as did another paper. That paper has given Wyoming Valley a new name: 'The valley with no heart.' Don't all reporters have mothers? And parents? Children?"

Mary Stinson was no doubt referring to the *Times Leader*. Under a front-page headline, JURY RULES DEATH WAS SUICIDE, the main article, by Marita Lowman, noted that Glen had been publicly identified as a suspect for the first time. A follow-up story by Lowman contained suggestions from unnamed investigators that Glen's story made no sense. For example, the story said that investigators "found it odd" that Glen had never called to learn the status of the investigation. Of course, the police had told him to his face that they thought he was the killer, and his lawyer had told him to keep his mouth shut. Nonsensical or not, the pillorying escalated, almost exclusively through the words of *Times Leader* columnist Steve Corbett. Although he had written about the case before the inquest, his column the following day marked a change in tone.

It was as if Corbett had been unleashed by Maguire's courtroom naming of Glen as a suspect. He called Glen "a wise guy," "a tough guy," and "a former golden boy." He made a major point of Glen's confrontation with the TV reporter, pointing out that "Glen threatened to hurt somebody."

This was the start of a troubling pattern. Corbett's vitriolic attacks would become stronger and more vicious as the investigation continued to be stalled. Selective leaks from the police were analyzed in a manner most detrimental to the suspect. On several occasions, without result, Corbett wrote that the authorities were closing in.

Gradually, Corbett injected himself into his story—a journalistic taboo. With each passing month, the word "I" crept more and more into his copy, as did suggestions that the case was fitting for a made-for-television movie or a crime novel.

No matter what was reported, Glen remained silent, so his sister, Lisa, took up the gauntlet more than ever. "I think it was the beginning of Glen's set-up. I think that was what the whole thing was used for, to start publicly pointing the finger at him," she said of the inquest.

In the ensuing months, virtually every newspaper article about the murder case would contain a seemingly obligatory background paragraph explaining that during Neil's inquest Captain Maguire had identified Glen as the only suspect in Betty's murder.

In the eyes of some elated law-enforcement officials, the finding of suicide was the best-case scenario. To them, it made Glen look more guilty. To them, Neil must have known about his brother's guilt—why else would he have killed himself? To them, the jury's finding of suicide proved that Glen was capable of doing anything to save his hide—and that, in fact, he had, by emotionally propelling his own brother to his death. It didn't matter that everything related to Neil's death would probably be inadmissible if Glen were ever brought to trial for Betty's murder. What mattered now, more than ever, was perception. And the perception, more than ever, was that Glen was guilty.

The portrait being painted was dramatic and titillating, but unsupported by evidence. More than ever, it included unattributed insinuations that Neil had played a significant role in Betty's murder, or at least its aftermath—Neil was involved, Neil knew all along, Neil covered up, Neil had something to hide, Neil couldn't face up to telling the truth, he couldn't take the pressure, he couldn't turn in his brother.

If Glen ever was arrested, the police and prosecutors would have the equivalent of an unindicted coconspirator by innuendo. And since this supposed accomplice was no longer around to defend himself, just about anything could be inferred about him, without fear of a libel or slander charge.

The evening following the inquest, Giovannini sought the Democratic nomination for district attorney. City Council member Bob Reilly, Neil's friend and a candidate for county clerk of courts at the time, said he talked to Giovannini about the inquest while waiting to address the nominating committee. "We went for suicide and we got it," Giovannini told him. Reilly said he swelled with anger.

When the committee nominated Podcasy for the D.A. slot on the ticket, Giovannini decided not to run, however. So much for timing.

Members of the Tasker family agreed with the inquest finding, but realized that the verdict wasn't going to bring about the arrest of Betty's killer. As a result, they took a more assertive posture, recognizing the news media as a necessary evil and becoming quasi-members of the police investigative team.

Jack Tasker's wife, Dorothy, for example, relayed to authorities how Barbara Wende had told her she had been very friendly with Betty through the dental auxiliary, but had never spoken to police about their conversations. Wende told Dorothy that she had never said anything because she figured that Betty had confided in plenty of other people. Soon thereafter Captain Maguire called Wende to request an interview.

The tip, ten months after the murder, turned out to be a good one. In two interviews, Wende provided significant details about what Betty had told her following Glen's breakdown in 1985. More important, she told the investigators about a conversation she had had with Betty the Tuesday before her murder, in which Betty had told her she was tired of being stepped on and was going to take a stand if Glen pulled his Friday-night shenanigans that weekend.

As their frustration with police inaction continued to grow, Betty's relatives began cooperating more with the news media. On Sunday, March 9, 1987, Fred Ney of the *Sunday Independent* wrote a lengthy story headlined, TASKER, DEMANDING JUSTICE, MAY GO TO ATTY. GENERAL. A veteran journalist, Ney had been following the case from the beginning.

Looking back on the previous August, the elder Tasker told Ney that he had begun to suspect that his son-in-law had killed Betty within the first fifteen minutes. "I wake up in the morning and go to bed at night thinking about it. I'll never rest until this thing is solved," he said, breaking out in tears.

Obviously frustrated, Tasker said he was appreciative of efforts by the Wilkes-Barre police and the district attorney's office, but wondered why more wasn't being done. He said he was thinking about taking the case to the Pennsylvania state attorney general's office. "I don't want to embarrass anyone," he said. "But a suspect has been named. He had motive and opportunity. If they're waiting for a signed confession, they'll never get it." Terming parts of Glen's story "unbelievable" and "incredible," Tasker said he couldn't imagine that an intruder would render a man unconscious, then go upstairs and commit a murder instead of making a rapid escape. He also said he couldn't accept the claim that neither Glen nor his brother had gone upstairs to check on Betty and Danielle.

Turning his attention to Neil specifically, Tasker said he believed that Glen's brother had taken his own life, recalling how Neil had been quoted as saying, "I don't want to do anything to hurt my brother." Tasker then suggested that there was still someone alive who could help solve the case—Neil's widow, Nancy. "I can't believe that a man can be married to a woman and she doesn't know his innermost thoughts, especially about something as serious as this case." Remembering the optimism he had mistakenly held in the hours before Neil died, Tasker said he found it difficult to accept that Neil wouldn't have told Nancy everything he was going to say to authorities that morning.

Ney went on to note that Nancy had "repudiated any suspicion that Glen is guilty," and instead had "challenged police and prosecutors to go out and find the real killer."

The next evening, the phone rang in Betty's parents' home around 6:30. It was Nancy. "I guess I'd be the last person you'd be expecting to be calling."

John Tasker tried to say hello. But Nancy wasn't in the mood for pleasantries. "I'm sick and tired of my name and my husband's name being dragged through the paper."

Tasker would later tell police that he felt Nancy wanted him to respond with "something derogatory," but said he remained pleasant. Nancy said she was nervous. "It's very difficult," she told him, insisting that she didn't know anything about the murder, that she did know her husband's innermost thoughts, and those thoughts were that he didn't know anything about the murder.

She insisted that Neil had agreed to come in and talk one more time simply in the hopes that everyone would finally get off his back.

Betty's father replied that he hoped the case would be solved soon so that everyone would be "able to have all this behind us."

Of course, in Nancy's case that was an impossibility. She feared that she would never be able to put "all this" behind her.

Although the police weren't moving against him, Glen was feeling the pressure elsewhere. He had lost a great many patients. Family and friends like Richard Miscavage continued to come, but business slowed so much that Glen began to wonder if it was even worth going into the office. He began pondering whether he should leave the valley entirely and move back to Virginia. He told friends such a move might be the best plan for Danielle, too.

Debbie Shipp, meanwhile, was preparing to move to take a nursing job at a hospital in Delaware. Glen told family members that he was through with Debbie. Nancy recalled, "He wanted to get on with his life; she wanted to get on with hers. She moved; he stayed here. He said it was completely over."

But Glen was soon surreptitiously driving back and forth to Delaware every other weekend. He and Debbie again talked of marriage and looked at engagement rings. But talk is all they did.

Glen insisted to Nancy that Carol Kopicki also was out of the picture. But that was not entirely the case either. Still officially married, Carol had joined another aerobics club, the Odyssey Total Fitness Center, since she had been snubbed the few times she went back to Aerobic World. Even though her connection to Glen had not publicly surfaced, the relationship was no secret to the Aerobic World crowd. Glen also joined the Odyssey. Then homicide investigators began getting reports of Glen and Carol being seen together elsewhere.

Embers also were flying at a new pace between Glen and Betty's brother, Jack. It seemed that some of Glen's softball buddies didn't want him on the Riverside Cafe team for the upcoming season. Plain and simple, they felt uncomfortable—especially the ones who had been closer friends with Neil. Regardless of what they thought of Glen's guilt regarding Betty's murder, almost all of them believed Glen was at least partially responsible for Neil's death and felt he should cooperate with the police.

The way Glen had heard the story, it was his brother-in-law, Jack, who had instigated the softball-team insurrection. To Glen, that was the last straw. He had had enough of the Taskers. This one time, he was angry enough to strike back—incredibly, about inclusion on a softball team roster. Glen wrote yet another letter, this one to his old drinking buddy/brother-in-law:

4/8/87

Jack,

It seems as though, through manipulation, that you have succeeded in preventing me from playing softball this season. It's too bad because all of the guys on the team are friends of mine and really want me to play. Is that what bothers you? What bothers me is not that I won't be playing ball, but that you think that you can control my life and what I do with it. That's not something that people who *care* about each other would do.

Whatever your reason may have been, you have also succeeded in preventing your parents and your family from seeing Danielle regularly. When your Mother calls for her, I'll tell her to ask *you* why Danielle is not coming up to see her. I would hate to resort to this action but this is part of the situation which you have decided to create.

The *choice* is yours, Jack, as to what is done, but unless I hear from a team representative before the roster goes in next week, then those are the rules you have decided to play by!

I never wanted to have Danielle's visitation used for anything other than to make your Parents happy. It was never easy to see her go, especially after reading all the nice things you and they had to say about me. I tried to be sociable because I was doing what Betty would have wanted me to do.

I'm done paying the price *to you*, for infidelity, which is something you guys should know *a lot* about.

For someone who claims to still care about me, you have a funny way about showing it. I guess we'll find out about how you care about your parents' relationship with their granddaughter. It's also funny that you would use someone, who you were stabbing in the back and bad mouthing less than a year ago, to make the softball decision.

The *decision* is *up to you* as to how things will come out, but I'm getting tired of being nice to people who treat me like dirt, and spread false information wherever they go, for something I had nothing to do with.

It seems that many of your family members feel that they are the only people who have lost anyone. Losing Betty and Neil was as devastating to our family as it was to yours. People who *claim* to have been close to Betty, don't even know how much Neil and Nancy and Betty and I depended on each other and sought friendship and comfort in each other's company. They never took the time to know, that's another story.

I'll be awaiting your decision as it not only affects me but also your parents and Danielle. It's a tough one to make.

Glen

P.S. If this goes any further than you, people are going to know the *real* Jack Tasker—count on it!

The letter, mailed to Jack Tasker's home, had a chilling effect and the stench of blackmail. The reference to the real Jack Tasker pertained to *his* extramarital activities. The threat raised the stakes considerably.

CHAPTER 21

The Monday after he received Glen's letter, Jack Tasker sat down at the Luzerne County Courthouse with D.A. Bernard Podcasy, Captain Maguire, Detective Mitchell, and Assistant D.A. Dan Pillets. According to a report that Maguire later filed on the session, "Tasker stated that he has had a conversation with Glen Wolsieffer recently in which he stated to Glen that he thought he killed his sister and that Glen stated 'he just wished the whole thing was over.' Glen also stated that he wanted to talk to Jack."

Jack went on to tell the officials about the letter he had received from Glen, about his not being able to play softball for the Riverside team in the Wilkes-Barre Recreation Board League. "Glen also states in the letter that Jack should do something before this weekend." Maguire's report did not mention Glen's threat to expose "the real Jack," and obviously what Glen meant by that.

Pillets instructed everyone how they should proceed legally, and Jack Tasker agreed to meet with Glen equipped with a hidden body recorder. Others would later say that it was Jack himself who suggested that he wear a body wire. Chief D.A.'s Detective Michael Dessoye contacted Major Mike Jordan, then the area commander of the Pennsylvania State Police, to arrange for two technicians to be on hand to install the recording device.

Two days later, shortly after 7:00 A.M., the state police team placed a body recorder on Jack and a transmitter in his Oldsmobile station wagon. Jack then proceeded to his office, on Old River Road in South Wilkes-Barre, to wait for Glen.

Once the two men started talking, there were times when the equipment would occasionally fail to clearly pick up all of the conversation. But this was the least important problem; the investigative team had failed to communicate to Jack Tasker the importance of his listening as much as possible, as opposed to his talking as much as possible.

Over the course of the next two hours, it would often be difficult to tell if Jack was trying to trap Glen, or if Glen was trying to trap Jack. Did Glen suspect that Jack was wired? Was Glen engaging in a spirited game of mental chess? Or was he genuinely concerned about his brother-in-law's state of mind? At times, the conversation bordered on the macabre.

They started with small talk, but the tension was palm sweaty. Jack had quit the South Wilkes-Barre Rotary Club in a huff when, shortly after Betty's death, Glen and Neil resumed attending meetings. Jack had been telling anyone who would listen that Glen was guilty. Now there was the softball-team fracas, and the nasty letter Glen had written only a week earlier.

As unlikely a scene as could be, the two men started talking like old pals, in spite of all of the rancor between them since Betty's murder.

"Hope you didn't lose any sleep over this," said Glen in a friendly tone.

"Oh, I can't sleep anymore. I don't know where to start."

"Let me just tell you how I feel about you, all right?" said Glen. "You know, before Betty got killed, you and I were, I think, like best friends. And that's the way I'd want to keep it. I mean, I care about you, and things that I said in that letter, I just said them because I'm tired of being pushed around. And I'm not going to do anything about it, because I care too much about you and your family. I mean, softball's a very minor issue when you're talking about shit like this."

Jack defended himself by listing different players who wanted him off the team.

"*Really?*" asked Glen in response to one of the names.

"That's the name I have," said Jack. "Swear to God to you. I'm not going to lie to you."

"No," said Glen.

"Nothing's going to go out of here, between you and I," Jack assured Glen, employing the standard electronic-surveillance denial technique used over the years by many an FBI operative wearing a hidden recording device. Glen said he realized that.

"Because I'll tell you," Jack continued, "I have my own problems to hide in my life, Glen. I got problems."

"If you're telling me that, then I believe you," said Glen.

Indirectly raising the possibility that Corbett the columnist had been applying the same threat of exposure that Glen had invoked in his softball letter, Jack said that Corbett had approached him directly, "busting my ass" for information.

"Corbett came to me, and he says to me, 'What do you have to hide?' I said, 'What do you mean by that?' He was like buddy-buddy with the family, okay? There was nothing in the papers. He says, 'What do you have to hide? What's with your parents? It seems to me they're protecting Glen. What's with your family? What do you know?' he says to me. He's on my case."

Jack explained that he told the columnist: " 'Steve, I don't know nothing. I can't tell you nothing. Just let it go at that.' And he says, 'I don't believe that.' He says, 'When I talked to your brother-in-law and I asked him about girlfriends, he said, "Why don't you ask Jack Tasker about that?" ' Bang, he hit me. Then he's snoopin' around over at the Riverside." Jack told Glen that the next thing he knew, Corbett was "snooping around" with two of their fellow Rotarians. "I have nothing to do with that."

"Neither do I," Glen replied. Apparently there were others at the Rotary Club who had Friday-night flings they preferred to keep hidden.

"And then I get the letter," said Jack. "And I'm in the middle of it. They said that they—"

"—You know what to do with that letter?" asked Glen.

"Yeah, I'm gonna tell ya—"

"—Rip it up!"

"No. I'm going to tell you where it is, and I want you to know something. Because the letter you sent me some time ago, I have that one," Jack said. "There's a letter that I have, that you just sent me. There's a couple cards, and, uh, some letters from Sharon [Jack's mistress]. They're in the trunk of my Monte Carlo. My Monte Carlo is across the street."

"Hey, don't be telling me this stuff, because I'm gonna be the one that would have to go find it," said Glen. He sounded concerned, as if he feared Jack might be planning to take his own life. "I mean, tell me you're not gonna do anything."

"I can't take it anymore," Jack replied.

"*Jack*, tell me that," said Glen, rising out of his chair.

"I can't— Listen to me, just sit down."

"Jack, Jack," said Glen, "I'm not going anywhere, I want to help you. You don't have to do anything, please."

"But see, you know what hurt me? The worst thing that hurt me?"

"What? Talk to me. Tell me," Glen coaxed.

"You see, it's not even that Betty's dead. I can't believe—I feel bad for you. Glen, I feel bad for you. They're pushing a premeditated murder case on you."

Glen said he was aware of that, and Jack said he could not believe it. "I can't ever believe *that*."

"Jack, it wasn't—"

But Jack didn't give Glen a chance to speak. He again cut him off. "—I'm tellin' you, I can't believe it. In my heart, I told my mom, if anything ever happened it's because someone put pressure on you. It's not your fault." Jack explained that he meant Debbie Shipp. "I look at her, and Glen, I blame her."

"Jack, I don't. Jack, I don't know who to blame. I wish I did. This thing'd be over with if I knew anything, if I knew who to blame. Believe me, I don't want to see you go through this or your Mom and Dad, or me, or my family."

Abruptly, Jack changed gears, perhaps hoping he could catch Glen off guard. "Glen, did Neil tell you, the day he died, that I saw him? Did he ever tell you?"

"No," said Glen. "No, I didn't see him after he left my mother's that morning."

"I'm living with too much in me," said Jack. Had he spoken to Neil that morning? Had he been following Neil? What was he talking about?

Glen didn't get a chance to inquire because Jack just as suddenly switched subjects again, this time to his fear of his affair being exposed. "I want you to know another thing, too, uh, I did call Sharon and told her to be very, very concerned for Herb [Sharon's husband] and her kids. I thought you were going off the deep end with me, I really did. I thought—"

"—With this letter?"

"Yeah. And I talked to her, I did talk to her, you know, I talked to her."

Glen claimed he hadn't meant any harm by his letter. Still, Jack pleaded with him not to reveal anything. "My parents, you know." He went on to speak of people grilling him for information. "I'm just leery of everybody."

"I see that," said Glen, adding that he wished Jack didn't have to be so distrustful. "Nobody—nobody—knows anything about you from me."

"But Glen, that's not the bottom line."

"Okay. But I'm just telling you that—"

"I'm not nervous about that, Glen, you don't understand."

"A long time ago, I told you: 'You and I know these things about each other,'" said Glen. Jack agreed. "And I said, 'You're my friend, and they're not gonna go any further.' And that's how it stands today, too, Jack."

"I understand that. We both got a lot of problems."

Again turning the tables, Glen offered to lend a hand. "Can I help you with any of them?"

"The whole thing is, you said to me one time—and this has really been buggin' me—it was over between you and her [Debbie]. You said how good you felt."

"When we were drivin' to the Poconos that day?"

"Yeah," Jack recalled. "You said, 'Ah, it's over.' And then you and Betty went to Florida. And you, and you said to me how good you felt. And I was having problems with her," said Jack, meaning with his mistress. "And I thought to myself, holy shit, I just don't want you to lie to me. That's all I ask you. I don't care what it is, don't lie to me."

"All right," said Glen. "What I was telling you: Debbie and I were kinda phasin' it out, y'know. I wasn't really serious about her anymore. What I wanted to tell you, to help you out, was that, you know, maybe you could do it, too. Maybe you could start seeing less of Sharon and really depending on her, and start being concerned about, you know, things that you wanted to be concerned about—your family and your kids. Believe me, I was behind you then and I'm still behind you as far as anything goes, as far as Sharon."

Jack explained that it was difficult for things to be the same between him and Glen. Just as quickly, Glen agreed. "No. Well, I'm not saying you and I can't—I mean just because of what everyone else says, you and I can't be as close as we wanna be or as close as I wanna be to you."

"I think I'm closer to you right now than I've ever been, but it might not look it," said Jack. "But I'm holding an awful lot in me, Glen."

"Do you think that I could help you by talking about it? Can I do anything for you?" asked Glen.

"No, it could only hurt you. And I want you to know that, and that's the truth. And if I'm lying about it, God will drop me dead right here. I don't know what to say." However, Jack continued, "But if the day comes there's a problem for you, I can help you. I can help you."

"Well, I'm sure if it did, you'd be there for me," said Glen.

Jack's depression, real or feigned, dramatically kicked in again. "It's just, I can't take it anymore."

"What are ya gonna do?" Glen asked. "What can't you take, Jack?"

"Just the pressure in me."

"Pressure about?"

"About you."

"About the investigation? Don't worry about me, Jack."

"Don't worry about *you*?"

"Yeah. Maybe I'm naive. Maybe I just believe that because I didn't have anything to do with it, that I have nothing to worry about," said Glen, unknowingly taking advantage of the opportunity to put a strong denial on the record. "I don't know. Maybe I'm stupid. That's probably what it is. You know what I worry about? Just Danielle. Danielle and my mother, that's what I worry about. I want to take care of them as best I can, and that's it."

"You better worry about yourself, too, a little bit."

"Well, I don't know what I can do about that."

In the ensuing exchanges, Jack continued to act buddy-buddy, warning Glen that people were talking behind his back. "Between you and I, I want to just be able to shoot from the hip with you," said Jack. "When everything's all over with, if I have one good friend, that's enough for me. I just don't want you to lie to me."

"I wish to hell we both could get everything straightened out," Glen consoled. "I mean for your life and for mine. The thing is we lost too many good people. And the dickheads are still around."

In efforts to soften, Jack admitted he had been drinking too much lately. And in an attempt to catch his prey off guard, Jack told Glen that he had seen him driving Nancy's car the other day.

Jack even tried the dramatic. "Glen, I'm the one being choked. It's easier for her to be dead. It is, I have to tell you that. I'm being choked every day and it's not 'cause I want you in some jail."

Standing firm, Glen said he knew that. "The police might, but I know you don't," he said. "They're choking me too, Jack. Not you, them. And the damn newspapers. You say you care about me?"

Jack said he did care, "or I wouldn't have you here."

"I care about you too," Glen replied. "Otherwise, I'd be writing fuckin' letters to twenty people, you know. I just wanted, just wanted you and I to get something going." Glen wished Jack a better, happier life. "But you're the one that's gotta do that. Nobody else can do it for you. I'm sure I can't. You got kids that you love, Jack."

Betty's brother turned the conversation to Glen's brother. "It was hard going to Neil's funeral, Glen. Hard not to look at you. I wanted to look at you, Glen."

"I know, that's why I said hello, because I knew that you wanted to. It was six months today," said Glen as the two men started to cry. "They were good people."

"How are you handling the pressure, Glen? Tell me, how do you do it?"

"I try not to think about it. I try not to think that people are following me. You try not to think about anything. You certainly don't think about work too much because there isn't a hell of a lot of work to do."

Jack expressed surprise. "No, it's real slow," said Glen.

Things were not much better for him, Jack added. "I can't get mine done. My business is pretty decent, but I'm screwing up. It's almost like I don't care anymore. I mean that. I've lost interest in my work."

Glen wondered if Jack still wanted him as an insurance client. Jack told his brother-in-law it was not a problem. "We gotta keep whatever ties we can. This is what I feel inside."

The more Jack tried to assure Glen that the Tasker family never meant to hurt him, the more emotional Glen became. When Jack promised to support Glen, the dentist cried, "I know. I believe you. I believe anything you tell me, Jack. I mean it."

"For you to come in here—I don't even know why you'd even trust me, to be honest with you. All the shit in the papers, everything you've seen."

"You know why?" said Glen. "Because we were almost like brothers at one point. That's why. And I don't care, I don't care what the fucking papers say."

"I do. I do, Glen." Both men could be heard crying by this point.

"Fucking buried me," said Glen. "What the fuck can I do about it, Jack?"

"Well, Glen—"

"—Fucking buried me. Betty's gone—I mean, they think I fucking—"

"—It doesn't matter, Glen. It doesn't matter."

"I still gotta learn to live without them, Jack," Glen replied, crying even louder into Jack's hidden microphone.

"It doesn't matter. I understand that, but the worst pain is to see what's going on with everybody else. I thought the death of my sister was one thing, just watching everybody else is unbelievable."

"Just that every time your dad comes down, I see him. I can't imagine what it does to him. I want to help him, and I can't."

"No," said Jack firmly. "He's very hurt, Glen."

"I mean what could— Oh, man."

"He has these thoughts in his mind, believe me. But go easy on him."

"Oh, I know."

"But he still cares about you."

"Oh God, he and me were good friends. Do you think if I asked him he would be my friend again? I want to just have a good time again," said Glen.

"All the papers, all the bullshit—Sharon, Debbie, and the job, everything, let me tell you something, when the shit hits the fan, you're still my brother-in-law."

"All right," said Glen.

"You can count on it," Jack promised.

"Now I do."

"You're still my brother-in-law, Glen. I don't know what I could do, really, I have ideas in my mind how to help. But that's my choosing. I have to be responsible for that, you know, everything. To listen to these people try to tell me or explain how you possibly could plan it—I don't believe it."

"*Plan?*" asked Glen.

"Plan the death of my sister—your wife, Glen."

"I can't even think of it."

Again Jack failed in his objective. The conversation circled around and around, but Glen seemed more concerned with maintaining strong family ties than with unburdening his soul.

Finally, in a reference to Captain Maguire's inquest identification of Glen as the prime murder suspect, Jack told Glen: "They dropped a bomb on you. You better get ahold of yourself."

"I almost wished they would have arrested me at one point, just to go to trial."

Jack said that was the last thing Glen should want. "Not right now you don't want that," he said. "Glen, if I was to sit down and show you the little bit that's been told to me, my mother, and my father, you wouldn't have a chance in hell."

"Is that right? In other words, it's stuff that they think they have against me?"

It sounded as if Jack didn't answer. Instead, he again stated that he didn't believe "this shit with premeditation stuff."

"I'm not *any kind* of fucking murderer!" Glen shot back.

Still, Jack tried to soften Glen up, saying he had tried, but had been unable, to put himself in the position of getting angry at his wife and making "a mistake."

Glen agreed. "You're talking about human life, Jack."

Looking back on his life, Jack lamented that he had "probably screwed up more things than anybody." The important thing now, he said, was "to be able to be straight."

As the conversation continued to wander from the agenda, Jack said he was keeping some of what he knew inside of him and, bizarrely, invoked Neil's name again. "I decided if I just keep it in me, and it's hard to take it all, and I know what Neil feels like. Um, I talk to him once in a while."

"Who?" asked Glen.

"Neil."

"Now?"

"Yeah. I really do."

"Do you?" asked Glen.

"I'm not nuts now."

"I know," said Glen, trying to assure. "I didn't mean to react that way. I wish I could talk to both of them. I know you and Neil were close."

Jack replied that he indeed had been very close with Neil. He said he wasn't trying to compare Glen with his dead brother, but observed, "He was like the softy and you were a little harder, ya know, in your approaches."

"Yeah," said Glen. "I couldn't have picked two better guys to be my brother and brother-in-law, let me tell you that."

The session continued in that vein for some time—hugs, promises to keep in touch, promises not to tell anyone of their meeting, promises to help each other in times of need. But Jack failed to elicit any sort of admission. On the contrary, Glen had cried, said he missed Betty, and insisted that he hadn't killed her. He sounded genuine. Jack, on the other hand, seemed obsessed with discussing his personal problems. If the confessional approach had been preplanned to loosen Glen up, it had failed miserably.

In fact, Glen had not suspected anything sinister in his meeting with Jack Tasker. That evening, Glen related to Nancy how he and Jack had talked, and how Jack had cried. Glen sounded concerned about Jack's health and state of mind. "I thought Glen took it all seriously," said Nancy.

Undeterred, the Tasker men regrouped. Four months later, with the approval of higher-ups but against the advice of those working the case full-time, Betty's father set out for the Wolsieffer dental office in Nanticoke to trap Glen himself.

Nancy had paid a visit to Betty's parents the previous week to tell them Neil's story in the hopes that they would understand her plight better. She told them how upset and torn Neil had been, and how he had been mistreated by certain law enforcement officials. "I wanted them to know that I had suffered a loss too, that they weren't the only ones."

When Nancy later heard about Glen's meeting with Betty's father she was sure that her chat had prompted the elder Tasker to meet with Glen. "I felt that I had had a positive effect on him. I thought maybe he felt bad, and didn't really think Glen did it."

Glen also subsequently viewed the meeting as a positive sign. "I told him everything. I told him what happened in the house that night," Glen related to Nancy, revealing an optimism that he had been believed and that now hopefully the Taskers would be more helpful.

Little did Glen and Nancy know, however. John Tasker appeared at Glen's office ostensibly to make arrangements for Danielle to see her grandparents. But under his clothing, he was wearing a recording device taped to his body by the police.

Unlike his son's wobbly effort at undercover work, John Tasker used his years of experience investigating insurance claims to pin Glen down on several points.

"Hi. Can I see you for a minute? The reason I'm here is Gramma is going nuts about seeing Danielle. She's afraid I'll be mad if she calls. So I just want to make any arrangements we can," said Tasker.

Glen said he did not want to run into Marian. "You and I will deal with it," he said. "I think we're better off. There's too much shit going on. I think there's too many parties involved that are keeping you and I apart."

Just like the conversation between Glen and Betty's brother, the small talk was remarkable, given the shots the Tasker family had taken at the dentist in the newspapers.

"Jack shaved," said the elder Tasker.

"Yeah, I saw him the other day," said Glen.

"He said he ran into you. You know, how he used to be in the party crowd, the real talker. He's getting meaner than shit, and we're all getting meaner than shit," said Tasker, shifting gears in a hurry. He wasn't about to let his agenda get off the track.

"I can understand that," said Glen. "I wish I could do something that could help everybody. You know what I mean, to do something to resolve this, whatever happened. I don't know if anybody wants to talk to me. I don't know if they believe what I say, if they ever will—"

"—Hey. I want to listen to you," said Tasker. "I mean, I feel that this thing has gone too damn far. We're divided, we sorta ought to be helping each other."

"Yeah. That's what I thought in the beginning."

"And whether or not the circumstances work out, me and Marian will always like you."

"I know that," said Glen. "And I care for you more than I show. More than I can show because I do. And, I loved Betty."

Tasker offered to help in any way he could. "I'm so locked in as to what I can say and do," said Glen, "because of the attorney and all of this other bullshit. I can't do anything on my own anymore. And it was like that from the first day. When I tried to talk to the police, tried to help them— All of a sudden they don't want to hear anything I have to say anymore. I wish the hell that we could get some kind of guy in there that could start over, I mean, from Day One."

Tasker said he had kicked that idea around himself and even had the names of two private eyes recommended to him. Tasker said they wanted money up front, but that didn't bother him.

"Money is nothing," Glen concurred. "As a matter of fact, I'd sell my house. I don't give a shit about my house. My house ain't nothing without Betty there, it doesn't mean anything. I might sell it anyway. I tried to stay there and I just can't do it."

And so it went. John Tasker kept after Glen, coming at him from different angles—talking about Neil, Debbie Shipp, Jack's anger—then bullying Glen about whether he knew anyone who possibly would have wanted to kill Betty. But Glen showed no guilt. There would be no confession. He even volunteered to recall the entire story of that fateful morning, adding several peculiar details to his version of events. "I got nothing to hide from you," Glen assured.

In his latest chronology, Glen contended he had had two conversations with Betty when he arrived home that night, a very brief one when he moved Danielle from the master bedroom to her own room, and an extended one when he returned after having milk and cookies in the kitchen. "When I came back up to sleep, Betty was still a little awake, so we were talking for awhile."

Tasker wanted to know if they had fought.

"Not at all," Glen insisted. "Not one fight at all. I was even joking around with her. I said, 'I know it's late, but do you want to play around, darling?' " He said Betty replied, " 'Glen, I'm still sleeping.' "

There were other tidbits. Now he was sure he had seen the intruder's features because "the curtain in the hallway was open," but still didn't know "if it was a bright night that night." Now he was sure he had looked in on Danielle and then closed her door. And now he was sure he called Neil because "that's the only number" he could remember "with a banged head, and lying on the floor."

Bizarrely, Glen talked about possibly moving to California, inviting Tasker and his family to join him. Misstating the obvious, he said he had asked Nancy if Betty had been raped because "that's the worst thing that can happen." And he also talked about spending nights at 75 Birch in hopes of catching Betty's murderer, as if he really expected someone to return. "I don't know if they want more money, I don't know what they want. If they want me, come and get me."

As he described the attack against him, Glen explained why he was still alive, and raised the prospect of there having been two intruders.

"By the time I got into the back room, that's when they grabbed me. I say they, because I don't think it could have been one. Because I got pulled from the back with something around my neck and I was trying—I had my *fingers in*. That's the only way I saved myself, by getting my hands in so that I was able to pull."

After Glen finished with the sequence, Tasker seized on Glen's theory of multiple intruders. "I can't understand that there was more than one—"

"—The only reason that I say that—"

"—The police think—well, you know what they think," said Tasker. "The police have you figured as the only suspect."

Glen said he realized that.

"And?"

"That's a problem for me."

"And they will continue, and probably push the issue."

Glen said that was why he wanted to be at 75 Birch when the murderers returned. "If they don't want to find anybody but me, I want to find them."

"I want to find them, too," said Tasker. "Just as bad as you do."

Glen invited his father-in-law to come stay with him at the house. "I'd be glad for the company. Because I'm sure you want a piece of their fuckin' asses as much as I do."

But along the way, Glen would utter several lies. When Tasker wondered if Betty had still been angry about Debbie Shipp, Glen insisted, "I swear, as far as Betty knew, I was not involved with anybody up until the day she died." Later in the conversation, he contradicted the earlier misstatement while explaining that he was the prime suspect "because of other involvements and Betty finding out, which, I mean— If I never told anybody anything, I'm going to tell you, Betty and I did not have an argument that night. I did not kill her." Then there was the matter of Glen previously having told the police that Betty had not woken up when he got home from the Crackerbox. Here he was now admitting that he had talked to Betty twice, before *and* after his milk and cookies.

When Glen discussed the status of his marriage just prior to Betty's murder, he also reconstructed history. "That last year that we had together was the best year that we had in a long time because, you know, Danielle was getting older, we had more time. Betty and I had more time for ourselves, you know, without having a baby around. By that time, everybody wasn't coming over to visit and, you know, it was a lot better."

And at one point, when Tasker talked about how brutal Betty's beating had been, Glen reacted with a story that suggested he had never looked at his wife's corpse. He told Betty's father that he had learned of the severity of the attack only a month earlier, during a conversation with Nancy at the cemetery, when he asked her, "Tell me more about what happened with Betty, because I haven't even been able to talk to anybody about it." She said, "They beat her up pretty bad." But Glen had to have known; he had looked at the body twice at the funeral home.

As the conversation circled toward its conclusion, Glen suggested Tasker might want to find out what the police knew, and enlisted support for his theory that Betty's murder could somehow be related to a rash of break-ins around the Birch Street area or the strange phone calls to Betty and Nancy. "That's the kind of shit that's going to get us somewhere."

But Tasker was unimpressed, and instead kept bringing the focus back to Glen's two-intruder theory. Glen said he saw only one attacker but said that by the sequence of events, "it almost had to be two. There might have been one guy downstairs, the other guy upstairs. I don't know if they came in the back door. I don't know where the fuck they came in, maybe the bathroom window."

At another point, though, he suggested that the two intruders would have had to have been standing next to each other. "I still remember vividly getting hit from behind right after I got released. Now, if this guy is hurt the way I must have hurt him to let me go, he's on the ground. I didn't even get time to turn around. After I got released, it was like you could feel the blood kind of coming back to your head again. And, like a little dizzy and all of a sudden it's whack, right on the head."

Ultimately, Tasker warned, "They got one suspect and it's you. I don't think they're going to let up. If I could come up with anything else, I would, really." Glen said he knew that.

"And I pray to God it wouldn't be you," said Tasker. "Really—not only for my sake and Marian's sake, for your mother's sake, and for Danielle's sake—because she's got to live a lot longer than we do."

CHAPTER 22

With Neil gone, Nancy started to see a great deal more of Glen. Their heightened relationship sparked gossip, but their closeness was emotional rather than physical. They were bonded by the unnatural deaths of their spouses, a mutual grief that prompted them to support each other's emptiness and join forces to face the challenges of single parenting.

The rumor mill had started churning as far back as the day of Neil's funeral at St. Boniface Church, the same parish where Nancy taught. As the service began, the widow sobbed gently, planting her head on Glen's shoulder. He wiped his eyes with a hanky. Nancy put her arm around him and squeezed tightly. Together, they helped the priest ready the Holy Communion wafers.

They were arm in arm as they exited the church, a poignant scene captured by the swarm of newspaper photographers camped outside. In the eyes and minds of those thinking below the waist, Glen and Nancy quickly became an item.

Since Danielle was in kindergarten mornings only and Nancy wasn't working, she frequently babysat Glen's daughter while caring for Bryn. In time, Phyllis returned to her job, and Nancy's babysitting role became even more regular. She picked up Danielle at 11:30 at St. Boniface, then went to her parents' house on Parrish Street, where Glen retrieved his daughter after work. In addition, Glen came to Nancy's parents' house two or three days a week to have lunch with Nancy and Danielle.

"I was seeing him on a daily basis," Nancy recalled. "My parents really went out of their way to help Phyllis through it, but they had other feelings about Glen, my father more so than my mother. They were doing it for me."

During this period, Nancy was Danielle's mother figure while Glen filled the father figure role for Bryn. "I remember telling him that once. That is how they perceived us. Danielle looked up to me like I was her mother. I mean she never called me that, it was just understood." Nancy recognized the pitfalls of this arrangement, though, telling Glen, "We're giving these kids a false sense of family."

Still, they were each other's support system. "I don't think I could have gotten through it without him. I felt that Glen was probably the only one who knew what I was going through," Nancy said. For his part, Glen told her, "I can't get through this without you. You are such a support to me. You are so level-headed." But then, as Nancy recalled, "He painted me as this poor widow who couldn't get by without him—and part of that was true. But it was a two-way street."

In the weeks immediately following Betty's death, Glen had bemoaned things Nancy couldn't relate to. For example, Glen would often tell her: "If only it didn't get dark at night." Now, with Neil gone, Nancy said, "All of a sudden, I hated when it got dark." He also had mentioned how walking back into his house was so difficult, and now she knew exactly what he meant.

Nancy found herself spending more time with all the Wolsieffers. "I had the most supportive family anybody could ever hope for, but they were all couples, every single one of them. And I couldn't go up there and look at couples. Plus, my brother was having a second child, and my sister got pregnant. I couldn't deal with that because it was everything I wanted, and it was taken away. I felt, at that time, more comfort in Neil's family because his mother was widowed. His grandfather, Bob, was widowed.

Lisa wasn't seeing anybody. So there was Lisa alone, Phyllis alone, Bob alone, Glen alone, me alone. I don't think it is hard to understand that I felt more comfortable being with Neil's family than being with my own, because my own was too painful, even though their support was so much better."

The police and press both tried to keep tabs on Nancy's relationship with Glen. One entry in the *Sunday Independent* stated: "Speculation about the case has raged in the community since the outset, and Mrs. Nancy Wolsieffer, Neil's wife, has openly professed her belief that authorities are suspecting the wrong man, even though police and prosecutors have consistently refused to say publicly whether they have a suspect in the case."

Officer Brian Lavan reported to Captain Maguire that on New Year's Eve, while he was at his mother-in-law's house, Glen and Nancy left together before midnight, ostensibly to visit his mother's house on Magnolia. Lavan said that when he left the Woods residence at about twenty minutes into the New Year, he spotted Glen and Nancy still sitting across the street in Glen's black Subaru. At least one of Lavan's superiors used the sighting as further confirmation of a supposed romance.

In time, word got back to Nancy that the police had seen her and Glen together in the parked car. "It was getting to be midnight and we didn't want to be in there for all the fanfare," she recalled. "I was so upset. I couldn't bear to be around there at midnight. We went out in the car and the next thing I knew Glen's lawyer said something about that the police saw us in the car. And so what? If they knew the reason why. I mean, I was crying my eyes out in the car. It was the first New Year's without Neil and I couldn't be in there. And it wasn't even a party. It was the family sitting around the table having shrimp. They probably made it out like I was at this wild New Year's Eve bash and went out in the car with Glen. It is just so unfair because that is not the way it was at all."

Trying to somehow reassemble her life, Nancy moved back into 84 Birch that spring, in April 1987. The winter had been cruel to the unheated house. "The table is still warped. It's like a reminder of days gone by," Nancy observed years later. Besides still grieving the loss of Neil, she had to contend with the unfinished, two-story addition in the rear of her home.

The plastic sheet still separated the old part of the house from the new. Just like with her life, Nancy needed to push the musty, semi-opaque divider away. It was time to step forward, to rebuild, to embark anew.

Stretched financially and feeling alone, Nancy accepted Glen's offer to do the work. That, in turn, isolated her even more from Neil's friends. They had planned to get a group together to finish the project. "But when they found out that he was here, they wouldn't come," Nancy said. "They wouldn't have anything to do with him."

Still believing fully in Glen's innocence, Nancy felt sorry for him. At times, it seemed like that was her new station in life—to feel sorry for Glen.

When Glen lamented he wished he had called the police instead of Neil, Nancy replied, "It's not your fault. You didn't know."

When she received hordes of sympathy cards for Neil, she felt compelled to hide them because Glen had gotten so few. "He would look at them and say, 'Well, geez, I didn't hear from him' or 'I didn't hear from her.' I started putting them away when I knew he would be here, so he wouldn't see them."

Or when Glen admitted to her that, in fact, he was still seeing Debbie, and had been since less than a month after Betty's murder, Nancy was a patient listener. "He would open up to me about Debbie. He did fall in love with her, but he made it like Debbie was so dependent on him," she said. "He would say I need to break this off and I would help him. I would be his ear, and his shoulder. He would cry that he felt so bad."

Glen claimed he had written Debbie letters on many occasions to break off the relationship, and that he had spoken to her about the need to go their separate ways. But the efforts were always unsuccessful. As usual, Nancy was sympathetic and understanding. "I would never condone adultery—no matter what, there is no excuse. But it pales when you are up on a murder rap. And I didn't believe that he was guilty of that, so his involvement with other women just paled in light of the whole picture."

The personal kinship between Nancy and Glen continued to

develop, far beyond serving as parental figures for each other's children. In many ways, Glen became Nancy's Neil figure. "I wanted him to be Neil," she admitted. "Those feelings just took over, like whatever I felt for Neil, I tried to transfer them into Glen, as a coping mechanism—like, 'Neil's not dead' or 'Neil is dead, but I have Glen so I'll get through this.' " When she needed advice, she found herself calling Glen. A problem with the car, call Glen. Need someone to talk to, call Glen. She couldn't do a thing without him. "He reminded me of Neil so much, more than he ever had. He hadn't reminded me of Neil when Neil was here."

Small instances brought a continual flood of recognition. For example, Glen would open the refrigerator and, standing there, look in the same way his brother used to. "The way he drove the car, the way he put his hand on the wheel, stuff I never noticed— all of a sudden that was just how Neil held the steering wheel," she said. "Or he'd go for a bowl of ice cream at nine-thirty at night, and I'd think, 'Oh, God, that's what Neil did.'

"It was such a comfort to have him here. I wanted him to stay all the time, I never wanted him to leave— He *would* leave, but I didn't want him to," Nancy said. "I thought how could people think this about him because look at how good he's being to me."

She said she will probably never know what Glen wanted out of their relationship. Despite unsubstantiated rumors, as well as innuendo in one of the local newspapers, Nancy swore the relationship never became intimate. She also contended that Glen never tried to seduce her. "It was all a comfort kind of thing, like he was going to take care of me because that's what Neil wanted."

One investigator suggested that Glen treated Nancy so well because he was afraid Neil had told her something important about Betty's murder. But, Nancy assured, "that didn't happen," because Neil had never told her anything.

There were plenty of whispers in the valley whenever Glen and Nancy were seen together in bars and restaurants. She was offended that people assumed something sexual was going on between her and Glen simply because she was seen out in public with him. In Nancy's eyes, it wasn't easy for her or Glen, after years of independence, to be back in their family settings. Sometimes she just needed to get away from all the well-meaning relatives and the intact families. "A lot of times on a Friday or a Saturday, Lisa and Glen and I would go out. And I don't mean out to a bar. I mean out to eat and back home again."

Of course, more gossip was spawned every time she and Glen were seen together. The most outrageous rumors had Nancy secretly married to Glen or pregnant with his child. There also was gossip that Nancy's affair with Glen had started *before* Betty's murder. As the story went, such a long-running relationship would explain Nancy's motives and behavior in defense of her brother-in-law.

Glen and Danielle continued to live with his mother and Lisa, although the child spent a great deal of time with Nancy, just across the street from the house where her mother was murdered.

In late July, the two widowed parents took their daughters on vacation together to Ocean City, Maryland, an excursion duly noted in the newspapers the following week. The trip sparked even more suspicion about a romantic link. "My every move was scrutinized because they thought I knew something. They thought I was going to pick up where Neil left off." Nancy said she and Glen took the children to the beach to get away from the pressure. The kids needed a vacation. She insisted there was nothing more to it than that.

In fact, one of their more frequent excursions was visiting their spouses' graves, in cemeteries about fifteen minutes apart, especially on holidays and anniversaries. Nancy always wanted the graves to look as nice as possible. In the winter, when it snowed, she often called Glen and pressed him to drive out with her to the gravesites to clean up the plots and headstones. Several days after the placement of fresh flowers, Nancy would return to remove them.

At Neil's grave, Glen's mood was always the same. "He just stood there," said Nancy. "Stoic." Some of his worst crying sessions, however, occurred standing over Betty's grave.

He also experienced an odd lapse of memory on one visit in the summer of 1987. Out of the blue, he asked Nancy about the extent of Betty's injuries. Nancy explained that her face had looked awful, that she had been beaten extensively. Glen appeared to be overcome with emotion. He said he couldn't drive. He had to sit for a while. And so he sat under a tree crying and crying and crying. "I just wanted to go back to Betty and look at her again," he later said.

Despite Nancy's concern for his well-being, Glen still managed an active social life. He played in a few golf and softball tournaments, and was even elected to the board of directors of the South Wilkes-Barre Rotary Club, the organization he had once headed. "Obviously, the fact that we elected him to the board would tell you what we think of him," Charles Eastwood, newly elected vice president, told a local reporter. Rotary International officials were asked by an outraged member of the press how Wolsieffer could be allowed to hold office. Organization officials pointed out that there had not even been an arrest, never mind a conviction.

In the months after the inquest, the two remaining Wolsieffer siblings held brainstorming sessions, gathered around a table at 14 Magnolia. Glen and Lisa would sometimes be joined by Nancy Wolsieffer and Gary Stinson. Always, Phyllis sat in another room.

Family members tried desperately to keep TV and newspaper reports from Phyllis, and for the most part, they succeeded. Protected and isolated, her support was unfailing and unquestioning. For example, she had never quizzed her son about the night Betty died. "He always says to me, 'I come home, go to bed and look what happened.' " When asked if there was any part of his story that she questioned, Phyllis replied: "*Me*? No, no."

She said she understood why the police held Glen's adultery against him, but argued that there was more to the story. "He was wrong in that, but he did not have the perfect home life that people paint the picture of." She contended that she left 75 Birch crying on many occasions because, in her view, her son was being mistreated by Betty. "She loved him. She was there. But he didn't matter. She called him freak of the week, in front of me, 'Oh, here comes freak of the week.' Many times I was there, he's sitting at the supper table, she's on the phone, Danielle is in front of the TV set. When I hear this stuff, how perfect they were—believe me, I loved her, she was like a daughter to me, she was my granddaughter's mother, but she was not perfect."

Nor did she think it was possible that Betty and Glen had argued, that in the heat of passion Betty ended up dead. Glen had often told his mother that Betty never communicated with him, so "they never argued. So why would I think that? I think if she argued, he wouldn't argue back."

For her part, Glen's younger sister was more combative. "I hated everybody and I didn't want to go anywhere. But then I wanted to go tell them, show them, that they are not getting to me." Lisa admitted that part of her attitude was a defense mechanism because so many people believed that her brother was a murderer and didn't go out of their way to hide their feelings. "This made me very cold," she said.

Though she usually managed to hold back, sometimes Lisa felt compelled to speak up. One time the family went out to dinner in Harveys Lake, where she figured no one would recognize them, and she overheard a man at the next table talking about "the dentist who killed his wife."

When the group got up to leave, Lisa rose also and approached them. "Look, before you open your big mouth, why don't you try to be considerate of people around you?"

"I'm sorry. I'm sorry," the man apologized.

"Yeah," Lisa replied. "That is my brother. Don't apologize to me. You owe him an apology, but I'm sure he doesn't want to hear it from you."

While protecting her surviving brother, Lisa tried to absolve Glen from any wrongdoing, at least in her own mind. His story of the intruder made perfect sense to her. All she saw was that the police were hounding Glen unfairly, the same police who had so much to do with her brother Neil's tragedy. She blasted Minnick as a "cocky cop" and contended that Glen had sustained the scratches on his chest when the officer let him slip from his hands.

Lisa had theories upon theories: the burglars had not intended to kill, and so that is why they left the jewelry behind. The man who made the mysterious calls to Betty and Nancy on Friday nights could be the killer. The intruder or intruders would have had no problem using the rickety ladder because she had used it herself to help Betty get into the house when she had locked herself out.

In time, Lisa also developed theories about Glen's infidelity. "I think it was more that somebody paid attention to him," she explained. "Glen loves to be liked, so whatever form that takes is what he takes. Sometimes he took third, fourth, fifth place with

Danielle and the neighbors that needed dinner and her mother's grass that needed cutting and 'Eileen Pollock is having a baby, so we need to have a shower,' or 'This dental auxiliary thing needs to be done.' There were eighty million things that Betty needed to do." Perhaps one of them, Lisa added, was playing tit for tat.

Lisa was a loyal sibling. As she told friends, she had already lost one brother; she was going to do everything she could not to lose the other.

CHAPTER 23

As Betty's unsolved murder approached the one-year mark, the local media took the opportunity to employ a tried-and-true newspaper tradition: the anniversary story. The *Sunday Independent* had received word that the *Times Leader* was planning to launch its new Sunday edition on August 9, three weeks before the actual anniversary, with a big splash on the Wolsieffer case. So the *Independent* dedicated parts of five pages to its anniversary package a week before that.

The front page of Section One carried a story headlined: THE WOLSIEFFER MURDER: UNSOLVED ONE YEAR LATER. The front page of Section Two carried a story headlined: TOP CITY POLICE BRASS NOW FEAR WOLSIEFFER MURDER PERFECT CRIME. Contrasting the troubling "web of purely circumstantial evidence," reporter Fred Ney quoted Police Chief Joseph Coyne and Detective Captain William Maguire as saying they would certainly arrest Glen Wolsieffer if given approval by D.A. Podcasy. But the district attorney continued to disagree. "I think we have to make a distinction here. Making an arrest is the easy part. Getting a conviction is a whole different story," Podcasy said.

The *Times Leader* package was even more dramatic. Carrying the headline, 'TIL DEATH DO US PART—WHO KILLED THE DENTIST'S WIFE? the stories took up half the front page and four more full pages inside. Podcasy told the paper: "To get a conviction on purely circumstantial evidence, that circumstantial evidence has to be particularly strong. You can't arrest on suspicion or public sentiment."

Despite Captain Maguire's inquest testimony, or perhaps in spite of it, Podcasy continued his longstanding refusal to publicly identify Glen as an official suspect. He said it was "inappropriate and unethical" to single out any individual prior to an arrest, and emphasized that no one from his office had ever indicated a suspect in Betty's death by name. As he had been forced to do on now countless occasions, Podcasy also denied his inactions were in any way connected with his tough political race to keep the D.A.'s job.

With the general election fast approaching, the Wolsieffer investigation became even more of a political football. Bernard A. Podcasy, the appointed incumbent, had won the Democratic nomination, and his Republican opponent was Correale Stevens, a four-term state representative.

Stevens had never tried a criminal case in his life, and some would argue that his biggest piece of legislation as a state representative was getting a bill passed honoring Bruce Springsteen, despite the fact that "The Boss" hailed from neighboring New Jersey. Stevens didn't let his lack of experience stop him, however. In 1985, he had run unsuccessfully for a judgeship on the county Court of Common Pleas, the trial level, and in later years expressed interest in becoming the region's U.S. Attorney and thereafter a federal judge.

Stevens was successful because he was a consummate politician. He looked good. He carefully cultivated senior citizens' groups. He helped balance countywide tickets and produced heavy vote totals from his home turf for his running mates. He knew how to determine which way the political winds were blowing. Seizing on an issue he knew was on the minds of voters, Stevens promised that if elected, he would make solving Betty's murder "a top priority." Stevens derided Podcasy's inaction virtually nonstop. "Some decisions should have been made by now," said Stevens. "The fact that they haven't stems from the continual inaction by the current district attorney. Podcasy just seems to be lacking direction."

Podcasy still wouldn't budge, despite growing accusations that he was too close to the Wolsieffer family. He also denied that he was afraid to prosecute a tough case for fear of losing it in an election year. He was hurt deeply by the accusations that he was protecting Glen, and he believed that the voters would understand that he was only being fair and just in not making an arrest on skimpy circumstantial evidence just to appease a collective lynch mob.

At almost every campaign stop, Podcasy was put on the defensive. High-ranking police officials hounded him to arrest Glen. The Tasker family continually asked for a meeting or an update. Even several of Podcasy's assistants, supporters of his, recommended an arrest.

During one campaign strategy session with his advisers, who included some of the valley's most politically powerful and astute citizens, Podcasy was warned that he would probably lose the election unless he authorized Glen Wolsieffer's arrest. Several in attendance pointed out that state law gave district attorneys 180 days after an arrest to bring the case to trial. By then, they said, the election would be held, "and you'll be D.A. You've got everything to win and nothing to lose."

But Podcasy would have none of it. "He really didn't think it was the right thing to do," said one adviser who attended the session. "He had strength of soul. He was very thoughtful and moral about it. He didn't feel there was enough evidence."

As the campaign neared its climax, Podcasy vainly tried to play the political game by comparing his ten years in the district attorney's office to his opponent's utter lack of experience. Podcasy charged that Stevens had been "out back-slapping, kissing babies and cutting political deals as the true politician that he is. In my ten years, I have never once seen Correale Stevens in a court of law, let alone involved in a criminal case."

In a reference to the Wolsieffer case, Podcasy pointed out that Stevens criticized investigations in the D.A.'s office without being privy to the whole story. "Where are his facts? He is making uneducated remarks to intentionally slant these matters for his own political benefit. I am sick and tired of taking public abuse from a political opportunist who cannot even represent his own constituency with any degree of dignity or distinction. My opponent has spent all summer taking cheap shots at me and my office. Let's look at his performance in a court of law—none! My opponent can, and does, make bold-faced allegations, but without knowledge and experience, it appears that the old adage rings true: 'Empty barrels make the most noise.' "

As Election Day drew near in the predominantly Democratic county, Stevens dogged Podcasy about allegations that his father's influence had helped him get the job in the first place, and battered the D.A. on his operation of the office, alleging that it was "in a state of confusion and chaos." He countered Podcasy's attack on his "undistinguished and negligent" legislative voting record by stating, "I'm running for district attorney, not the state legislature."

Stevens said it would be better for everyone if Podcasy focused on his own local problems. And indeed, there were problems. The office was in disarray. Charges against three codefendants were dropped in a highly publicized murder case when the star witness "announced" in one of Corbett's columns that although she had already testified at the trial of the fourth codefendant, she wasn't going to testify again. Several of Podcasy's advisers recommended that Corbett be arrested on charges of tampering with a witness, but Podcasy "couldn't pull the trigger," said one of them. "He's a deliberate guy."

Come November, Stevens proved the more persuasive. He was elected, and the Wolsieffer murder story was to take a new direction.

Throughout the bitter campaign and transition period, the Wolsieffer investigators, basically Mitchell and Sworen, continued to track leads from the serious to the ridiculous. Each tip had to be checked out, though. It was becoming difficult to separate what witnesses knew firsthand, what they had read in the newspapers, and what they had heard on the street. One of the more outlandish theories had Glen killing Betty with dental floss. Another suggested a special kind of tubing found only in dental offices. A third involved the strapping used to secure dental x-rays and other dental supplies. One neighbor heard that Betty had been strangled with a telephone cord, her body discovered in Danielle's bedroom.

One scenario heard even by Nancy suggested that the Wolsieffer boys had switched wives: Glen with Nancy, and Neil with Betty. Under that theory, something had gone awry and either Glen or Neil had committed the murder.

A police report was even duly filed after a waitress at a popular downtown Italian-American restaurant reported that while serving dinner to Dr. Wolsieffer and another well-dressed man, the dentist asked her if she had seen the movie *Fatal Attraction*. And Mitchell contacted the magician who had performed at Eileen Pollock's house the Friday afternoon of Betty's murder. Pat Ward, who lived just six blocks away from the murder site, confirmed that he had performed a trick using three pieces of clothesline rope and had given one of the pieces to Betty Wolsieffer's daughter. Mitchell wanted to know if the piece had been strong enough and long enough to strangle someone. Ward said the pieces ranged in size from several inches to less than two feet and that he had not given Danielle the largest one.

Before the investigation would conclude, many days would be spent on the inevitable "other" suspect, Tracie Witner, a twenty-two-year-old woman who slit her wrists and told her probation officer she had murdered Betty as well as several other people across the country. Mitchell tracked her down and learned that she had drug and alcohol problems and a long criminal record. The woman confessed, claiming she had choked Betty and hit Glen with a beer bottle, but her story was full of holes. It was ultimately determined that Witner, who said she worked at the Close Encounters Massage Parlor, had spent the night of Betty's murder eating at the Big Wrangler, drinking at Carter's Bar, and passed out at her boyfriend's home, with her nephew as an additional alibi.

There had been rumors that a car had been heard, and possibly seen, traveling up Birch Street in the wrong direction during the early-morning hours of the night of Betty's murder, potentially important if it could be linked to the trip investigators believed Glen made to the riverbank to dispose of evidence. Mitchell telephoned Michael Schwab in Tucson, Arizona. An employee of the University of Arizona, Schwab confirmed that he had been visiting his mother in Wilkes-Barre on the weekend in question, that at about 3:00 A.M. he had parked his car in the driveway of 98 Birch, the home of a relative, and that he and his wife, Dorothy, then got out of the car and started walking toward his mother's house at 109 Birch. While still in the driveway, the Schwabs heard a car squealing around the corner of Birch and Pickering streets, and saw it go up Birch the wrong way at a fast rate of speed. Schwab said that by the time he and his wife walked from the driveway to the street, the car was no longer in sight. He had the impression the vehicle was "a smaller-type car," but was unable to provide any description of the driver or say if there had been any other occupants. His wife, meanwhile, thought the vehicle was "a bigger car." The lead was another dead end.

Bizarrely disregarding his attorney's standing orders, Glen accepted Captain Maguire's out-of-the-blue telephone invitation to discuss the investigation at his Nanticoke dental office on March 10, 1988. Maguire later acknowledged that during the chat he told Glen that Neil's "reputation was also in question because of all the unanswered questions, that people were calling in with information that Neil could have been the killer." Glen said he felt bad about the rumors, but insisted that Neil had done nothing other than come over to his house after Betty was dead and call the police. Maguire also contended that Glen explained at one point that he could not talk on the advice of his attorney: "I'll have to take my chances with a jury. You understand, don't you, Bill?"

Meanwhile, efforts by the FBI continued to yield inconclusive results. No semen was found in any of the eight swabs sent by Dr. Hudock from the autopsy—two each from Betty's mouth, back of the throat, rectal area, and vagina.

Human blood, "probably" from Betty, had been detected on the pillow, the pillowcase, and one of the bed sheets. There were links, but to an even lesser degree, between Betty's blood and the human blood found on the bedspread. But just as the presence of Glen's hairs in his bedroom was of no legal usefulness, so too were the discoveries of Betty's blood on neutral objects in her bedroom or on her body.

Although blood testing had been attempted on a whole slew of items, the FBI reports went on to state that all other grouping tests "were inconclusive or precluded due to the limited amount of sample." Also, no blood was found on Glen's gray belt sent for analysis, the .22-caliber Ruger or its holster, the five towels, his clothes, or nine of Betty's fingernail clippings. A sample from the first finger of her left hand was found to be human blood, but it could not be further identified. The experts also failed to find any blood on the mysterious blue washer-type object that had been found embedded in Betty's neck. Portions of the blue rubber were missing, suggesting that fragments might have still been adhering to the item it was originally attached to. Despite metallurgical examinations, though, the FBI was unable to determine the manufacturer or intended use of the object. As for fiber samples removed from the carpet in the master bedroom, the upstairs hallway, and the family room, the FBI declined to compare them with fibers recovered from Glen's clothing because such a match would prove nothing. It was Glen's house.

The tests were a bust, but the federal agency became involved in another important aspect of the case when the Wilkes-Barre police filed a Crime Analysis Report with the FBI's National Center for the Analysis of Violent Crime (NCAVC). A criminal profiling and consultation program, NCAVC is responsible for reviewing crimes of violence and providing a criminal investigative analysis for the purpose of establishing motivation for the crime, as well as providing an offender profile of the perpetrator. The unit's reports are based not only on information supplied for a particular case, but also on research involving thousands of crimes of violence.

The fifteen-page Violent Criminal Apprehension Program (VICAP) questionnaire is designed especially for homicides that involve an abduction; are random, motiveless, or sexually oriented; or are known or suspected to be the work of a serial killer. But, the Wilkes-Barre investigators figured, anything that had even a chance of helping, no matter how remote, was worth the effort. Because a suspect had been identified—Glen Wolsieffer— a suspect personality profile could not be compiled under FBI rules. But there was another avenue to pursue that could be just as helpful: Could the FBI determine whether Glen's story was false?

On October 9, 1987, Mitchell took the request a step further, asking if the FBI could determine "if the crime scene was staged. . . . If it is determined that the crime scene was staged, we would like an expert to testify to that fact."

Various reports and interviews, crime-scene photographs, the video of the crime scene, and even newspaper clippings were packaged together for review by the FBI experts. Mitchell typed out a seven-page, single-spaced summary of the case, mixing the key circumstantial facts with those requiring favorable nuances.

For example, Glen "smiled" when his lawyer arrived at the hospital, Glen's scratches "appeared to be fresh," when asked why he had not gone upstairs, Neil had "a serious look" on his face, the night of the murder Glen was drinking "at a singles bar," Glen "tried to act surprised" when the deputy coroner told him his wife had been murdered, Glen "never tried or asked to see his wife and child" before going to the hospital.

Matter of factly, Mitchell also stated: "A short time after Neil's death, his wife, Nancy Wolsieffer, began going out with Glen Wolsieffer. The relationship is continuing to the present, along with Glen's relationship with the two other women."

Mitchell concluded with what he characterized as "a very important fact about Glen Wolsieffer," the continuous mark around his neck. "It extended from the sides of his neck to the rear of his neck. There were *no marks on his throat*. It appeared as though he placed a rope or chain around his own neck and caused the mark. The mark was pink in color and about ⅜th of an inch wide," Mitchell wrote. "For a person to be choked and become unconscious, the marks on the neck were on the wrong side."

The request for a crime-scene analysis was eventually directed to John E. Douglas, the nation's premier behavioral scientist and an internationally recognized expert. Douglas had worked on the intricate fiber analysis aspects of the Wayne Williams child murders in Atlanta, the shooting of civil rights leader Vernon Jordan, the Yorkshire Ripper case in Great Britain, the Green River killer in the Pacific Northwest, and dozens of other serial and high-profile cases. He later served as chief consultant to the hit movie *The Silence of the Lambs*.

When he issued his four-page report several months later, investigators in Wilkes-Barre were ecstatic.

> CONCLUSION: It is the opinion of SSA John E. Douglas that the crime scene was "staged." It is my personal experience, through work in the NCAVC, that crime scenes are "staged" or altered when a subject, well-known to the victim, wants to distract an investigation and set it off in a direction that will eliminate him as a primary suspect.
>
> Unfortunately for the subject, and opportunately for anyone experienced in crime analysis, this "staging" is easily observed. The subject "stages" a scene to make it look like a crime that *he* thinks it should look like. Of course, when this is done, the subject is under a great deal of pressure and stress and does not have the time to logically fit all the pieces together. When you analyze a crime such as this with a lot of apparent activity on the part of the subject but without any clear idea as to the motivation of same, you question the statements provided by any witness/victim.
>
> If the motivation was burglary, the crime . . . was "high-risk" and improbable. If the criminal intent was homicide, the intruder would have looked for his intended victim(s) upon entry into the second-floor window. Instead, he immediately went downstairs. If the subject intended to kill, he did not have a knife or gun, and did not display or use same. The victim died of strangulation. Manual strangulation is a very personal-type crime.

Douglas remarked that the ladder "appears to be badly rotted and is leaned against the roof with the rungs placed in the wrong direction." He also noted the lack of indentations in the ground beneath the ladder, the lack of "debris transference onto the roof," the lack of indentations in the rain gutters where the ladder had been leaned against, the lack of foot impressions on the moss-laden rungs, and the lack of footprints on the windowsill.

He noted that both of the Wolsieffers' cars were parked in the driveway "in full view from the road," and since they were sleeping in their bed on a Saturday morning, they were at "low-risk" to be "targeted by someone motivated to kill, rob, or both." The crime, as described by Glen and based on what Douglas read in the various police reports, "would be considered extremely 'high-risk,' " he said.

> If the subject entered the residence, he knew from the vehicles parked in the driveway that someone was home. The time of day (daybreak) and day of week (Saturday) also makes this a "high-risk" type of crime. Some people could already be awake in the neighborhood who may observe this intrusion—including the people residing in the residence he is about to intrude. If the subject, in fact, entered the second-floor window, he would check all rooms on that floor prior to going downstairs to the first floor. It doesn't matter what his motivation for going there was; this is just common criminal procedure observed within the NCAVC. If Mr. Wolsieffer was choked unconscious, and at this point his wife is still alive upstairs, it does not fit the logical crime scenario that the intruder would return upstairs and kill Mrs. Wolsieffer—leaving Mr. Wolsieffer alive downstairs.

To summarize, Douglas said, "Mrs. Wolsieffer was killed by someone who knew her very well. After the homicide, the crime scene was 'staged' to give the appearance that the residence was intruded by some unknown subject."

Douglas's analysis was just what this circumstantial case needed. Clearly, his work pointed the finger at Glen. If prosecutors could somehow get the specialist on the witness stand, he could make all the difference in the world. But getting him there would prove to be no easy task.

CHAPTER 24

Still close to Glen, and still trying to put the pieces of her life back together, Nancy Wolsieffer returned to her first-grade teaching job at St. Boniface in the fall of 1987. Danielle was one of her students.

After attending a seminar on how children deal with death and other personal problems in the home, Nancy conducted a mini-lesson on the subject. "You know how kids blame themselves for everything. One little boy had a turtle and he went away for the weekend and he left the window open. When he came back, the turtle had died. He thought it was his fault, but the turtle had this disease."

Danielle wanted to talk about her mother's death. "I thought it was my fault—" she started to explain. But Nancy cut her off. They would discuss it at home, in private, she instructed. Nancy later told the youngster there was no way she was responsible for her mother's murder.

Accepting Glen's assurances that he was no longer seeing Debbie Shipp, and still convinced of his innocence regarding Betty's murder, Nancy continued to commiserate with her brother-in-law, often advising him that no matter how difficult the challenge, he should start looking to the future.

One day that fall, while working on Nancy's addition, Glen mentioned that a friend of his from his Virginia days had called to say there was a woman he wanted Glen to meet. He could come down for the weekend, and they could double-date on a daylong cruise in Maryland.

Glen and Nancy talked about how hard it was to start over. "I can't imagine dating, you know, small talk in a restaurant," Glen said, with Nancy agreeing. Still, she wanted to be positive. "How bad could it be? You've got to do it. You've got to get on with your life."

Glen told Nancy how sorry he was about having been with Debbie, and how he wished he could tell Betty how sorry he was.

Nancy empathized. "You made your mistake. You know it's over. You can't live with that." It was time to move ahead, she said. Appearing to do so reluctantly, Glen agreed to the trip.

When he returned, he told Nancy that he'd made it through the ordeal all right, that "the girl was nice," but that it had been "really cold on the ship."

In fact, Glen had spent the weekend with Debbie Shipp.

As 1988 began, Glen no doubt began to feel the world closing in on him, though. He began to seriously consider moving away from Wilkes-Barre. His dental business was virtually non-existent. He and Danielle were never going to return to 75 Birch. They were still living with his mother and sister on Magnolia Avenue. The homicide investigation had been quiet for so long, leading the Wolsieffer family to hope that nothing would come of it. But now the new D.A. was promising to make the Wolsieffer case his top priority, and they couldn't be so sure.

Exploring his employment alternatives, Glen met with an old friend and colleague from the Washington, D.C. area who needed help and said Glen would be welcome. Testing the waters, Glen began working part of his week in an office building in Arlington, Virginia, the other half still in Wilkes-Barre. While in Virginia, he slept at a friend's house. It wasn't the best of situations, but it netted him the most money and enabled him to still see Danielle.

If things worked out, Glen decided, he would move to Virginia permanently.

"I'd like to take everybody with me," Glen told Nancy one day. "My mother, my sister, you, Bryn, all of us."

Nancy, emotionally attached to Glen more than ever, contemplated moving with him. "I have nothing to keep me here," she said. Everyone gave her dirty looks, as though she was some kind of criminal. But then she would waver and decide she didn't want to leave. "That's how it evolved. We just talked like that occasionally. But plans were never made, or 'We're going on this day, or this year, or after Christmas.' It was nothing like that."

At times, Glen was just as ambivalent. He said he didn't feel right about picking up and leaving because he was the "root of everything."

"How could I leave my whole family in a state like this and take off?" he asked. When there were headlines and increased pressure, Glen would say, "I'm going. I'm not staying here." Then he would say, "I can't." One day he was going, the next day he wasn't. Nancy instructed him that he had to think of himself sometimes, too.

On the days that Glen felt that he was going, he often asked Nancy about her plans. "He would say, 'What do you think about going down?'" And Nancy would reply that maybe she would go back to school for her master's degree, and she could watch the kids while Glen worked.

It didn't matter to Nancy that the police and her friends had been telling her since Neil's death that they had seen Glen around town with each of his two girlfriends. She believed Glen when he said he was through with both of them. Furthermore, she had come to rely so much on Glen. "He was the only one that I felt comfortable with, that understood me," she said. "I was so desperate for some kind of a life that I thought, 'What do I have to lose? Here, there is such a war between the families, and everybody is talking about Neil and Glen and me; the best thing is to run away.'"

Nancy hadn't thought the matter through, however. She insisted that her relationship with Glen was purely platonic, regardless of the rumors throughout the valley. "We didn't become involved, and we didn't have plans to get married like people said we did," she said. "There was no way I was going to marry him."

So what did all this mean?

"I can't say I was in love with Glen because now I look at it and can see it for what it really was—dependency. But at the time, I told Glen I loved him. But I didn't love him like I would tell Neil I loved him. I couldn't be without him, but I knew what love was with Neil, and it wasn't the same feeling with Glen. It was a comfort. It was totally emotional," she said. "I didn't make a move without him, I didn't make one decision. I did nothing without consulting him—and I was so, so dependent on him. I couldn't imagine him going and leaving me."

Glen could envision such a scenario easily, however. His bi-state work schedule, with Sundays off in Virginia, left him time to maneuver his clandestine side trips to Delaware to visit Debbie. And, incredibly, during this same time frame Carol Kopicki began making weekend visits to see Glen in Virginia. She also began making plans to extricate herself from her marriage. Eventually, Glen stopped pushing Nancy about her plans. Having her around to watch over him all the time would certainly force him to alter his social life. And that was the one thing, most of all, that Glen Wolsieffer did not want to do.

That spring, Glen sold 75 Birch, coincidentally to one of Ferguson's partners. Since no charges had been filed against Glen, under Pennsylvania law he inherited Betty's share of the sale. Marian Tasker later said that Glen discarded what remained of her daughter's things without even asking if she wanted them.

There was no mortgage to pay off because Glen and Betty had purchased "joint spouse protection" on their accidental death mortgage insurance. Ciavarella pointed out to the insurance company that Betty Wolsieffer's assailant was unknown. Under the terms of the policy, the insurance company was obligated to pay the Franklin First Federal Savings and Loan Association the balance of the loan.

While Glen began renting a condominium in Falls Church, Virginia, Danielle spent the summer with her grandmother in Pennsylvania, but transferred in September 1988 to Saint James, a parochial school in Falls Church, Virginia.

Danielle didn't immediately accept her new surroundings. She experienced anxiety attacks, which often required her father to pick her up from school early. Clearly, she did not like after-school day care. She needed a home environment. Mary F. DeLaney, one of the teachers at Saint James, began taking Danielle home with her. This required an extra hour's commute for Glen each evening, but he did it happily, since Danielle began to calm down and excel in the classroom. She started attending Rainbows for Children, a support group for children of separated, divorced, or deceased parents. "Falls Church is my home now," Danielle told DeLaney that spring.

By moving to Virginia, Glen essentially prevented Betty's parents from seeing their granddaughter. Clearly, the child had become a pawn in the constant battling between the two families. As tensions continued to escalate, the Tasker family considered taking the matter to court. They never did, though, fearing such an action would have a worse effect on the child.

Whether she would have ultimately been welcome in Virginia or not, Nancy decided to stay put. "My common sense was in check, and I thought, 'You can't run from this. It's going to go with you wherever you go.' "

More important, Glen's lies finally began catching up with him.

One morning in early 1988, the simple matter of a piece of misdirected mail led Nancy to uncover a little lie, which uncovered a bigger lie, which uncovered a series of major lies stretching back to the morning of Betty's death. Before it was over, Nancy would conclude that Glen had murdered Betty.

When Glen and Nancy had moved out of their Birch Street houses back in 1986, he had had his mail forwarded to his mother's house, while Nancy had hers sent to her parents'. With transfers being called for from two Birch Street addresses bearing the same last name, it was not uncommon for Wolsieffer mail to be misdirected. It also followed that on several occasions, an envelope or two was opened mistakenly by the other Wolsieffer.

Nancy, of course, had resumed getting her mail at 84 Birch once she moved back. But she continued, from time to time, to get a piece or two of Glen's mail. On the morning in question, when Nancy sat down to pay her bills and balance her checkbook, she opened a bank statement and began reading. Her eyes zoomed to the listing of an ATM withdrawal from a MAC (Money Access Center) machine in Delaware. She knew the entry had to be a mistake. She had never been in Delaware in her life, save for maybe driving through it. The only thing she could come up with about Delaware was that Debbie Shipp had moved there.

But Glen had assured her he was done with Debbie.

Nancy's eyes scanned the top of the page, where she noticed the statement was addressed to Glen, not her. This was Glen's withdrawal in Delaware.

She confronted her brother-in-law. "Are you still seeing Debbie?"

"*Debbie?* No. *Gawd*, no," said Glen with a piercing stare that disconcerted Nancy.

"Oh," she said, withholding her discovery for the time being. "I thought you were—I heard you were."

"You know, people are out to get me. They are just saying all kinds of things about me," Glen replied. He assured Nancy that Debbie was ancient history.

Neil's widow retrieved the bank statement and showed it to Glen. He denied it. He looked at the document and denied it again. "I was never there," he assured her.

"I don't believe you," Nancy said. "If you're lying to me about this, what else are you not telling me?"

"Maybe she took my card out of my wallet."

"Yeah, right," said Nancy.

Pressing him hard, one of the few times she ever did, Nancy wondered aloud if Glen had been somehow involved in Betty's murder.

"How could you think that about me?" Glen replied.

Quickly, Nancy apologized. How *could* she think that?

As Glen started to cry, Nancy felt terrible. Still a pushover, she felt sorry for Glen. She comforted him.

The bank statement stuck in Nancy's mind, though. She grew increasingly incensed about Glen's explanation, as well as his casual indifference to having been confronted. Several days later, with the statement in hand, she again cornered Glen and accused him of lying.

"I'm not lying," Glen insisted.

"I don't believe you," said Nancy. "Why would that appear on a bank statement like that?"

As he had done the first time, Glen suggested Debbie might have taken his card without his knowledge.

Nancy was incredulous

And then it came out. Just like that, Glen relented. "I was down there."

Although Nancy had physically shown Glen the bank statement, he obviously hadn't focused on the date of the ATM withdrawal. And when Nancy demanded, "When were you there?" Glen cited a different date.

"Well, I did go down a weekend in January. That's the only time I was there. And I only went down to tell Debbie, you know, that we had to end things."

The bank statement indicated the withdrawal had been made on a Monday in February. Nancy seized on the discrepancy. She handed him the statement, suggesting he take a good look at it. "Well, what about this?"

"Oh," Glen replied. "I guess I was there then, too."

"That means you were there all along!"

"Yeah," said Glen, breaking into tears. "I was."

Nancy felt a great deal of embarrassment over her failure to see through Glen sooner. She had been so blind. "See, I didn't know that Glen was like two different people. The Glen I knew before, when he was married to Betty, I didn't know he was capable of lying left and right. And all of a sudden, when I caught him in little lies here and there, then you look at the whole picture. If he could look me straight in the face and lie about a stupid bank statement that doesn't really mean anything, what else is he lying about?

"It was like bombs dropping," she observed. "I realized that he *was* a liar. It was so deep, it was scary. Like, 'What is he made out of? How could he be this good at what he's doing? How could he fake me out like this?' " She especially remembered his lancing look. "He could just penetrate you with his eyes and tell you, 'I'm telling you the truth.' "

Nancy thought back to the weekend in 1987 when Glen had said he was going on the cruise with his friend from Virginia. "I don't believe that you were ever on a cruise with someone, that they wanted you to meet this new friend."

Cornered, Glen admitted that he had been with Debbie that weekend as well.

Nancy began to recall dozens of incidents involving Glen— statements that made sense at the time but now deserved a second look. Things she had overlooked, or given Glen the benefit of the doubt on, or accepted his improbable explanations for, or simply not questioned him over the first time around. She realized Glen had been lying all along. "What a con man he was, how easy it was for him to lie, and how convincing he was when he lied, and how he could cry, cry—like sob crying—and it didn't mean a thing."

She tried to recall the occasions when Glen cried in front of her. She vividly recalled the day, while Neil was in the hospital following his collapse, that Glen came to her house to visit. Nancy had been sitting in the living room, folding the laundry, thinking about her husband lying in a hospital bed. Glen took a seat and proclaimed: "No one understands what I'm going through. I feel so lost without Betty." Then, as Nancy recalled, "He cried and cried."

She consoled him. "I felt so bad. I thought, 'How could anybody go through this, losing a spouse? Like I would die if it ever happened to me.' "

Now, remembering that day, she recalled what the police had told her all along about Glen's uninterrupted involvement with Debbie during that exact same time period. Nancy felt so empty that she had not believed the investigators. "Those are the instances that were so profound to me, where he could cry to me, because he knew I was giving him the sympathy, but really, he walked out the door and probably went to her house."

For the first time, Nancy began to see Glen for "how he really was"—a calculated charlatan and a cunning user. There was only one conclusion she could reach from all of this: Glen not only had murdered Betty, he had been responsible for Neil's death as well. "He killed him, and I don't see how you could get around that," she said.

Nancy felt even worse that she had caught Glen so many times, only to get suckered in by his baloney explanations, especially concerning Debbie or Carol. "People would see him and they'd say, 'God, I didn't know Glen was still seeing Carol,' " Nancy recalled. " 'Well,' I said, 'he's not.' 'But I saw them driving down the street in the car.' And then I would ask him, 'Now, I said I would support you, but now you're making a fool out of this whole family by still doing what you were doing before.'

"Every time I went in for questioning, the police told me he was still seeing these women and I was defending him. Not only about that, I was defending him about everything," said Nancy. "He was making a fool out of me because I really believed he was innocent and I believed that he was getting such a raw deal."

Looking back over their relationship since Betty and Neil died, Nancy realized that "everything he did, I gave him the benefit of the doubt."

Nancy started to compile a list. First, she recalled how Glen's moaning that fateful morning had prevented Neil from going upstairs. She remembered that Neil also had been bothered by Glen's asking for a glass of water instead of about his wife and child.

She also recalled that Glen had repeatedly failed to remember that she had been in 75 Birch the morning of the murder to get Danielle. "Oh, you were there?" Glen would often say in supposed surprise after Nancy would recall details of, for example, the paramedics treating him on the floor. She would then tell him that she had already told him many times that she had been in the house that morning.

Now she realized she had been hoodwinked on that score as well. "It wasn't that he didn't remember that I said I was there, he was playing dumb."

His pretended vagueness hit other sensitive areas as well, such as his supposed unawareness of precisely where Betty had died. Nancy had cleaned up the house after it was released by the police. In the process, she had ripped the tape off the floor where the police had marked the location of Betty's body. In trying to help Glen visualize what had happened, Nancy pointed it out one day: "Here is where she was."

"How do you know where she was?" Glen wanted to know.

She hated to explain, but she told him that she was the one who had removed the police tape from the floor.

"I thought she died in bed. I didn't know that she died on the floor," Glen said.

More than a year later, when Glen decided to move to Virginia, he told Nancy he didn't want to keep the bedroom set and planned to sell it.

Nancy objected, reminding Glen that the furniture had been a wedding present from Betty's parents.

"Betty died in that bed," he claimed.

"No, she didn't," answered Nancy.

"Oh, I thought she did," Glen added.

Again, Nancy had to show him where Betty's body had been found.

That in turn led Nancy to recall the time at Betty's grave when Glen had claimed not to know the extent of the injuries to her face. Nancy remembered how surprised, and then broken up, Glen acted when she told him. But he had looked in the casket just as she had before the funeral. And the newspapers had been writing all along that Betty had been beaten. "So how could he not have known?" she wondered.

This reflection prompted another doubt that had nagged her: Glen's lack of curiosity about the events the night Betty died. "I was always wracking my brain trying to think of what happened in the house, like why would the intruder go in that bedroom, and go up on the roof at dawn, things like that." But when she had asked Glen, he had simply replied: "I don't know."

"Everything was 'I don't know,' " said Nancy.

Nancy herself had been witness to Glen's odd disappearances. Many times he simply was not where he said he would be. "He would say that he was going to play golf or something, and I would always find out from someone that that was not where he was." This pattern was obviously similar to the one that Glen had practiced on Betty for so long. Like Betty, Nancy had bought Glen's explanations whenever he got caught.

For example, the day after Glen had taken his daughter to an Alabama concert, Danielle told Nancy: "Debbie must be Daddy's girlfriend because he kissed her on the lips and she got her hair done."

"*Debbie?*" asked Nancy.

"Yeah, we went to the concert with her."

Looking back, Nancy remembered how she had accepted Glen's explanation that he hadn't gone to the concert with Debbie, that she had actually attended with a receptionist from the office. He had said he was going with Danielle, and he had. "Omission isn't the same thing as a lie," he had explained back then, "I just left some parts out."

As Nancy reviewed her relationship with Glen, she recognized that he possessed an ability to instantaneously feign drastic mood changes. First, there was the day he was released from the hospital, when he turned back in her driveway to get his neck collar before taking a ride to Richard Miscavage's cabin. Then she had felt sympathy for him; now she believed he had been faking and had remembered to get the brace to supplement his public image as wounded victim. "It struck me at the time, but I rationalized it away."

Then there was the afternoon he had been working on the upstairs part of the addition at 84 Birch when Nancy came home from school and heard him whistling. "I yelled up, 'I'm home.' When I went up, he had a hammer in his hand, and he was crying. I know he was whistling before that, and that really bothered me. I thought, 'Are you crying for my benefit?' "

But the crying, as always, softened her, and so she comforted Glen. "Look at how hard you're working," she told him. "You don't have to do this. This is too painful for you."

Glen looked up and said, "But Neil would want me to do this." He cried some more, and Nancy comforted him some more.

As she recalled that day, bitterness crept into her voice. "That happened too many times for me. When I think about it, you can't imagine the betrayal in that."

CHAPTER 25

Even though she was now convinced of Glen's guilt, Nancy still had difficulty separating from him. "It was like somebody else had died. The feeling was like another loss: 'This is all true—what everyone has said all along is true.' That was very hard to accept."

During the spring of 1988, as Glen made the full-time move to Virginia, Nancy's thoughts coalesced. She decided she would be better off without Glen in her life at all. "I wanted to spill my guts," she said, to tell Glen everything she thought about him, to confront him about Betty's murder. But she thought better of it. When he came to visit her on Father's Day, she simply told him: "I can't support you at all anymore. I need you out of my life. I need to get on with my life. Do not call. I don't want any contact with you."

"I understand. I'm sorry about everything that happened," Glen said without elaboration.

The two of them sat in silence. "It was the end of the road. There was nothing more to say," said Nancy. "He knew how betrayed I felt. He knew that I knew what he was all about."

Without another word, Glen got up, departed his brother's house, got into his car, and drove off to Virginia. "I think he was relieved. It was one less ball to juggle," said Nancy. "It was empty for me. I was totally drained. I had nothing in me."

In time, Nancy's split from Glen would have official consequences as well. Taking office in January 1988, Correale Stevens, the new D.A., moved into action. Never one to be accused of being shy, the new D.A. held a "get-acquainted" session with the Tasker family, then met with reporters, reviewed the case with police investigators, then held a news conference "to let the people of Luzerne County know the status of the case." Stevens said he wanted "to see justice triumph," but observed that there was a lot of "fact-finding" to be done. He said he didn't want to raise false hopes of a quick arrest, but emphasized that his administration was committed to a "full-scale effort."

With Chief Coyne at his side, the new D.A. announced a "new strategy" in their efforts—only he wouldn't say what it was. He acknowledged that there were "some legal problems" with the case, which he described as "an open investigation full of unanswered questions." Stevens hadn't solved the murder, but he wanted everyone to know he was on the case. He was quickly starting to sound like the man he had run out of office.

At least Stevens knew his limitations. He decided to have others more qualified do the courtroom work but still take the credit himself. And so Stevens reached out for help.

His "new strategy" was to consider asking state Attorney General LeRoy S. Zimmerman to submit Betty's murder to a special statewide investigative grand jury; Luzerne County did not use a local grand jury system. Not until May of that year, however, did the D.A. formally make his request, and only after several unsuccessful meetings in Harrisburg, the state capital, with reluctant officials, who did not believe that the Wolsieffer case qualified under the narrow requirements for intervention by the attorney general's office.

"It is my specific request that we need to utilize the investigative resources of the multi-county grand jury in this particular matter, and my office lacks such necessary investigative resources," Stevens wrote. He said the special grand jury was needed because it had the power to compel testimony from witnesses such as "police, relatives, medical technicians, and other individuals who may have knowledge of the death of Betty Wolsieffer." Stevens also asserted that the panel would have the power "to require the production of documents, records, and other evidence, including but not limited to, possible medical reports, bank statements, etc."

While there might have been questions about Stevens's abilities in a courtroom, he certainly wasn't a neophyte concerning the politics of the situation: "Moreover, I request that my administration remain in control of and in charge of the prosecution, unless you prefer otherwise." Stevens said he wanted the case submitted to the grand jury by that November.

But officials at the state capital balked at the legality of Stevens's approach, and so the statewide grand jury was not used. Instead, at the request of Wilkes-Barre Police Chief Joseph Coyne, the Pennsylvania State Police formally joined the two-year-old Wolsieffer homicide investigation that October. Two experienced veterans, Troopers Carl M. Allen and Stanley J. Jezewski, were assigned as the main investigators to assist Wilkes-Barre police and the Luzerne County District Attorney's Office.

There was more than six decades of law enforcement experience between the two state policemen. Considered to be the best homicide investigators in the Wyoming Valley and beyond, Allen and Jezewski were almost always assigned the toughest cases. They worked well together. They were tough, too. Years ago, Jezewksi had sustained five bullet wounds during a run-in with an accused murderer.

Since Wilkes-Barre authorities were cut off from so many potentially important witnesses because of the bitter accusations of unfairness and underhanded tactics, Jezewski and Allen were told to reinterview key witnesses and help assemble the case for possible prosecution. Accordingly, the two troopers spent several days reviewing the Wolsieffer file. It took more than eight hours just to read the several hundred pages of police reports already compiled.

For their first interview, Allen and Jezewski chose Nancy Wolsieffer. As soon as they entered her home, Nancy could tell that the troopers were different—kind, respectful, and compassionate. "Just air your bitches. Get out everything that's wrong," Nancy was instructed. And so, with her neighbor-attorney Richard

Ferguson at her side, Nancy talked both about the inquest and a wide range of earlier incidents involving police treatment of Neil.

Nancy said she and Neil had talked about the murder many times during the seven weeks before his death, especially about how Neil was "in a terrible position," contrasted with Glen having hired an attorney. Showing a new boldness to speak out, Nancy told the troopers she was certain that Glen had not told Neil he had killed Betty, because Neil had subsequently wondered why Glen had asked for a glass of water while moaning on the floor instead of asking about Betty and Danielle.

Allen and Jezewski sensed they were onto something important. "Without asking you point-blank, has your opinion about Glen changed over the years?"

"Yes," Nancy replied without elaborating. She insisted she didn't have any concrete evidence, but she still provided a wealth of information and gave the troopers a psychological boost. Most of what Nancy told them confirmed information previously gathered, but she did point out that Glen had told her he had money for his income taxes and $400 cash in an envelope for the trip to upstate New York, and that it was in the desk in the rear bedroom, about $900 total. She said he told her several times that the money had been stolen by the intruder or was in the possession of the police. He also said that he had deposited checks in the bank, but never told her that he had accounted for all the money supposedly missing after the murder.

This was important information because, in fact, Detective Mitchell's seizure of the family checkbook on the Saturday of the murder had led him to discover that Glen had made two deposits in the week before Betty's murder, challenging his claim that $1,300 had been stolen. The deposit tickets indicated that on the Friday before the murder, Glen deposited $409.25, and on the day of the murder, at 9:01 A.M., he deposited $947.95, for a total of $1,357.20.

Trooper Allen asked Nancy what Glen told her when she questioned him about the small details of his statements to police. Nancy then gave the troopers the version of the story that she had heard from Glen. Again, it was fairly consistent with his other statements, with one new twist. Now Glen believed that the in-

truder was someone he and Betty knew. Nancy said that to many
other of her questions, Glen had simply answered, "I don't know."

The troopers didn't press much more. They departed on good
terms and headed for the Tasker home.

Marian Tasker told the investigators that Glen had "a short
fuse," and that Betty had to make all the decisions because Glen
was unable to. She said Betty had wanted more children but Glen
did not. Betty's mother also said that Betty had told her she had
found three or four letters that Debbie Shipp had written to Glen,
and that her daughter had said she was keeping them "in case
anything ever happens."

She said Betty never told them that Glen hit her. "But she
wouldn't tell us if he did," she added. She did recall one occasion
when Betty had a mysterious lump on her back, and another time
when she cut her leg and Glen stitched the wound up.

The next day, Allen and Jezewski headed for Phyllis Wolsieffer's house, where they interviewed Glen's mother and his aunt,
Mary Stinson. They also interviewed Lisa at her office. Desperate
to find someone who would help, the Wolsieffer women had
agreed to cooperate as long as Detective Mitchell wasn't part of
the interview team. Lisa said the troopers told her they were working on "all these leads, and looking at other people." She said she
cooperated because she believed them.

Aunt Mary told the troopers that when she and other family
members were denied the opportunity to visit with Glen early the
Saturday afternoon after the murder, she parked herself in a chair
outside his room. She then alleged that when D.A. Bernard Podcasy came to Glen's room, about 2:00 P.M., a detective came up
and announced: "We got our man." She said she then advised the
others to get Glen a lawyer. "I don't think they looked for anyone
else after that."

Lisa and her aunt both mentioned that Glen had treated patients
from Clear Brook, a drug and alcohol rehabilitation facility.
Though neither woman knew of any serious problems Glen had
encountered with those patients, they suggested his contact with
the facility was an investigative lead worth pursuing. Maybe someone had broken into 75 Birch looking for drugs.

Lisa also offered the theory that Betty had followed Glen

downstairs, saw the intruder—"possibly recognizing him"—ran back upstairs, and was chased by the intruder, who engaged Betty in a terrible fight that left her dead.

Perhaps most revealing about the Wolsieffer family comments was Phyllis's admission that the son she had supported so unceasingly "never went into details about the incident with me."

And so it went.

Frank D. Lisnow, Clear Brook's executive director, confirmed that Glen had treated patients from the rehabilitation center since 1984. He added, however, that he was sure, "with a level of certainty, that no significant complaints were received concerning his services."

Allen and Mitchell talked to Deputy Coroner Bill Lisman, who told them Glen did not respond as he would have expected when he informed Glen that Betty was dead, and during two subsequent chats that Saturday—the second to talk about funeral arrangements, the final one when the family decided to switch funeral directors. "Glen's reaction was just not a normal reaction," said Lisman, a funeral director for over twelve years. "He never asked me any questions, and he never asked about his child."

Jule Cook, who lived next door at 77 Birch, now told the investigators that she had seen Glen use the beat-up red wooden ladder "many times, a lot, three times or more," to get in that same back bedroom window "when he had been locked out of the house."

To start their second week of interviews, Allen and Jezewski traveled to Newark, Delaware, to talk to Debbie Shipp. She too said Glen had treated people from Clear Brook, and, like the others, recalled that none had ever caused any trouble. She said she had last seen Glen less than two weeks before, on October 23, when he came to her apartment in Delaware for dinner. Debbie also said she was aware of the anonymous calls Nancy and Betty had received when their husbands were not home, and had been told Nancy received such calls even after Betty's murder, which was true. But Nancy had dismissed them as cranks. Also, the calls had come in early evening, not after midnight as the ones before Betty's murder.

Debbie continued that she herself had gotten an anonymous call from a man on the Thursday before Betty's death, and two on the day of the slaying. Debbie told the investigators that the calls stopped after Betty's murder, but she did not think they were in any way related. Jezewski asked Debbie if she had any other boyfriends who might have been jealous. No, Debbie said, she hadn't seen any other man for several years. The phone calls were a puzzling mystery, then. Had Glen been making all those calls?

Perhaps Betty's girlfriends' memories were improving with time, because in a reinterview with Eileen Pollock, she stated that right before her death Betty told her things were going "very badly again." She alleged as well that Betty told her that Glen had punched a hole in his office wall in anger. Another friend, Miriam Cannon, said she saw Betty with a black eye once, but Betty insisted she got it when she bumped into something.

In their quest to determine how—or, more to the point, whether—an intruder could have entered the Wolsieffer home through the upstairs window, Allen accompanied Detective Sworen, Assistant D.A. Richard Hughes, and Mitchell to 75 Birch, where they reenacted poking a hole in a new screen they had purchased. The hole looked the same as the one in the screen removed from the crime scene. The test proved nothing. But the visit to the murder scene was not a total loss. Noting that the kitchen floor was covered by linoleum, and assuming that an intruder would have worn sneakers, the investigators noted that it would have been impossible for anyone to have snuck up behind Glen from the basement door in the kitchen without making noises.

In their quest to refine the time of death, the state troopers and others met with Dr. Robert Catherman, a former chief medical examiner for the city of Philadelphia. The respected pathologist reviewed the pertinent records and stated that he believed Betty Wolsieffer had been dead four to six hours before Dr. Hudock had examined her at 10:30 A.M. the morning her body was discovered. He said he believed the time of death would have been closer to the six-hour end of that range, meaning about 4:30 A.M.

After further review of the documents, Dr. Hudock said he agreed with Dr. Catherman's assessment. These expert opinions were problematic for a potential prosecution, however. Had Glen and Betty argued for two hours or so after the bars closed? The time of death needed to be pushed back, not forward.

Finally, in their quest to dispel allegations by the Wolsieffer family that the Birch Street area had been a hotbed of break-ins in the months preceding Betty's murder, the investigators conducted a comprehensive review of police reports concerning burglaries and attempted burglaries for all of 1986 in the general area. On Birch Street, there had been six burglaries or attempts, one threatening phone call, and one theft of bicycles from a garage. Not one of the burglaries could be considered to be consistent in modus operandi with the circumstances of Betty's murder. In most of the cases, no one had been home at the time of the break-in or attempt. No one had been attacked or severely injured. Still, there were a couple of interesting reports that a creative defense attorney might try to use: in one case, a hole was found in the screen door at the rear of the home at 55 Birch at 7:00 A.M. on July 4. In the other case, which took place three months before Betty's murder, Linda Escarge of 45 Birch told police that when she had heard a noise in her backyard, around 10:40 P.M., she turned on her back-porch light and saw a man carrying a fourteen-foot wooden ladder in her yard. Her fourteen-year-old son, James, said that when the man, blond and clad in blue jeans, saw him looking out the window, he dropped the ladder and ran behind the garage.

Although the renewed investigation raised hopes on all sides, the breach in the relationship between Nancy and Glen spilled over to Glen's sister and mother. Nancy found that very sticky, given that she still wanted Bryn to have as fulfilling a relationship as possible with her grandmother. In time, the most noticeable separation occurred between Lisa, Glen's unflinching supporter, and Nancy. When asked about the severed relations, Lisa admitted the strain, but claimed not to know why. "I just don't ask. As long as I see Bryn, and when I see Nancy everything is civil, that's fine."

Lisa also grew more uncomfortable with Glen's continuing liaisons with Debbie and Carol. She wanted him to drop both of them. "I kept telling him, 'Everything you do, you can't breathe without being watched, so just think. It doesn't matter to me, but think about it.'

"At that point he was just pathetic. I felt so sorry for him that I could look at him and tell he thinks no one else will ever want anything to do with him, so if he has one of these two that will stick with him then that's what he is going to stick to. He is not somebody that could be by himself."

Although there were suspicions in official circles that the relationship had never stopped, Carol Kopicki began admitting to close friends in August 1988 that she had resumed relations with Glen. In September, Carol's husband filed for divorce, and she began making plans to move to Virginia as soon as the decree was issued. It was clear Carol did not know what she was getting into.

One day at the Odyssey health club, Carol suggested to Nancy, who also belonged, that she and Glen should write a book about their experiences.

"I don't think Glen and I see things from the same perspective," said Nancy.

"Like what?" asked Carol.

"Like he's still seeing Debbie. He's a liar." Carol went off to call Glen in Virginia.

Throughout that summer and fall, Glen continued to see Debbie Shipp in Delaware, but their encounters were drastically reduced. After her conversation with Nancy, Carol really put the squeeze on Glen, demanding exclusivity. But he still managed to sneak away here and there to see Debbie.

With the murder investigation revived full-steam, even Glen must have realized he had to whittle down the field. Debbie had told him of the visit from Troopers Allen and Jezewski, and soon thereafter, Glen invited Debbie to Virginia so they could have a heart-to-heart chat.

"We can't see each other anymore," Glen explained.

"Why not?" asked Debbie.

"Because they're saying you're the motive for everything that's been going on."

As always, Debbie understood.

Of course, Glen made no mention of the fact that his relationship with Carol was continuing to grow, or that she was in the process of getting a divorce, or that she now had definite plans to move in with him in Virginia.

When Phyllis Wolsieffer learned of Carol's intentions, she decided she could no longer remain silent about her son's love interests. She was under a psychologist's care already, trying to cope with the losses of Betty and Neil, plus the withdrawal from Danielle after caring for her for two years. She wouldn't have minded if Glen had developed a lasting relationship with Nancy. But clearly that wasn't going to happen. Instead, her son was going to live in sin with Carol.

Phyllis was outraged. "Carol pushed her way in—pushed and pushed—that's all she did, and I didn't approve of it." In the middle of the Christmas season, she summoned Carol to her house. "I came right out and told her. Well, she ended up crying, and I was crying. I said to her, 'I don't know how you could push your way in there with him like you did, knowing all that he has against him.' I mean it was obvious to me that they weren't going to let this thing go, and she never said she loved him to me or anything. But she was bound and determined to be with him."

Phyllis said she most objected on moral grounds, and didn't want Danielle exposed to such living arrangements. She said she told her son repeatedly how she felt, "but who am I?"

Nancy and Glen had a confrontation of sorts that Christmas season as well, starting with an emotional telephone conversation. Phyllis had come over to Nancy's house and started crying her heart out. Nancy became angry at always being stuck in the middle, so she picked up the phone and called Virginia. "You're gone, and I still have to live with this every minute of every day. You are removed, and I have your mother here."

For the first time, Nancy directly implicated Glen in her husband's death. "Neil's dead because of you," she said. "I blame you for Neil's death completely."

Nancy said Glen cried profusely at that point. "I guess I know how you feel about everything else," said Glen, meaning Betty.

Nancy had been advised not to back Glen into a corner, so she left the conversation at that. "How do you think I feel about things?" Glen protested. "If only I had called the police instead of Neil, he would still be here."

No longer impressed with his pitiful explanations, Nancy told Glen that when he came up to Wilkes-Barre for Christmas to come over and clear out the sporting equipment and other things he had stored in her basement.

Several days later, when Glen came to get his belongings, he walked in as if nothing had happened and announced, "I love your wallpaper. Everything looks so good."

Nancy was stunned. Her harsh accusation about Neil's death was certainly still fresh in her mind. Staring at Glen, she thought to herself: " 'Don't you remember what happened just three days ago on the phone?' But that's what he was like. He would cry here, walk out the door, see some guy, and talk about the weather or golf."

Nancy came to question altogether Glen's motivation for completing the construction work on her house and offering to help her financially. "All of that was not sincere at all," she concluded. "This sounds funny to say, but I don't think I could have gotten through it without him. When I look back on it, though, I just wish he had left me alone. I don't believe that any of it was real. I don't know what makes him tick, but I wondered if he felt guilty because he knew he caused Neil's death so, 'Do I owe her this? Do I owe her to help her finish her house?' "

Worst of all, however, was the peculiar stare that Glen had given her the first time he professed his innocence about the Delaware bank statement. Now she was able to decipher that look. She had seen it on his face on many other occasions since Betty's murder. It was the gaze of a liar, scared that he had been caught with his pants down.

Of all the times Nancy had seen the stare, the most frightening was the day she had prodded him: "Just tell me you had nothing to do with Betty's murder." Glen had looked up at her, "and that same look came on his face."

"I said to Glen one time, 'You're no different than the police; you have betrayed me as much as them—only you are family, and I would never have expected it from you.' " Nancy viewed Glen's familial betrayal as treason of the worst kind. She had put her "ultimate trust" in Glen, only to conclude "that he let Neil die, that he buried himself in so deep into his web of lies that he cost somebody else's life. That to me is as tragic and as criminal as strangling Betty. There's no doubt in my mind that he loved his brother. I mean, okay, maybe he didn't love Betty—and I don't even know if that's true, but maybe he didn't. But he did love

Neil. He's that self-centered, though: 'I have to survive at all costs and I am not going down, and anybody else around me is going down, but I'm not. And that's it.' I still agonize over that to this day. How could he let his brother die?"

CHAPTER 26

IN HIS WORDS

After Betty was killed, I was up in Delaware one time and Debbie and I were walking through a mall, and she started looking in jewelry store windows. She said, "Let's look at them." I kind of played along. I said, "Yeah, that's nice." And I'm thinking, "This is great." I think we even got one of the guy's cards, you know, to call him. But, of course, I never called the guy back. She figured I was free, so why not push a little bit? I didn't budge.

She was really a quiet person. Carol and I have laughs and we're very compatible, whereas Debbie and I—obviously we were physically attracted to each other—but before or after that, the conversation was, you know, about work or just small talk. She was very professional.

Carol didn't know I was still seeing Debbie. She just assumed that I wasn't. I think Nancy told her. Nancy and I were talking—we were close—and she found a receipt from somewhere in Delaware.

It was a cash card or a cash receipt. It was some weekend that I was up seeing Debbie. Nancy knew I was seeing Carol, so she was telling Carol, "Hey, you know, Glen is still seeing Debbie." And Carol hit the roof, she called down here and called me everything in the book.

I said, "Hi, honey. How are you doing?" "Don't call me honey," she said. "You are the biggest prick that ever lived. I just got done talking to Nancy and she told me you are still seeing Debbie. How can you be doing that to me?"

She said, "If you are going to get serious about me, dump Debbie." So that's when I started the process of dumping Debbie. Because I knew Carol was going to leave her husband and I wanted to be with her. I guess that was when I knew Carol was really serious about me. The following February, Carol and I got engaged down in St. Croix.

Debbie never wanted to talk about Betty or what happened that night. The only thing she ever did say to me is that she was really sorry about what happened to Neil. That was the most she talked about anything. She wrote me a letter and told me that she was in counseling and all that. I never told Carol that I got that letter. I didn't think it was anything that was going to make her too happy either. Debbie sent it to the office. The cops were around questioning again and they had told her that I was engaged.

Basically it said, you know, thanks to me she's in counseling and she wishes that she didn't hate me because that means that she still has some kind of feelings toward me, and that someday she is going to get over me altogether and then she won't hate or care or, you know, at that point she'd be able to focus on her own life, that kind of thing. And she said that she could hurt me, you know, during a trial if I was ever arrested. She said she doesn't want to do it because of Danielle, but she doesn't care if she hurts me. I guess that's her way to screw me over.

PART THREE

SARCIONE

Correale Stevens had boxed himself into a corner by having promised to solve Betty's murder. The man who ran Bernie Podcasy out of the district attorney's office for failing to bring the killer to justice had failed to produce for twelve months now. "We're getting closer and closer to an arrest," Stevens said. "But it's not going to be in the next two weeks or two months."

Stevens's much-publicized request to the state attorney general for a special grand jury quietly disappeared. In fact, Zimmerman had rejected Stevens's application and was now out of office. There were other problems building in Stevens's office as well. There were complaints of disorganization and botched prosecutions. Stevens wasn't spending any time in the courtroom.

But he had a plan. He was a longtime friend of the new Pennsylvania attorney general, Ernest D. Preate, Jr. They had talked informally even before Preate's election. Stevens asked Preate to authorize use of his office's manpower to assist in the ongoing investigation and, he hoped, an eventual trial.

In mid-April of 1989, Stevens and the investigators traveled to Harrisburg for a meeting with the attorney general. The next day, the officials held a news conference at police headquarters in Wilkes-Barre to announce the formation of a new task force. Preate said he agreed with Stevens's request that his office be a part of the investigation. Much was made of the fact that city and state police, as well as the Luzerne County D.A.'s office, would participate in this latest law-enforcement effort. State police officials pledged that department's "full resources."

So what was new? Essentially, the appointment of a chief prosecutor. Preate disclosed that he had assigned the director of his criminal-law division, Executive Deputy Attorney General Anthony Sarcione, thirty-five, to personally serve as his representative on the team. Sarcione, a veteran lawyer with an excellent courtroom presence, was designated the task force's coordinator. If the expanded investigation resulted in the filing of criminal charges, the case would be prosecuted by Sarcione and Luzerne County Assistant District Attorney William Keller, another first-rate prosecutor with experience in more than one hundred criminal trials, including guilty verdicts in several high-profile first-degree murder cases.

Keller agreed to be a member of the team provided he didn't end up being Sarcione's waterboy. Keller had been a private attorney and part-time assistant D.A. for years, leaving in 1982 when he was passed over for the vacant D.A.'s job. He had rejoined the staff in 1988 as a senior trial attorney. There was only one concession to be made: Sarcione wanted to present the closing arguments if, and when, there was a trial. Astute enough to appreciate the politics of the situation, Keller agreed.

To get around the major legal hurdle that had hindered Preate's predecessor, that of satisfying the narrow provisions required for state intervention, Sarcione was sworn in as a special Luzerne County assistant D.A. without pay—solely for the Wolsieffer case. Technically, then, Sarcione would be working for Stevens.

When confronted, Stevens snarled at reporters whose questions insinuated that the help from Harrisburg was designed to take the heat off his failure to solve the case. Stevens contended that the key issue was teamwork and cooperation. "We have hundreds and hundreds of cases," he said. "But from time to time, there is a case that requires assistance from the attorney general's office. . . . This is an unusual case. We need the extra resources."

Stevens, the master politician, had done it again. Now he was in a position where, if matters went poorly down the road, he could point a finger at the attorney general's office. If things went well, he could take some of the credit. The most important gain for Stevens, though, was that he no longer had to worry about being cornered into prosecuting the case himself.

Tony Sarcione, just under six feet tall but only one hundred fifty pounds, wasn't the kind of guy to worry over being cornered about anything. He was a tenacious, dedicated professional with an inexhaustible supply of energy and ideas. In the courtroom, he was hyper, always pacing, gesturing with his arms, swatting away with his hands the preposterous claims of a defendant. During particularly strong lines of questioning, he was known for his powerful gaze, the look of a wild animal hunting down his prey. Aggressive and obsessed with case preparation, he was determined to bring Glen Wolsieffer to justice. "To me, here was a guy who committed murder and was laughing at the authorities," he said while explaining why he volunteered to take the case. Luzerne County was fortunate that Preate had gone along with Stevens's plan.

Sarcione grew up outside of Philadelphia, in Penn Winne and Villanova, with an older brother and a younger sister. He had attended a Jesuit boys school and a strict Roman Catholic high school. His father, Alexander—a graduate of West Point—had worked as an attorney with the Pennsylvania State Department of Transportation for nearly twenty-five years, holding the rank of deputy state attorney general.

Taut and athletic, with a penchant for jogging, and surfing near the family's duplex in Ocean City, New Jersey, the younger Sarcione graduated with a political science degree from Glen Wolsieffer's alma mater, the University of Scranton, in 1975, the same year as Glen. He then joined his brother, Alexander Junior, at the University of Delaware Law School.

After law school, Sarcione served as first assistant district attorney in Chester County before joining Preate's staff just two months before the formation of the Wolsieffer task force. In his ten years with the Chester County D.A.'s office, Sarcione personally handled more than a thousand criminal prosecutions, including murder cases.

It was in law school that Sarcione focused on what he wanted to do for the rest of his life—put criminals behind bars. In March 1976, Tony's brother was murdered during an armed robbery at a gasoline station where he worked nights to support his wife and two-year-old daughter.

Tony and his brother had been best pals. Alexander had taught him football, basketball, and surfing. He had been his big protector. Tony couldn't believe the news; he put his fist through a drywall.

After a friend drove him from school to his parents' house— passing the crime scene along the way—Tony went to the morgue to identify his brother's bullet-riddled body. To this day, he thinks of his brother whenever a coroner takes the witness stand and starts describing the condition of the deceased.

Four suspects were picked up the night of the shooting, but the investigating authorities felt they did not have enough to make any charges stick, so the men were released. "Since then, the case has languished, just like the Wolsieffer case," said Sarcione, his Philadelphia accent still intact. "If someone would put in the effort, it would be solved." He said he believed that his brother's murder was never solved because the overworked D.A.'s staff was unable to commit the time and resources needed to crack the complicated case. What an irony: here was Tony Sarcione years later being assigned to help local authorities in Wilkes-Barre for the same reason.

And so, he was a man on a mission, hell-bent on being Betty's avenger, so that her parents and brother could sleep a little easier knowing that her killer had been given his due.

To Sarcione, as always, there would be satisfaction in being "the last voice for the dead person." He knew too well the anguish that a mother and father feel over the loss of a child through such violent means. He could appreciate how Betty's family felt during holidays, knowing that more than a decade after his brother's murder his mother still cried terribly whenever the family gathered to mark a special occasion. He had a motivation that was unique, and it would serve him well.

Sarcione dug into his new assignment with vigor and tenacity.

He retraced every step of the investigation. He took a tour of 75 Birch. Like Allen and Jezewski, he quickly became convinced that part of the problem was organization. This case needed someone to assemble the evidence and package it into a viable prosecution.

"It was an organizational nightmare in the beginning. I looked around and said, 'What did I get myself into?' After the news conference, I went up there and started looking at the material. I didn't realize how many reports there were and how much evidence had been gathered. But as I started reading and reading, I became more convinced of his guilt."

Sarcione made a list of people who needed to be talked to again, and during the ensuing months he met for marathon sessions with investigators. He kept access to new developments under closer watch, which resulted in fewer leaks. Virtually every witness was reinterviewed, and he personally participated in the most crucial ones. With his relentless pursuit, Sarcione gained the respect of the locals as one of the hardest workers they had ever seen.

During the ensuing months he would spend countless days away from his family—wife Janet and two adopted daughters, Jessica and Laura. There were times when the only way for him to see his children was for Janet to drive them up to Wilkes-Barre, where the playpen would be set up in the tight quarters of his motel room. Whatever the challenge, he stayed on his course.

The process of reinterviews wasn't the only important legwork that needed to be done. A review of test data and the evidence indicated that several obvious chores had not been conducted. The forty-eight belts and straps seized from 75 Birch the day of the murder had yet to be analyzed for blood. The source of the hairs on the windowsill in the second-floor back bedroom—where the intruder would have entered—remained unidentified. The source or sources of the two palm prints lifted from the desk in that room also remained unknown. At the least, samples could have been taken from the most obvious possibilities, to eliminate them from contention.

Hair samples were collected from everyone who could have been in the back bedroom—including Carol, Debbie, Danielle, and Glen, who explained that he was cooperating in this limited degree because he believed the probe was taking a new direction.

Jezewski and Detective Mitchell proceeded to the FBI Crime Lab in Washington with the hair samples, while Corporal Centi from the Pennsylvania State Police sent the FBI the lifted palm print samples, plus the rolled impressions of palm prints of about twenty law-enforcement officials who were in 75 Birch the morning of the murder, as well as those of Tracie Witner and her boyfriend. The last problem the police needed was for a defense attorney to suggest that a careless cop had leaned against the desk, or that a potential suspect had not been sufficiently investigated.

Upon examination, federal agents were able to obtain "one latent palmprint of value" from those lifted from the desk. They said, however, that it did not match any of the palm prints submitted, including Glen's. So whose palm print was it? Two potentially important comparisons could not be attempted; fingerprints had been taken from both Betty and Neil, but officials in Wilkes-Barre had neglected to take their palm prints when they had the chance.

As for the hair samples, the FBI experts reported, "It is pointed out that several years have passed since the crime date and the known hair sample collection. Inasmuch as hair characteristics can change with the passage of time, meaningful hair comparisons can be difficult and extremely limited."

The check for blood on the belts and straps, conducted at the Pennsylvania State Police Regional Laboratory in Wyoming—and three years late in coming—also was negative.

Sarcione was not worried, though. Yes, his case was almost all circumstantial. But that hadn't stopped him before. That was part of the challenge. He knew in his heart that in a relatively short period of time, there *would* be an arrest.

Tipped that investigators were indeed finally moving in on Dr. Wolsieffer, Corbett the columnist jumped back into the fray at the end of July 1989 with two columns that introduced a "druggie" angle to the public. Corbett claimed this was an exposé, but in fact, the possibility of a suspect from the Clear Brook rehab facility had been one of the first leads Troopers Allen and Jezewski had investigated back in October of 1988. Playing up the "druggie angle" as a huge development in the case was a classic example of news that is news because it is new to the news gatherer.

In the first column, Corbett said he had asked the dentist

during a February 1989 telephone conversation if he had ever tried to figure out who could have killed his wife. The dentist was quoted as having answered, "I wish to hell I knew. Maybe it was some druggies I treated from Clear Brook." Corbett thought the suggestion incriminating as to Dr. Wolsieffer's credibility, since he had failed to mention the possibility to police during their interrogations shortly after the murder.

Corbett did not spell out why he had kept his supposed exposé a secret for nearly six months, allowing only that the interview had "bothered me for months." So, in the week before writing the column, he explained, he had called Dr. Wolsieffer back.

More troubling was the incriminating interpretation Corbett attached to a statement Dr. Wolsieffer made in the follow-up conversation: "It could have been a druggie, or a non-druggie, from anywhere." Corbett wrote in explanation: "Now Wolsieffer is saying he is *convinced* that the murder was committed by 'druggies I treated from Clear Brook.'" But Dr. Wolsieffer had said no such thing.

The purported exclusives would eventually cause the case to explode, but in a very negative way. It was the kind of dangerous journalism that gives rise more and more to calls for a tightening of the First Amendment and a licensing system for reporters and columnists.

Mark Ciavarella had had enough. He had instructed Glen repeatedly not to talk to the news media. It was obvious Glen was unable to follow his orders. As a criminal attorney, if he couldn't control the situation, then he didn't want to be part of it. Ciavarella relayed word to Glen that he was quitting.

Glen asked Carol Kopicki's attorney, John Moses, to take over, but he demurred, citing a possible conflict of interest because of his representation of Carol. In the event Glen was ever arrested, Moses said, he would reconsider his position. Moses instead recommended Frank W. Nocito, an aggressive young attorney from Kingston, and Glen agreed.

The intensified investigation continued into the fall of 1989. Sarcione was almost ready to move. It hadn't taken him that long. Among other evidence to cap the case, the state police took aerial photographs of Birch Street and its relationship to the Susquehanna River. A possible argument at trial could be that after the murder, Glen drove to the river and dumped his bloody clothing, the murder weapon, and any other incriminating materials. That also would explain why his car had no dew on it.

In their final round of interviews, the investigators stayed away from Carol Kopicki because she had moved into Glen's Virginia condo with her son that August. Her daughter, several years older, stayed behind, choosing to live with her grandmother.

But Allen had paid another visit to Debbie Shipp in Delaware, along with Sarcione and Keller. Still trying to play Glen's women off of each other, Allen dutifully informed Debbie of Carol Kopicki's new address and roommate. Now that Debbie was out of the loop, another dose of Glen's deceit just might loosen her up.

Debbie related how Glen had planned to leave Betty the weekend of the murder but called it off because of the cut screen door, and how their relationship had ended in the wake of the first state police interview, with Glen telling her the authorities thought she was "the motive for everything." That last line was a zinger as far as the prosecutors were concerned.

On Halloween, Allen, Jezewski, Mitchell, and Sworen drove to Virginia to meet with local police officials. The investigators then took a reconnaissance trip past Glen's townhouse and his office building. They ran a license plate check on Glen's 1988 black Chevrolet Blazer. The Pennsylvania team told their Virginia counterparts that they would be back.

Meanwhile, in Pennsylvania, Sarcione and Keller were putting the finishing touches on the arrest warrant and an accompanying fourteen-page affidavit of probable cause. The document highlighted the best of the circumstantial evidence, which, for the most part, had been shielded from public view: Betty's face had been washed; the sexually charged admissions of Debbie Shipp and Carol Kopicki; Betty's vow to "take a stand" regarding her husband's gallivanting; Glen's minor injuries and lack of a choke wound in the front of his neck; no dirt or grease on the roof; analysis of the hair found on the windowsill and the blanket; tests showing blue cotton fibers under Betty's fingernails; and a summary of the report from the FBI's John Douglas that concluded that the crime scene had been staged and that Betty knew her killer "very well." For the first time, it was officially stated that the rickety wooden ladder had been found resting backwards against 75 Birch, as depicted in the videotape made of the crime scene.

On the morning of November 2, Sarcione convened a meeting at the D.A.'s office with Keller, Mitchell, Sworen, Allen, and Jezewski. They reviewed the arrest warrant documents one last time, then Mitchell and Sworen signed them. Bill Keller, the assistant D.A. from Luzerne County, approved the warrant, and District Justice Michael J. Collins signed it. After thirty-eight months, the time had finally come.

Under what they assumed was a shroud of secrecy, Mitchell, Sworen, Allen, and Jezewski headed for Virginia in a pouring rain. The plan was to make the arrest the following morning, surprising the defendant as he prepared to leave for work.

When Sworen arrived at the hotel, there was an urgent message from his wife, Corine, to call home immediately. "You're not going to believe this, but it was just on the news," she said.

"What was on the news?" Sworen asked.

"That a contingent of county, state, and local police have left Wilkes-Barre and are on their way to make the arrest."

The detective called Bill Keller back in Pennsylvania, who in turn conferred with Sarcione. The situation was complicated by the fact there was a dentists' convention over the weekend in Hawaii. No one was sure if Glen might be attending.

"You better go now. Don't wait," Keller instructed.

Needless to say, the members of the arrest team were livid. "I mean, we're trying to get him with the element of surprise, and all of a sudden somebody leaks the information up here and it's on the news and it's broadcast all over," Sworen later recalled. "You don't know—what the hell—if the guy's sitting in there with a shotgun or whatever. He's got time to think: 'These guys are going to come. They are going to try to take me away.' What's he got to lose? You don't know. The way it happened wasn't right. It should have never went down that way."

But whatever big shot leaked it obviously didn't care.

Chapter 28

Shortly after five o'clock, Glen was working on a patient in his office in the shadow of the Pentagon when he was told he had a telephone call. It was his Aunt Mary, calling to tell him that she had just heard on TV that the police were on their way to Virginia to arrest him. Calmly, Glen finished up with his patient, informed his coworkers, then headed for his townhouse in Falls Church.

Assuming the arrest team was still on its way, Glen asked Lisa to drive down to help with the kids and other details. Carol had no legal right to Danielle, and there was no telling how the authorities might handle that. But there would be no time. The knock on the door came with the conversation in progress.

"They're here," Glen said, handing the phone to Carol.

The arresting officers came in, moving swiftly past the Halloween decorations still gracing the door and steps. Danielle and Carol's son watched from the top of the second-floor steps.

Back in Wilkes-Barre, Lisa sat on her kitchen floor listening on the phone as Carol described the unfolding scene. "They have him against the wall, they're putting cuffs on him, they're taking him out the door," she said nervously.

Technically, Glen was arrested on a fugitive from justice warrant. He didn't understand that, since his new attorney, Frank Nocito, had offered to surrender him if the authorities ever decided to make an arrest. But this was standard procedure. As Glen was put into the back seat of a police car, Mitchell got in the front with a uniformed Fairfax County police officer, who drove. Mitchell then read Glen his constitutional rights. One by one, Glen said he understood.

After some small talk about the TV news leak, about Neil, and about Glen's dental business, Glen told a story of a particularly nice day he remembered spending with Danielle and Betty. Mitchell listened to the story, then expressed his sympathy to Glen. "I'm sorry all this happened—Betty's death and your arrest," said the detective.

"It happened so fast. We got into it. Everything was a blur," replied Glen. He paused for a couple of seconds, then continued: "I can talk to you, can't I, Bob?" Mitchell assured his charge that he indeed could talk to him.

"I don't know who to talk to anymore," Glen continued. But just as suddenly, he changed the subject, to talking about his dental practice again, and the high prices of homes in the Washington, D.C. area as compared to Wilkes-Barre. Mitchell would later say that he believed Glen changed subjects because he realized he had said something incriminating.

Everyone at Phyllis Wolsieffer's house was hysterical. For Glen's mother, her feelings were indescribable. She was about to lose another son. "When you know something isn't true, and have to live, and know that other people think it is . . . ." Her voice trailed off, not completing the thought.

Immediately, she blamed the Taskers for the arrest. "I don't dismiss the fact that they have gone through a horrible, horrible time, but if they had any love for Danielle, they would not have pushed this with Glen," she said. "They pushed it because they wanted the revenge of Glen for not being faithful to Betty."

Over at the Tasker home, there were subdued, empty emotions. "I have no feelings for him. My feelings are for the little girl," Marian Tasker said. "It's not anything to be happy about."

"It's been a nightmare. I don't think it helps," added Betty's father, John. "It's not the conclusion. It's the beginning of another series of events."

The Tasker family had felt cut off from the information flow since the state attorney general's office entered the case and had learned of the arrest from reporters. They said they had no idea Glen's apprehension was being planned, even though Sarcione and Keller had met with them earlier in the week to review the sequence of events in the case.

Stevens and Preate held a news conference. It was announced that the Commonwealth would not seek the death penalty. Stevens said the case would be prosecuted by Sarcione, and Bill Keller from his office. There would be no change in his hands-off approach to the Wolsieffer case. Instead, the D.A. announced that he would continue to serve as "coordinator of activities" in his office and work on other cases, mainly those involving narcotics.

Glen waived extradition and was back in Wilkes-Barre by 2:30 the following afternoon. He was taken to police headquarters to be processed. As the dentist was being taken out of the back seat of the gray unmarked police car, his aunt, Mary Stinson, made her way through the crowd of reporters, photographers, police, and onlookers to give her nephew a hug and kiss. "Glen, I love you."

"I love you, too," Glen replied, unable to hug back since his hands were cuffed in front and his feet were shackled.

As she was pulled away from the embrace, Aunt Mary turned to Detective Mitchell, standing alongside. "You son of a bitch, you'll be hearing from me."

Later that afternoon, Glen was brought before District Justice Collins for a ten-minute arraignment. After his handcuffs were removed, his mother, Phyllis, gave him a tight hug and kiss. She sobbed loudly as she stroked the back of his neck and complained about the failure of the authorities to provide Glen with a coat to put over his short-sleeved shirt.

A preliminary hearing was slated for the following week. Afterward, in a bail hearing before Judge Robert Hourigan, the presiding judge in the county, the amount of $200,000 was decided on, and Nocito said the Wolsieffer family was trying to get the proper documentation to use family real estate as security. Phyllis Wolsieffer and her sister, Aunt Mary, both agreed to offer their houses as collateral, but the details would take some time to be worked out. Judge Hourigan recessed the hearing until the following morning. Glen had no choice but to spend that Friday night at the Luzerne County Correctional Facility.

Carol Kopicki arrived from Virginia during the bail proceeding. Her ex-husband had driven down to take care of his son and Danielle. The Fairfax County police had decided not to refer Danielle to a child protection agency because she appeared to be in no danger under Carol's care.

In court, Carol embraced Glen's mother and Aunt Mary and touched hands with Glen as she walked over to John Moses, her attorney, who had been invited to the proceedings by Nocito.

As she departed the courtroom, and as the TV and newspaper cameras recorded her every step, Carol was served with a subpoena by Wilkes-Barre police captain Chester Dudick to testify at the preliminary hearing.

Special guards ringed the roof and grounds of the jail the next morning, and security was beefed up at the courthouse as well for the second bail hearing. With the real estate technicalities still not worked out, Glen was released with the pledge of a bail bondsman. However, he was ordered not to leave Luzerne County pending another bail hearing the following Wednesday, and not to contact any member of the Tasker family. Nocito told Judge Hourigan that he planned to ask the court to amend the bail conditions so that Glen would be allowed to resume his dental practice in Virginia pending trial.

From this point on, though, Nocito would not be acting alone. There had been an understanding from the start that if Glen was ever arrested, Carol Kopicki's lawyer, John Moses—or an experienced trial attorney like him—would have to be hired to assist Frank. A hard worker and a quick study with a great future, Nocito had never handled a case this complicated. The cigar-chomping, publicity-conscious Moses, on the other hand, knew his way around the criminal courts and was said to be one of only two defense attorneys to win acquittals in a first-degree murder case in the last two decades. But Moses's longtime representation of Carol Kopicki constituted at least the appearance of a conflict of interest. He told the Wolsieffer family he had to research the issue.

Stevens quickly made his objections known, contending that Moses had a conflict because he was professionally associated with Peter Paul Olszewski, a former assistant D.A. who had worked on the early stages of the Wolsieffer case. Olszewski had quit the D.A.'s office when Stevens took over and was mulling a run against him in the next election. Stevens complained that Olszewski maintained a law office in the same building as Moses, and that his name was listed on stationery for the Moses firm as "of counsel." Moses denied his relationship with Olszewski had anything to do with his dilemma, insisting the former prosecutor had never been a member of his firm.

Kicking his campaign off a bit early, Olszewski blasted away. "I think it is rather interesting that D.A. Stevens raises this issue considering the fact that Mr. Stevens isn't trying the case, nor is in any way personally involved in this case."

After consulting with his partner, Charles Gelso, Moses decided that if he joined Glen's defense team, his prior representation of Carol Kopicki would constitute, at the least, an unacceptable appearance of a conflict of interest. He informed Nocito of his decision, and the two men, meeting with Glen, began raising the names of other competent defense attorneys.

One of those was Anthony M. Cardinale of Boston, Massachusetts, an established protégé of F. Lee Bailey and a childhood friend of Moses. Cardinale had represented Mafia kingpins and other big-time felons in courtrooms all across the country, but the real attraction in the Wolsieffer case was that Cardinale was a hometown boy. He had lived in South Wilkes-Barre as a child, and had returned to attend Wilkes College, where he was a star athlete.

Moses told Glen he would be lucky to get Cardinale, but he gave him a call. Of burly build, soft voice, and thick black mustache, Cardinale agreed to come take a look. When Glen met him, he was visibly unsettled by Cardinale's uncanny physical resemblance to his brother, Neil. But as they talked, Glen's confidence skyrocketed. They hit it off.

When Glen returned home after meeting Cardinale, he told his family, "Well, we got ourselves a lawyer." He told his mother and Lisa to be prepared for when they met him, though. "I walked in, and it was like Neil came back to save me," Glen explained. "He looks just like him, he acts just like him, he's great. I love him."

Addressing a more immediate concern, acquaintances of Glen's back in Virginia were informed that Dr. Wolsieffer needed some written testimonials that could be used, if necessary, to help convince the judge that he should be allowed to return to his dental practice while awaiting trial. There were twenty-five signatures on a petition that expressed confidence, utmost respect, and faith in Dr. Wolsieffer, "not only as a dentist, but as an individual for whom we can trust. . . . We still believe in him as a human being and would like to fight for his right to freedom." Among others, letters of support were written by Glen's tax consultant, pointing out his "scrupulous concern with regard to satisfying all Internal Revenue Service requirements"; the operators of several laboratories dependent on his business; and a banker friend who said Glen had "never tried to hide anything from anyone. . . . His honesty and frankfulness is above reproach."

Mary F. DeLaney, the teacher from Saint James who cared for Danielle after school for the first year, wrote that she felt it would be "devastating to remove Danielle from her deep friendships and ties. . . . Danielle and her father have endeared themselves to the school community. That support is still here for them, and we welcome them back."

On the other side, subpoenas were served during the next few days on more than a dozen potential witnesses. Starting a trend that would permeate much of their remaining coverage of the case, the *Times Leader* accorded great prominence—the third paragraph of its story about the subpoenas—to the fact that Corbett the columnist was among those summoned, to discuss the "druggie" conversations he had with Glen. Adding to the coronation, the newspaper ran a large photograph of Trooper Jezewski actually handing Corbett the subpoena in his newsroom. Obviously, Corbett's superiors approved of his grandstanding.

Two days later, in a column that contained the words "I," "me," or "my" a total of fifty-eight times, Corbett explained why he wouldn't testify about his telephone conversations with Glen beyond saying that his columns about them were accurate. He refused to meet with Sarcione and Keller, and said if he testified beyond confirming the accuracy of his columns he very well might "lessen the role of a free press in a free society. This isn't the Soviet Union, where journalists function as an arm of the state, doing the state's bidding." In an attempt to explain his independence from the court and law enforcement, though, Corbett admitted having worked with the authorities, indirectly revealing them as being among his confidential sources. That in turn raised the question of whether he was technically a police agent. "I shared information with some of the same people who now want me to jeopardize my confidential sources—which might very well include them," he wrote.

As he would do repeatedly in the coming year, Corbett left the impression that Glen had given great emphasis to the possibility that "druggies" might have killed his wife, while, in fact, Glen had said that he really didn't know, that it could have been druggies or non-druggies. Corbett also inaccurately characterized as a discrepancy the supposed difference between Glen's so-called "druggie" statement and what he told the police when they found him on his kitchen floor and interviewed him at the hospital. In fact, there was nothing contradictory about the various statements. Nothing said in those earlier statements precluded a scenario in which former patients from the drug rehab center could have been the intruders.

The parties were back in court the following Wednesday, with Judge Hourigan authorizing Cardinale to appear in Pennsylvania for the Wolsieffer case. Over the objections of Sarcione, Glen was given permission to return to Virginia to practice dentistry, with the conditions that he telephone Wilkes-Barre police at 10:00 A.M. and 10:00 P.M. daily, not apply for a passport, and refrain from use of alcohol and drugs. Judge Hourigan also allowed the $200,000 bail bond to be substituted with the Wolsieffer and Stinson homes, a $20,000 certified check, and a judgment note in favor of the State of Pennsylvania for property Glen owned in Virginia.

The Wolsieffer case offered Cardinale a chance to strike up old acquaintances and strut his big-city stuff. A football star for the Wilkes College Colonels, he had gone on to Suffolk University Law School in Boston, and then began his professional law career working for F. Lee Bailey. He quickly got a taste for the big cases, the ones offering the biggest challenges. He saw that in the Wolsieffer case. Because it had taken so long to make the arrest, he said, he knew it was going to be "one hell of a trial."

Cardinale was a colorful man with hundreds of stories to tell. In 1988, he was voted "best mob lawyer in Massachusetts" by *Boston* magazine, and gained notoriety in New York, and before the U.S. Supreme Court, when he represented reputed Genovese crime family chief Anthony (Fat Tony) Salerno in the notorious "Mafia Commission" case.

Every bit as much of a workaholic as Sarcione, Cardinale immediately started his search for a chink in the prosecution's armor, beginning with a check to find out if relevant weather data really showed that the ground at 75 Birch would have been as soft on the morning of the murder as the police were saying. He wanted to know if the police had adequately followed up all leads pertaining to other possible suspects, how extensively the neighbors had been interviewed, what was Pennsylvania state law as it pertained to the admissibility of forensic tests like hair analysis and fiber analysis, and the rest of the nuts-and-bolts work that comprises a strong defense.

After consulting with Bailey, Cardinale hired Dr. Cyril H. Wecht, a noted pathologist from Pittsburgh who had worked on such high-profile cases as the congressional investigation into the assassination of John F. Kennedy, and began sending him relevant hospital records, the autopsy report, and the affidavit that accompanied the arrest warrant. "This case is a political football," Cardinale wrote. "The former district attorney was defeated in his attempt for reelection based upon the failure to 'solve' this case. In my view, there is no more likelihood that Dr. Wolsieffer is guilty of this crime now than there was three and one-half years ago."

For those who kept watch on such things, Nancy Wolsieffer had been conspicuously missing from Glen's side since his arrest. Her absence was viewed as puzzling, given her vocal support during Neil's inquest and in the months immediately following.

In fact, Nancy had not been seen or heard from in public

since her brother-in-law's arrest. The newspapers knocked on her door, but she didn't answer. She was served a subpoena to testify at the preliminary hearing, and Sarcione spoke to her several times about the parameters of her potential testimony.

Sarcione told her to stay loose, that if she didn't hear from him she should plan on going to work. The phone call never came. The prosecutor decided to keep her under wraps for the time being, and at the same time, give the defense something extra to think about.

CHAPTER 29

With the electric atmosphere of a gala opening night, Glen's preliminary hearing began on November 14, 1989, nearly two weeks after his arrest. The protracted proceedings would include the titillating testimony of his two mistresses, Betty's thoughts about her troubled marriage—as told through the testimony of her friends—and a contumacious attack on the court system by Corbett and the *Times Leader*.

Because Luzerne County did not use grand juries, the Commonwealth of Pennsylvania would present its case based on the arrest affidavits. Justice Collins would then decide if there was sufficient evidence—a *prima facie* case—to send the matter to the Court of Common Pleas for trial.

Because of the overwhelming public interest in the case, the hearing was transferred from Justice Collins's small office to Orphans' Court, in the new annex across the street from the county courthouse.

As court convened, Glen reached for his wallet and pulled out a small color photo of Danielle. He stared at it lovingly and kissed it. Then he blessed himself.

Cardinale asked that the first-degree murder charges be dismissed on the grounds that the affidavit of probable cause contained insufficient evidence. He also contended that Sarcione had joined the prosecution team without having satisfied any of the provisions of the Pennsylvania Commonwealth Attorneys Act, which allows participation by the state attorney general's office for a limited number of circumstances, such as a lack of resources or a conflict of interest at the local D.A. level. Cardinale contended that the deputizing of Sarcione as a local assistant D.A. was "more form than substance." He asked that the state official be removed from the case, and that the local D.A.'s office handle the matter. Justice Collins rejected both motions.

Cardinale then asked that all scheduled witnesses be sequestered, meaning that they had to leave the room so that they could not hear the testimony of those before them. As everyone else left, Corbett approached the bench to declare that as a journalist, he objected to being made to leave. In the alternative, Corbett asked that the proceedings be halted so he could contact his lawyer.

"Is there another representative of the *Times Leader* present?" asked Justice Collins. Corbett said there was.

When Sarcione said he might not call Corbett, Cardinale observed: "He seems significant enough—or has made himself significant enough—that if they don't call him, we will. So we would like him sequestered."

Justice Collins told Corbett to leave, and Debbie Shipp, now thirty, was sworn.

To those hearing it for the first time, Debbie's story was shocking. Clad in a white-and-black-checkered suit and breaking into tears on two occasions, she revealed the inner workings of her love affair, notably Friday nights at the Imperial and Glen's plans to leave Betty the weekend of the murder if not for the cut screen door. For the climax of her testimony, Debbie quoted Glen as telling her in November 1988 that their relationship had to be terminated because "an investigation had started up again, and they were saying I was the motive."

Sarcione had one final question: in all those seven years of their relationship, how many times had Glen told her he was going to leave Betty for her? "Quite a few," Debbie allowed. Yes, more than once a year.

"And did he ever keep that promise?" Sarcione wondered. Ever the optimist who could see the silver lining, Debbie thought of the weekend at the Red Roof Inn and responded: "Just for three days."

Although Stevens wasn't doing anything in the courtroom regarding the Wolsieffer case, he was busy elsewhere. He sent Carol Kopicki, the next witness, a letter granting her immunity from prosecution, a move designed to allay her lawyer's concerns about her admitting to violation of Virginia's cohabitation laws pertaining to unmarried couples.

In form-letter style, Stevens thanked his hostile witness "for her cooperation" and "courage" in helping "our investigation and prosecution." Even worse, Stevens did not have the authority to grant immunity. Apparently he didn't know that.

With her attorney, John Moses, at her side, Carol took the stand and promptly took the Fifth. When she declined to say even if she knew the defendant, Keller protested that there was nothing incriminating in the statement that Kopicki had given police a week after the murder.

Moses stepped in. In addition to the Fifth Amendment issue, he cited sections of the Pennsylvania Constitution and a Pennsylvania Supreme Court case regarding one's right to protect his or her reputation. There also was the matter of Virginia's morals and cohabitation laws. "As long as this witness reasonably believes that any testimony she might offer would be a link or could be a link in the chain of incrimination, she has the absolute right to invoke her rights. And that's exactly what she's doing," he maintained.

Keller brought up the immunity letter from Stevens, and Moses replied that Stevens "cannot grant immunity." He said the D.A. had failed to follow the proper statutes and procedure, and asserted that Justice Collins did have the authority to decide on an immunity dispute. Justice Collins announced that he would decide the issue during the lunch break.

When the magistrate returned, he first had to deal with Ralph Kates, the attorney for the *Times Leader*. Cardinale demanded that Corbett remain out of the courtroom, even for the arguments challenging his sequestration. He also suggested that the matter had been disposed of, and that if Kates wanted to argue some more, he should do it to a higher court.

Kates, who carried himself with the pompous arrogance of his client, started talking about the origins of sequestration orders, dating back to common law in England in 1696. He suggested that Cardinale was trying to tell the newspaper who could and could not cover the hearing. "I suggest that you not give that power to the defendant, that you not let him decide that simply because a columnist has castigated him in the press, has castigated his counsel in the press."

Cardinale replied that the purpose of the sequestration rule was "to avoid corruption of the fact-finding process. And that's why both parties agreed on sequestration of witnesses. I didn't name Mr. Corbett as a witness, but I expected him. My brother in the prosecution team did." He said that unlike other exceptions to sequestration orders—family members or chief investigators—Corbett simply worked for a newspaper, one that was capable of sending two or three other reporters to replace him. The press wasn't being kept out, just a member of the press who had deliberately "injected himself into these proceedings beyond the position of a simple newsman. And that was his choice."

Kates claimed that Sarcione had told him he had no objection to Corbett staying. But Keller was quickly up to say that the Commonwealth had "no position one way or the other."

Justice Collins eventually tired of the silliness and ordered Corbett to remain out of the courtroom. Kates asked if there was some way to immediately get a typed transcript of what had just been discussed. Justice Collins told him no. Kates again asked for a hearing. Again, he was turned down. The attorney then asked that the proceedings be delayed until a transcript was prepared and he could file an appeal—"before any further irreparable harm occurs to my client."

"Okay," said Justice Collins, testily. "The Court will deny your request for a delay of these proceedings." For the time being, at least, Corbett would remain out.

Quickly, Moses was standing before the bench entering his appearance on behalf of the Northeast Pennsylvania Professional

News Media Association, and Kates was back representing the *Times Leader*. They were challenging an order barring photos in the hallway. The hearing had taken on the feel of a carnival, complete with zany side shows.

Following another dose of oratory, everyone compromised. Photos could be taken as long as they were taken by the elevators, not in front of the courtroom door.

Finally onto the Kopicki matter, Justice Collins agreed with Moses that she had a right to take the Fifth, and that he did not have any contempt powers to compel her to testify.

Keller objected, then asked Justice Collins to keep the preliminary hearing open pending an appeal in the event Kopicki was later ordered to testify. The justice agreed.

The assistant D.A. then called Joyce Marie Greco to the stand. She brought along her lawyer, Carmen J. Latona, and she too was mum. But for a different reason. "On advice of counsel, I'm asserting my constitutional rights not to answer because my good name and reputation may be jeopardized," she said when asked if she knew Dr. Wolsieffer. When Keller tried to argue that there was nothing in Greco's 1986 statement that would incriminate her, Latona argued that he wasn't citing the Fifth Amendment, but Article One, Section Nine of the Pennsylvania Constitution, the part that gave his client "the right not to answer questions which would bring disgrace, infamy, shame, or reproach, or questions that would also accuse her of possible immoral acts or impugn her reputation."

Justice Collins said that under the circumstances he would not require Greco to testify, but again made provisions to keep the hearing open until the issue was decided by the higher court.

Although Cardinale tried to bar the next witness, Barbara Wende, from testifying on the grounds that she would be delivering unacceptable hearsay, Sarcione argued that the testimony should be allowed under the "state of mind exception," where hearsay evidence is allowed to show the state of mind of the deceased just prior to death. Cardinale countered with the contention that in order for such testimony to be admissible, the Commonwealth would have to establish that his client knew his wife's state of mind. In the end, Wende was sworn and related what Betty had said about her terrible summer in 1985 and the conversation just three days before her murder—the one in which Betty said she was going to "take a stand" if Glen came home late that Friday.

With Carol Kopicki and Joyce Greco gone, the prosecution team called Richard Miscavage to cover some of the same ground. He admitted he knew about Debbie Shipp and Glen, and Carol and Glen. Keller asked the witness if he had ever seen Glen and Carol together. Miscavage answered that he had. The prosecutor asked where. Trying to wiggle out of identifying the Busy Day Motel, the witness replied: "In a local establishment."

"What do you mean, 'local establishment'?"

"I was in her company one night in a motel. . . . I was with Glen and Carol and myself and another individual," Miscavage said, chivalrously keeping Joyce Greco's name out of it.

Eileen Pollock was next, to recount her conversations with Betty at Aerobic World about Glen's slow dancing with Carol at the Crackerbox. She also testified that she frequently saw Dr. Wolsieffer in the company of Carol and Joyce Greco before Betty arrived for class.

"And what would happen when his wife got there?" Sarcione asked.

"The whole little threesome would split up."

Cardinale objected. "Move to strike the characterization."

"I don't think it's characterization," replied Sarcione.

Justice Collins overruled the objection, inadvertently leaving a serious misimpression as it applied to Joyce Greco's relationship with Glen.

Then Barbara Dombroski, wife of Dr. Wayne Dombroski, the dentist Glen shared offices with, testified about her conversation in August of 1985, when Betty told her she had confronted Glen and he had admitted having an affair.

The first day ended with medical testimony, first from Dr. Hudock, the county coroner, regarding the time of Betty's death, the condition of her body, and how long it would have taken her to die. Dr. Hudock went on to testify that from a medical and pathological point of view, he would have expected to have found blood on Betty's face, given the beating on her face. "There was no blood, and there should have been blood."

Keller wondered how long it would have taken to strangle Betty. "Three to five minutes. That's all a person can be without air before they die."

Then Dr. Dennis Gaza, who had treated Glen in the Mercy Hospital emergency room, told of finding the bump on Glen's head, "the equivalent of a collection of blood under the scalp." He said it "looked like a hematoma, a bruise," and recounted that he had taken the injury seriously because it conceivably could have killed someone with different physical characteristics. Dr. Gaza also mentioned that he had found an abrasion on the back of Glen's neck, but nothing on the front.

In trying to push the point that the location of Glen's head wound was an unlikely spot for one to self-inflict such an injury, Cardinale got Dr. Gaza to acknowledge that the occipital region was "rather vulnerable" and could affect one's vision, balance, gait, heart rate, and respiration. "If you have a blow to that area, you can have loss of consciousness," he said.

"And that's the area that you observed the injury to Dr. Wolsieffer?" asked Cardinale.

"*Near* that area," the doctor replied.

The next morning's front-page headlines declared: WOLSIEFFER'S WOMEN TAKE THE STAND, EX TESTIFIES, CURRENT LOVER TAKES THE FIFTH. The disparity in coverage between the two dailies showed clearly. The *Citizens' Voice* headlined its main sidebar: DOCTOR: WOLSIEFFER'S HEAD WOUND WAS SERIOUS, a story about Dr. Gaza's testimony. The *Times Leader* blared: TL COLUMNIST CORBETT IS BARRED FROM COURTROOM. The newspaper also printed an editorial entitled, FREE PRESS BLOCKED OUT OF WOLSIEFFER HEARING. There were ironies noted about the "crumbling Berlin Wall," and Justice Collins's decision was characterized as "a dagger in the heart of the First Amendment."

The *Citizens' Voice*, meanwhile, covered the Corbett angle in a collection of incidental courtroom anecdotes by noting that the sequestration order "did not sit too well with a *Times Leader* representative." Trying hard not to acknowledge his existence, the newspaper called Corbett "the man" on several other occasions. The acrimony between the two journalistic camps would continue throughout the proceedings.

The preliminary hearing resumed with the summoning of Jule Cook, followed by her husband, George, both of 77 Birch. Because of their poor medical conditions, their testimony was videotaped for possible use at the trial. The Cooks' testimony unveiled a perplexing inconsistency in the government's case: did Glen use the rickety ladder whenever Betty locked him out, as the Cooks now seemed to be saying? Or was the ladder in such bad condition that it would never have supported the weight of a two-hundred-pound intruder? Generally speaking, Mrs. Cook said, "When Glen got locked out, the ladder was usually there on a Saturday morning."

At one point, Sarcione asked Mrs. Cook how well she knew Betty. As she started to answer, Cardinale objected. "If there's a basis for this line of questioning, I'll be glad to let it go forward. If I may just have a second with my brother."

Cardinale had been doing it for hours now, calling Sarcione his "brother." The prosecutor hated it. He had objected during one of the bail hearings, pointing out, "I'm not his blood brother, Your Honor." He had hoped Cardinale would get the hint, but obviously he hadn't. "Your Honor, if I may just put on the record, I would object to defense counsel calling me a brother. I've never heard that term used in a Pennsylvania court. I've tolerated it for a full day."

Cardinale tried to explain. "I don't think my brother has to be so—what's the right word for it—upset. It's certainly not meant in any non-endearing way. It is a fashion of Massachusetts lawyers. It's something meant out of total respect."

Sarcione replied: "Your Honor, the definition of brother in one's dictionary is that I'm a relation of this man, and I'm not." The tension lifted as everyone in the courtroom broke out in laughter. "I don't believe it's proper, in all seriousness."

Justice Collins said there were other possible definitions for the word. "It could be used in a much larger sense, that we're all brothers. The Court doesn't find it improper."

Because of the limited powers of Justice Collins, several of the legal issues in the Wolsieffer hearing had been placed before Court of Common Pleas Judge Gifford S. Cappellini, who had been notified that he would handle any trial of Dr. Wolsieffer. Judge Cappellini had already convened a hearing on the D.A.'s demand that Carol Kopicki and Joyce Greco be compelled to testify. But Stevens's office had failed to file the required paperwork, so the judge ordered that the entire petition be refiled.

Now Collins's proceeding was being interrupted so Judge Cappellini could hear arguments about the court order keeping Corbett out of the preliminary hearing. The judge asked both sides if they planned on calling the columnist immediately or not at all, in which case the sequestration dispute would be moot.

Corbett didn't get a helping hand from either side. The prosecutors, who were miffed that he had declined to speak to them in preparation for the preliminary hearing, were noncommittal about their plans. By now Cardinale had grown angry about the whole affair because in his mind it was helping Corbett gain the attention he was so desperately seeking. In Cardinale's mind, there wasn't the slightest First Amendment issue. The newspaper could send as many reporters as it wanted, just not the one who was going to be a witness because he had injected himself into the case. As he had previously told Collins, Cardinale told Judge Cappellini that if the government didn't call Corbett, he definitely would.

The judge reserved his decision pending a full hearing. Since he again let the preliminary hearing continue, he, in effect, made a decision.

With all parties back before Collins, the focus of the hearing turned to law enforcement, as Keller and Sarcione began their parade of police and prosecutors. The testimony provided the public, as well as Cardinale and Nocito, with a glimpse of the various parts of the prosecution puzzle.

After hearing from the policemen and paramedics who responded to 75 Birch that fateful morning, Keller announced a surprise witness for Day Three, Mercy Hospital security guard William Emmett. Glen's softball buddy detailed how Glen told him that he had been asleep on a downstairs couch when awakened by a noise, not upstairs in bed with Betty. Emmett also quoted Glen as telling him that after having been out drinking the night before at the Crackerbox Palace, he "felt like getting into a fight, but never expected this." During his visit that Sunday, Em-

mett continued, he recalled Glen introducing him to his Aunt
Mary, then looking out the window to proclaim: "It's a nice day
for golf. We'll have to get out sometime." The witness said he
distinctly recalled Glen telling his aunt that before he went to bed
that Friday night, he had locked all the windows in the house.

Detective Bob Mitchell, the police department's chief investigator
on the case, was next. Among the host of evidence and statements
he testified about, the most potentially damning was his recitation
of the strange remarks Glen made in the police car minutes after
being arrested in Virginia: "It happened so fast. We got into it.
Everything was a blur."

Cardinale cross-examined for one hundred minutes, ham-
mering at Mitchell's ability to remember specific details at the
hearing that he had not written into his reports back in 1986. The
defendant's improved memory on the Saturday of the murder was
supposed to denote inconsistency, and therefore a lack of truthful-
ness. But here was Mitchell remembering things seemingly out of
the blue more than three years later. "This is a report made for
me, not for you," Mitchell fought back at one point. "I remembered. It's in my mind. I don't have to put it down." At one point,
he used a finger on his right hand to point to his skull. "It's right
here, in my head."

"I'll bet," Cardinale retorted.

After Mitchell was finished, the prosecution called Corbett, who
testified to the accuracy of the two "druggie" columns. Keller then
read into the record the key paragraphs from each of the columns,
with the operative quote being "It could have been a druggie, or
a non-druggie, from anywhere."

The entire process didn't even last one third of Andy Warhol's
fifteen minutes. When it came time for Cardinale to cross-
examine, he simply stated, "I have no questions at this time."

That Sunday, Cliff Schechtman, the *Times Leader*'s managing
editor and Corbett's personal editor, wrote a column contending
that his man had been "gagged by the gavel of a local district
justice and the transparent motives of a Boston defense attorney.
In Corbett's absence is the resounding void you see on the left of
this page." To the left, under Corbett's photo and a headline,

WHAT I CAN SAY ABOUT WOLSIEFFER, was a column of blank space.

Two days after the amateurish stunt, Corbett was back writing, however, calling Frank Nocito "the lightweight half of Wolsieffer's defense team" and Cardinale the "Human Blockhead, a side-show attraction who, for a fee, pounds nails into his face without showing pain." He said Dr. Wolsieffer "resembles the geeks who sleep in barns with dancing pigs and bite the heads off chickens." And he referred to Justice Collins—hospitalized that weekend in critical condition with heart problems—as "the Luzerne County midway's 'Rubber Band Man,' tying himself in knots and struggling with heady legal issues that, as a low-level magistrate, he had never encountered before." Any remnants of journalistic standards were vanishing quickly.

The next morning, Joyce Greco's attorney told Judge Cappellini that his client had changed her mind about talking in court and now wanted to testify—for the same reason she originally refused, to clear her reputation. Latona told the judge that Greco's efforts to protect her good name had been compromised by the news media. "There were several reports that she was a girlfriend of the doctor. That was not her statement, that was the media's statement," he said.

It was inevitable that Greco's tangential involvement would get blown out of proportion. First, there had been Eileen Pollock's titillating testimony about "the little threesome" at aerobics class of Glen, Carol, and Joyce. Then there was Richard Miscavage's testimony that he, Carol, Glen, and "another individual" he did not identify had spent time at a motel. And in his petition to the court on the immunity-testimony dispute, Stevens had contended that Greco had had an extramarital affair, without identifying the other party.

But it got worse. Without naming names, one TV station reported that "two former girlfriends of Dr. Wolsieffer took the Fifth Amendment." Another suggested that Greco did not want to testify because she was hiding the fact that she was one of Dr. Wolsieffer's lovers. Elden Hale, the general manager of WNEP-TV, told the *Times Leader* that his reporter had received the information from Stevens. "We asked Correale Stevens who she was, and he said a girlfriend," Hale explained.

Outside of court, Latona said his client was considering suing several members of the news media. In the meantime, three national TV tabloid programs, "A Current Affair," "Hard Copy," and "Crimewatch Tonight," sent crews to Wilkes-Barre to cover the latest developments.

After Judge Cappellini ruled that Carol Kopicki could properly cite the Fifth Amendment in refusing to testify, Stevens filed a six-paragraph petition requesting that she be granted immunity as a matter of "public interest." The judge promptly signed the order, and after nearly a month of wasted time, Carol agreed to testify. "I have one question in this matter," said Moses. "Why didn't the Commonwealth file this motion three weeks ago? They certainly could have done so, and the matter would have been resolved then and there."

Although still technically *persona non grata* because of a defense subpoena, Corbett the columnist was in attendance when the hearing resumed with Carol Kopicki on the stand. Cardinale saw him, but didn't bother to object. He was surprised by the outlaw arrogance, but he had more important things to worry about.

In terms of razzle-dazzle, Carol's appearance was anticlimactic. From the prosecution team's perspective, her admissions brought them closer to demonstrating a motive for murder. From the defense's view, she testified truthfully about her "loving" relationship with Glen. If there was a trial, the jury was going to hear about the affair one way or the other.

As for Joyce Greco, she confirmed Carol's motel visits with Glen, and made clear that her friendship had been with Betty. She was not asked specifically about her relationship with Rich Miscavage.

"So it's clear, you didn't have a relationship with the defendant, did you?" asked Sarcione.

"No," the witness replied firmly. "I hardly knew Glen Wolsieffer."

For the defense case, Cardinale called Corporal Eugene J. Centi of the Pennsylvania State Police, whose initial reports indicated he had lifted two partial palm prints off Glen's desk in the rear second-floor bedroom, the supposed entryway for the intruder. The photographer and fingerprint analyst testified now that he had lifted a partial palm print, *singular*. Centi said the print was of the bottom part of a palm, and that the lift was large enough that he could have made a match if a matching sample had been provided.

Centi said he and the FBI had tried to match the lift with about twenty-two exemplars, including Dr. Wolsieffer, Danielle Wolsieffer, and the police officials who were in the house the day of the murder. He said he did not have palm print samples for Betty or Neil Wolsieffer. Under additional questioning by Cardinale, Centi said he never processed the rickety ladder "because it was too pitted and it had some rotten areas around it. It was an impossibility to process for prints." Cardinale did not raise the discrepancy between the two palm prints in Centi's report and his testimony. There would be time enough for that at a trial.

With Keller cross-examining, Centi said that when he lifted the partial palm print he believed it to be "fairly new," estimating ten to fifteen hours—"twenty-four hours or less." He said he based his estimate on the fact that the older a print, the more it deteriorates. The print on the desk had come up quickly, usually a sign of freshness.

But under his questioner's prodding, Centi backed away, saying the condition of the print could be affected by the temperature, the condition of the house, and whether the person leaving the print perspired more or less than normal. By the time Keller finished, Centi was saying the print could have been there a week, two weeks, even six months.

In an attempt to disassemble the prosecution's strategy, designed to show that Glen's story about a break-in was unlikely, Cardinale questioned Detective Mitchell about similar crimes in the Birch Street area during 1986. He was hoping to tie in police records of similar crimes with the fears expressed by the Cooks. This would lend credibility to what Glen had told the police the Saturday of Betty's murder. There was one big problem with all of that, though. The police reports didn't reveal any cases of "signature crimes," offenses where the modus operandi was very similar to the one espoused in the Wolsieffer case.

"When I examine reports, I look for similarities of the whole crime, and I didn't see any similarities in any of these reports that match 75 Birch Street. That was unique," Mitchell said.

"Were there any ladder entries to a second-floor window which resulted in an occupant in the home being murdered?" Sarcione asked on cross-examination.

Cardinale objected, so Sarcione tried another way. "Going through all of those files, did you find any case in which a ladder was used to gain entry to a second floor?"

"I found no other incidents with a ladder," Mitchell said.

Sarcione wondered if the detective could recall a homicide on Birch Street during his two decades on the force. Mitchell said that as far as he knew, the Wolsieffer murder had been the first.

Without warning, Cardinale turned and called Steve Corbett to the stand. He gave his name and address, then asked to speak to the court. "Since I had no idea when, or even if, I would be called by the defense, I had no idea when my attorney should be here to assist me in my appearance. Would I be able to contact my attorney prior to involving myself in Mr. Cardinale's proceedings?"

Cardinale was steaming. "Your Honor, if Mr. Corbett needs the assistance of counsel for any purpose, and knowing that all I'm asking is if he can give some truthful answers to my questions, if he needs an attorney for that, let him take all the time he wants."

"Yes, sir. I need an attorney for that."

"I'm not going to call him as a witness, then," said the defense attorney.

Justice Collins wanted to know if Cardinale had any other witnesses. He replied that he did not, for the moment.

Corbett had not moved himself from the witness chair. Cardinale glanced over at him and pronounced, "I'm not going to waste any more of the Court's time."

Justice Collins said he didn't know what Cardinale was talking about.

"As far as this witness is concerned, I'm not going to wait for his lawyer. If he's not willing to answer questions truthfully, I don't want to wait. . . . As far as I'm concerned, he can leave the stand."

Now Corbett was indignant. "Will somebody please explain to me why I was called to the stand? Thank you for your kindness."

Cardinale was more than happy to answer. "You were called to answer some questions under oath, sir."

Corbett stepped down.

Both sides agreed to let Cardinale conduct depositions of the Cooks at their home the following morning due to their poor health. Justice Collins told everyone to return to his courtroom afterwards for final arguments. The preliminary hearing, often a one-day event, had taken on a life of its own, a trial before the trial.

The next afternoon, Cardinale spoke first, calling the case "totally speculative." He pointed to the unidentified palm print and the lack of any incriminating forensic link between Dr. Wolsieffer and the murder. He maintained that the inconsistencies in his client's statements to police were "so small" as to be insignificant, especially in light of the "constant attempts" throughout that Saturday to get Dr. Wolsieffer to incriminate himself. On the other hand, Cardinale contended, the "mere existence" of the palm print was significant because it demonstrated "that somebody, whoever it was, was in that house at some point prior to Betty Wolsieffer's death." According to Cardinale, the injuries his client sustained were consistent with having been attacked, and hospital records showed him being "markedly shaken" and that he was in a "shock-like state."

Sarcione began softly, then dramatically raised and lowered his voice at key moments. He said the premeditation required under Pennsylvania law could occur "within a second," as he swiftly turned around and pointed an imaginary gun at a TV reporter sitting nearby. He spoke of Dr. Hudock's testimony about three to five minutes needed to strangle.

He wondered why there were no marks on the front of Dr. Wolsieffer's neck if he was attacked from behind, as he had claimed. "I submit, Your Honor, if there was an intruder in that house that night, when the police got there, Dr. Wolsieffer would have had two rounds, or a round in the back of his head, from that intruder; he's not going to leave an eyewitness."

Sarcione mocked the defendant's version. "An intruder enters the second floor, goes down to the first floor and then back up to the second floor. Your Honor, a second-story entry as well. Second-story entry in an occupied home?" With two cars in the driveway. "I could see if this was a museum with Rembrandts, but this is a regular, modest home. There hasn't been a murder on Birch Street in twenty-four years."

Why would an intruder leave Dr. Wolsieffer downstairs with a loaded gun and go upstairs and kill his wife? Sarcione wondered. "Does that have the ring of truth to it? That's ridiculous. And for this man to have this Court believe that, it has no ring of truth. It is illogical."

He said Dr. Wolsieffer was present at the time of the murder, he had opportunity, and he had a motive. "He's telling Debbie Shipp a weekend before, 'I'm going to be with you.' The weekend before the murder," said Sarcione. "We have plenty of motive established. Not only through Debbie Shipp, but also through Carol Kopicki, his other lover at the time."

The prosecutor pointed out that the defendant never tried to go upstairs to check on his wife and daughter, and contended that Dr. Wolsieffer slipped the two times he asked Officer George, "How's my daughter?"

He also spoke of the pressures no doubt building in the defendant's life at that time. Betty wouldn't give him a divorce. He was worried about leaving Danielle. He was telling Debbie Shipp the week before the murder that he was going to move in with her. Then he saw his other lover at the Crackerbox. "I submit it's logical to infer he saw Carol Kopicki there with her husband, and that irritated him a little bit, putting him in a little bit of an angry mood.

"I submit the totality of everything—the cuts on him, the blood on her, the denim—the totality of it all points right to him, right to him," Sarcione said forcefully, jabbing his finger in the direction of the defendant.

The prosecutor from Harrisburg had started out by saying this was only a preliminary hearing. But the words that followed had certainly sounded like a summation at trial.

CHAPTER 30

The longest preliminary hearing in the history of Luzerne County ended on December 11, 1989, with Justice Collins ordering Dr. Wolsieffer to stand trial on charges of first-degree murder, third-degree murder, and voluntary manslaughter. (The charge of second-degree murder, a homicide committed during the commission of a felony, was not applicable and therefore not included in the charges sent to the county court.) The standard of proof needed to get the case held over for trial was not that rigorous. The trial, with its standard of reasonable doubt, would be the real test.

Stevens surfaced to tell reporters that he was satisfied with the work of the investigators and Sarcione and Keller.

For the Taskers, the decision was welcome, but they realized each ruling was a single step in a long, difficult journey. "The hardest thing for me to do is sit in that courtroom and look at the *alleged* murderer sitting there," said John Tasker, Betty's father. "Let me give you a clue—look up the word 'sociopath' in the dictionary."

Thinking about the loss of their daughter, the Taskers thought of the hardships endured by Phyllis Wolsieffer as well—the loss of her husband, the loss of a daughter-in-law, the loss of her son, and now her only other son was facing trial on charges of murdering his wife.

Danielle Wolsieffer was allowed to spend three hours with her maternal grandparents on the day before New Year's Eve. It was her first visit with the Taskers since May. The grandparents and their attorney said they hoped the visit would mark a resumption of encounters, but it was not to be. Part of the problem was that Danielle did not want to see the Taskers, no surprise given what she must have been hearing about them since her mother's murder and the public identification of her father as the prime suspect.

Glen's arraignment in county court was scheduled for January 19, 1990, but the day before, the defense team filed papers challenging Justice Collins's decision. When that strategy failed, Cardinale and Nocito filed a motion again challenging Sarcione's involvement in the case. Judge Bernard J. Podcasy, father of the former D.A., halted Glen's arraignment pending resolution of that dispute. "I don't know why they want me out," Sarcione said. "I think Wolsieffer's running scared."

Stevens clung to a section of the law that allowed state intervention when a district attorney "lacks the resources to conduct an adequate investigation or the prosecution of the criminal case." He insisted that Sarcione was serving as an assistant D.A., working under his "direction and control."

But the D.A.'s position was on less than firm ground. During a hearing on the matter in late March, Sarcione suggested from the witness stand that Judge Cappellini make "a good-faith exception" to the state law, contending that there was nothing on the books preventing a deputy state attorney general from serving as a special assistant county D.A. And when Nocito cross-examined Stevens, the D.A. acknowledged that he had requested "investigative assistance" from the state attorney general's office, not prosecutorial assistance.

The argument failed, however, as Judge Cappellini ruled that Sarcione technically worked for Stevens and could therefore stay on as chief prosecutor.

Meanwhile, investigators continued to track down leads, incriminating or exculpatory. Sue Vohar told Mitchell and Sworen that she had worked for Dr. Wolsieffer as a dental assistant part-time in 1986 and full-time the following year. She contended that Glen had received cards, letters, and telephone calls from Carol Kopicki as early as March 1987. Vohar also told the detectives that her boss displayed his anger by throwing dental instruments, including on occasions when she wouldn't respond to him. She quoted Glen as having once told her: " 'If there was any woman I would like to hit, it would be you.' "

Vohar said Glen tried to put the make on her in April of 1988, just before he permanently moved to Virginia. She contended he told her that his attorney had advised him he should not be seeing the same women all the time. "He told me he was attracted to me, and that he wanted me to go to bed with him."

According to a police report Mitchell prepared of the interview, Vohar quoted Glen as saying that he "thought about sex all the time. He thought that there may be something wrong with him. Glen stated that he likes oral sex, likes to give it and receive it. She said that Glen got down on his knees in front of her and begged her." The report quoted Vohar as saying she told the good doctor that he should get some therapy.

As part of his rounds of reinterviews, Mitchell had another chat with Susanne Neher, age sixty-six, the owner of the Granite Motel, one of the establishments Glen had used for his encounters with Carol Kopicki in July and August of 1986. She provided the original sign-in cards, and recalled that Dr. Wolsieffer always used Room 12. Neher said the first time he used the room, he left it dirty.

"What do you mean?" Mitchell asked.

She explained that she had found the bedsheets bloody, giving her the impression a female guest had had her period.

Neher told Mitchell that the next morning, while cleaning the room, Dr. Wolsieffer returned by himself, looking for his watch. Neher said she told him he was going to have to pay extra for the mess he had left. She said he agreed to pay without debate.

At least part of the trial promised to be a battle between forensic titans. Sarcione and Keller were hard at work with their expert pathologist, Dr. John I. Coe of Minnesota. He had been one of nine pathologists to serve on a panel for the House Select Committee on Assassinations that investigated the death of John F. Kennedy, and was one of three pathologists to review the death of Martin Luther King. During forty years of practicing forensic pathology, he had testified all across the country.

Dr. Coe, who toured 75 Birch as part of his preparation, told Sarcione he believed Betty Wolsieffer had died between five and eight hours before Dr. Hudock's temperature readings, meaning between 2:30 and 5:30 A.M. This moved the time frame even farther away from Glen's statement that "it was just getting light out," and closer to the required closing time for taverns in the valley.

Dr. Coe determined that death was caused by "mechanical asphyxia due to ligature strangulation, with probable manual strangulation as a contributing factor. Death was not instantaneous. The photographs further indicate that something was wedged in the mouth." Testimony of this sort would help support a first-degree murder charge on the grounds that an object was used as deadly force.

Based on photographs of the back of Dr. Wolsieffer's neck and "information provided by the attending physician," Dr. Coe contended, "There is no good evidence that he was throttled from behind." On top of that, Dr. Coe said that Glen's neck wounds were "more consistent with the lesions being self-inflicted."

Meanwhile, Cardinale and Nocito were busy with their expert, Dr. Cyril H. Wecht of Pittsburgh. Most important, Dr. Wecht would be expected to explain how Glen could have been choked from behind without leaving marks on the front of his neck.

With unresolved side issues, a trial in the spring was obviously out. Meanwhile, Glen kept drilling teeth down in Virginia. That only served to make many people in the Wyoming Valley angrier than they already were.

The defense filed a motion seeking to keep secret Glen's medical records from Mercy Hospital and his psychiatric records from his 1985 hospitalization. The records had been obtained by search warrants within days of Glen's arrest. "It is hard to believe that there is anything more personal or privileged than the communication of one's personal thoughts or emotions to his psychiatrist or physician," the lawyers wrote in court papers. Ultimately, the Mercy Hospital records would be allowed, but introduction of the psychiatric documents would not be permitted at the trial.

The defense leveled another half dozen arguments as to why the murder charges should be dismissed, including Stevens's use of the case in his political campaign and a contention that "a witness crucial to the defense, Neil Wolsieffer, has died and is consequently unavailable."

Hearings begot hearings. Proceedings were postponed several times due to Cardinale's commitments in other courthouses. That stopped the clock on the Commonwealth's deadline to bring Glen to trial. As July turned to August, Cardinale revealed that Betty's father and brother had worn body recorders in attempts to trap Glen. The defense attorney later told reporters that his client had cried on the tapes, but he declined to provide additional details. He said he was contemplating turning the tables on the government and using the tapes as part of his defense.

On August 8, in his final pretrial order, Judge Cappellini ruled that statements the defendant made to police before and after his arrest were admissible, including the comments he made to Detective Mitchell in the police car following his arrest. The judge said evidence retrieved from 75 Birch without a warrant also could be used at the trial. He said the police had been invited to the house by the call from the defendant's brother, Neil.

Judge Cappellini agreed with a defense contention that it would be impossible to select an unbiased jury in Luzerne County with the media saturation—especially the onslaught from those who preferred to dispense with a trial altogether. In a compromise, both sides agreed to a change of venire; the judge and lawyers would go to another jurisdiction to select a jury, then bring the jurors back to Wilkes-Barre and sequester them to sit in judgment before a local audience.

This precipitated yet another delay, albeit the final one, because the Pennsylvania Supreme Court had to designate the county from where the jurors would be selected.

On November 5, 1990, one year and three days after his arrest, the trial of Dr. E. Glen Wolsieffer got under way in Harrisburg, the state capital, with jury selection. It took a week to pick the panel. They were sent home for the weekend to say good-bye and pack, loaded onto a bus that Sunday evening, and shipped off to their temporary home in Wilkes-Barre, the Ramada Hotel On The Square, across the street from the *Times Leader* offices.

Anticipation filled the air as an overflow crowd squeezed its way into Judge Cappellini's third-floor courtroom the next morning, November 12, 1990. A large crowd remained in line outside for the next available seats.

A former public defender, assistant D.A., and criminal defense attorney, Judge Cappellini had a reputation of being fair and very competent. Neither side objected to the fact that he and Nocito had once been members of the same law firm or that while he served as a special deputy state attorney general, he had worked under Sarcione's father. Judge Cappellini, who lived just one street over from Birch, usually allowed defense attorneys a great deal of leeway, but from a prosecution point of view, that kind of trial usually left little for the defendant on appeal.

The judge and lawyers entered the beautifully appointed courtroom. The seven men and five women on the jury, along with four alternates, were escorted in and sworn. The jury box ran against the left wall of the large courtroom. Directly in front of the railing were two sets of tables facing the front of the courtroom. The prosecution team of Sarcione, Keller, Mitchell, and Sworen were seated in the front tier. Behind them sat Dr. Wolsieffer, closest to the jury box, with Nocito in the middle and Cardinale on the right outer edge. In the usual Luzerne County accommodation to the news media, reporters were allowed to sit in two rows of uncomfortable wooden chairs arranged along the right wall of the courtroom, inside the well of the court, directly across from the jury box. Judge Cappellini issued an order allowing cameras on the third floor outside his courtroom, but photographers were instructed not to take pictures of the jurors.

The battle lines were most distinctly drawn in the courtroom proper. The Tasker family sat in the front row on the right side, assisted by Sworen's wife, Corine, the county's victims' rights coordinator. Across the way, directly behind Glen, sat Glen's family, anchored by Phyllis, clutching rosary beads, Lisa, and Mary Stinson.

All the alliances of yesteryear—Jack Tasker playing golf with

Neil, or going out drinking with Glen; Lisa running a crafts show with Betty, or trying to help her save her marriage riding around looking for Glen in all the wrong places—all that was gone.

Betty was gone. Neil was gone.

This was family against family, with no in between. You were either for Glen or against him.

CHAPTER 31

Turning to the jurors, Judge Cappellini carefully instructed them that the defendant, Dr. E. Glen Wolsieffer, had the right to remain silent and to present no evidence. "You must not hold it against the defendant if he happens to choose not to testify." The judge's advisory was an instruction always given, but almost never followed.

Sarcione began his "bird's-eye view of the facts" by explaining his theme for the trial. "This case is about *marriage*, it is about *infidelity*, on behalf of the defendant, especially on Friday evenings into Saturday mornings, and it is about *murder*, and covering your tracks after a murder. That's what this case is about, those three words."

The prosecutor spoke eloquently for another twenty minutes—about the perseverance of the investigators, about Glen's numerous statements to the authorities, about his initial lies to the police about Debbie Shipp, about his life-style, the "backwards" ladder, the undisturbed "heavy dew," and the lack of evidence showing forcible entry.

He also spoke about the Cooks having seen Glen use the ladder at least once when he was locked out, about the FBI's involvement, about the forcibly removed head hairs consistent with the defendant's, about his Friday nights with Debbie, about his Friday nights with Carol, and about Betty telling Barbara Wende that she wasn't going to take Glen's Friday nights out anymore.

And he spoke ever so briefly about the defendant's dead brother meeting the police at the front door. "You will hear that Neil Wolsieffer, approximately six weeks after this incident, is dead. He is no longer with us."

But it was Sarcione's introductory salvo that said it all. Three words: Marriage. Infidelity. Murder.

Cardinale started his longer remarks by explaining that criminal trials are often cluttered with "layers of distortion." He said jurors had to decipher between what his client believed happened in the early morning hours of August 30, 1986, what the police believed happened, and, finally, what the prosecutor believed had happened. He contended that the investigators looked at the case through a bifocal lens, with one part wanting to find out what really happened, and the second part of the lens acting as a filter. "What the filter does, it takes away anything that's inconsistent with any preconceived notions the police may have, or any theories that they have developed."

The prosecution, Cardinale continued, worked with distorting trifocal lenses, adding to the mix "a deep desire and need—a want—to find and to believe that the defendant is guilty. In this case that belief, that third of the trifocal lens, can't be just that he's guilty, but he is big, bad guilty. . . . He has to be premeditated." As for the taped conversations with Dr. Wolsieffer's father-in-law and brother-in-law, Cardinale asked the jurors to pay close attention to the Tasker tapes, where "he and his brother-in-law are both crying over their losses," and the part where Dr. Wolsieffer explained to his father-in-law that the reason he had no marks on the front of his neck was because he had his hands in between the ligature and his throat. "But, of course, that doesn't fit in the theory, that doesn't fit into their preconceptions, so that's ignored." It was clear, Cardinale said, that the police never had any other suspects, that their case was built around "a fixed preconception" and "a theory they never let go of."

Cardinale spoke until the lunch break, at which time, outside the presence of the jury, Judge Cappellini granted a defense motion to sequester Corbett, whose name appeared on the prosecution's list of potential witnesses. The move precipitated another hearing on the First Amendment.

When the jurors returned, Cardinale continued bashing evidence they had yet to hear. He characterized the prosecution's case as "a lot of excuses," "a complete brush-over," and a distortion. Turning to what was going to be the most crucial aspect of his defense, Cardinale asked the jury to "pay close attention" to evidence about the "two unknown palm prints," plural. He said the police had recovered the evidence right after the murder. Put that together, Cardinale said, with his client's explanation, during the secretly taped conversations with his in-laws, that after giving it some thought, he realized there must have been two intruders, not one. "He says he believed there were two people there. And what do we have? Two palm prints that cannot be matched. . . . There is no way to get around that."

Furthermore, he argued, "No amount of evidence they present about my client's infidelity should make you look through the same blurred lenses they do to dismiss this evidence just because my client was unfaithful to his wife." The issue was not infidelity, Cardinale said, but whether the evidence showed that his client's infidelity constituted a motive for murder.

Keller showed the jury twenty-five photos, including one of Betty Wolsieffer's body on the bedroom floor and a close-up of the victim's head. Two diagrams, one of each floor of 75 Birch, were set up on a stand facing the jury box. The prosecution team then played the videotape taken of the crime scene by the police on the morning of the murder.

Following a recess, testimony finally commenced. What better way for Sarcione to start the prosecution's case than with Barbara Wende? Betty's friend from the dental auxiliary essentially repeated her testimony from the preliminary hearing, recounting Betty's stated intention three days before her death to "take a stand" if Glen went out gallivanting that Friday night.

To the packed courtroom, Wende outlined their friendship, their conversations about Glen's breakdown and hospitalization, and about Betty's "pretty rough summer" of 1985. "Betty, in the course of that conversation, had told me that Glen had asked her to set him free, and that she was not about to give Glen a divorce. Betty told me that Glen said that he was a burden to both she and Danielle." Cardinale objected to the last sentence, and Judge Cappellini concurred. But there was more damage on the way, as Sarcione now focused his questions on the conversation Wende had with Betty on the Tuesday before her murder.

"Mainly, we talked about Betty's unhappiness in her marriage," said Wende. "Betty surprised me by her tone of voice, because she was very angry in this conversation."

"Can you describe her voice for His Honor and the members of the jury?" asked Sarcione, skillfully guiding his witness through her very compelling testimony.

"Betty was not speaking nicely about Glen at all. Betty was angry in the way she was talking about Glen. Betty was upset about Glen."

"What did the discussion entail?"

"Betty told me that things had not been going well at all in the last year of their marriage," said Wende. "Betty told me that Fridays were becoming an especially difficult time. And the reason she told me this is because at one point in the conversation I had told her to 'Cheer up, the weekend is coming.' She said that Fridays were an especially bad time and that the weekends were not a good time in their marriage. Betty told me that Glen stayed out until the wee hours of the mornings on Fridays. I actually asked Betty why she didn't try to go out with Glen on Friday evenings, and Betty told me that Glen knew that Betty didn't drink and she would not be able to stay out as late as he liked to. Betty also told me that she was sure now that Glen must be seeing someone on these Friday nights."

Wende said that Betty went on to express how unhappy she was in the relationship. "I asked Betty why she had not expressed this unhappiness to Glen. Betty told me that if Glen came in late that particular Friday night, she was going to take a stand and say something to him. Then Betty said she was not going to be able to take this anymore, and she was going to have to do something about it. She was not going to allow herself to be stepped on anymore. That's what she said."

Wende said the conversation had taken place over the phone and had lasted no more than thirty-five minutes. "Did you talk to Betty Wolsieffer at all after that Tuesday phone call?"

"No," she replied. "I never talked to Betty ever again."

It was pretty dramatic stuff. Sarcione let it sink in, then sat down.

Cardinale had repeatedly made known his opposition to testimony from any of Betty's girlfriends about statements she made to them. However, Judge Cappellini ruled that he was going to allow them under an exception to the hearsay rule that permits second-hand testimony when it documents the victim's state of mind just prior to death. If Dr. Wolsieffer was convicted, this issue would no doubt be a key part of any appeal. But for now, Cardinale was obligated to contend with the contents of those conversations.

Under cross-examination, the defense attorney first asked Wende about Betty's comment during their final conversation that she was "sure Glen was seeing someone else." Wende said the subject had come up while Betty was discussing how terrible Friday nights were for her marriage.

Cardinale wanted to know how Wende had responded. "I didn't press her for who it was, or anything like that," Wende replied. "If she wanted to divulge it, that was her business. She confided in me. I was there for her support, that was it."

Hoping to raise a credibility issue with the witness, Cardinale sought to suggest that it was unlikely that such a supposedly good friend would not have pushed Betty for more details. Wende explained that she had previously heard rumors about Glen but had not gone to Betty with them "because I respected her and did not want to embarrass her."

Wende said she realized during the conversation that Betty had finally "put enough together to know for herself." But, she insisted, that was still not enough for her to override the bounds of their friendship. "If she wanted to offer the information on who it was, that was fine. But she wasn't offering that. I was there for support. I was not there to embarrass her or cause her to divulge anything that embarrassed her."

Seeking to raise another credibility issue, Cardinale sought to establish an inconsistency between Wende's trial testimony to Sarcione and her testimony at the preliminary hearing regarding what she had originally told police. "I recall that there's a discrepancy on my statements from that period of time with regards to that," she acknowledged.

"When did you discover this?" asked Cardinale.

"I discovered that when I was able to review my statements," she replied.

Under persistent questioning, Wende contended that she had not made her discovery that morning, but was forced to admit that she had spoken to Bill Keller just hours before taking the witness stand. Yes, they had discussed the fact that her testimony at the preliminary hearing regarding Betty's statement that she was "sure Glen was seeing someone else" was something she had failed to specifically mention back in 1987.

Cardinale showed Wende a statement she gave police in June 1987. There was no mention of such a statement. Then he showed her a police report dated July 10, 1987. Again, the defense attorney wanted to know where it stated that she had told investigators that Betty had told her "she was sure Glen was seeing someone else."

The line of questioning was a potential nightmare for Sarcione's game plan, but Wende was well prepared and far from intimidated. Reading from the report, Wende said, " 'Betty told Barbara she loved Glen and she would fight to keep the marriage going. Betty said there was another woman involved with Glen.' " It was hard to see the discrepancy.

In fact, the root of the problem was with Wende's incorrect recollections during her testimony at the preliminary hearing, not with any failure to have mentioned Betty's statements about Glen's infidelity to investigators in 1987.

Wende explained that she had been "extremely nervous" at the preliminary hearing and misspoke. "I did the best I could," she said. "As time goes by, I am more clear on it. I know what transpired."

"Your memory, you think, is better today than it was back in 1987?" Cardinale asked.

"My thoughts are very clear on this," Wende replied firmly.

Again, the witness offered that it had not been her place to embarrass Betty. "I feel that friendship comes from the heart. This was just something that I felt I was not going to press Betty on."

Going back to Wende's final conversation with Betty, the one where she revealed her plan to "take a stand" if Glen stayed out late that final Friday, Cardinale tried to get the witness to admit that it was she who had suggested that Betty confront Glen.

"I totally disagree with that statement," Wende said. "Betty is the one who said, 'I am going to have to take a stand. I am going to have to say something.' "

As she had done at the preliminary hearing, Wende did admit that she had "encouraged Betty not to allow people to take advantage of her," but asserted, "I didn't tell her to 'take a stand' against her husband that night. I asked her why she had never expressed her unhappiness, and that is when she told me if he came in late that Friday night, she was going to 'take a stand,' she was going to say something."

Cardinale was finished. He had tried, but failed, to make any significant headway. Over at the Commonwealth's table, the tension appeared to ooze right out of Tony Sarcione. Wende had provided a very powerful and encouraging start to the prosecutor's parade of witnesses. Sarcione had that look of his, the gaze of a hunter with his prey locked into the cross hairs.

The rest of the afternoon and early evening was consumed with the confusing, sometimes embarrassingly so, testimony of Officer Dale Minnick—first on the scene and still sounding as though he had solved the case single-handedly.

He got Neil Wolsieffer's name in quickly, recounting how Neil had let him and Officer Anthony George into 75 Birch that morning. Unsolicited, Minnick recalled that "when I approached Neil again, he insisted that we go upstairs."

Cardinale objected to hearsay from the deceased, and Judge Cappellini concurred.

Throughout his testimony, Minnick, who had retired from the force that February, continued to answer straightforward questions of fact with his opinions. Each time, Cardinale objected, and Judge Cappellini sustained. The problem got so serious that at one point, Keller had to beg his witness: "Officer, just tell us what you did. Don't give us editorials."

Minnick changed his testimony from the preliminary hearing about never leaving Dr. Wolsieffer unattended. He now claimed that both paramedics had joined him and Officer George upstairs. He contended that "we" searched the house for an intruder *after* the defendant had been removed to the hospital, which would have meant Officer George had left by that time. Then he corrected himself on that point, too.

As he had done at the preliminary hearing, Minnick insisted that the ladder was leaning backwards against the house. Keller turned toward the ladder, which was resting against a pillar in the right corner of the courtroom, next to the water cooler. Keller wanted to bring it over to the jury box. Judge Cappellini would have none of it. Instead, the jurors were allowed to leave their seats to get a close-up look.

One side of the ladder and a piece of wood were now taped together. A photo taken on the day of the murder showed that the ladder was broken. "The minute we moved the ladder, it separated," said Minnick. However, he insisted, it was already cracked, just not separated, when he first saw it. He also insisted that no one had moved the ladder before Detective Mitchell did. Then it sounded as if he was saying that he personally had been up on the roof within the first hour of his arrival, which would have meant before Detective Mitchell started his analysis of the ladder.

Under cross-examination, the clutter continued. In response to a series of pointed questions from Cardinale, Minnick was unable to explain how the ladder had been carried from the side of the Wolsieffer garage to the back roof without splitting, but then somehow split the minute he moved it. Also, the witness had insisted to Keller that Neil had kept bugging him and Officer George to go upstairs. Yet, right in Minnick's original report—the one that failed to mention that the ladder was backwards—it was stated that upon asking Dr. Wolsieffer if anyone else was in the house, the dentist replied that his wife and daughter were upstairs.

Running through a series of police photos of 75 Birch, Cardinale successfully raised the possibility that items like the shade in the back bedroom window had been moved by someone during the time between Minnick's arrival and the taking of the photos about two hours later. Shown a photo of the roof taken at 9:30 A.M., after he had supposedly left grass clippings in the morning dew, Minnick was unable to pick out the supposedly damning cuttings. Cardinale pointed out that there were no grass clippings or footprints visible on the roof portion of the police video either. "I know there was grass on my shoes. Whether I left it on the roof, I don't recall," Minnick now conceded.

It was not a stellar performance from the first officer on the scene. But getting it out of the way made for a good strategy.

Day Two started with another argument in chambers over Corbett's newspaper wanting to make a fuss over the sequestration order. Rather than get sidetracked with another time-consuming hearing over what he considered to be a spurious First Amendment argument, Cardinale dropped his objection for the time being, thus allowing Corbett to return to the courtroom.

The rest of the morning, and part of the afternoon, was consumed by the testimony of Officer Anthony George, who joined Minnick first on the scene, paramedic Richard Powell, and his partner, firefighter John Ostrum. They all held up their end, and Minnick's performance quickly faded from everyone's memory.

Officer George tried to give his opinions at first, such as when he offered that Dr. Wolsieffer had given "a fake cough." Judge Cappellini ordered him to stick to the facts.

There were still discrepancies. George told the jury that Dr. Wolsieffer had asked him on two occasions, "How is my daughter?" Powell testified that the defendant had asked him, "Where are my girls?" Ostrum seconded that Dr. Wolsieffer inquired of him on two occasions about his daughter and wife. The testimony from Powell and Ostrum pretty much destroyed the prosecution's attempt to paint the defendant as indifferent and uncaring about his wife because he knew she was already dead.

In the main, though, the testimony from the three men was consistent as it pertained to the chronology of events. There were other benefits, too. When asked, Powell and Ostrum both said that in their conversations with Dr. Wolsieffer about what had happened, he never mentioned that there had been two intruders.

*   *   *

After lunch, the jurors heard the tape of Neil Wolsieffer calling police headquarters on the Saturday morning in question. The transcript distributed to the jurors did not contain any passage in which Neil was instructed to stay where he was, as Cardinale had contended in his opening remarks.

The jurors then heard the sad tale of Deborah Shipp. A reluctant witness, she related her sordid story of Friday nights at the Imperial or her house, the broken marriage promises, how Glen had introduced her as his fiancée when he went to look for an apartment, the time Glen ran away for a weekend, Glen's inability to make a commitment because of fear of being cut off from Danielle, the cancelled plans because of the slit screen door, and the fact that she didn't know about Carol Kopicki until after Betty's murder. The jury was shown the pearl earrings Glen had given her for Christmas in 1984, when she quit Temple University to be closer to her paramour. They also looked at a watch and bracelet, also gifts from Glen.

Debbie told of the breakup in November 1988, when Glen summoned her to Virginia to tell her they couldn't see each other anymore. "He said that I was looked at as the motive."

"During that seven-year period, did the defendant ever promise you he would marry you?" Sarcione asked.

Debbie replied in the affirmative.

Sarcione inquired how many times.

"Several. I didn't count them," she said.

Had they ever made preparations? "No, not any real plans."

Seeking to bring closure to the bittersweet walk down memory lane, Sarcione asked a seemingly simple question: "After that conversation in Virginia in 1988 that you had with the defendant, where he told you the reason why he couldn't see you, did you ever talk to the defendant again?"

"I saw him twice after that."

Instead of stopping at that point, Sarcione forged ahead. "You weren't intimate with him after that?"

"Yes."

"You *were*?"

"Yes."

"I have no further questions, Your Honor."

*   *   *

As if having to dredge up her personal missteps in a packed court-room wasn't enough, Cardinale proceeded to heap even more disrespect on Debbie's relationship with his client.

Yes, she said, Glen had asked her "several times" to marry him. No, they never made plans for a wedding. Yes, she continued to see Glen even after she found out he was seeing someone else.

"You would go out with him, go places with him?"

"Not really go out places with him."

Focusing on the Wolsieffer family, Cardinale asked Debbie if she was aware of Glen's "very deep love" for his daughter, Danielle. Debbie said she was.

"And you knew that through all the experiences you had, that Glen wasn't going to leave Betty and his daughter, was he?"

"That's not what he told me."

"I understand that. But you had experience with him and you knew that no matter what happened, at least during the times you were together, he didn't leave them, correct?" She said yes.

"And even after she died, he didn't marry you?"

"No."

"You didn't get engaged?"

"No."

Following a recess, Commonwealth Exhibit 85, a tape of Glen's call to Betty Jane Kelley at Wilkes-Barre Police Headquarters the Sunday before the murder, to report the cut screen, was played for the jury. The tape was the linchpin of the prosecution's theory of preplanning and premeditation, a necessary requirement for first-degree murder.

Carol Ann Kopicki took the stand next. Keller had her walk through her relationship with the defendant. Using motel registration cards, he had her confirm five encounters—two at the Busy Day Motel and three at the Granite Motel up in Mountaintop. Keller extracted a sixth admission by asking if she and Dr. Wolsieffer had visited any other motels. "Yes," Carol replied. "The Red Roof Inn." The prosecutor did not ask about the nights on the dental office floor.

She also detailed that when she and Glen got together, it was usually on a Friday night. Glen usually left around 2:00, and never once stayed until the next morning.

Keller had one final question. "Miss Kopicki, who are you living with now in Falls Church, Virginia?"

Cardinale objected on the grounds of relevancy. "Overruled," said the judge.

"With Glen," she said.

"With the defendant?" Keller asked for the sake of clarity.

"Yes."

On cross-examination, Cardinale had his client's mistress paint an image of a loving family living down in Virginia—Glen and his daughter, Carol and her son. There was no mention of her daughter, who had chosen to stay behind in Pennsylvania.

"Who takes care of them?"

"I do and Glen does."

Cardinale asked how long they had been living together. Carol said about a year. However, she remained as fuzzy as ever about precisely when the relationship had resumed following Betty's murder.

She said her son was in the sixth grade, while Danielle was now in the fourth.

"Is Dr. Wolsieffer a good father to both?" Keller had reached his limit with the testimonial and objected. Judge Cappellini sustained.

"I have no other questions. Thank you," said Cardinale.

CHAPTER 32

Day Three began with great anticipation as Neil Wolsieffer's widow took the witness stand. This was going to be her first substantive statement in public since her brother-in-law had started working in Virginia nearly three years earlier.

At a pretrial interview, Nancy had asked Sarcione why he had said he was going to call her at the preliminary hearing, but never did. "Are you going to do the same thing? I need to get mentally prepared." The prosecutor told her they had decided to save her the first time around. Implicit in that decision was the unrelenting hope that Nancy knew more than she had professed and would decide to open up at the trial.

But Nancy continued to insist she had told investigators everything she knew, a contention Sarcione ultimately came to accept. "When I first started investigating the case I thought she knew more. But as I got into it, I didn't think that any longer," Sarcione said.

The focus of the prosecution's interest in Nancy's testimony, then, was important but not tantalizing. In the days immediately following Betty's murder, she had helped Glen compile a list of missing items for his attorney. The list included several pieces of Betty's jewelry that Nancy had been unable to locate. At the time, she had no idea what, if anything, Glen and his lawyer had done with the list. In fact, they had turned it over to the police. Within the next week or so, while cleaning up at 75 Birch, Nancy located several of the pieces of jewelry, and again informed Glen.

Now Sarcione wanted her to testify about the jewelry that she had found because her discoveries supported the Commonwealth's contention that there had been no burglary.

For the uninformed, speculation was rampant about what she would say. There was talk that she was the prosecution's surprise "smoking gun." But it was not to be. The jury would hear none of Nancy's personal story of betrayal, her emotional transformation from Glen's sympathizer and supporter to an unswayable nonbeliever. Those details would not be admissible.

The jurors would later say they were curious for more information about Neil Wolsieffer, since they kept hearing about him. But because of restrictions on what could be discussed concerning Neil, Nancy provided little illumination in that regard. Hers was more a psychological boost to the case as she filled in some blanks regarding Glen's version of events, and provided powerful new details about Betty's final days.

Sarcione set the stage with his very first question. "Nancy, could you tell us, please, where you live?"

"I live at 84 Birch Street in Wilkes-Barre," she answered with a nervous quaver in her voice.

"Where is that in relation to 75 Birch Street?"

"It is across the street."

Asked when her husband had passed away, Nancy replied: "He was killed in a car accident October 16, 1986."

She said that after she and Neil moved to Birch Street in 1983, she saw Betty daily. "We were very close friends."

In response to questions, Nancy explained that she had often discussed with Betty the troubled condition of Betty and Glen's marriage.

As Cardinale's objections on the hearsay issue continued to be overruled by Judge Cappellini, Nancy quoted Betty as telling her in early August 1985 that she was "worried about Glen possibly having an affair, but she wasn't sure." By the end of the month, meaning after Glen had been hospitalized at First Valley Hospital, Nancy said Betty told her "that she had asked Glen if he was seeing someone—early in the morning she asked him—and he said yes."

She said Betty told her that Glen usually stayed out until after 2:00 A.M. on Fridays, and that she usually waited up for him, busying herself with crafts or soaking in the tub. "After she found out that he was seeing someone, she said she didn't want him to go out on Friday nights anymore."

Nancy said that Betty was particularly angry when she talked to her on Saturday morning, August 23, 1986, one week before her murder. "She said that Glen had gotten home at 3:30 and she was really upset because that was so late." If the jurors were keeping track of the dates—a difficult task without the aid of pen and paper—they would have realized that the reason for Glen's tardiness that night was that he had been up at the Granite Motel in Mountaintop with Carol Kopicki.

Nancy said they discussed Betty's marital discord a few days later, too. "She said that on Monday night, prior to the murder on Friday, that she and Glen had been up all night talking because it was around that time a year earlier, the anniversary of when she found out about another woman, and she said she was really upset and reliving all that. She said they stayed up practically the whole night talking. She called me Tuesday morning to tell me he wasn't going to work, and they were going to Betty's parents' house to cut the grass, do chores and work outside."

They had spoken again that Friday morning, Betty's final morning, Nancy said. Her sister-in-law told her she was taking Danielle to a birthday party. "I just said, 'Are you okay?' She said, 'I am upset.' She said, 'Things aren't right.' She said, 'I will call you when I come back, and we will talk about it.' But we didn't."

Sarcione proceeded on to another topic of their discussions, Debbie Shipp's love letters. Nancy said Betty told her about them near the end of 1985, and even showed her one of the cards at the kitchen table at 75 Birch. "She said she found them in Glen's briefcase and she said that they were little cards and things that she had sent him when she was away at school, and she said she was going to just put them away and save them." During that same time period, Nancy recalled, Betty also had told her that she had found a receipt for a security deposit Glen had put down on an apartment.

Turning to her and Neil's activities the morning of the murder, Nancy said they were awakened at 7:15 A.M. by the ring of the telephone. Her story was consistent with her earlier statements, and she told it briefly and with confidence. Sarcione then moved on to the technical reason for her being there, the issue of Betty's jewelry. Nancy said she was aware of the "good jewelry" that Betty had, which was few in number. "When I first looked, I just looked in the jewelry box, where I assumed it would be. So, I reported it was missing. But then when I went back in and started to straighten up the house, I found the diamond earrings and the different things that I said were missing. They were there but they were in different areas of the house that I never looked before."

For example, Nancy said, she found a pair of Betty's diamond earrings in an ashtray on a desk in the kitchen. She knew Betty had purchased a pearl necklace for her mother for a gift, and knew that she had not given it to her mother before she died. Nancy said she found the necklace in a decorator box on the kitchen counter.

One last thing, Sarcione wondered—had she ever had a conversation with the defendant, in January 1987, about what had happened? Nancy said she had.

"Did the defendant ever say to you he saw two intruders?"

"No," she answered, as Sarcione returned to his chair with an air of satisfaction.

Cardinale had to negotiate a mine field in his cross-examination. He certainly did not want to unnecessarily open any trapdoors.

Nancy acknowledged that during all the years she had known Glen and Betty, she had never seen Glen be violent with Betty or strike her. She also had never seen them fight.

She conceded that Neil had often gone out with Glen on Friday nights in 1985, but only "sometimes" in 1986. Yes, she admitted, there had been crank telephone calls to 84 Birch on the Friday nights that Neil had been out with Glen. Yes, they had an unlisted phone number. But Cardinale's queries on that point begged the issue of how and why a supposed stranger had gotten access to the number. Had Glen made the calls?

As for the state of Glen and Betty's marriage, Nancy said that she was aware of the affair with Debbie but was under the impression that Glen and Betty had been "in counseling" and were working at saving their union.

Cardinale asked Nancy about a piece of wood she said she had found on the bed in the master bedroom of 75 Birch while cleaning up a few days after the murder. Nancy said she believed the wood had come from the shade in the rear bedroom. Yes, she said, she had found the wood before Glen was released from the hospital.

But that was as far as Cardinale could go on the subject. Of course, his intent was to plant the suggestion that the intruders had somehow transported the piece of shade into the house and on to Betty's bed. But the theory seemed implausible. How had the dozens of cops and other officials missed the wood while scrutinizing the murder scene that Saturday? Had the cops been that sloppy? Common sense dictated that someone had placed the wood on the bed after the police had released the property. But if Glen didn't do it, then who?

As for the jewelry, Cardinale got Nancy to concede that in addition to the pieces she had recovered, she had not found Betty's diamond V-necklace.

Then he inquired about missing cash.

"*Glen* told me that," replied Nancy, for once being able to reveal a hint of her feelings of mistrust toward the defendant.

Cardinale did not pursue any other topics and sat down.

Sarcione decided to briefly conduct a redirect examination, however. He had Nancy reiterate that in 1986 Neil did not go out with Glen every Friday night. "Once in a while, not often," Nancy said. "Maybe once a month he would go out, to one place where they went, for a few hours and he would come home about 10:30."

In a display of gamesmanship, Sarcione scored splendidly with a sudden loss of hearing. "What time? I'm sorry—10:30, did you say? That he would come home?"

"That's what she said," bellowed Cardinale from his chair at defense table.

"I'm sorry," Sarcione pleaded. "I didn't hear."

The prosecutor closed his second round of questions by making sure that it had been "the defendant" who had told her that money was missing from the house.

"Yes," Nancy answered.

The "loss of hearing" exchange would not be the only time the adversaries would toy with each other. During one sidebar, Cardinale and Sarcione argued over what a Birch Street neighbor who walked her dog the morning of the murder could and could not testify about.

Cardinale warned Sarcione, "If you have testimony about the dog, you'd better have the dog ready to testify." Judge Cappellini ultimately ruled that the woman could testify.

As the two attorneys walked back to their respective tables, Sarcione whispered to Cardinale, "The only fucking dog in this place is you."

Finished with her testimony, Nancy wanted to hear the rest of the trial. But because Betty's friend Jane Ann Miscavage was scheduled to testify next, Cardinale still wanted Nancy kept out of the courtroom under the sequestration order. He had been informed that Mrs. Miscavage was going to quote Betty as having threatened Glen that he would never see Danielle again if he left her.

Cardinale said he was considering calling Nancy to say that Betty would never have said that. As a potential defense witness, she could not remain in the courtroom. Of course, another by-product would have been that she would have been unable to hear any testimony she might recognize as untrue.

But it did not work out that way. Nancy sent word through her attorney that if she were asked about Betty's comments she would testify that she didn't believe Betty had really meant it. With that, Cardinale dropped the issue. "In the heat of anger, I might say the same thing," Nancy said later. " 'If you leave me, you are never seeing this child again.' She did tell me that she said that."

Jane Ann Miscavage, who spent some of her lonely Friday nights talking on the telephone to Betty Wolsieffer, testified that she also had talked to her friend about Debbie Shipp's love letters. She said Betty was devastated to learn Glen was having an affair. Just weeks before her death, Miscavage said, Betty told her she believed the affair was still going on, despite Glen's assurances to the contrary.

Miscavage said she asked Betty why she just didn't divorce Glen if she was that upset. She quoted Betty as saying she would never divorce Glen, and that she would "drag him through the mud" and "never let him see Danielle" if he ever filed for a divorce.

Under cross-examination, Miscavage acknowledged that Betty had complained to her constantly about Glen's cheating ways. But, Cardinale pointed out, she had told police just ten days after the murder that Betty was a very private person and had not complained lately about Glen. The defense attorney hammered away at other inconsistencies and changes in her statement.

"In September of 1986, you told the police that she had no complaints lately about her husband?"

"She was upset."

"But she had no complaints, is that what you told them?"

"She was upset."

"If someone was upset and says, 'I am tired of you going out on Friday nights,' is that not a complaint to you?"

"Yes, I guess so."

" 'I think he is still fooling around, even though he told me he isn't,' isn't that a complaint to you?"

"Yes, but she didn't say it in that way," Miscavage maintained.

"However she said it, it is still a complaint no matter what words she used?"

"She was quite devastated, yes."

Cardinale pointed out that Miscavage herself had learned of certain information in September of 1986, namely that her husband was having an affair with Joyce Greco. "That caused you some devastation, isn't that true?" Miscavage agreed.

"And it caused a lot of resentment in you?"

"Toward some people, yes."

"Including my client?" Miscavage denied the charge.

"*No?*" Cardinale mocked.

"No."

"You like him, I take it?"

"No," the witness conceded.

Cardinale wondered if Miscavage remembered telling Carol Kopicki: "You wait, because if this ever gets to court, I am going to drag you all through the mud." She swore she hadn't.

Miscavage was reminded that she was under oath, but she wouldn't budge.

"You are not that bitter or you weren't that bitter that you would have made a comment like that?" No, she said.

"Not at all," said Cardinale, building his sarcasm. "But you are bitter enough, are you not, Mrs. Miscavage, to take your two daughters—"

"I don't have two daughters."

"Sons?"

"I don't have two sons either."

"A son and daughter. We have eliminated everything else.— To take your son and daughter and bring them to your husband's sister's home, when he was there with Joyce Greco and Carol Kopicki, and put your children in front of your husband and those people and tell your children, 'That's going to be your new mother. That's what your father's been doing.' That never happened?"

"No."

"Objection," yelled Sarcione.

Judge Cappellini wasn't about to step in here. "Overruled."

"Your Honor—" Sarcione tried again, but in vain.

"Your testimony today, Mrs. Miscavage, is that you deny that that occurred?" asked Cardinale of the day when three-fourths of the Miscavage family found the fourth member sitting poolside with Joyce and Carol.

"I didn't say it didn't occur," said Miscavage. "I *was* there. I did not say that was going to be their new mother. My daughter was looking for her father. I, at the time, did not know that the girls were there."

The witness confirmed that she and her husband were no longer living together, and conceded that her learning of her husband's affair was a major contributing factor.

"As a result of all that, would you agree with me that your feelings against your husband and any of his friends, particularly Dr. Wolsieffer, is such that you would make good on promises you made to drag people through the mud if you ever had a chance to do so in court?"

"I never made that statement."

"You never did?" She insisted she had not.

Cardinale asked for a moment, looked at his notes, then suggested that instead of "drag everybody through the mud," she had said she would "bury people if she got a chance to go to court."

"No. I have nothing to bury somebody with."

"You tried your best today, I can tell," said Cardinale walking away. "No further questions."

Sarcione only had one question on redirect. "Mrs. Miscavage, are you here today pursuant to a subpoena issued by the Commonwealth?"

The witness replied in the affirmative, as if to discount any possibility that she might have an ax to grind.

The procession of girlfriends continued with Barbara Dombroski, who recounted Betty crying on the phone to her about Glen and Debbie. "She told me that that Saturday night they had been out to a birthday party for a friend and they had a good time. On Sunday, Glen got up and he told her he was going to move out. She said she asked him if he had been having an affair with Debbie Shipp and he admitted that he was. . . . She told me that she hated her for ruining their lives."

Moving ahead to the months just prior to Betty's murder, Dombroski said her friend told her she was upset about Glen going out on Friday nights. "She told me that she couldn't sleep until he got home because she was worried about where he was."

On one occasion, early in the summer of 1986, Betty told her of an overnight shopping trip she reluctantly took with her parents. "She told me that she didn't want to leave Glen alone. She said to me it was the first time she had left him alone since she found out about Debbie."

"Did she tell you why she didn't want to leave him alone?" Keller asked.

"She told me that she didn't trust him."

Eileen Pollock testified that in the summer of 1985 Betty told her on several occasions that "she was suspicious of Glen's behavior.

He was keeping odd hours and going to the office on Sundays to collect his mail, different things that she was becoming suspicious of his behavior. . . . She had told me that in regard to the late hours, that he was helping his secretary paint her home and so was his hygienist. They would both be there to midnight painting, and she didn't really believe that they were painting this home until midnight. She had gone to his office, she found cards and letters that the hygienist had written to him. She referred to them as love letters."

"Did she tell you what she did with those?" Keller asked.

"She told me she was going to hold onto them and sometime when the occasion arose, she would confront him with them. She never told me where she put them or what she did with them, just that she was going to hang onto them."

Pollock said that following Glen's hospitalization, Betty had come to her to explain things. "She had told me that she wanted myself and Barbara Dombroski to hear these things from her. She told me about Glen getting an apartment, she had found out that he had tried to get an apartment and that he wanted to go out on his own. She didn't want him to do that. She said that she didn't want him to leave. If he left—I guess he had suggested a trial separation, and she said she wouldn't have that. 'If he walked out, he wasn't coming back.' She didn't want him getting this apartment and going through this trial separation."

Pollock said that Betty had also confided in her in February 1986, following Glen's runaway weekend with Debbie. "She told me that he checked into the Red Roof Inn and called her several times during the weekend." The witness went on to explain that one of Betty's main concerns since learning of the Shipp affair the prior summer was that Debbie had kept working for Glen. "After this weekend he spent at the Red Roof Inn, Debbie supposedly quit—she left his employ—and at that particular time, Betty thought that things were getting better. They seemed like maybe the problems were all resolved."

But then, Pollock said, in the summer of 1986 Betty "alluded that things were happening again. . . . She told me that someone had told her about Glen being at the Crackerbox and slow dancing with Carol Kopicki."

She said Betty then told her, "It will be a long time before I will be able to trust him again."

Under cross-examination, Pollock said Betty had never told her that if she and Glen divorced, she would drag him through the mud. Betty also never told her that if they divorced, she would prevent Glen from seeing Danielle. "She would not do that."

Planning ahead for the forensic battle he knew loomed about the blue fibers found under the victim's fingernails, Cardinale got Pollock to say she thought Betty had worn a blue vest and pants to the birthday party at her house the afternoon before she died.

After a break for lunch, the prosecution called the last of Betty's girlfriends, racquetball and exercise colleague Jean Kwiatkowski. She was summoned essentially to share her account of a party that she, Betty, and Glen had attended at Lesley McCann's Aerobic World in the spring of 1986.

"What night of the week was this party?" Sarcione asked.

"It was a Friday evening," she said. Most of the people there knew each other, and so "the people were just talking with each other." She said that Betty wasn't ready to leave when, about 11:00, Glen suddenly announced his plans to depart.

"I was facing both Betty and Glen, and Glen just said, 'I am leaving now.' Betty asked Glen if he would like to get something to eat instead of leaving. Glen's answer was, 'Friday nights are mine.' He then left."

The saddest part about the testimony from Betty's friends was how all the women recalled Betty telling them she still loved Glen and was sure that they would work things out. The testimony from the friends also raised another good point: what ever happened to Debbie's cards and letters?

The prosecution called Dr. George E. Hudock, Jr., the county coroner, to the stand next. His testimony was lengthy, complicated, and important for the jury to hear. It consumed the rest of the day and a good deal of Day Four.

Dr. Hudock said he believed that Betty Wolsieffer had died between 2:30 and 6:30 A.M. on the Saturday in question. He made no mention of the estimate of between 4:00 and 7:00 A.M. that he had given reporters at a news conference in 1986, immediately following Betty's autopsy. The wider margin better fit the prosecution's scenario that Glen came home from the Crackerbox at about closing time and started arguing with Betty. No one was going to suggest that they argued for two to five hours. Starting the range at 2:30 A.M. fit the scenario perfectly.

After detailing the bruises and lacerations on Betty's face and neck, Dr. Hudock was asked by Keller if the injuries would have caused bleeding.

"Yes, sir," said the witness, launching into a technical explanation. But had the doctor found any blood? Dr. Hudock replied that other than red markings on the left hand that may have been blood, he failed to detect any from the head to the waist.

As for the cause of death, Dr. Hudock said, Betty Wolsieffer died from "asphyxia due to strangulation" by a combination of hands and a ligature. "The irregular abrasions and contusions of the neck are consistent with the irregular marks that I see on the neck when somebody grabs somebody around the neck, and some of these abrasions had a linear pattern that's consistent with some object being applied around the neck."

He said the injuries around the victim's mouth had been caused by "some kind of force or injury," and added that some kind of object had been placed over her mouth.

Keller wondered how long it had taken for Betty Wolsieffer to die "once the strangulation started."

"It took about three to five minutes. She didn't die instantly," the witness replied.

Under cross-examination, Dr. Hudock was quizzed about lividity, livor mortis, rigor mortis, and blanching. The defense strategy was to get the time of death moved closer to sunrise. Even though he agreed with several of Cardinale's suppositions, which would have put the death after 4:00 A.M., Dr. Hudock refused to waver on his 2:30-to-6:30-A.M. range.

Dr. Hudock said the object used to kill Betty could have been a belt, or a curtain cord, if it was wide enough. But, he continued, he had no idea what was used, or whether it was rough or smooth. Still, Cardinale seemed pleased that a belt was in the running, and that the injuries to Betty's neck were specifically consistent with the type of injuries caused by the use of a belt.

The pathologist talked of the mysterious blue object he found on the bedsheet when he turned the victim's body over, saying that when he turned the body back over, the object corresponded to an abrasion on the back of Betty's neck, below the hairline. Under Cardinale's questioning, he pointed to a different spot on the neck, though. Even later, he implied that the object could have been unconnected to the murder and fallen out of the victim's hair.

Corporal Eugene J. Centi, supervisor of the records and identification division of the Pennsylvania State Police, was full of surprises during his visit to the witness stand on Day Four. On the heels of Cardinale's mention of two partial palm prints and two intruders in his opening statement, the one, and "only one," palm print that Centi had testified about at the preliminary hearing had been transformed back into two—Commonwealth Exhibits 112 and 112A.

As a result, Cardinale lost the ability to make ground with the discrepancy. He also was unable to get Centi to duplicate his preliminary hearing testimony that the palm print had been "fairly new—less than twenty-four hours." But his inquiry on that point was not totally without value to the defense.

With Keller repeatedly objecting to the line of questioning without any success, Centi conceded that after he had dusted the desk with special volcanic ash powder, the prints "did develop fairly well."

"When you say 'fairly well,' I am talking about how fast, 'fairly fast,' did you mean?" asked Cardinale.

"After I applied the powder and started working with the brush, they came up, they developed."

Cardinale wanted to know if Centi had noticed the ridges from the palm prints "immediately."

"I object, Your Honor," barked Keller, who obviously did not want another soul near that back bedroom window.

"Overruled," said Judge Cappellini.

"Yes, I did," the witness responded. "After I started using the brush."

Attempting to establish a crucial aspect of his two-intruder defense, Cardinale got Centi to acknowledge that one of the partial palm prints was horizontal to the front of the desk while the other was vertical. The defense attorney also established that a groove in the desk could be seen in the lift of Commonwealth Exhibit 112A, as well as "two objects right next to the groove."

"Those two objects came up and attached to that lift when you took the lift?" Centi agreed.

"And anything that someone had on his hand when he put his hand on that desk would come up with that lift, correct?"

Again, the witness agreed.

In between all this, Cardinale asked if Centi recalled that the flat roof leading into the second-floor back office was "covered with a roofing material that looked similar to shingles on the side of a house." Centi agreed that the roof was asbestos with a granular substance. He also acknowledged that if someone left a latent palm print anywhere, they also would leave whatever substance they had on their hand.

A series of photo blowups of isolated portions of the two palm prints was produced from the defense table. Cardinale handed them to Centi with a magnifying loop. The photos appeared to depict several pieces of a granular substance trapped in the lifts.

"Has anybody ever asked you to check the substance from that roof against what is depicted in the photograph, Defense Exhibit Number 8?"

"I object, Your Honor," said Keller. "Overruled," said the judge.

Centi responded that no one had ever asked him. And he answered with the same "No, sir" each time when Cardinale asked him if anyone had ever asked him to see if the items in the lift were wood, or specks of red paint, or fibers, "particularly blue fibers."

"No, sir," Centi answered after the judge disallowed Keller's series of objections.

Turning to a different photo, a blowup of part of Commonwealth Exhibit 112, Cardinale asked Centi if he could see "markings or indentations" in the middle of the palm print lift.

"Yes, sir," said Centi.

"And those indentations resemble, do they not, the buckle of a belt?" asked Cardinale.

Keller objected, and this time Judge Cappellini sustained. But the jury had heard the line of questioning.

Looking at another photo enlargement, Centi conceded that there "appears to be" a fiber in the palm print lift. No, Centi said, no one had ever asked him to look for fibers in the lifts.

Pushing for every inch he could get, Cardinale asked Centi if he agreed with him that the fiber in the lift was blue. "I can't determine that," Centi answered, later adding that he could with the proper magnifying equipment.

Preparing to conclude, Cardinale wondered if Centi had ever taken palm prints at an autopsy, like the one he had attended for Betty Wolsieffer. Centi replied in the affirmative.

"Nothing difficult about that?"

"No, sir."

Had Centi ever taken palm prints from an exhumed body? "I can't remember that, no," the witness replied, adding that the process had been done, to his knowledge.

After Judge Cappellini sustained a series of objections about related exhumation palm print sequences and whether the prints were consistent with someone having climbed through the back bedroom window, Keller asked some questions on redirect. No, Centi said, he had never been instructed to do anything with the palm prints other than compare them to the known samples. He didn't do anything else with the lifts after they were sent to the FBI. Nor did he even know for sure whether there were any fibers in the palm prints. He had not magnified or blown them up in size. Keller's questions and Centi's replies were strong denials of a cover-up, but a prima facie case for lack of thoroughness.

Asked why he had failed to take Betty Wolsieffer's palm print at the autopsy, Centi replied: "It was an oversight on my part." He said no one had ever instructed him to take Neil's palm print.

Cardinale's defense was becoming clearer, using the unidentified palm prints to raise reasonable doubt about possible intruders. But he had to worry whether the jury was picking up on all the technical nuances. And, he had an even bigger problem: the circumstantial sandwich being prepared by Sarcione and Keller was starting to come together very well. It looked like the trial was going to come down to a battle between common-sense logic versus complicated interrogations about the possibility of roof particles in a latent palm print. Sometimes jurors don't worry about reasonable doubt; they just worry about being reasonable.

The day was not over. After a lengthy recess, the trial resumed with more of the supporting players.

With some slight elaborations, William Emmett, the security guard at Mercy Hospital, repeated the testimony he had given at the preliminary hearing regarding his conversations with the defendant: Glen said he had gone to the Crackerbox and "felt like getting into a fight, but he said he never expected this," he was sleeping on the couch downstairs when he heard a noise and "it was hot down there," he told his aunt he had locked all the windows, and, of course, Glen told him they would have to get out and play some golf.

Several neighbors—from Tom O'Connor coming home from work to Harold Galey walking his dog, Sunshine—testified about being awake near sunrise on the Saturday in question, and none of them heard or saw a thing, especially any intruders. Interestingly, Jim Escarge, Glen's paperboy, said he had put the paper between the screen door and the front door. Glen had told the police that when he came home from the Crackerbox he found the front screen door locked. Officer Minnick said he found the newspaper on the front porch. How did the paper get there? And better yet, why?

CHAPTER 33

As large crowds, including packs of high school girls, gathered hours before the start of court each morning to battle—sometimes literally—for the 150 or so seats, the combatants in the valley's newspaper war slugged it out with paper and ink. DISCREPANCY ran across the front page of the *Citizens' Voice* one morning. Another offering simply stated: LOVERBOY. The *Times Leader* joined in with KOPICKI, SHIPP TELL LOW-BUDGET HOTEL SEX TALES. Corbett called the defendant "Dr. Love" and made a pointed characterization of Cardinale as "the Boston wise guy." TV newscasts throughout the day and night usually led off with coverage of the trial. The press was having a field day.

On the battlefield, Corbett's in-again, out-again travails were more than amply covered by his employer, complete with photos of his "discussing" his problems with his attorney, while the *Citizens' Voice* continued to go out of its way to avoid using his name, referring to him as "a local reporter" in its stories. The *Citizens' Voice* seemed to get more quotes from the Wolsieffer family; the *Times Leader* kept its edge with access to the Taskers.

Because of the dizzying pace of developments, the *Sunday Independent* could not keep up with the two dailies, but prepared in-depth reviews of the testimony and analyses of what loomed ahead. The only thing journalistically more invigorating than three newspapers in a city of 50,000 was a crazy, sexy story to fight over.

In fact, Judge Cappellini had reached his breaking point in his dealings with the press. The strobe lights bouncing off the courtroom walls as witnesses entered and exited had to be stopped. He reconvened court that Friday and announced that he was handing down an order to "maintain appropriate order and decorum, and proper procedures to ensure that both the Commonwealth and defendant are afforded a fair and just trial." Judge Cappellini banned TV cameras and equipment, recording devices, and photographic cameras from the entire third floor.

The morning session of Day Five consisted of testimony from Dr. Dennis Gaza and Dr. Robert Czwalina, who both had treated Glen at Mercy Hospital the morning of the murder. In between, the jury heard from Richard Reem, the first of several FBI agents.

Dr. Gaza said he had admitted Dr. Wolsieffer to the hospital for a loss of consciousness with a head injury. In answer to a question from Sarcione, Dr. Gaza said that following his complete workup, he would have discharged the defendant if he had not been told about the unconsciousness, which was a subjective finding based on the claim of the patient.

On cross, Dr. Gaza acknowledged that his records failed to show any notation about scratches or abrasions on Dr. Wolsieffer's chest, or anywhere on him, for that matter. The witness acknowledged that because of the size of Dr. Wolsieffer's head wound, "a significant force" had to have been applied. He said it was consistent with the type of wound that could cause loss of consciousness. It could have been caused by a fist or a blunt object. Or it could have been caused by banging his head against the wall.

Asked by Sarcione if the wound could have been self-inflicted, Dr. Gaza replied: "I can't assume that." Cardinale suggested that if someone did want to inflict a wound on himself, the area of the back of the head where his client sustained injury "would be a very dangerous place to be trying it." Dr. Gaza agreed. "It would be a rather tenuous area to try to do that, yes."

On more redirect, Sarcione wondered if the medical training that a dentist receives would make him or her familiar with that area of the back of the head. Dr. Gaza agreed to that, too. "He would have had the initial anatomy and physiology."

Back to Cardinale, who asked if a dentist would know how dangerous it would be to sustain an injury in the area in question. The witness again agreed.

The questions, now back and forth from both attorneys, were at the heart of the case. Had Glen hit himself on the head? Had an intruder bopped him? Or had Betty injured him during a final fight?

Dr. Gaza told Sarcione that the medical training received in dental school would make one aware that a claim of loss of consciousness would lead to his being admitted to the hospital. He acknowledged to Cardinale, though, that such medical knowledge would not lead one to inflict a wound to such a vulnerable area of the head "unless you wanted to die."

"*Die?*" asked Cardinale in return.

"Die in the process inadvertently."

Sarcione fought back. "Obviously, doctor, the defendant didn't die, correct?"

"No."

Cardinale made the final move. "Was he at risk of death where the injuries you observed occurred?"

"Yes, within a twenty-four-hour period," replied the doctor.

Dr. Czwalina recounted his treatment of the defendant, and noted that by the time he examined Dr. Wolsieffer the bump on the back of his head had shrunk from 2½ inches square to about three-quarters of an inch square. On the major question, Dr. Czwalina said that if he had not been told that the patient had lost consciousness, he also would not have admitted him. He also said he considered the abrasion across the back of Dr. Wolsieffer's neck to have been "superficial, but well marginated."

FBI Special Agent Richard Reem, a body fluids expert with eighteen years' experience in the laboratory, testified extensively, and impressively, about the blood analysis and testing he had done. For example, he said the genetic markings in Betty's blood would be matched by .07 percent of the white population, or about "one individual out of 1,428 individuals randomly selected off the street corner." But the bottom line was that Reem had not found any of Glen's blood anywhere. He had found Betty's blood, but not anywhere or on anything that would incriminate Glen, such as the clothing he said he wore that night.

During a recess in the middle of Reem's testimony, Judge Cappellini conducted yet another First Amendment hearing, pointing out to the assembled media that "there are twenty amendments to the United States Constitution." He modified his order, allowing the cameras to be stationed across the rotunda from his courtroom. The compromise would last for only a day though, when another violation forced the judge to bar photographers and TV cameras again from the third floor entirely.

After lunch, the jury heard testimony from Joseph P. Sobel, a senior vice president of Accu-Weather, Inc., a private weather forecasting company. Sobel, with a Ph.D. in meteorology, described the weather conditions present in the Birch Street area the Saturday morning of Betty's murder. He talked about dew and water vapor. He said a car used at 2:00 A.M. would have less dew on it than one not used at all. Under cross-examination, some of his answers raised questions as to how long any dew would have remained on the unobstructed back roof past the 6:27 A.M. sunrise.

Peter Paul Olszewski, the young former assistant district attorney who participated in the Saturday afternoon hospital interview with the defendant, provided key details of that session: Dr. Wolsieffer said he had watched the intruder go down the stairs; he could have shot him; he gave no answer when asked why he had not; he did not have any conversation with Betty before going to bed. Olszewski acknowledged that his final question was, "Did you kill your wife?" to which, he said, the defendant answered, "No."

Given the fact that Dr. Wolsieffer was read his *Miranda* rights before the afternoon interview, Cardinale asked if his client was considered a suspect at that time. "He was not a suspect when I walked into his room, but in my mind he certainly was when I walked out," Olszewski replied.

"That's why you accused him of killing his wife?" Cardinale demanded.

"I did not accuse him. I asked him if he killed his wife."

The next witness, Detective Gary Walter Sworen, testified both that he saw the scratches on Dr. Wolsieffer's chest and that he didn't find any mark across the front of his neck. He said that during the afternoon interview at the hospital, he had checked the defendant's hands and found no marks on them. The absence of scratches on Glen's hands cast additional doubt on his story. If Glen had been able to slip his hands between the ligature and his neck, how had he been able to save his life without injuring his hands?

Sitting in the right rear of the courtroom with her mother and father, Nancy recollected that Glen had never mentioned any scratches on his chest to her. In fact, the testimony about them was the first she had heard of them. "I didn't remember the mark on his neck either. The only thing that he and I ever discussed about his physical injuries was the head and the feeling of blacking out." And he had once showed her the "bump" on his head, months later.

Testimony about Glen's physical condition wasn't the only revealing news Nancy had picked up during the trial. By listening to the various police witnesses, she learned that Glen told authorities the day of the murder that Betty had not woken up when he had arrived home from the Crackerbox. This was not what Glen had told her. He had contended to her that he was certain Betty had woken up when he got home because he had "wanted to fool around." Nancy also remembered how Glen had broken into tears when telling her how he had kissed Betty on the nose, "like he did every night," then said, "I love you" before going to sleep.

"Why did he tell me about this whole thing, kissing her on the nose, crying?" Nancy wondered. "He was crying his eyes out telling me how much he missed her. He was reliving that final night and telling me."

A rare Saturday session began in chambers, where Cardinale requested that Corbett the columnist be excluded for the next portion of the testimony: the tapes secretly made of conversations his client had with Betty's father and brother. The defense attorney pointed out that Corbett's name was mentioned numerous times in the conversations, and there was no telling where things might end up on his cross-examination, if he eventually took the stand. The issue, Cardinale said, was that his client had not called the columnist out of the blue to suggest druggies might have been involved in his wife's murder, but instead his client had called to give Corbett "a piece of his mind" because of Corbett's questionable behavior. Cardinale said he did not want to go into detail for the record, but pointed out that there was mention on the Tasker tapes of what Corbett had been up to. This would have included Corbett pressuring the Taskers to cooperate with him.

Attorney Ralph Kates of the *Times Leader* asked if Corbett could receive a copy of the tape transcripts. Judge Cappellini pointed out that if Corbett got access to the transcripts before he testified, there would be no point in keeping him from hearing the tapes.

Kates next wondered if his client could get a copy of the transcript after he testified. Bill Keller grabbed the floor. "The Commonwealth's position is we are not going to hand out any transcripts of these tapes to anybody." Keller had reached his fill with Corbett, especially when he had refused to come in for a pre-trial preparation interview. Besides, the transcripts were not part of the evidence, only the tapes.

Kates wanted permission for his client to listen to the tapes after he testified. Judge Cappellini said that was an altogether different issue that would require the filing of a separate motion.

The newspaper lawyer mistakenly contended that once the transcripts were given to the jury, they were part of the evidence. "No," said Judge Cappellini, his patience beginning to wane as well. "The transcript is merely an aid. It only becomes evidence when it is offered as a proper document to be admitted, but it is not going to be offered."

Because he had no idea what was on the tapes, Kates was forced to admit that he had no valid argument for Corbett being allowed to stay in the courtroom. But, Kates continued, the problem with Corbett could have been avoided. "He could have been called to the stand two days ago, because both the prosecution and the defense know what's on those tapes." Kates obviously had missed the message. At this point, no one on either side was going to go out of their way to help the *Times Leader* team.

Said Cardinale: "So it is clear, I am not agreeing to giving him access to anything at this point." On behalf of the Commonwealth, Keller agreed.

Kates then said that since the judge was not signing a formal order, the newspaper and Corbett were agreeing to the columnist's absence while the tapes were played. "We will simply ask him to step out of the room."

When told to leave on prior occasions, Corbett had risen from his chair ever so slowly, fixed his tie and his suit jacket, then turned for his overcoat—either putting it on or resting it over his left arm. Then he took a slow walk, not to the judge's chambers, but through the well of the courtroom, past the defendant, the two families, and all the spectators, heels clicking all the while on the marble floor. It was a scene that Cardinale, for one, did not wish to see again. "We don't have to do any formal pronouncement. I don't care how he leaves, just have him leave," said defense counsel.

The session in chambers had consumed a half hour. Judge Cappellini's tipstaff, George Brussock, entered the courtroom and walked over to the two rows of chairs filled with reporters. Quietly, he summoned Corbett to come into the judge's chambers. "Bring your coat," Brussock added, a broad smile on his face.

After Judge Cappellini told Brussock to bring back the jury, Keller moved to introduce the tape recordings made during the April 16, 1987, conversation between Betty's brother, Jack, and the defendant. Transcripts were handed out to the jury. Because of the need to prevent Corbett from getting a copy of the transcript before he testified, all the other reporters were refused copies, although such a distribution is a common courtesy at criminal trials.

At that point, Detective Sworen began playing the first of the two reels holding Jack's conversation. If the prosecution hadn't put them on, the defense surely would have.

Knowing what was coming, Lisa Wolsieffer began snickering from her seat, front row, left side. Gloating, she looked over at Jack Tasker, seated front row, right side, and smiled. He did not look back. Instead, he stared straight ahead.

Jack's wife, Dorothy, was missing, at least for the start. His mother sat with her eyes closed. His father bit the nail on his right thumb.

Even though the courtroom was deathly quiet, the conversation was very difficult to discern. "We were almost like brothers at one point," Glen was saying as both men began crying on the tape. Then there was a mention of "Sharon" and "Debbie." Everyone knew about Debbie, but "Sharon" was a new name. From the conversation, she clearly was connected with Jack, not Glen. "There's a couple cards, and, uh, some letters from Sharon," Jack said at one point. "I want you to know another thing, too, uh, I did call Sharon and told her to be very, very concerned for Herb and her kids. I thought you were going off the deep end with me, I really did," Jack said later, when expressing concern about Glen's threat to expose "the real Jack Tasker."

Lisa Wolsieffer continued to smirk.

As Sworen changed tapes, Nancy Wolsieffer got up to leave. She kept hearing Neil's name but couldn't understand exactly what was being said. From the part she could pick up, it sounded like "Glen was taking Jack under his wing. Jack fell for it." Nancy got that sick feeling all over. "He's doing it to everybody," she thought to herself. Listening to Glen handle the conversation with Jack, she thought: "That's how he treated me."

Out in the hallway, during the recess, Nancy's eyes met Glen's. "He couldn't look at me. He had that look," she recalled. "I remember him saying to me once, 'Now you know what I'm really like.' He knew I was on to him. He knew, 'I can't fool her anymore.' "

Moral issues aside, the sad irony of the public disclosure of Jack Tasker's personal life was that it was his doing, the unfortunate by-product of his relentless quest to trap his brother-in-law.

Back in court, the jury heard the conversation between Glen and Betty's father. It gave the jury much more to concentrate on. Of particular importance to the government's case, as it related to Glen's credibility, was his assurance: "I swear, as far as Betty knew, I was not involved with anybody up until the day she died." The jury had heard otherwise from the parade of Betty's girlfriends.

John Tasker wondered if Glen and Betty had fought that

night. Glen insisted they had not, but he revealed that they did "talk for a while," and that he had wanted to have sex but she declined. That differed from what Glen had told the police.

Also of significance, the jury heard Glen talk of his two-intruder theory and about the break-ins in the Birch Street area. For Glen, it was like testifying without having to undergo the scrutiny of cross-examination.

Judge Cappellini announced that the jury was going to be transported to 75 Birch for a tour of the house. They would not be allowed to ask questions, however. He said that afterward, the jury would return to the Ramada Hotel for the rest of the weekend. They would be allowed to go out to a restaurant, but in a group, under court supervision.

The judge warned the news media that 75 Birch and its surroundings were to be considered part of the courtroom. He said that in view of his latest order banning all cameras and TV equipment, he would consider any intrusion on the privacy of the jurors during the tour to be a violation of his order.

As everyone prepared to depart the courthouse, Marita Lowman of the *Times Leader* asked if it would be okay for a photographer to fly over the house in an airplane. Judge Cappellini was taken aback by the question. "I don't care if he's in an airplane or a spaceship. That doesn't make it okay."

Outside 75 Birch, neighbors and reporters gathered in bunches. The defendant waived his right to be present. The jurors split into two groups to go upstairs. In the master bedroom, several of them got down on their hands and knees to re-create Glen's version of crawling to the steps. It was a tough sell.

The relatively small size of the house was illuminating to several jurors as well. Where could the intruder—or harder to imagine, two intruders—possibly have hidden?

Chapter 34

While most of the jurors watched the Notre Dame-Penn State football game on TV that Saturday, on another floor of the Ramada, Glen Wolsieffer and Cardinale sat down to discuss their case. According to the defense attorney, there was no forensic evidence to connect his client to the murder, not even a motive, just opportunity and presence. Here was a guy with two women on the side, Cardinale explained. "Whatever spark he didn't have, he made up for it. There's no way he would have jeopardized that life."

Asked how he thought the trial was progressing, Cardinale said, "I feel good that a lot of their witnesses are becoming our witnesses, like Centi, the two doctors, the blood man. Where there's nothing to show, how are you going to show it?"

Cardinale would not say if Glen was going to take the stand. "People do want to hear his story. But they have his version on those tapes," he said. "There is no significant discrepancy."

"Don't you think most people are wondering why you're not dead?" Glen was asked.

"I almost was," he replied.

Cardinale stepped in, explaining that the issue wasn't why Glen was still alive. "How do you know they didn't think he was dead? And how do we know that they knew Betty was dead?"

The conversation turned to the plethora of disbelievers, who pointed to the lack of injury to the front of Glen's neck as proof he had not been attacked.

Suddenly, Cardinale stood up and removed his belt. As if on cue, Glen removed his feet from the bed, stood up, and turned himself around, so that Cardinale was behind him, holding the belt. Cardinale launched into an explanation about two possible ways it could have happened. He had a wrap-around-once theory, then a wrap-around-twice theory.

The wrap-around-once theory seemed impossible without even addressing any questions about the front of the neck. A continuous mark could not have been left across the back of Glen's neck if a belt, or whatever, had simply been thrust over his head, then pulled back. It also would not work if the ligature was thrust over his head and then crossed over, to say nothing of the acrobatics required for the hand switch.

No, the only possible way for an attacker from the rear to leave no mark in the front and one in the back was the wrap-around-twice theory.

But as he tried to demonstrate the concept, it was quickly clear that it was not going to work with Cardinale's belt. "It would have to be something longer than this," he acknowledged while failing to complete the second wrap.

"Like what?"

"A cord or a rope," answered Cardinale, seeming to dismiss the possibility of a belt, an idea he had fought so long and hard to plant during his cross-examination during the week.

Glen was asked what the ligature around his neck had felt like. "Like a rope or a chain," he replied.

Cardinale said he believed the ligature around Betty's neck had been wrapped around twice as well. The attorney was actually trying to choke Glen now, hard, really pulling on the belt ends. Again, without being told, Glen played his part. The idea was to demonstrate that Glen had put his hands between the ligature and his neck, thereby preventing an abrasion from being made on the front of his neck. Glen slipped his hands into the right location, but only after Cardinale loosened his grasp and allowed access, something an attacker was considerably less likely to do.

Cardinale explained that the abrasions on the back of Glen's neck were not consistent with a belt having been used. He said the abrasions would have been caused by Glen moving his neck side to side while trying to break loose, with his fingers protecting the front of his neck.

Glen moved his neck side to side, letting the belt slide against his neck. Cardinale explained that there wouldn't be any marks on Glen's hands because the ligature would gravitate to the grooves in the fingers, "where there are lines already."

It was a bizarre scene, an accused strangler going through the motions of strangulation foreplay at the hands of his attorney.

In light of Cardinale's insinuation that granules from the back roof might have been picked up in the palm prints from the desk near the window, forensic experts from both sides gathered early at the courthouse that Monday, Day Seven, to examine the lifts. In the course of his analysis, one of the FBI agents extracted some of the material in question, described as "a black powdery substance." He then announced that the material, which had been the focus of Cardinale's attention on Friday, had dissolved. Cardinale accused the FBI of destroying evidence. His pieces of "roofing material," real or imagined, were gone.

Sarcione countered by pointing out that the defense's forensic expert, John Balshy, had been in the room with the FBI experts.

Judge Cappellini sounded displeased by this latest screwup. He said he had been unaware that any of the evidence was going to be altered during the examination. It was going to be another long day.

When court resumed, John Swan of 47 Birch Street, a friend of Betty's brother, claimed that he was up cooking 150 pounds of shrimp the night of the murder. He said he went to bed about 2:30 A.M. but was unable to sleep because he "had a lot on my mind."

Swan said he heard a bang coming from down the street, in the direction of the defendant's house. "It lasted—bang, stop, bang, bang, bang, stop, bang, stop—for a good five minutes. I know it was between 3:30 and 3:39 because I looked at the digital clock. I didn't recall the last minute of the time. There was no reason to. I thought somebody lost their keys or was locked out."

Under cross, however, it was pointed out that there were three houses and a cross road, Locust Street, between the Swan residence and 75 Birch. There were plenty of houses on Locust as well. Swan said he first talked to the police in February 1988, soon after he told his story to Jack Tasker.

Although it did not become an issue in Swan's testimony, the time of the banging was inconsistent with the prosecution's theory of the crime. If it had been Glen banging, where had he been from 2:00 until 3:30?

Special Agent Gerald F. Wilkes, a tool-mark expert for the FBI, testified that he used a binocular microscope to examine the strands adjacent to the hole in the screen removed from the upstairs back bedroom at 75 Birch. Based on his examination, he was unable to determine what type of tool or object had been used to make the hole. Furthermore, he found that the strands "were protruding in both directions, to the inside and to the outside of the screen, as if some object had been forced through it and then removed. Because of that fact, I was not able to even determine from which direction the damage originally occurred."

Not counting a break for lunch, the next three hours were consumed watching videos of Jule and George Cook at the preliminary hearing and their subsequent depositions under defense subpoena. They both were too ill to testify again.

The jury listened intently as the Cooks described Glen using the rickety red ladder on a Saturday after being locked out. Almost unnoticed, in the midst of the tapes being played, District Attorney Stevens made a brief appearance in the courtroom.

Late that Monday, FBI Special Agent Douglas Deedrick, a hair and fiber expert, took the stand, marking the start of an excruciatingly technical stretch of the trial, accounting for one-fourth of the total testimony, and boring anyone who tried to listen to it all.

Most important, the witness said it was possible but not essential that a "forcibly removed" hair had been removed violently. He also contended that despite scant scientific literature on the subject, the FBI lab could distinguish between blue cotton fibers and blue cotton denim fibers such as those comprising the clothing Glen wore on the night of the murder. That news was potentially very damaging to the defense.

Cardinale was still trying to put someone else in the house, preferably two men. In addition to the palm prints, he could try to do it with the hairs that were recovered or with the blue fibers found under Betty's fingernails, assuming it could not be shown that the fibers were from Glen's clothing.

From the blanket in the murder room, there were two forcibly removed male hairs that were microscopically like Glen's, and two that had similarities and differences to Betty's hair. For example, they appeared to be too long. Because the two male hairs were of different length, Deedrick was forced to concede they possibly, though not probably, could have come from two different men. In explaining "forcibly removed," Deedrick said such hair was not ready for natural shedding. He said force was required for its removal, "enough to cause pain." But at another point, he testified that a comb or a brush could forcibly remove hair.

This evidence was not going to prove that Glen and Betty had been involved in a fight. There also was nothing in all the hair testing to put someone else in the room, except perhaps Danielle, which made sense since she watched TV on the bed all those Friday nights waiting for her father to come home.

Cardinale felt he had been sandbagged on the denim evidence, given what the FBI had written in its report back in 1987 about the commonness of such fibers. Now it sounded like the blue cotton denim fibers recovered from Betty's fingernails were an exact match to Glen's clothing. Even Deedrick had to admit that it was possible that other pants and jackets could have the same characteristics in their fiber makeup. But to have any impact here, any outside intruders would have had to have been clad in the same kind of jeans, with the same indigo dye.

On the other hand, if Glen killed Betty, and he really was wearing those clothes, and Betty scratched out some blue denim fibers, why wasn't there the slightest bit of her blood on his clothing? To muddy the waters more, Deedrick said he was unaware that Betty wore blue pants and a blue striped top the Friday of her death. He said he also was unaware if the kind of indigo dye commonly used in blue jeans was commonly used in the manufacture of other cotton clothing.

As for the palm prints, Deedrick said he found a blue-gray fiber in one of them, but in answer to a question from Sarcione, the agent said the fabric was "not typical" of the kind used in sweatshirts, an item Glen said he thought the man at the top of the stairs had been wearing. Deedrick also stated that he had not found wood, asbestos, or the impression of a belt buckle in the lifts. He also noted that he had not found any blue-gray fibers under the victim's fingernails.

So where did that leave the defense vis-à-vis forensic issues? In a fairly weak position.

One interesting tidbit struck a chord in Nancy Wolsieffer as she listened: an unknown substance containing orange cotton and orange rayon fibers had been removed from Betty's neck.

Nancy almost jumped out of her seat when she heard the word "orange." The cops had asked her repeatedly about how many pillows were kept in Betty's bedroom. Nancy had remembered two throw pillows, but had been able to find only one of them. She remembered that both pillows were orange or rust-colored. "It hit me like a brick," she said later. "It just came over me, that there had to be something to this." Perhaps the missing pillow had been used in Betty's murder, then thrown in the river. Strangely, there was no mention in any of the records from the investigation that the available throw pillow had ever been seized or tested.

As with almost all criminal trials, the judge's chambers were not only the venue for tedious arguments about technical matters. It was often the place where the most important, and interesting, issues were decided.

During a break in Deedrick's testimony, Judge Cappellini held a private hearing on the prosecution's plan to call the FBI's premier behavioral science expert, Special Agent John E. Douglas, to testify that in his opinion the crime scene at 75 Birch had been staged by a killer who knew Betty Wolsieffer "very well." The argument pitted the ever-advancing state of criminal investigative technology against the fundamental right of a defendant to a fair trial. The stakes were extremely high for the defendant, given what Douglas was prepared to say.

"The position of the defense is that there is no possible admissible basis for this expected testimony," said Cardinale. "Nowhere in the country has this type of evidence ever been admitted." The defense attorney contended that the testimony was designed to do only one thing: provide an "expert opinion" as to Dr. Wolsieffer's version of events, namely that he had murdered his wife.

"What this purported expert is going to do is talk about things that are completely credibility-oriented," Cardinale said, maintaining that such issues are "solely the province of the jury."

He said Sarcione was free to argue at the end of his case about the particulars of Glen's story, "but that's about all. There is no way he can put on a witness . . . who will get up on the stand and say, 'I believe the Commonwealth's theory, she was strangled. . . . I believe that whoever killed this woman knew her.' "

Calling Douglas a "voodoo man," Cardinale characterized some of the special agent's assumptions as incredible. For example, Douglas had contended in his report that no criminal would have broken into 75 Birch because two cars were in the driveway. "Why isn't it any less likely that people are on vacation?" asked Cardinale. He said the agent's bottom line was " 'I don't believe the story that the suspect gave.' "

Sarcione said he had found a case in Georgia where an expert in crime-scene reconstruction was allowed to offer conclusions as to how a murder was committed. He also maintained that Douglas had analyzed more homicides than anyone in the United States, anyone in the world, for that matter. He said Douglas had been qualified as a crime-scene reconstruction expert in the states of Louisiana, South Carolina, and Connecticut. "It is a new area of expertise, obviously," the prosecutor said. "The jury should have help if it is needed," adding that most jurors were unaware of the fact that strangulation is a personal-type crime.

But Douglas had never testified in a manner that so directly pointed a finger at a defendant. He had never testified that a crime scene had been staged and that the victim had been killed by someone very close to them.

And that contention was precisely what bothered Judge Cappellini. "In this case it has to be the doctor. It can't be Danielle," the judge said. "Is that what you mean by personal?"

Sarcione said no. He pointed to his brother's murder, where an unknown perpetrator had shot a stranger. Such homicides, he said, are rarely strangulations.

"You are indicating his testimony will clearly and unequivocally put into this case only one person who could have committed this crime," said the judge. "It has to be Dr. Wolsieffer. He is saying, 'Ladies and gentlemen of the jury, I am a certified expert. I am going to tell you who killed Mrs. Wolsieffer, Dr. Wolsieffer.' "

"He is going to say it was a personal-type crime, not saying who killed her, and he is going to say that the scene was staged. That's all I want him to testify to," Sarcione pleaded.

"There's nobody there except Dr. Wolsieffer and Danielle. That's all who were there," the judge reiterated.

"Also Neil Wolsieffer was in the home that morning," Sarcione argued. Thank God that Nancy didn't hear that one.

Judge Cappellini observed that Neil had been inside 75 Birch only after the murder, unless at this late stage the Commonwealth was going to argue otherwise. "I have trouble with this theory. How can we have an expert tell that jury at this point, whatever words you want to use or whatever manner, that there's only one person who could have committed this crime?"

Realizing his fight was futile, Sarcione argued that in the alternative, Douglas should be allowed to say that the condition of the house—the turned-over ottoman, the desk drawers open, the briefcase open—was not consistent with a ransacking, and therefore the crime scene was staged. "That's definitely within his field of expertise," he said. "This is a completely circumstantial case, as everyone well knows, and here we are with a very vital part, which the Commonwealth needs. This is a murder case!"

But the judge wasn't buying it. "You are back to the same proposition. You are back to one person, and one person only, who could have committed this crime, Dr. Wolsieffer," he said.

Officially, Judge Cappellini reserved decision. He eventually ruled that Douglas would not be allowed to take the stand.

*   *   *

After Deedrick completed his testimony on Day Eight, November 20, 1990, George D. Wynn, a fingerprint technician with the FBI, testified that he had been unable to match the latent palm prints lifted from Glen's desk with any of the "thirty-some-odd" samples he had been sent by the local authorities. He said one of the lifts, Commonwealth Exhibit 112, was a small portion of the palm in Exhibit 112A, the other lift. He said they were from the same person and the same hand, the left hand. At the preliminary hearing, Trooper Centi had testified the print was of a right hand. At the trial, he said he did not know which hand was involved.

Looking at a photo blowup of Commonwealth Exhibit 112A, the larger of the two lifts, Wynn said he believed that two black dots in the photo, one of which had been "cut out and dissolved," consisted of "clumps of fingerprint powder that were not brushed out."

What about the section of Commonwealth Exhibit 112 that Cardinale thought might be the impression of a belt buckle? Wynn said it also was consistent with the natural creases found in that area of the palm, "part of the natural folds and natural flex creases."

Of four other areas on photos of the lifts, Wynn said he believed the materials were "substances probably picked up by the lift, by the tape, from the surface on which the latent print was developed." He opined that other substances, previously identified as fibers, were probably on the tape itself before the lifts were made. He went through virtually every possibility except that any of the substances could have come off the hand of the person leaving the lift.

As for the rickety ladder, Wynn acknowledged that in his opinion it could have been checked for latent prints. He obviously was not in a position to say why Corporal Centi had opted not to perform such testing.

Asked about age testing of latent prints, the witness said there was no way to determine how long ago a print had been left.

Under cross-examination, he acknowledged that he had been asked by Sarcione, Mitchell, and Sworen only seven weeks before to determine which hand the prints had come from, and also acknowledged that he and other FBI specialists had been asked about the foreign matter inside the lifts only the previous week. All he had been asked to do prior to 1990 was to compare thirty-five samples with the lifts.

In response to questions, he confirmed that there were "things" in the Pennsylvania State Police photos of the lifts that had a reddish tint, a rust-colored tint, and a brown-colored tint. He admitted that he had not been given the opportunity to analyze any of the substances on the lifts, but was nonetheless confident that the black material was fingerprint powder.

The war of scientific experts continued on Day Nine with another closed-door hearing in Judge Cappellini's chambers about the next witness, Dr. John I. Coe of Minnesota. The esteemed forensic pathologist told the judge that he was prepared to say, "within a reasonable degree of medical certainty," that the wound on the rear of Dr. Wolsieffer's neck was more consistent with being self-inflicted than with the defendant's story.

Dr. Coe said that he had based his opinion on the nature of Dr. Wolsieffer's injuries—an uninterrupted, relatively straight line from earlobe to earlobe—and how the attack had supposedly occurred—from the rear, with a ligature placed around the defendant's neck.

Cardinale, who did not want Dr. Coe to testify at all, asked him if he had been told that the defendant contended that he had both his hands under the ligature, and that the attack had come from behind. Dr. Coe said he was aware of those claims.

"Is it your testimony that there is no way that an attack from behind could have resulted in the marks and injuries you observed, or had reported to you?" Cardinale asked.

"In my opinion, that would not be possible."

Cardinale got up to demonstrate his theories, to see if he could convince Dr. Coe to change his opinion. The defense attorney used a belt and the neck of his co-counsel, Frank Nocito.

Cardinale conceded that a belt had not been used, that the ligature must have been something thinner, based on the width of the injury to his client's neck. He tried out his two methods, the wrap-around-once and the wrap-around-twice, with Nocito moving his neck from side to side, to help everyone watching imagine the ligature rubbing into the back of Dr. Wolsieffer's neck. Cardinale said the victim's hands would be inside the front of the ligature, protecting the front of the neck from being harmed.

"That could produce that linear mark if enough pressure is applied so that the individual is becoming nearly unconscious from it," said Dr. Coe. He added, however, that an attack in such a manner would still cause bruising on the front of the neck or leave marks on the hands.

On that basis, Judge Cappellini qualified Dr. Coe as an expert witness, and the trial resumed in the big room. Sarcione started the questioning by asking if an injury to the rear of someone's neck, with no injury in the front of the neck or on his hands, was consistent with that person having been attacked from behind.

"I feel this is inconsistent," Dr. Coe replied, explaining that he would expect to find "marks on the front of the neck" and a "crossover pattern of whatever instrument was used on the back of the neck," even if the victim had used his hands inside the front of the ligature to protect himself.

Sarcione summarized all the reports, medical records, and photographs Dr. Coe had reviewed, then graduated to the more important question: "Are those abrasions consistent with the abrasions being self-inflicted, within a reasonable degree of medical certainty?"

Cardinale objected, but Judge Cappellini overruled.

"Yes, they are."

"Why do you say that?" Sarcione asked.

"The lesions in the back of the neck could be easily produced by a person using the instrument, and would be inconsistent with their being produced, as I have described in the previous hypotheticals, from an assailant attacking from the rear."

"Cross-examine," said the lead prosecutor, returning to his chair with a glow of satisfaction.

The main thrust of Cardinale's questioning, supported by the Mercy Hospital records showing Glen to be "markedly shaken" and in a "shock-like state" on the Saturday of the murder, focused on whether his client could have mistakenly overstated that he "felt he was losing consciousness."

If true, Dr. Coe conceded, he might have a different opinion. He pointed out, however, that those same medical records stated that Dr. Wolsieffer had spoken clearly and appeared to be thinking properly.

No matter how Cardinale tried to make his point, and he tried assiduously, Dr. Coe always came back to the same conclusion: there were ways that an attack from the rear could produce an abrasion on the back of the neck, but there should be lesions on the front of the neck, too, or on the hands.

Perhaps a relatively light amount of pressure had been applied, Cardinale suggested, disregarding his client's claim of feeling a loss of consciousness from the press of the ligature. "It would be hard to believe that one could get marks on the back of the neck, no matter how it is produced, without producing marks on the front of the neck," said Dr. Coe. "There has to be something touching the front of the neck. . . . You are not producing any asphyxia if you are producing pressure only on the back of the neck." The suggested defense scenario also sounded inconsistent with the expected actions of a vicious killer.

Before he gave up, Cardinale borrowed a rope from Sarcione and, once again, the neck of his co-counsel to demonstrate his theories to the jury. It did not matter what method was used or how Nocito simulated trying to prevent injury by using his hands within the ligature—Dr. Coe said he would still expect injury to the front of the neck.

Cardinale had raised possibilities, but very remote ones. As Dr. Coe had told Cardinale in chambers: "Counselor, we never can say never." But nothing had been put forth even approaching a probability. From a strategic point of view, unless Dr. Wolsieffer was going to take the stand and somehow talk his way out of all of this, the trial was over. Dr. Coe had inflicted nearly the same kind of damage the FBI's Douglas would have, only it sounded less speculative and more scientific.

Chapter 35

Steve Corbett's wait was over. He had wanted his fifteen minutes; he was going to get exactly a half hour. He strolled confidently to the witness stand to testify against the man he had pilloried for so long without regard to fairness or the judicial process.

After eliciting the necessary biographical information, Keller asked him about the accuracy of his two "druggie" columns. Corbett said both were accurate. Keller then read the appropriate excerpts again, with the operative phrase being, "It could have been a druggie, or a non-druggie, from anywhere."

Those who defended putting Corbett on the stand contended that he provided the jury with yet another version of events from the mouth of the defendant. Those who were opposed contended that calling him to the stand was nothing more than a high-profile thank you from D.A. Stevens, who, after all, was running the case.

As Cardinale rose to conduct his cross-examination, not even he could have imagined the seeds of scandal about to be planted.

"Mr. Corbett, in your conversations you say you had with my client, were they tape-recorded?"

"Were they tape-recorded?" Corbett asked back.

"Yeah," said Cardinale.

"No, sir," Corbett answered firmly.

"Did you take notes?"

"Yes, sir."

"Do you have them?"

"No, sir."

"Where are they?"

"I don't know exactly where they are, sir."

In truth, Corbett had surreptitiously taped at least the second telephone conversation in question, in violation of Pennsylvania's strict wiretap law. And others at his newspaper, the *Times Leader*, knew it, too.

Cardinale had no idea, though, and so he forged ahead. He wanted to know if the first column contained quotations from a conversation that had taken place in February 1989, six months before the supposedly incriminating remarks were first published.

Corbett said he did not recall the exact date and responded with a non sequitur. "It was prior to the second article— The second article was prior to the publication of that, yes."

Two more times, the columnist was asked the question, as the newspaper's attorney, Ralph Kates, nervously walked back and forth in the front of the courtroom.

"You are obviously having trouble understanding. Let me see if I can break it down," Cardinale said.

Step by step, in response to single-issue questions, Corbett agreed that the first column was published on July 30, 1989. He agreed that the column contained parts of a conversation with Dr. Wolsieffer. He agreed that the column was accurate.

"And you told me you don't have any notes, or if you do, you don't know where they are, correct?" asked Cardinale.

Corbett started to reach into his pocket, but he did not pull out his notes. "I cannot answer your question because it requires me to disclose unpublished information or confidential sources, which are protected by the Pennsylvania Shield Law, the First Amendment to the United States Constitution, Article 1, Section 7 of the Pennsylvania Constitution of the Commonwealth of Pennsylvania," he said, reading off a card.

"It is an interesting response," said Cardinale. "But, please, listen to my question." Cardinale again asked whether the first column was based on "a conversation you purportedly had with my client in February of 1989, six months earlier. Do you understand that?"

"Excuse me. Your Honor, may I ask a question?" Corbett asked. "I don't know what I am supposed to do once I invoke this shield."

Judge Cappellini had said nothing up to that point. He had not reacted at all to Corbett's claim of journalistic privilege. "Just a moment, please," the judge now interjected. "What is the problem with the question that's being asked? You are not revealing any confidential information. The only question that's being asked, and you can consult with your counsel, the only question that's being asked, and I think it is simple—maybe you don't understand it—there's an article that appears in the *Times Leader*, dated Sunday, July 30, 1989, that has been read into evidence and stipulated by counsel. All that counsel for the defendant is asking you is whether the information that forms what is set forth in the article was obtained by you on or about February of 1989. Do you have any problem with that?"

Kates stepped up to the judge. "I can solve the problem."

Judge Cappellini was not so sure. "Is there any problem? With him now raising the Shield Law, that's what I am asking. What is the problem?"

Kates suggested his client was not certain of the date of the interview and could reply if he were given the article to look at.

"He can answer whether he knows or not, it is simple," said the judge. "Can you answer that, Mr. Corbett? Do you understand what the question is?"

He said he did.

"It has nothing to do with the Shield Law," said Judge Cappellini. "Nobody is putting you in a position that you are invoking the Shield Law. This is not a Shield Law issue."

Cardinale jumped back in. "Would you like to answer the question now?"

"Repeat it, please."

"Please listen this time and maybe you can remember and give us an answer. Listen to the question for the fourth time. In July of 1989—July 30, 1989—you wrote an article in which you just had portions of it read to you by Mr. Keller, which you claim are accurate, correct?"

"Correct."

"Do you understand so far?"

"Yes, sir."

"And the conversation purportedly had occurred six months prior to your article in July 30, 1989?"

"I don't believe that's the case," said Corbett. "If I can see the article to which you are referring, I can clear that up for you quickly."

Again, Cardinale stepped back. "Let me see if I can refresh your recollection. In the beginning of the article, sir, you state that you were recounting a conversation you had in February of 1989, does that help you at all?"

"Is that in the second article?"

"July 30, 1989."

"There are two separate columns. Is that in the later column, the later column, the second column? And does that refer to the first conversation I had with your client, or the second conversation I had with your client? If you would let me see that, I will be happy to help you."

Back and forth they went. Oddly, Corbett was repeatedly unwilling to say precisely when his first "druggie" conversation with Dr. Wolsieffer had occurred. In fact, it had taken place twenty-one months before, making it three months shy of the wiretap statute of limitations, if Corbett had also secretly taped that call.

"I asked you if you recall when the conversation took place, whether or not you tape-recorded it, and you said, 'No.' I asked you if you had any notes reflecting the conversation and you said you did, but you didn't know where they are, isn't that correct?" asked Cardinale.

Corbett said he was confused and wondered if he could consult with his attorney. Judge Cappellini stepped in, and again instructed the witness that the Shield Law did not apply to Cardinale's "simple question."

The defense attorney tried again. "Let me repeat the question," he said. "Do you know where your notes are? That's all I'm asking. Can you answer?"

"I have my notes somewhere."

"Do you remember where?"

"No, sir, I do not," said Corbett. "May I clear something up with regard to your question?"

"My question simply was this, and you have answered, you have no idea where your notes are."

"Specifically I have notes a lot of places."

Judge Cappellini had had enough. "Let's not go back and forth. Let's resolve this. It is very simple." He asked Cardinale if he wanted the notes.

Cardinale said he did. "If he is able to put his hands on them."

The judge turned back to Corbett: "Can you produce these notes by searching in the various places you have already indicated, and if you can, you can come back and produce your notes and then we will determine whether they are relevant to this case."

Cardinale said that he could still continue with his cross-examination. The issue of the notes would not be raised again. Over in the news media seats, the reporters and editors from the *Times Leader* were squirming in their chairs. Several of the other local reporters were unable to restrain their giggles.

Cardinale said he did not want the witness to discuss any conversations he may have had with his sources, because of his right to confidentiality regarding the origin of his information. The defense counsel suggested, though, that Dr. Wolsieffer had told Corbett during the interview that the director of the Clear Brook rehab facility, Frank Lisnow, had been interviewed by the state police in October 1988, prior to the first interview. "Did he not say that's where this information was coming from, that, in fact, he had been told by the people at Clear Brook that the police were out asking whether or not he had been giving dental care to patients at this Clear Brook facility?"

"No, sir," said Corbett. "I don't believe he said that."

"You don't?"

"No, sir."

"You are relying upon your memory of the events?"

"May I clarify something, because I believe I misspoke and I believe it is important that I clarify this."

"Wait, pardon me," Judge Cappellini interjected. "You mean on this question?"

"On a related issue with regard to these conversations," said Corbett, his lawyer still silent.

"No," said the judge. "If it comes up. You have been called—"

"—I believe it came up."

"Pardon me, Mr. Corbett. You have been called by the Commonwealth," Judge Cappellini resumed. "If there's an issue that has to be resolved when you are finished with your cross-examination, the Commonwealth will ask the appropriate questions. That's the way we proceed."

At this point, Judge Cappellini felt compelled to instruct the jury that what was taking place was "not an adversary proceeding between a defendant and the press. So that we understand each other, it is a proceeding in which evidence is attempted to be obtained for the jury." He again instructed Corbett that if he could not answer a particular question, he should indicate that.

Trying now to focus on the exculpatory aspects of his client's interviews, Cardinale asked Corbett if he had accurately reported his own question to Dr. Wolsieffer—"Have you ever tried to figure out who could have done such a thing?"—and his client's response: "I wish to hell I knew."

"If that's what I wrote, that's what he said," Corbett replied.

"Then later in the conversation, I take it you heard him say, 'Maybe it was some druggies I treated from Clear Brook.' You said, 'Huh?' He said, 'I don't know, I don't know who and how many.' Is that what he said?"

"That's what he said."

Again, Cardinale wondered whether one of Corbett's sources had told him about the state police's interest and interviews out at Clear Brook, and if he, in turn, had brought up the subject to Dr. Wolsieffer.

"I never heard anything like that," Corbett contended, thereby admitting to having been woefully uninformed. "I was shocked when your client talked about druggies."

Cardinale suggested that his client had told Corbett that he had had a contract to provide dental services to patients of the facility and that the state police had inquired as to whether there had ever been any problems between Dr. Wolsieffer and Clear Brook people.

"I don't recall the specifics of the conversation," said Corbett.

"If I didn't write about it, he didn't say it—and I don't recall him saying anything like that."

"That's because we don't have anything to refer to that we can check the accuracy or the completeness of that portion of this purported conversation, isn't that true?" asked Cardinale.

"I object, Your Honor," said Keller. The judge overruled, and allowed the question to stand.

"There were two conversations, and I must say this, because I believe I misspoke: There were two separate conversations with your client, and I wrote, I believe, one column about it, but it was continued into two columns," said Corbett, explaining what he had "misspoken" earlier, avoiding another opportunity to reveal his deceitful taping tactics.

"My question is you don't have any notes with you right now that we can check the accuracy?"

"No, sir, I do not."

Finally getting to the end, Cardinale got Corbett to acknowledge that at least in the second conversation it was he, not Dr. Wolsieffer, who brought up the topic of "druggies."

"What my client said, and you agreed it was accurate, is, 'It could have been a druggie, or a non-druggie, from anywhere,' " said Cardinale.

"If that's what it says, that's what he said."

"That's what it says," Cardinale confirmed.

"Then that's what he said."

Cardinale was through. Judge Cappellini looked over at Bill Keller, who at that moment was not a happy man. "The Commonwealth has no further questions," Keller said.

Judge Cappellini declared the morning recess.

Outside in the hallway, Jack Tasker told reporters, "Steve Corbett is the most honest person I've ever met." Little did Tasker know how much the testimony would haunt his family in the months to come.

Cliff Schechtman, managing editor of the *Times Leader*, approached. "That was kind of goofy, huh?" After a pause, he added, "I think I'm going to go talk to our lawyers."

CHAPTER 36

Margaret Fraley, formerly of 74 Old River Road in Wilkes-Barre, testified next. She told the jury how her two sons, then age eleven and thirteen, had dressed up in dark ninja-style clothing with up to a dozen of their friends during summer nights in 1986 to play a game called "Chase." The game, a kind of team hide-and-seek, was played on the block of Miner Street, Old River Road, Locust Street, and Birch Street.

"Would they wear black hoods?" Sarcione wanted to know.

"Some of them did, ninja-style, Halloween costumes, basically," replied Fraley, who had called authorities after she read of the Cooks' testimony at the preliminary hearing regarding frightening bands of strange people in the neighborhood.

"One team would hide and the other team would go out and look for them. They would have to be caught and run from one another, and run through the yards, hiding in the bushes, jumping over fences—that kind of thing," she said.

Fraley said the game continued until the fall of 1986. "I would say after school started, it slacked off."

*   *   *

The prosecution intended to call only one more witness, the chief investigator on the case, Detective Bob Mitchell. He would tie up all the loose ends, complement the other witnesses, and give the jury one more opportunity to hear about all the things that were wrong with Dr. Wolsieffer's version of events. Unfortunately, the day was Thanksgiving, so Mitchell would have to wait until the following Monday. As usual, Judge Cappellini instructed members of the jury not to read any newspapers or watch TV reports about the case. Despite the elaborate sequestration and news blackout system, the judge sent the jurors home for the holiday weekend.

On Day Ten, Mitchell spent several hours on the stand, giving the jury another dose of all the reasons why the unstable ladder had not been used—could not have been used, really. The testimony contradicted the essence of what the Cooks had said about seeing Glen use the ladder on other occasions, a discrepancy in the testimony that the jury would have to live with.

The chief investigator, who had sat there through all the other witnesses—the usual procedure in Pennsylvania—also helped ingrain in the minds of the jurors the best parts of the sometimes laborious expert testimony, especially the key points from Dr. Coe.

Mitchell gave the gist of the two hospital interviews, recounting how Dr. Wolsieffer told him he "started going black" and "felt dizzy," and how he said he had been attacked from behind. He reviewed how Dr. Wolsieffer originally claimed the Shipp affair had ended a year earlier, how he later admitted he made love with her the afternoon before the murder, how he told of chatting with his male friends at the Crackerbox without mentioning his talk with Carol Kopicki, how he claimed he had $1,300 in his desk drawer but how Mitchell had found the bank deposit slips for the same amount, and how, after his arrest, the defendant had blurted out: "It happened so fast. We got into it. Everything was a blur."

Mitchell also detailed the more damning physical evidence—the scratches on the defendant's chest, no marks on his hands, no abrasions on the front of the neck, the ottoman being turned over deep into the family room, the defendant had just happened to put his blue-jean clothing in the rear office, the victim's checkbook and purse left untouched on the dining room table, her jewelry box open but its contents intact.

Nancy Wolsieffer cringed again when Mitchell mentioned, "I recall that there was an orange piece of lint, or something, on her neck, which was taken off." Later, he testified, "There was also an orange throw pillow on the floor near the back of the victim, near the foot area, an orange throw pillow." This would have been the pillow that was not seized or analyzed.

Under Cardinale's cross-examination, Mitchell disclosed for the first time that in the first hospital interview Dr. Wolsieffer gave him a demonstration of how he supposedly had been attacked, how the ligature had been "wrapped around his neck."

"There's nothing in any testimony you have given before today about a demonstration, is there?" Cardinale asked.

"No, there wasn't. But I recall that," said Mitchell.

"Does it have something to do with the testimony that came in from Dr. Coe?"

"It has nothing to do with Dr. Coe," Mitchell insisted.

At another point, Cardinale asked the witness if he had listened closely to the Tasker tapes as his client said he loved his wife and had not killed her.

"I heard him say he knocked off the affair with Debbie Shipp the year before, when, in fact, he continued it on up until the time she died. That was on the tape, too," Mitchell snapped back.

Cardinale tried to ask the chief investigator about the politics of the lengthy probe, starting a question with "It took a change of district attorneys for you to come up with a charge—," but Sarcione objected and Judge Cappellini sustained. "Ladies and gentlemen of the jury, that has absolutely nothing to do with the case, whether it's three district attorneys, two, or four. Strike that from your mind. It has nothing to do with the case," the judge instructed.

Mitchell said the police did not try to find evidence solely against Dr. Wolsieffer. "What we did was, we tried to develop evidence, and all the evidence pointed to him."

Cardinale retorted that the investigators had not even bothered until the previous week to ask the FBI if there were any substances in the palm prints that could be identified. "You didn't even bother to check that before last week, isn't it true?"

"That's because you just mentioned all those facts last week, so I checked it after you made those assumptions that all these things were in the prints," Mitchell replied, helping make the defense attorney's point about police conduct, at least on that issue.

Although he had argued successfully in chambers to be allowed to question Mitchell on whether the police had adequately checked for similarities between Betty's murder and the numerous break-ins throughout the Birch Street area, Cardinale completed his five hours of cross-examination without addressing the issue. In his heart, he knew it was an empty box. As Mitchell had said at the preliminary hearing, when he reviewed the other break-ins, he had found none using a ladder. And in all his years on the police force, Betty Wolsieffer's had been the first murder on Birch Street. From Cardinale's perspective, the jury did not need to hear that kind of testimony.

"Your Honor, the Commonwealth rests its case," Sarcione announced.

Cardinale made the standard request for the outright dismissal of all charges. Judge Cappellini refused.

The defense then called its first witness, John Balshy, former head of the Pennsylvania state police's fingerprint and photograph section, who at one time had trained Corporal Eugene Centi, the prosecution's fingerprint expert.

As expected, Balshy supported the positions Cardinale had taken during his cross-examination of Centi and the various FBI experts. It was Balshy who had discovered most of the "foreign substances" in the two partial palm prints.

As the testimony droned on, the prosecution team objected whenever possible. Except for the role reversals, nothing in the case really changed.

Balshy, who had been allowed under a special dispensation to the sequestration order to sit with the defense counsel to assist during most of the FBI's forensic presentation, said that he thought Commonwealth Exhibit 112A, one of the palm print lifts, had been made by a right hand, not a left. He said he was still not sure that both prints had come from the same hand. He thought he saw blue fibers in the palm prints, too. He did not think the black material was fingerprint powder, but something that had been on the hand of the person who left the print.

Perhaps the most memorable moment of Balshy's testimony was the first question of cross-examination by Sarcione: "Mr. Balshy, were you sued, along with two other people, in the United States District Court for the Middle District of Pennsylvania, which is Harrisburg, Pennsylvania, in 1980?"

Balshy confirmed that the civil case involved charges of "fabrication, dye spoilage, destruction, and concealment of evidence" lodged by a man acquitted of murder. He confirmed that he had been defended by the state attorney general's office, and that the jury had returned a judgment in the amount of $18,500. Yes, Balshy said, the verdict in that case came in 1980, and he retired in January 1981.

The witness then denied Sarcione's insinuation that he had not known how to work the FBI's microscope on the day when everyone was taking a closer look at the substances in the palm print lifts. "All I was asking was if they had a fine adjustment on theirs. Mine has a coarse adjustment in a different place. I was asking him where it was at."

That was all for Balshy. The jurors had been picked from the Harrisburg area. Perhaps they had heard of his well-publicized case.

The next morning, Day Eleven, would have been Glen and Betty's fourteenth wedding anniversary. Instead, it was to mark the final day of testimony and the delivery of closing arguments.

Cardinale called his other expert witness, Dr. Cyril H. Wecht of Pittsburgh, Pennsylvania, also of JFK congressional committee fame. One juror later observed dryly that the fit and well-tanned witness "looked like he just flew in from Florida."

Dr. Wecht's testimony essentially boiled down to a theory that if one put one's hands inside a ligature to prevent choking and bruising to the front of the neck, the pressure of one's fingers against the neck—depending on where they were placed—could adversely affect the important vagus nerve, which runs from the brain down the side of the neck as part of a network controlling heartbeat, blood to the brain, consciousness, and, ultimately, life and death.

Pressure on that area, Dr. Wecht contended, could accelerate a feeling of dizziness and near-unconsciousness, while the ligature would leave a straight-lined injury to the back of the neck, but not to the front.

At a sidebar, Keller objected to the testimony, pointing out that the only time Dr. Wolsieffer had made the claim that he put his hands inside the ligature to protect himself was during the taped conversation with Betty's father, a conversation Keller obviously could not cross-examine. Cardinale argued that it did not matter where the evidence had come from. He said that Dr. Wecht's testimony was required to counter Dr. Coe's theory that the neck wound could have been self-inflicted. Judge Cappellini said he was skeptical, but allowed Cardinale to go forward.

Back in open court, Dr. Wecht insisted that his theory was feasible because of the structures in the neck. First, stimulation of the vagus nerve could cause the heart to beat more slowly. "If you begin to cut off air, then you produce a state of hypoxia, decreased oxygen supply, or anoxia, the absence of oxygen supply." Less oxygen caused by the compression would lead to a decreased blood supply. Involvement in a struggle, "a state of hyperexcitability," would increase demands on the body's systems—"the pulse goes faster, the brain needs more oxygen, you are breathing faster." The end result could be "light-headedness," "dizziness," or "fuzziness," Dr. Wecht said. "The vision begins to become poor, you can say it is black, blacking out, and so on, and that may or may not lead to unconsciousness." There was that word "anoxia," which Glen had used to describe Neil's collapse.

Dr. Wecht insisted that his "extremely plausible scenario" could occur without marks on the front of the neck or the hands, provided the ligature was not sharp-edged enough to lacerate the fingers. He said the mark on the rear of the neck would be caused by the ligature coming in contact with the skin. The more the ligature was pulled in the front, and the more pressure applied by the assailant, the greater damage to the victim's neck. The witness also opined that he believed the lack of a frontal neck wound was not corroborative of the rear wound having been self-inflicted.

Cardinale provided yet another demonstration with Nocito, this one much closer to the real thing. Dr. Wecht explained that "only about seven pounds of pressure is sufficient to compress the carotid artery, and that's not much at all." As Nocito's face turned redder by the second, his hands inside the ligature clearly fighting off Cardinale's stronghold, Dr. Wecht added, "You have a lot more than seven pounds of pressure involved there."

Preparing to conclude, Keller wondered if Dr. Wecht could rule out that the wound on the back of Dr. Wolsieffer's neck had been self-inflicted. Wecht conceded, "It is possible."

"If someone had a necklace, a gold necklace, around their neck—"

Cardinale objected as Keller kept on talking.

"—and pulled it—"

"Objection!"

"Overruled."

"—And pulled it, would that cause the injury consistent with what you saw on Commonwealth Exhibit No. 31?" meaning the photo of the back of Dr. Wolsieffer's head.

"It could," Dr. Wecht admitted. "If you put something around your neck and you pull on it hard enough, you could produce an area of some discoloration."

Cardinale rested after calling just the two witnesses. As everyone expected by that point, the defendant was not going to take the stand.

The end result of the appearances by Balshy and Dr. Wecht was that the jury had heard more than enough of that type of testimony. Unavoidably, it had all started to sound the same. All the scientific witnesses went through long stretches that were difficult to understand. The strangulation demonstrations were not that much of a help either. Once around, twice around. Loop, no loop. Crossover, no crossover. None of it seemed logical.

More to the point, the important question wasn't why Glen had a mark on the back of his neck but not in the front. What really mattered was why he was alive with such minor injuries while his wife was so brutally murdered.

CHAPTER 37

As Nancy Wolsieffer sat there in the courtroom trying to figure it all out, she knew what made the most sense to her as soon as she heard Bill Keller ask the question. Finally, the issue of a gold necklace had been brought up. Nancy had been waiting to hear such a question because she knew that her brother-in-law did, in fact, wear a gold chain, regardless of the fact that he told Carol Kopicki after the murder that "they're not for me." But what did Carol know at that point? Only what Glen had told her after the fact.

Nancy's mind tried to quickly process the interviews she had had with the police—what she had said, what she had heard, what she had read. She realized that no one had ever asked her whether Glen wore a gold chain. To her, it offered a solid possibility of solving the mystery of what had really occurred in the master bedroom of 75 Birch. "If they struggled, then Betty would have pulled the chain," she said. "I think he had his chain on."

The government's case had offered little else to suggest a crime of passion scenario, though, despite Betty's promise to confront her husband if he stayed out late, despite Glen's alleged previous use of the ladder when she locked him out, and despite the fact that a great deal of the physical and forensic evidence bolstered such a position. It certainly fit that the wound to the rear of Glen's neck could have been made by Betty yanking at his gold chain during a final argument over his infidelity. She would have been pulling and grinding it into his neck until it broke. The width, length, and, most importantly, the location of Glen's wound were all consistent with that scenario. In fact, it was the most consistent of all the ligature scenarios suggested during the trial. The scenario would be completed if Glen had used the now-missing orange throw pillow to silence Betty, especially if she had been the one to hit him on the back of his head.

But if the jury was to hear any suggestion that such a personal confrontation had occurred, the panel would have been less likely to convict on first-degree murder. So instead of talking about a spontaneous fight between a compulsive womanizer and his emotionally drained and abused wife, Sarcione's closing argument would consist of talk about preplanning, and premeditation, and self-inflicted wounds.

Under trial procedure, Cardinale went first, beginning with emotion in his voice and direction in his delivery. But he soon fell into a rambling scattershot approach, taking aim at what he perceived to be weaknesses in the prosecution's case in the hope that someone on the jury would grant him a reasonable doubt.

He contended that the prosecution lacked a motive, that the "relationship" with Debbie Shipp and the "fling" with Carol Kopicki were not important enough for Glen to have committed murder. "There's no question that Dr. Wolsieffer cheated on his wife," he said. "But there's also no question that whatever was going on in his life, with whomever other than Betty, was not threatening to him in any way, and wasn't giving him any pressure that he had to do something about it, let alone something so drastic as kill his wife.

"Whatever reason he fooled around outside of his house, that is not a reason for you to find him guilty of murder in the first degree. It just isn't enough," he continued. "No matter what his wife knew, Friday nights he went out and came home late. He did what he wanted. How can the Government say to you that all of a sudden, after years of this, Betty Wolsieffer says, 'I am going to put my foot down'? She puts her foot down hard enough that my client is going to kill her? And kill her over what, the relationship with Debbie Shipp that would never have ended?"

If there was any doubt of Glen's unrelenting love for his wife, Cardinale continued, the jurors should listen again to his voice on the Tasker tapes, crying and claiming, " 'I wish I was dead instead of her' and 'I wish she were here so I could talk to her.' Those aren't the words of somebody who didn't love his wife no matter what he did with Shipp, Kopicki, or fifty other people."

Moving on, the defense attorney accused the police of misconduct, saying they focused exclusively on his client because he was left alive and his wife was beaten and strangled. "I am sorry that he wasn't beat to a pulp, but that's not how you can base a conviction of first-degree murder." Any inconsistencies in Dr. Wolsieffer's statements were due to shock, Cardinale contended.

The defense attorney went on to contend that the entire police effort was improperly focused on his client. "From Jump Street, it was 'let's nail the doc.' " He mocked Minnick's testimony about "he better have a bump on his head," and questioned the credibility of the police testimony by referring to crime scene photos showing the rickety ladder in two different positions and the kitchen phone hung up.

Several of the jurors fixed their stares on Glen Wolsieffer sitting frozen in his chair, unwilling to show any kind of emotion as Cardinale continued to belittle the circumstantial case.

"What evidence?" the attorney asked. "Are they talking about fingerprint evidence? The only evidence about that shows that someone *other than my client* was in that back room that day." Cardinale said the blood evidence and fiber evidence, such as the "forcibly removed" hairs or the blue denim fibers found under Betty's fingernails, were equally nonincriminating to his client. He said the time of death was most consistent with Dr. Wolsieffer's version that it was "just getting light." He disparaged the testimony of Betty's friends as having been colored by newspaper reports about the Shipp and Kopicki affairs, and pointed out that not one of them mentioned any violence between the victim and her husband.

Cardinale said the case came down to one simple fact: the

investigators simply didn't believe Dr. Wolsieffer. "The Government will put a witness on the stand and leave the impression he never asked about his wife, and, therefore, ladies and gentlemen, you can conclude he killed her. That's not the way this should work out in a case of this magnitude. You cannot put blinders on, you cannot accept, without testing against other evidence you have seen in the case, the theories that have been put forward by the Commonwealth."

He maintained that the demonstrations with his belt showed that Dr. Wolsieffer could have been attacked just like he said and sustained precisely the neck injury that he did, solely to the rear of his neck.

Moving to the palm prints, Cardinale expressed anger at the prosecution's failure to examine the matter stuck on the print lifts until he raised the issue in the middle of the trial. Even now, Cardinale said, the color and nature of the material on the lifts was unknown. "Does the Government know? They want you to guess that it has no impact on this case, that it didn't come from material on the roof of that rear family room, that it didn't come from the ladder. They want you to guess that. Don't do it. I am begging you on behalf of my client. Keep the Commonwealth to its burden."

Cardinale then presented his strongest arguments, about the prosecution's unsupported claims of premeditation. "They say my client is diabolical, that he planned all of this, premeditated all of this, was smart enough to know just how much to whack himself in the head so he wouldn't die and smart enough to self-inflict some kind of injury to his neck that somebody later would be able to come in and say it is consistent with just the way he described it," said Cardinale with dripping sarcasm. "He was that smart— but he was that dumb that if he was going to set this up, he took a ladder and put it the wrong way? You can't have it both ways."

Cardinale kept at it for a total of ninety minutes, gradually losing his audience in the process. He tried valiantly, but in the end he was handcuffed by the material he had to work with, a silent client with an implausible story. Houdini he was not.

Sarcione had listened carefully to Cardinale's speech, and had found it lacking. "I was not that impressed, quite honestly. I thought Mr. Cardinale appeared nervous, not very fluid, and he was choppy. All of that helped my own confidence."

Sarcione rose from his chair slowly. His closing argument at the preliminary hearing *had* been his warm-up, and a good one at that.

But this was the real moment. And Tony Sarcione, the last voice for Betty Wolsieffer, did not disappoint.

Sarcione played on very simple themes in his closing—common sense and logic. "No one requires jurors to leave their common sense back at home. You bring that with you. You gather that from everyday experiences and apply that when you look at the facts of a case such as this. You use your everyday ordinary common sense. What has the ring of truth to it? Do the statements of the defendant that are in this record have a ring of truth?"

Disagreeing with Cardinale, he maintained that the case *was* about pressure, the kind exerted on the marriage as a result of Betty knowing about Glen's infidelity. "Can you imagine the devastation, not just Debbie Shipp, but now he was dancing at the Crackerbox with the other girl, Kopicki? Now there's another one. Is that pressure? I submit that it certainly is."

He argued that the pressure had built until Betty told Barbara Wende the Tuesday before she died, " 'I am not going to take it anymore. I am sick of him going out on Friday nights. I am not going to be stepped on anymore. I am going to put an end to it.' "

As Sarcione moved on to another point, Phyllis and Lisa Wolsieffer got up and left the courtroom. If they didn't hear it, they wouldn't have to deal with it.

Along with common sense and pressure, Sarcione continued, there was a series of coincidences, the ladder for one. "This intruder happened to pick the same ladder that the defendant utilized when he was locked out of the house? A coincidence?"

He noted that Betty was going to confront Glen "that Friday night—or early Saturday morning, depending on when his gallivanting ceased. This is another coincidence—a major coincidence. This intruder, or maybe intruders he now says, happened to pick out of the 365 days in a year the same night that Betty was going to confront him? That's a major coincidence. Does it have the ring of truth to it? Just when she was going to confront him?"

Sarcione moved directly to the defendant's story. "Forget all these technicalities. This is a common-sense logic case. Is it logical what he wants us to believe? The intruder not only goes to the same window out of all the windows—you saw the house, there's windows downstairs, there's windows on the other side of the house, two doors, all these modes of entry—but he goes to the same window the defendant utilizes. And you know what else? You heard the Cooks, when the defendant would go in and use the ladder, he would put the screen to the left of the window. Another coincidence, the intruder put the screen to the left of the window. I submit to you there's too many coincidences."

Sarcione jumped back to some more common sense, pointing out that Dr. Wolsieffer had said it was getting light out when the intruder or intruders struck. "Now, you are a burglar. Are you going to sit there and wait until daylight to pull a job like this? Does that make logical sense to you, you wait until daylight?

"There were two cars in the driveway. No one can rebut that," he continued. "Think about it. It is ridiculous. What can you assume when you see two cars in the driveway? The house is occupied. Then you are going to go to the second floor? Look at it logically from an intruder's viewpoint. You are going to go to the second floor when it is daylight? You have been to the neighborhood. You saw how close-knit the houses are. So you can be seen climbing up a ladder when it is daylight, with maybe your fellow intruder following you. Does that have the ring of truth to it?

"Let's look at where the intruder goes in. In a back bedroom. And we all heard testimony about the shade being down and draperies. Now the shade wasn't all the way down but it was down. This guy, this intruder, for all he knows, is maybe putting his foot in that window on somebody's face. Does that make any sense? Seriously? Logically? Common sense? You don't know if a professional wrestler is in that house and you may be stepping on his face. It just doesn't make sense.

"Then let's take it a step further with the logic. The intruder, if you believe there was one, comes in, goes through the problem and hassle of getting in upstairs by lugging that ladder from between the garages, across the driveway into the back of the house, up against the wall, puts up the ladder, over the roof, pops the screen in the window, goes through all that problem to get up there—which is a lot when you are an intruder in daylight—and then runs right downstairs. That is what he said, comes in and runs downstairs. It is not logical."

The prosecutor said his common sense also made him doubt Dr. Wolsieffer's claim that he had "crawled out of his room" after hearing the "metal crashing" noise from the rear bedroom. First, Sarcione doubted the description of the noise. The second-floor outside of the house was wood, save for an aluminum gutter. "And you have this fan on, this big heavy fan that's on in the room, and he hears metal-like crashing?"

While Dr. Wolsieffer had mentioned on the Tasker tapes that he had checked on Danielle, he never told Mitchell or the others he had done so. "Your own flesh and blood, five years old, you're in the hallway and you see a man going down, and you're going to crawl by her door and continue down, not knowing if that intruder was in your daughter's room? She's five years old, your blood. Is that logical?

"You know what else isn't logical? He told Detective Mitchell he left his wife asleep, that he didn't wake her up. Does that have the ring of truth to it?"

Sarcione was building now. His voice was loud and steady. He wanted to walk the jurors through Dr. Wolsieffer's supposed journey that morning behind the man with the stockinglike mask. "He goes downstairs. . . . No one is in the living room, no one is in the dining room— You were in the house. It's not a large house by any sense of the imagination. He is in the kitchen, he knows no one is around and he says to this detective, 'I took one step, one step from that divider in the kitchen there, one step, and something is wrapped around my neck from behind and I am being strangled.' But you know what? Where does he tell us he woke up? He is lying across the divider and near the telephone. Is that logical if the confrontation took place a foot into the family room? Does that have the ring of truth to it?"

Then there was the problem in Dr. Wolsieffer's story of his holding the gun in one hand but somehow getting his hands inside the ligature to prevent himself from being fatally choked. "Is it possible for this man here to be able to beat the rope or chain, as he called it, to his neck? Think about it."

Cardinale objected, but Judge Cappellini ruled it was proper argument, even if speculative.

"Maybe after the rope or the chain, as he described it, is applied to the neck you might be able to get a finger in. But we are not that quick. We are not cats, we are human. And you are talking about a six-foot, two-hundred-pound guy doing this."

Sarcione was sticking and jabbing now. There was no blood on Betty's face. Did that make sense?

Comparing the photos of the injuries on Betty's face and neck to the defendant's "perfect linear marks from ear to ear," Sarcione wondered, "Does that indicate a death-and-life struggle with a six-foot, two-hundred-pound goon? Absolutely not. It is not logical. The physical injuries that this guy says he suffered are totally inconsistent with a life-and-death struggle. You don't have to be a brain surgeon to realize that."

Then there was the testimony that Dr. Wolsieffer was admitted to the hospital only because he claimed he had been unconscious. "What did he have? The perfect linear abrasion from ear to ear to the rear of the neck and—everyone talks in his medical terms—a hematoma. 'What's that, Doctor?' 'It's blood from a bruise.' I said, 'Is it a lump, in laymen's terms?' 'It is a lump.' That's what a six-foot, two-hundred-pound intruder did. I submit it is incredible."

Equally as implausible, Sarcione continued, was the defendant's claim that the intruder left him downstairs lying near a loaded gun, unconscious or not, to return upstairs to Mrs. Wolsieffer. "Is that logical? Is that how an intruder is going to act?"

Sarcione then pointed to Mitchell's testimony about finding the deposit slips matching the $1,300 Dr. Wolsieffer claimed had been taken from his desk drawer. Then he contended that none of Betty's jewelry had been taken. "There was a TV in the house, that was still there, a VCR in the family room, that was still there, two portable radios in the second-story bedroom that this intruder came in. You heard Nancy Wolsieffer testify about the good jewelry found downstairs in the ashtray—one was in the ashtray, the diamond earrings right in the ashtray in the kitchen, there was another set of jewelry up on the counter in the kitchen."

He additionally suggested that it wasn't logical that Betty had not been sexually assaulted. "And it all happened on the night that Betty was going to confront him, all that night."

Sarcione argued that Dr. Wolsieffer's remark to security guard Bill Emmett, that he "felt like getting in a fight," was especially germane because of the defendant's encounter that evening with Carol Kopicki at the Crackerbox, with "a little booze" in him. "Who was Carol with? Her husband. Did that have an effect on him, make him angry?"

Acknowledging that his case was circumstantial, Sarcione next contended that substantial direct evidence had been presented as well, the blue denim fibers in Betty's fingernails, the forcibly removed head hairs, the backwards ladder, the dew. He described how the officers had made footprints in the dew when they walked on the roof, but again the question unanswered was whether a dew print made at 2:00 A.M. would still be there six or seven hours later. Disposing of his other problematic area, he dismissed the palm prints in four crisp sentences and moved on: "We put our case on. We put on the palm prints. Did we hide that from you good people? We put on the palm prints."

Sarcione said the defendant's credibility was another point in need of attention. First, Dr. Wolsieffer had said he broke off the affair with Debbie Shipp the year before. Then he said he had seen her on the day of the murder. The defendant said the intruder wore a dark sweatshirt, but no sweatshirt fibers were found anywhere in the house. He told Emmett he was on the couch, not upstairs in bed, when he heard the noise. "Let's put it all together like a puzzle," Sarcione suggested. "When you pour the puzzle out on the table, it looks like junk, but when it all fits in and you put everything in perspective, it is a beautiful picture. This man's statements are in evidence. You have to assess whether or not you are going to credit them. That's your job, that's your prerogative, that's your duty as a juror."

Sarcione reminded the jurors about the telltale signs they had heard concerning Dr. Wolsieffer's real condition on the Saturday morning of the murder. When Officer Minnick had yelled at him, he sat up. When the ambulance crew arrived, he sat back down and closed his eyes. "Is that an injured man?" When Dr. Wolsieffer slipped from Minnick's hands, he broke his fall. "Does that tell you he is okay coordination-wise? That he has got it together?

He didn't want himself getting hurt because he broke his fall. He knew what was going on."

Bouncing back to Glen the man, Sarcione recounted testimony about Glen's proclamation that "Friday nights are mine." His voice building in volume, Sarcione observed, "He said that right in front of his wife. You don't think that's pressure? You don't think that hurt that woman? . . . That's the type of man we are dealing with here, that has three women at once, his wife, Debbie Shipp and Carol Kopicki. And did either of them know about one another? Did Debbie Shipp know about Kopicki? Does that tell you something about this man's deception? Kopicki didn't know about Shipp, Shipp didn't know about Kopicki, Betty found out about both of them."

The prosecutor mocked the defense contention that Debbie Shipp was just a whim, recalling the gifts of jewelry Dr. Wolsieffer had given her. "Do you think Debbie Shipp wanted to be his Friday-night special for all those years? You don't think she had hopes?"

When Cardinale objected to Sarcione's mention of Dr. Wolsieffer's promises to Shipp, the prosecutor simply switched gears to Carol Kopicki. "Then there were the Friday nights with Kopicki. Another thing that tells you about this man, this defendant here, who you have to assess his credibility. Glenn Wilson, do you remember he signed in at some of those motels, that's on this record?"

Now Sarcione was back to the defendant's statements, zooming in on the comments he made to Betty's father. " 'The last year we had together was the best year that we had in a long time.' He is telling his father-in-law about him and Betty. Does that tell you about his credibility? 'Betty and I had more time for ourselves.' That's what he is telling the father-in-law. 'I swear Betty knew that I was not involved with anybody up until the day she died.' "

With a look that appeared almost menacing, Sarcione's face showed his contempt for the defendant's lies. His delivery was riveting. His right hand slashed about, dismissing each of Glen's false statements. Alternately, he poked his right index finger toward the defendant when he uttered the word *he*, as in, "That's what *he* is telling the father-in-law."

Cardinale sat there rocking back and forth in his chair, staring at his client, who was seemingly preoccupied taking notes on a yellow legal pad. The defense attorney then stood to object to Sarcione's piercing remarks, but Judge Cappellini overruled.

Now it was time for Sarcione's toughest test, his argument in favor of the most severe charge of homicide, first-degree murder. He started with Dr. Hudock's testimony about a ligature having been "wrapped around her neck." Under Pennsylvania law, the ligature constituted use of a deadly weapon. Then there was the "three to five minutes" that Betty struggled to save herself. He forewarned the jurors to listen to Judge Cappellini's instructions that premeditation can be formulated within seconds, certainly within the time frame it took to strangle Betty. The prosecutor contended that after the slaying the defendant went outside and set up the ladder. Because of tension and pressure, he put it up backwards and forgot to step on it to make an imprint in the ground beneath it. He said the ottoman and coffee cup that were turned over in the family room also were mistakes committed by the defendant because they were found too far into the room from where the struggle supposedly took place.

"He also forgot the physical evidence. The scratches on the chest. Betty had on her wedding band and her engagement ring," he said. "There was blood, the FBI agent testified, on both the engagement ring and the wedding band, and the defendant had scratches on his chest. That, I submit, was consistent with the scratches."

Cardinale objected again, and the judge again overruled.

Suddenly, Sarcione was finished. "I would just ask you—I am not going to remind you of the oath, I know you took the oath, I am not going to read it to you—to give the case a fair look, utilizing your common sense and remembering that Betty Wolsieffer, ever since she had that conversation with Barbara Wende— she wasn't going to take it anymore—never saw another Friday night."

The courtroom was bone-chillingly silent. Sarcione returned to his table with a glow of satisfaction. He had consumed less than an hour. Keller had dropped a pencil to signal the fifty-minute mark, and Sarcione heeded the pre-arranged cue.

Judge Cappellini told everyone to remain in their seats. He

told the jurors that they would receive his final instructions in the morning, just before they began deliberating the case. He sent them back to the Ramada and summoned the lawyers for both sides to the bench. For the record, Cardinale said he did not want the judge's charge to include any explanation of the fact that his client had not been obligated to take the stand. He personally thought it was better not to draw any additional attention to that point. With that, everyone adjourned for the evening.

There were handshakes all around over at the prosecution table. Sarcione was still pumped, as if he needed to go jog for an hour to burn off the excess energy. Sarcione's mother chatted with Marian Tasker. Both women fought back their tears. "Thank you so much," Mrs. Tasker told the prosecutor.

The Wolsieffer side was very subdued. But back at the hotel, Cardinale repeated his long-standing optimism. "There's no way this jury will convict Glen of anything, especially if they ask to hear the tape of him talking with Jack," the defense attorney said. That evening, Cardinale and Nocito went out to the Crackerbox for a couple of drinks with one of Cardinale's college football pals. Enjoying the temporary break from the tension, the lawyers called their client from the bar—as Glen later explained—"to bust my balls."

The following morning, with a heavy dew covering the valley, Judge Cappellini instructed the jury on malice, intent to kill, and premeditation. He said preplanning was not necessary for first-degree murder, just enough time to fully form an intent to kill and a conscious recognition of the intent by the killer.

He said a lack of affection in the marriage could be considered as part of a motive, although that was not a necessary element of proving the crime. Finally, Judge Cappellini advised the jury that their evaluation of the circumstantial evidence in the case should depend on "common sense and human experience.

"Remember, you can find malice and murder only if you are satisfied beyond a reasonable doubt that the defendant was not acting under a sudden and intense passion resulting from serious provocation by the victim," he said. "The law recognizes that the cumulative impact of a series of related events can lead to sudden passion and amount to serious provocation. The test is whether a reasonable person confronted with the same series of events would become so impassioned that he would be incapable of cool reflection." Again, although a crime of passion had not been the centerpiece of either side's strategy, it was looming in the background, as always.

As the jurors went to their special room to deliberate shortly before 10:00, Glen Wolsieffer—dressed in a gray and black wool blend jacket, black slacks, white shirt, and a paisley tie—alternated between standing around nervously making small talk and sitting in his chair, hands folded in front of him, the tips of his index fingers touching his lips.

Nancy walked over to Phyllis Wolsieffer's row to sit and talk.

"How are you doing?" Nancy asked, marking the first time she had gone across to the left side of the courtroom.

"Thanks for coming over here," Phyllis told her.

It wasn't that Nancy had tried to avoid her mother-in-law; she had been saying hello in the hallway during recesses. But this was different.

Like everyone else, Nancy had sensed the electricity in the invisible wall down the middle of the courtroom. "And I didn't want it to be like that with Phyllis," she explained. "I knew what I was going through. I felt really sorry for her."

After a few minutes, the two women left the courtroom along with Nancy's mother, Mary Ellen. They went for a cup of coffee in the lunchroom downstairs. "We talked about everything but," said Nancy. "It was strained and tense. No one talked about the possible outcome." They all fought back their tears.

Three hours into the process, the jury sent out a note requesting written definitions of their three guilty choices: first-degree murder, third-degree murder, and voluntary manslaughter. The judge walked across the rotunda to the jury room to inform the panel members that he could not fulfill the request and would instead orally repeat the definitions he had provided in his final instructions. Everyone filed back into court and Judge Cappellini again read the appropriate material, reciting it ever so slowly. The jurors nodded their heads that they had heard what they needed to hear and returned to their deliberations. It wouldn't be long now.

Word of a verdict swept through the third floor several minutes after 4:00. They had only been given the case six hours before. There was lunch, and waiting for the exhibits to be delivered, and then the rereading of the judge's instructions. Judgment had been determined swiftly.

The hallway outside Courtroom Four was packed with spectators wanting in on the final act of the trial. The courtroom was cleared as the usually relaxed and polite sheriff's security force suddenly became very stern and official. Although it was not publicly announced, there were whispers that there had been a death threat. Everyone entering the courtroom was going to be searched with metal detectors.

In fact, a friend of one of Judge Cappellini's sons said he had overheard Jack Tasker say, "If it's not guilty, I'll kill him." When the judge was informed of the threat, he realized he had no choice but to take it seriously.

Forced to battle their way through a horde of spectators, Phyllis and Lisa Wolsieffer were livid as they made their way back into the courtroom. Because of the crowd at the front door, the Taskers were being escorted through the judge's chambers. Lisa charged at Cardinale, demanding action. She couldn't believe that with all the precautions being taken, Jack Tasker was coming in the back way. Cardinale calmed her down, assuring her that the Tasker men had been thoroughly searched in the judge's outer office.

In the wake of the death threat, the prosecution team moved itself from the table in front of the defendant to the right side of the courtroom, facing the jury box. D.A. Stevens had shown up for the finale.

Cardinale looked stunned. He had expected the jury to take a full day at the very least. A reporter from the *Citizens' Voice* shook hands and extended good-luck wishes to members of both families.

With sheriff's deputies ringing the standing-room-only crowd, Judge Cappellini reconvened. Mel Glenn, the jury foreman, stood to read the verdict. "We, the jury, find not guilty on the first count, murder of the first degree." A loud gasp came from the Tasker side of the courtroom. "Guilty of murder in the third degree," the foreman continued. Instead of mandatory life in prison, the defendant would face a maximum of twenty years, but probably considerably less given Pennsylvania sentencing guidelines.

"Yeah!" said Corry Stevens, clenching his right fist in the air in triumph as those around him calmly broke out in smiles.

The Taskers were all crying. Across the aisle Phyllis Wolsieffer wore the look of a woman who had just lost another son.

Judge Cappellini polled the jurors, thanked them for their service, and dismissed them. He then summoned Dr. Wolsieffer and the attorneys to his bench, where he informed the defense that it had ten days to file post-verdict motions for a new trial or an arrest of judgment, which would constitute a dismissal of the charges on the grounds that the evidence had been insufficient to warrant a conviction.

In response to a series of questions, the defendant said he understood his rights. Judge Cappellini then wondered about everyone's position on bail. Cardinale was stunned again. Based on his experience elsewhere, he had assumed that with the conviction, Dr. Wolsieffer would be hauled off to prison automatically. But third-degree murder was a bailable offense in Pennsylvania, through the entire appeal process under certain circumstances, and Dr. Wolsieffer had appeared at every court proceeding as required.

On behalf of the Commonwealth, Bill Keller requested that the $200,000 bail be raised to $500,000 in view of the verdict and the fact that Dr. Wolsieffer was now a resident of Virginia. Cardinale insisted that given his client's history, he was not a risk to flee. "While I understand the Commonwealth's position and its need to make such an argument, I respectfully and humbly request that bail remain the same, that he not have to use funds that could otherwise be used for his appeal."

Judge Cappellini ruled that bail would remain at $200,000, and directed the defendant to continue to telephone the Wilkes-Barre Police Department every day at 10:00 in the morning and 10:00 at night, and to notify the D.A.'s office within forty-eight hours of a change in address or telephone number.

With the technicalities disposed of, Glen Wolsieffer calmly and silently walked out of the courtroom. Holding his sister's right hand, he then swiftly made his way through the crowd of people and cameras, down the steps, and out into the parking lot, where several admiring high school girls followed him to his car.

CHAPTER 38

IN HIS WORDS

I went into the trial with the knowledge of being innocent off the testimony. These people were trying to fit what they had, or what they thought they had, as a case. It's been portrayed that I am cocky. I have never heard the word "confidence" come up. I have the utmost confidence in the gentlemen who are representing me, and I know the truth.

I certainly never got any confidence-boosting from Betty, you know. I would say we got along—I guess that was our relationship. We were very good friends, and I loved her, and I guess she loved me. But certainly not a real intimate type of love. But she would never, you know—like Carol will buy or pick clothes out for me and she'll say, "Oh, that looks great on you. You really look good in this." Or even getting a haircut, "Yeah, your hair looks nice." Something as superficial as your appearance, or even something as personal as, "I really like the way that you make me feel," or "I really like how good you are with the kids," or "I really like how you do this or that." People like to be complimented, let's face it, it's

human nature. Just something that makes you think that you are noticed, or worthwhile. I think that has a lot to do with two people
getting along or making each other feel good. I think we found that.
As far as confidence goes, I don't think I've ever lacked that.

I know the courtroom was filled with people who hate me, people
watching my every move. A lot of people who were my friends are
no longer my friends. I saw people glaring at me. But if I put
myself in their positions and read the propaganda that these people
have put together, what else should they think?

Debbie stated in the preliminary hearing the fact that she was
the motive. I knew that I had said that to her, so I didn't really
look at that as anything really that interesting. I felt that her testimony was very accurate.

The supposed closeness of these other women to my wife?
Nancy and Betty were extremely close. My sister, Lisa, and Betty
were extremely close. If there were any confidences, they would
have been placed with Nancy or Lisa. I'd like to find a way to put
Eileen Pollock in storage. Jane Ann Miscavage didn't like herself.
You got to like yourself to have somebody else like you.

As Frank or Tony says, "The guy," meaning me, "is quiet for three
years. Now all of a sudden he's going to get in a squad car and
blab to Mitchell?" I didn't have anything to blab to Mitchell. He
starts saying small talk, so I'm telling him, "Yeah, yeah. Things
happened quickly that night." But he wants to choose that it's in
relation to me and Betty, rather than what it was meant—to relate
to me and the intruder or intruders.

It is just like the inquest. It was convenient. The inquest was
convenient for them to allegedly prove that Neil killed himself so
that it would make me look bad. So you know, this is just another
little thing they can throw in the fire.

I'd like everyone to believe me, but I know it's not going to
happen. I can't prove I wasn't in the house.

CHAPTER 39

More than eighteen months after the trial, Glen Wolsieffer continued to be a free man, living with Carol Kopicki in Virginia and practicing dentistry. If the Taskers were ever to launch a custody or visitation fight, they would probably have to file the legal papers in Virginia, Danielle's legal residence.

Dr. Wolsieffer steadfastly maintained his innocence while acknowledging that his story was difficult to believe. Technically, he and Carol were still engaged, but he said he would not get married without his attorneys' approval.

As for swearing off another bout of infidelity, Dr. Wolsieffer expressed hope, but made no promises. "I think that I would feel a lot more guilt than I did with Betty. I think I would get a pang. I don't rule it out, but I don't go looking for it." As usual, Dr. Wolsieffer's explanations were contradictory or convoluted. "I see what that stuff does to you now. What it does, not just to me, or to the one that I would be hopping into bed with, but also to the one that I'm in love with. Yeah, I'd say it might be the first time that I'm actually in love with someone. I'm in love with Carol. I feel now that I want to be loyal and faithful. I don't want to lose her because of that."

At D.A. Stevens's request, the Pennsylvania State Board of Dentistry commenced disciplinary proceedings against Dr. Wolsieffer even though he had not renewed his license when it expired in March 1989. Dr. Wolsieffer was represented at the dental board hearing by attorney Frank Nocito, who in the coming months would assume the Wolsieffer case full-time as Cardinale became involved in Mafia cases in New England and New York City, including the 1992 trial of John Gotti. Officials in Virginia, where he had a separate license, announced that they would not move against Dr. Wolsieffer until after he was sentenced. Even then, the officials continued, license revocation was not mandatory.

Meanwhile, several of the public officials involved in the Wolsieffer prosecution went on to higher office. Despite his campaign promise to complete his term, D.A. Stevens decided to run for county judge. He won a primary nomination, and before the November 1991 election, he was appointed to a vacancy on the bench. On Election Day, he easily captured one of the four available ten-year slots. Joseph Giovannini, the coroner's solicitor, lost in the judges' primary, while Bill Keller, with the most experience of all, lost his bid for a judgeship in November's general election to a candidate with as little courtroom experience as Stevens. Peter Paul Olszewski, the young assistant prosecutor who interviewed Dr. Wolsieffer at the hospital the Saturday of Betty's murder, won election as the new D.A. Dr. Hudock, the coroner, easily won reelection. In Harrisburg, there was talk that if Attorney General Ernest Preate were to run for governor, Sarcione would campaign for the AG's post. Sarcione, however, rejected that suggestion, saying he instead was interested in someday becoming the Chester County D.A. Then, he could see to it that his brother's murder was solved.

In March 1992, Janet and Tony Sarcione's third adopted child, Alexander, celebrated his first birthday. The child was named after Tony's brother.

In early 1992, Nancy Wolsieffer left her job at St. Boniface to replace a teacher on sabbatical leave in the Wilkes-Barre public school system. She hoped that in the next two years she would be able to obtain a permanent position.

Nancy continued to be haunted by her husband's death and the politicized inquest. "People still do not realize the scapegoat that Neil was made out to be," she said. The inquest jury's vote was never officially announced, but one of the jurors later said it was five to three, suicide versus accidental death. When confronted with the fact that eight jurors had voted instead of the usual six, Dr. Hudock, the county coroner, and Giovannini, the coroner's solicitor, maintained in separate interviews that they were unaware of the two extra voters. Each also maintained that they were under the impression the vote had been unanimous. Dr. Hudock referred additional legal questions to Giovannini.

When pressed on the subject, Giovannini insisted that nothing improper had taken place. Asked to explain the unprecedented change in procedure, he acknowledged that the two alternates should have been dismissed. He then maintained that it was irrelevant whether the required majority of four votes would have been obtained for suicide if the panel had been kept at its regular size of only six members. "There could have been fifty jurors. All it says is six, so that means at least six," he claimed.

Nancy wasn't the only one who remembered Neil. Bob Reilly, who went from the city council to county clerk of courts in the period after his friend's death, organized an annual golf tournament for the benefit of Bryn Wolsieffer. Several others were working behind the scenes in 1992 to revive a proposal to name a city park after Neil, a plan that had been tabled in the politicized atmosphere immediately after his death. "That's another betrayal in itself, that the town could turn on somebody," said Nancy. "There are so many betrayals. That's why I don't have trust in people. It's coming back, but it's such a slow process.

"I'd do anything to get my old life back, but I'm to the point where I know there is a life out there. I know that nobody is going to do it for me. I have to do the work to get there."

In a related issue that received no publicity, a three-member arbitration panel in Scranton ruled that Neil Wolsieffer's death was accidental. The decision culminated in one of several civil actions Nancy filed after insurance companies denied payment on modest life-insurance policies because of the inquest verdict. The other lawsuits were settled out of court. The arbitration decision represented a major victory for Nancy, but she acknowledged that it did her little good in Wilkes-Barre. For example, Dr. Hudock, who testified at the Scranton proceeding, confirmed in an interview that he was aware of the panel's finding, then coldly added, "I didn't change the death certificate."

As for her relationship with Glen and the other Wolsieffers, Nancy said she and Neil's mother, Phyllis, don't talk about the murder or Glen. She said she was uncomfortable with Phyllis's unwavering support of her surviving son, but said she wanted desperately to continue a relationship with her daughter's grandmother. "As much as I care about her, I think, 'Don't you see what he did to Neil?' "

Nancy said she planned to have nothing to say or do with Glen ever again. "His story is full of holes," she now says firmly. She is so thankful that she saw through him before she ever began making serious plans to move to Virginia with him. "Now it makes perfect sense to me because my thoughts are so much clearer. Then I was desperate. I was dependent. I was just so scared I didn't know what I was going to do for money because I didn't have any and he was going to start this new practice. It just seemed like that was the thing to do."

Looking back, she said she didn't focus on the precise details of Glen's story at first because she had her back up over the way the police were treating the Wolsieffer family. "I was so defensive about the way that I was treated, Neil was treated, Glen was treated.

"When you find out how wrong you are about a person, you kick yourself. You say, 'Why didn't I see that?' " But, she said, she didn't regret how she managed after Neil's death. "I know it doesn't look right, but I don't care what it looks like. It's what I did to survive." Also, she said she was grateful for the close relationship she developed with Glen following Neil's death. "If I had never sought comfort in Glen I never would have realized what he was really like. I never would have seen all the sides of him. I never would have uncovered what a liar he was."

For example, she recalled the day that she confronted him about the arrogance of his adultery. "I have a feeling this has been a pattern of yours all your life," she remembered telling him.

"Well, not all of my life," Glen had replied.

Nancy had been stunned by the brashness. "He was kind of proud of it, I think, proud of the fact that he could get anybody that he wanted." Even while letting Neil drive to his death. "I can't imagine that anyone could allow their brother to die over something they did," she said. "I didn't do anything wrong and I know that Neil didn't do anything wrong. We were just a family that was caught up in the middle of this against our own will."

For Nancy, the healing would not come easy.

Over on Magnolia, Phyllis and Lisa Wolsieffer continued to believe in Glen's innocence in 1992, at least publicly. Allowing themselves to begin to ask the tough questions remained their most difficult task.

On Gilligan, the Taskers were still thinking of Betty every day. Beautiful photos of her graced the living room tables. The wedding album was no more. They continued to long for a relationship with their granddaughter, but acknowledged that by this point the youngster's mind had been poisoned against them.

When they visit the cemeteries, they visit two Wolsieffer gravesites: Betty's and Neil's.

With delay upon delay, it was difficult for Marian and John Tasker to keep the watch, but they prayed that some day soon justice would be administered.

Both of them said they have no doubt that Glen Wolsieffer was responsible for their daughter's murder.

Meanwhile, little bits of evidentiary information continued to surface.

The palm prints officially remained a mystery, but during an interview in early 1992, Dr. Hudock, the county coroner, said he was fairly certain that the palm prints on Glen's desk had been left there by his now deceased son, who had assisted him taking photographs at 75 Birch the morning of the murder. "I think I even saw him leaning on the desk looking out the window," he said. "I'm almost sure they were his."

The post-verdict motions were delayed for months as the defense waited for the tardy delivery of the trial transcripts. The main issues raised were the legality of the involvement of the state attorney general's office and the admissibility of hearsay testimony from Betty's girlfriends.

Then there were postponements and extensions, followed by a bombshell that would threaten the Wolsieffer conviction. On the afternoon of July 25, 1991, Steve Corbett, the *Times Leader* columnist, paid Tony Sarcione an unscheduled visit at the attorney general's office in Harrisburg. As Sarcione later recalled the conversation, in the midst of small talk Corbett suddenly began discussing his trial testimony. He reminded Sarcione that he had answered "no" when Cardinale had asked him "whether he had any *tapes* of conversations with Dr. Wolsieffer." Corbett told Sarcione that he was of the "firm belief" that he had answered the question truthfully because "Cardinale asked if he had any *tapes*, not whether he had a single tape."

Corbett then stunned Sarcione by revealing that he in fact did have a tape of *one* of the conversations he had with Dr. Wolsieffer. Within the next twenty-four hours, Sarcione informed Judge Cappellini and the defense team of his conversation. He then contacted Corbett and told him to preserve the tape.

The recording presented several potential legal problems. If it had been made without Dr. Wolsieffer's permission, it violated Pennsylvania's strict wiretap statute. Second, Cardinale and Nocito had been denied use of the tape at the trial to aid in their cross-examination of Corbett. It could necessitate a new trial. Third, there was the possibility that Corbett had committed perjury. Fourth, if others at the newspaper knew, charges might be brought for obstruction of justice and conspiracy. "In retrospect, with the issues that have arisen, I wish I had never used him," Sarcione later said of Corbett.

The following Tuesday, the 30th, Judge Cappellini signed an order directing Corbett to preserve the tape and to surrender it to the court "as soon as is reasonably practical."

The court order, of course, made Corbett's disclosure an issue of public record. The next morning's *Times Leader* carried the page-one headline, WOLSIEFFER ATTORNEY WANTS TO HEAR CORBETT'S TAPE. The story quoted the newspaper's attorney, Ralph Kates, as saying that the tape confirmed the accuracy of Corbett's column, and made no mention of any of the potential legal problems. The story inaccurately quoted Dr. Wolsieffer as having told Corbett flat out that "he believed" druggies from Clear Brook had killed his wife. Despite Judge Cappellini's order to turn the tape over, the *Times Leader* brazenly also announced on page one that it intended to publish the complete transcript of the telephone conversation in the following day's paper. The announcement prompted Nocito to hand-deliver a letter to Allison Walzer, the editor of the *Times Leader*, warning her that "publication of what may be an illegal wiretap may in itself be illegal, and give rise to possible civil and criminal sanctions."

The letter had no effect, though, as the *Times Leader*, cocksure of its position, printed the text of the conversation. Among the more embarrassing disclosures, during a discussion of his diet, Corbett told Dr. Wolsieffer, "I'm drinking juice like I'm some homo or something."

The transcript essentially matched the Corbett columns, but the characterization of "verbatim" was overstated, to be sure. Such journalistic issues were of no import for the moment, however. The question that really mattered was asked across the front page of the *Citizens' Voice*: WOLSIEFFER VERDICT IN JEOPARDY? It was a question without a simple answer.

As Corbett's paper was printing the transcript of his conversation with Dr. Wolsieffer, the *Citizens' Voice* used its front page to print the key Cardinale-Corbett exchange from the trial transcript under the large headline CORBETTGATE.

"Mr. Corbett, in your conversations you say you had with my client, were they tape-recorded?" Cardinale had asked.

"Were they tape-recorded? No, sir," Corbett had replied without elaboration.

The *Citizens' Voice* coverage also contained an admission from *Times Leader* managing editor Cliff Schechtman that "some of us" knew of the existence of the tape prior to Dr. Wolsieffer's trial.

The *Times Leader* coverage was filled with excuses and explanations. The newspaper quoted Sarcione and Keller as saying the conviction was not in jeopardy provided the tape supported what was written in the columns. Front-page excerpts included a portion of the trial where Corbett asked if he could clarify something, implying that he had wanted to clarify his unequivocal reply, "no," to the question about possible tape recordings. There was even a front-page editorial, entitled "Living Up to Our Responsibility," that defended the newspaper's actions while potentially making things worse by admitting "we knew he had a tape."

Then there was Corbett himself. Under the headline IF SOMEONE HAD BOTHERED TO ASK, he tore into Cardinale for supposedly asking the wrong question and Judge Cappellini for not allowing him to clarify his answer. He contended that if Cardinale had been "a smarter, better lawyer" the entire mess could have been avoided. He said that he had conducted two separate conversations with Dr. Wolsieffer about "druggies" and therefore was completely truthful when he replied, "Were they tape-recorded? No, sir." In the column, he explained, "THEY were not tape-recorded." He lamely maintained that any "first-year law school" student would have been expected to follow with the question, "Do you have a tape recording of either conversation?"

As spurious as that argument was, Corbett's credibility was damaged more by his repeated contention that his misleading trial testimony had upset him so much, "It felt like fire tearing into the pit of my stomach. And I felt sick. I had told the truth. But I wasn't able to tell the whole truth." *What?* "I had tried so hard to tell the truth during my appearance on the witness stand that I got sick after my testimony was complete," he went on.

Unexplained was why, if Corbett was so pained and anguished by all of this, he had waited so long—two years after the taping, and eight months after the trial—to tell anyone on the prosecution team, especially since Cardinale had used the singular word "tape" in several follow-up questions. If Corbett had been so upset by the judge not allowing him to clarify on the witness stand, why hadn't he told Sarcione or Keller during the next recess? Or at the end of the day? Or at the end of the week? Instead, a murder conviction now potentially hung in the balance, and the First Amendment was embarrassingly being invoked in blasphemous tones as a defense for this nonsense.

From Boston, Tony Cardinale characterized Corbett's trial testimony as an "outright lie" and mocked his differentiation between singular and plural as an attempt to "hide behind semantics. What else can you expect from someone like him? The question was simple and straightforward." He called for Corbett's arrest.

As to be expected, Frank Nocito seized the opportunity to

submit an additional post-verdict motion seeking a new trial or dismissal of the charges on the grounds of the secret wiretap. Nocito contended that the illegally made tape and the "deceptive, misleading, obtuse, obstructive and less than candid testimony" had denied his client a fair trial.

During a hearing convened to explore the matter, Corbett, Walzer, and Schechtman all declined to take the Fifth Amendment, despite Judge Cappellini's warnings, and admitted on the witness stand to key details about the tape's existence and the subsequent publication of the transcript. Meanwhile, Detective Gary Sworen from the D.A.'s office interviewed the participants as part of an official investigation. The pressure was building, but the newspaper people presented themselves as if the entire process was a lark, and that they were above the law. One day in court, as Judge Cappellini summoned Corbett to the bench to discuss his failure to cooperate, he looked to the rear of the courtroom at a smiling Cliff Schechtman, the managing editor. "Do you think there is something funny here?" the judge demanded. "If there is, tell me. I don't find anything funny here. There is serious business. . . . I don't want that kind of affront. This is a court of law." The judge was particularly incensed that the newspaper had printed the transcript of the tape after he had ordered that it be turned over. He couldn't believe that the newspaper's editors and lawyers had had the audacity to make a copy of the tape.

In another twist, Corbett claimed he had simply followed his lawyer's advice in remaining quiet immediately after his trial testimony. Fearing at the least a potential conflict of interest, attorney Kates hired his own counsel. This time, the *Times Leader* and Corbett made no mention of the fact that Charles Gelso, the prominent attorney hired for Kates, had represented organized crime figures in the past, just like Cardinale.

While Judge Cappellini wrestled with the problem of how the illicit taping might affect the Wolsieffer verdict, the sticky problem of what to do about the taping itself and Corbett's trial testimony rested with Jerome Cohen, who was appointed by the county judges to temporarily replace Stevens in the D.A.'s job during the very week the taping controversy broke. Cohen assured the public that he would do whatever was needed, whether it was popular or not.

Within a week, Cohen and Sarcione announced that Corbett had not committed perjury because no one had specifically asked the columnist if he had tape-recorded that particular conversation. Nocito said he "almost gagged on the explanation."

It would subsequently be announced that there would be no wiretap prosecution, either; Cohen ruled that the two-year statute of limitations had expired. Corbett had waited exactly two years from the date of the taping to tell Sarcione.

Nocito, supported privately by several judges and prominent attorneys, felt that the two-year period did not start to run until the time of notification, meaning the day of Corbett's "surprise" visit to Sarcione's office. At the minimum, it was argued, a statute of limitations claim is an issue to be raised by a defense attorney after an arrest, not by the D.A. as an excuse not to make the arrest.

Cohen, however, could not be moved. He ruled that the time clock under Pennsylvania law started running from the commission of the crime, not from the point of notification.

That left the publication of the transcript, a matter that Detective Sworen continued to work on arduously.

Meanwhile, Nocito continued to make his presence known by threatening to file a private complaint on behalf of Dr. Wolsieffer under a provision of Pennsylvania law that provides such a remedy when the D.A.'s office declines to prosecute.

As the columnists and editors of the other two newspapers in town attacked the *Times Leader*'s actions, Corbett and his editors embarked on a vigorous public relations campaign in their defense. The newspaper published stories saying only fifteen states had laws requiring the consent of all parties to a conversation before it could be taped, and quoted freedom of the press experts as saying that such laws were "hardly ever enforced." There was a front-page editorial suggesting that everyone ought to drop the whole thing and put the "focus back on the dentist." Kates, the *Times Leader* attorney, contended that federal law, which allows one-party consent, should apply. And Corbett continued to write columns about himself and the controversy, contending in one piece that "jurors"—plural—had told him the "druggies" testimony "helped them decide a murderer's guilt." But when Nocito sent an investigator out to confirm that morsel for his appeal, he came up empty, and Sarcione obtained a court order requiring that the interrogations be terminated. When asked at one of the post-verdict hearings about his claim that jurors thought his trial testimony had been key, Corbett backed away, saying he had gotten that "impression" from one juror.

Milking the situation for all the publicity possible, the *Times Leader* used its call-in line to invite readers to discuss the Corbett controversy. One of the callers was Dr. Wolsieffer's mother, Phyllis. "What goes around, comes around. The time has come. I've lived long enough to see you squirm like the snake that you are. You have hidden behind your journalism shield. Well, there's no such thing as a mother's shield and God only knows the countless times you've caused this mother's heart to break. So if there's any justice in this world, you will get what you deserve. And I hope your attorney and your editors squirm with you."

And so it went until December 12, 1991—with just three weeks remaining in Jerome Cohen's interim term as district attorney—when columnist Corbett, editor Walzer, managing editor Schechtman, and publisher Dale Duncan were arrested and charged with conspiracy to violate the state wiretap law by disseminating information obtained from an illegally taped conversation. Walzer was additionally charged with directly violating the law by publishing the transcript. Each count carried a seven-year prison term and a $15,000 fine. The *Times Leader* reported that the arrests marked "the first time in this country that a newspaper and its top management have been charged with publishing information in connection with wiretap laws."

The newspaper proceeded with its public defense. Duncan called the arrests outrageous. A lengthy editorial published the day after the arrests, and accompanied with photos of the four defendants, carried the headline, FOR REPORTING THE NEWS THEY WOULD IMPRISON US. The editorial traced its powerful role in the community back to the aftermath of the 1978 labor strike and the purchase of the paper by Capital Cities/ABC Inc. Claiming that its "aggressive reporting and commentary" had forced elected officials from office, the editorial offered yet another explanation for the purported persecution—political retribution and harassment. "What better way to calm an angry electorate than to silence the messenger of governmental wrongdoing?" Without making even an insinuation of an allegation against Cohen, the editorial contended that the interim D.A. was "a product of a system we have criticized for years."

In a statement released to reporters across the country, Duncan said, "While the convicted murderer in this case is free thirteen months after conviction, the newspaper is being harassed merely for reporting the news." Several out-of-town newspapers and TV programs, unfamiliar with the newspaper's questionable conduct throughout the Wolsieffer case, lent credence to Duncan's pleadings about the First Amendment. The publisher told associates he could not understand why the other local media had not come to the defense of the *Times Leader*.

The *Times Leader* defendants appeared for their arraignment with new attorneys, including the noted Philadephia lawyer and former prosecutor Richard Sprague. They smiled for photographers as they entered and exited the proceeding.

Two days before Christmas 1991, District Justice Martin R. Kane conducted a brief preliminary hearing, ruled that a *prima facie* case existed, and bound the matter over to county court for trial.

At times it appeared that the newspaper defendants still did not recognize the seriousness of the matter at hand. Corbett and Duncan chewed gum during most of Justice Kane's morning session. They again smiled at photographers on the way in and out of court. They laughed at some of the testimony and the sparring between attorneys.

Their behavior prompted *Citizens' Voice* columnist Mike McGlynn to write a column the next day entitled, "Why Are These People Laughing?" In his piece, McGlynn said he could not help but see "the newspaper's proclaimed devotion to the First Amendment as a case of finding a convenient tree to hide behind in a heavy windstorm. . . . Right or wrong, the newspaper and its staff continue to flaunt the holier-than, wiser-than, and better-than-the-rest-of-us-idiots-here-in-the-Wyoming-Valley attitude which has won the newspaper the ill will of enough area residents that it remains unable to make good on its 1978 vow to 'inflict a newspaper' on the community." He called his competitors "conceited, arrogant and self-proclaimed journalistic heroes" who have "no clue as to what this community is all about, choosing to regard it as a haven of simpletons and sheep who would be easily led to slaughter. It was a bit of a miscalculation."

With the first week of 1992, Cohen was out of office, replaced by Olszewski. A political ally of the newspaper higher-ups, he nonetheless promised to do what was right. The new D.A. moved quickly. Under another barrage of *Times Leader* editorials, Olszewski recommended that the charges be dismissed, contending that Dr. Wolsieffer had "no reasonable expectation of privacy" when he agreed to be interviewed. In late March, county President Judge Patrick J. Toole Jr. had little choice but to formally dismiss the charges.

Such were the ways of the Wyoming Valley.

Oral arguments on the Wolsieffer post-verdict motions were finally heard by Judge Cappellini, with Nocito adding the Corbett taping controversy to his list of issues. But none of it worked. After reading the 2,196-page trial transcript, and considering the implications of Corbett's less than frank testimony, Judge Cappellini denied Dr. Wolsieffer a new trial on April 23, 1992. The judge continued bail pending sentencing.

As Glen maintained his innocence, he added another bizarre twist to his explanation of the events surrounding his wife's murder. More than five years after the supposed attack, he still had a bump on the back of his head.

Detailing how he had kicked the intruder with his right foot and gotten hit on his head, Glen suddenly interrupted an interview at his Falls Church, Virginia, residence to offer a close-up look and a feel of what he contended was the remains of the 1986 assault.

"Feel my head," he instructed. "This side's got nothing, this side's got a dandy." There was a tight bump on the left side of his head, just off-center.

Dr. Wolsieffer was asked if the doctors had told him whether the bump would ever go away. "They never said anything about it."

"Did you ever ask the doctor?"

"It doesn't bother me," he maintained. But a minute later, he said he still got severe headaches from time to time.

Dr. Wolsieffer was asked whether he had been tested. "No, you know what, I was getting headaches for like a week after. I called Dr. Czwalina, the guy who saw me in the hospital. And he said, 'Let's see if they'll go away.' There isn't really a test they can do on it. Eventually, the headaches subsided." But again, a minute later he was talking about still getting headaches.

He was asked next about the relative size of the bump. "Is it the size now that it was then?"

"No, it's bigger," he replied.

When that response was met with skepticism, Glen amended, "Bigger then—but I'm not sure."

He went on to explain that when he got a headache now, he felt the pain in the area of the bump. "Sometimes the headache will thump there. Sometimes it's just a tension headache. What I'm thinking is part of my brain is probably going out into that cavity."

CHAPTER 40

IN HIS WORDS

Other than for sexual reasons, Betty and I were very happy together. That last year, things were great. She was happy. I was happy. We had mutual friends, we had mutual family, you know—I don't know how it was perceived that I got along with Betty's family. But they accepted me. They did a lot of things for me, and in turn I wanted to do a lot of things for them, and I think I did.

It wasn't like I was out at a motel every Friday night, most— I'd say half to two-thirds—of the Friday nights I was out with my brother, or my cousin, or both, or just friends. We'd be up at Eddie's. There was this traditional thing where my father used to go out Friday nights, not to get away from the house, but just that was his night out. He enjoyed kicking back and going out with his friends. Not necessarily to get drunk, but just to socialize, you know, have a few beers. It wasn't a big deal. And I guess my brother and I both followed the same pattern, and most of our friends did, too. I just want to point out that it wasn't, like, every Friday night.

I was at home except for a softball game or two during the week, which Betty was certainly welcome to come to—she chose not to most of the time—with or without Danielle. I was home during the week, and Saturday nights was when Betty and I would go out to dinner, either by ourselves or with friends or family, and then Sundays we were together. So I didn't think one night of the week was unreasonable.

I used to work Saturdays, so when I first moved back I went out Friday nights for maybe two weeks before I learned my lesson: if I'm going to go out, I'd go out and have maybe a few beers, and then some club soda, or Coke or something. I learned my lesson quickly with that. You can't work the next day, especially in this profession, with any type of the-night-before shakes or anything.

If Brian [Lavan] and Neil and Brian's brother, Billy, and I were out, Neil and Brian would be the ones that would get the heat on Saturday from the women, especially if they were hung over. "You got to rake the grass" or "You have to rake the leaves and mow the lawn. You're hung over, yeah, too bad. Get the hell out of the house and do your job." Betty and I would do whatever we were going to do on Saturday anyway, without her giving me any shit about it. So I figured, "Well, I'm lucky, I guess." Maybe she was just a more understanding person.

I loved her from the beginning, you know, right out of high school and during college. The worst thing that I felt that I could do to her was leave her to go to dental school. I guess what I think, now that I know something like with Carol, as far as being in love—I'm not saying my feelings weren't as strong for Betty, but what I knew then, that consumed me. The feeling that I had for Betty, it was love. It was a different kind, a younger, more naive-type love.

I wouldn't say I married Betty for the wrong reasons, but I would say that it was easier to be married than to not be married. Yeah, she wanted to be with me. I wanted to be with her. So I didn't feel that I could put that stigma on Betty, that she wasn't good enough to keep her husband.

I think that I respected Betty enough that I was the one who told her about Debbie, you know. I don't know whatever kind of respect people would have perceived me to have for her after screw-ing around on her.

In my own way—I guess that nobody would ever understand— I loved her.

I miss her now.

If I saw her tomorrow, I would say, "I love you."

CHAPTER 41

The burden of the day's itinerary was etched on Judge Cappellini's face as he convened court on the morning of June 4, 1992. It had taken so long for the system to catch up with Dr. E. Glen Wolsieffer. Public interest in the case, as well as public pressure for justice to finally be administered, had flowered once again. The courtroom was packed, standing room only, with spectators crunched into every available square foot.

The families were in their usual front-row positions, Betty's family on the right side, Glen's on the left. Marian Tasker read Bible passages while Phyllis Wolsieffer leaned forward in her seat, her daughter, Lisa, at the ready with smelling salts. The courtroom grew silent as the defendant entered, clad in a tan suit, rust-colored shirt and flower-patterned tie. He appeared as stoic and unemotional as ever.

Cardinale rose to speak first, suggesting a prison term of four years, the lower end of the Pennsylvania sentencing guidelines for third-degree murder. The defense attorney contended that deterrence and rehabilitation were irrelevant issues. "This was a one-time event. It never happened before, and it will never happen again," he said, acknowledging the accuracy of the jury's verdict for the purposes of his remarks.

Visibly shaking and with an unsteady voice, Cardinale then read from a letter written to Judge Cappellini by Danielle Wolsieffer. The eleven-year-old wrote, in part: "It was very sad after my mom died, but my dad and I had each other to be with. . . . We really have it nice now even after all that has happened to our family. My dad and I are very close and depend on each other for a lot of things. Please, when you give my dad his sentence, remember how much he means to me. I really love him and need him for everything."

After Dr. Wolsieffer declined Judge Cappellini's invitation to say a few words for himself, Sarcione began his remarks by recalling how Betty's father had told him the day before of his recurring nightmares about the exact details of his daughter's murder, and how he had pointed out that Betty should be the focus of the day because she was gone forever.

"And," Sarcione continued while turning toward Dr. Wolsieffer to point his right index finger at him, "the jury found that *he* was the cause of it."

Switching into the tough tone and strong volume of his closing argument at trial, Sarcione blasted the defendant for having killed his wife while his daughter slept in the adjacent bedroom, only to "have the gall to come in" and use Danielle as an excuse for leniency. Angrily, Sarcione declared that Dr. Wolsieffer's intruder theory was "a fabrication. He lives a life of fabrications. . . . Danielle will never know her natural mother because of this guy."

In order for a reduced sentence to be justified, Sarcione argued, the defendant should admit his crime and show remorse. But in Dr. Wolsieffer's case, there had been neither, "because he's cool and he continues to be calculating. It has been five years, nine months, and five days since Betty Wolsieffer was murdered. It is time for justice to be served."

With family members on both sides of the aisle now crying, Betty's father approached the bench. "With all of the issues before you, Betty is still dead, and she was murdered, brutally so. I don't want to be emotional." With that, John Tasker returned to his seat.

Judge Cappellini then expressed his discomfort with the judicial decision he was now required to make. Not only was there the history of his professional relationships with prosecutor Anthony Sarcione's father and defense attorney Frank Nocito, but he himself had gone to school with Betty's father, and one of his children had gone to high school with Betty and Glen. "This is truly difficult because the relationships run so deep," he said. "When I say my heart is heavy with what I have to do today, so be it. But I still have an oath to fulfill."

With Dr. Wolsieffer standing before him, his arms behind his back, his fingers intertwined, Judge Cappellini summarized the defendant's otherwise impeccable record—his professional status and success, his excellence in sports, his lack of a prior criminal record, "your love and care of your daughter, Danielle, and your close loving relationship with your family members." He said that each of the thirty-seven letters submitted by the defense "express disbelief of your involvement in your wife's death." Nonetheless, he said, the jury had determined otherwise.

"I have considered the gravity of the crime, the manner in which and the means by which your wife was strangled, as found by the jury," the judge said. "The death of your wife was not instantaneous as it was described by witnesses for the prosecution. Death did not come quickly. It took a period of time in which your wife suffered before she died.

"There can be no greater crime than taking the life of another without justification or legal reason. The trauma to the family of Betty Wolsieffer as well as to your own family can never be erased. Time may soften the tremendous loss and anguish suffered, but it will never erase it."

Taking a deep breath, the judge then declared that he was sentencing Dr. Wolsieffer to a minimum prison term of eight years and a maximum of twenty, just short of the statutory maximum of ten-to-twenty. "Total confinement is necessary because of the nature of the crime, the impact it had on our community, and your need for rehabilitation."

Cardinale then petitioned the court to reject Sarcione's previously submitted motion for an immediate revocation of his client's $200,000 bail. He contended that substantial issues would be raised on appeal, giving rise to the possibility that a new trial would be ordered.

Sarcione replied that the presumption of innocence was now gone and that the risk of flight increased dramatically upon sentencing.

Cardinale pleaded with Judge Cappellini. "He's not going anywhere. He's not going to abandon his daughter. Give him a chance to get a new trial. Give him a chance to save his professional life. Give him a chance to save his family life."

The judge observed that Dr. Wolsieffer's argument for bail had diminished considerably following his decision denying the post-verdict motions. The key factor now, he said, was determining whether there was a reasonable expectation that an appeals court would overturn his ruling. "I do not feel the defendant is raising any substantial questions of fact or law that would require a reversal by an appellate court, and the awarding of a new trial."

The judge then revoked bail and ordered Dr. Wolsieffer to be taken into custody. As sheriff's deputies prepared to move in, Cardinale gave it one more try. He asked that his client be allowed be remain free until the following Monday—four additional days— so that he could make arrangements for his daughter's care and spend some time with her in a nonprison setting. As he proceeded to make his case, Cardinale asked that the deadline be extended for yet another week, until Monday, June 15, 1992.

Sarcione opposed any delay, pointing out that the post-verdict motions had been denied six weeks earlier. "He's had plenty of time to get his things in order."

Judge Cappellini relented, however, agreeing to prolong Dr. Wolsieffer's surrender for a twelfth day, until the 16th, because of a court holiday on the 15th.

Final delay aside, Dr. Wolsieffer had run out of time. More than eighteen months after the jury's verdict, he was at last on his way to prison. For once looking stunned, but still keeping silent, he left the courtroom briskly with Cardinale and Nocito. The lawyers said they would proceed with their appeals and would even attempt the unlikely maneuver of getting bail reinstated.

Two by two, members of the Tasker family filed into the well of the courtroom to shake hands with members of the prosecution team. Sarcione expressed satisfaction with Judge Cappellini's "cou-

rageous decision." None of Betty's relatives opposed the temporary reprieve on the execution of sentence; the delay wasn't viewed
so much as a favorable development for Glen as a necessary opportunity for Danielle to say goodbye to her father and to be
assured that she would be well cared for by others.

Forgotten amid the hubbub, Nancy Wolsieffer departed the
courthouse with members of her immediate family. Her husband's
name had not been mentioned once during the proceeding. No
one had taken notice of her loss. They still didn't know her story.

The sentencing had only magnified Neil's "senseless death"
for her. She felt that the length of Glen's sentence was what it
should be, but in comparison, she still felt cheated by the results
of the coroner's inquest. "I think of how the legal system was very
fair in this sense but so unfair in Neil's sense. It's such a conflict.
I am filled with all of that. . . . When Sarcione kept making the
point that despite the media attention and the national attention
that this has brought, we can't lose our focus and we have to
remember the bottom line is that Betty's dead, I just wanted to
stand up and say, 'And so is Neil!' and 'What about Neil?' Then
he said, 'There's this child that is left to fend for herself,' and I
wanted to say, 'I have one too who is living without her father
because of this.' So everything that they were saying about Betty
I was transferring to Neil. I felt so heavy that people weren't
recognizing that. And even if they did, they would say it couldn't
be brought up, they'd say, 'It's not the place.' Which makes it
even more obvious that Neil's death was in vain."

Nancy said that she will never understand why Glen didn't
admit to Betty's murder immediately, thereby avoiding the ensuing
years of extra agony. "He's not going to admit it to anyone. He
hasn't admitted it to himself. If I could say just one thing to Glen,
if I could see him face to face, I'd ask, 'Why? Why did you ever
let it go this far?' All these lives are ruined."